Your Personal HOROSCOPE —2006—

The only one-volume horoscope you'll ever need

Joseph Polansky

The author is grateful to the people
of STAR ★ DATA, who truly fathered
this book and without whom it
could not have been written.

HarperElement
An Imprint of HarperCollins*Publishers*
77–85 Fulham Palace Road,
Hammersmith, London W6 8JB

The website address is www.thorsonselement.com

and *HarperElement* are trademarks of
HarperCollins*Publishers* Ltd

Published by HarperElement 2005

1 3 5 7 9 10 8 6 4 2

© Star ★ Data, Inc. 2005

Star ★ Data assert the moral right to
be identified as the authors of this work

A catalogue record for this book is
available from the British Library

ISBN 0 00 719774 8

Printed and bound in Great Britain by
Clays Ltd, St Ives plc

Contents

Introduction

Welcome to the fascinating and intricate world of astrology!

For thousands of years the movements of the planets and other heavenly bodies have intrigued the best minds of every generation. Life holds no greater challenge or joy than this: knowledge of ourselves and the universe we live in. Astrology is one of the keys to this knowledge.

Your Personal Horoscope 2006 gives you the fruits of astrological wisdom. In addition to general guidance on your character and the basic trends of your life, it shows you how to take advantage of planetary influences so you can make the most of the year ahead.

The section on each Sign includes a Personality Profile, a look at general trends for 2006, and in-depth month-by-month forecasts. The Glossary (*page 3*) explains some of the astrological terms you may be unfamiliar with.

One of the many helpful features of this book is the 'Best' and 'Most Stressful' days listed at the beginning of each monthly forecast. Read these sections to learn which days in each month will be good overall, good for money, and good for love. Mark them on your calendar – these will be your best days. Similarly, make a note of the days that will be most stressful for you. It is best to avoid taking important meetings or major decisions on these days, as well as on those days when important planets in your Horoscope are retrograde (moving backwards through the Zodiac).

The Major Trends section for your Sign lists those days when your vitality is strong or weak, or when relationships with your co-workers or loved ones may need a bit more effort on your part. If you are going through a difficult time,

1

take a look at the colour, metal, gem and scent listed in the 'At a Glance' section of your Personality Profile. Wearing a piece of jewellery that contains your metal and/or gem will strengthen your vitality; just as wearing clothes or decorating your room or office in the colour ruled by your Sign, drinking teas made from the herbs ruled by your Sign, or wearing the scents associated with your Sign will sustain you.

Another important virtue of this book is that it will help you to know not only yourself but those around you: your friends, co-workers, partners and/or children. Reading the Personality Profile and forecasts for their Signs will provide you with an insight into their behaviour that you won't get anywhere else. You will know when to be more tolerant of them and when they are liable to be difficult or irritable.

I consider you – the reader – my personal client. By studying your Solar Horoscope I gain an awareness of what is going on in your life – what you are feeling and striving for and the challenges you face. I then do my best to address these concerns. Consider this book the next best thing to having your own personal astrologer!

It is my sincere hope that *Your Personal Horoscope 2006* will enhance the quality of your life, make things easier, illuminate the way forward, banish obscurities and make you more aware of your personal connection to the universe. Understood properly and used wisely, astrology is a great guide to knowing yourself, the people around you and the events in your life – but remember that what you do with these insights – the final result – is up to you.

Glossary of Astrological Terms

Ascendant

We experience day and night because the Earth rotates on its axis once every 24 hours. It is because of this rotation that the Sun, Moon and planets seem to rise and set. The Zodiac is a fixed belt (imaginary, but very real in spiritual terms) around the Earth. As the Earth rotates, the different Signs of the Zodiac seem to the observer to rise on the horizon. During a 24-hour period every Sign of the Zodiac will pass this horizon point at some time or another. The Sign that is at the horizon point at any given time is called the Ascendant, or Rising Sign. The Ascendant is the Sign denoting a person's self-image, body and self-concept – the personal ego, as opposed to the spiritual ego indicated by a person's Sun Sign.

Aspects

Aspects are the angular relationships between planets, the way in which one planet stimulates or influences another. If a planet makes a harmonious aspect (connection) to another, it tends to stimulate that planet in a positive and helpful way. If it makes a stressful aspect to another planet, this disrupts the planet's normal influence.

Astrological Qualities

There are three astrological qualities: *cardinal*, *fixed* and *mutable*. Each of the 12 Signs of the Zodiac falls into one of these three categories.

Cardinal Signs	Aries, Cancer, Libra and Capricorn The cardinal quality is the active, initiating principle. Those born under these four Signs are good at starting new projects.
Fixed Signs	Taurus, Leo, Scorpio and Aquarius Fixed qualities include stability, persistence, endurance and perfectionism. People born under these four Signs are good at seeing things through.
Mutable Signs	Gemini, Virgo, Sagittarius and Pisces Mutable qualities are adaptability, changeability and balance. Those born under these four Signs are creative, if not always practical.

Direct Motion

When the planets move forward through the Zodiac – as they normally do – they are said to be going 'direct'.

Grand Trine

A Grand Trine differs from a normal Trine (where two planets are 120 degrees apart) in that three or more planets are involved. When you look at this pattern in a chart, it takes the form of a complete triangle – a Grand Trine. Usually (but not always) it occurs in one of the four elements: Fire, Earth, Air, or Water. Thus the particular element in which it occurs will be highlighted. A Grand Trine in Water is not the same as a Grand Trine in Air or Fire, etc. This is a very fortunate and happy aspect, and quite rare.

Grand Square

A Grand Square differs from a normal Square (usually two planets separated by 90 degrees) in that four or more planets are involved. When you look at the pattern in a chart you will see a whole and complete square. This, though stressful, usually denotes a new manifestation in the life. There is much work and balancing involved in the manifestation.

Houses

There are 12 Signs of the Zodiac and 12 Houses of experience. The 12 Signs are personality types and ways in which a given planet expresses itself; the 12 Houses show 'where' in your life this expression takes place. Each House has a different area of interest. A House can become potent and important – a House of Power – in different ways: if it contains the Sun, the Moon or the Ruler of your chart, if it contains more than one planet, or if the Ruler of that House is receiving unusual stimulation from other planets.

1st House	Personal Image and Sensual Delights
2nd House	Money/Finance
3rd House	Communication and Intellectual Interests
4th House	Home and Family
5th House	Children, Fun, Games, Creativity, Speculations and Love Affairs
6th House	Health and Work
7th House	Love, Marriage and Social Activities
8th House	Transformation and Regeneration
9th House	Religion, Foreign Travel, Higher Education and Philosophy
10th House	Career
11th House	Friends, Group Activities and Fondest Wishes
12th House	Spirituality

Karma

Karma is the law of cause and effect which governs all phenomena. We are all where we find ourselves because of karma – because of actions we have performed in the past. The universe is such a balanced instrument that any act immediately sets corrective forces into motion – karma.

Long-term Planets

The planets that take a long time to move through a Sign show the long-term trends in a given area of life. They are important for forecasting the prolonged view of things. Because these planets stay in one Sign for so long, there are periods in the year when the faster-moving (short-term) planets will join them, further activating and enhancing the importance of a given House.

Jupiter	stays in a Sign for about 1 year
Saturn	2½ years
Uranus	7 years
Neptune	14 years
Pluto	15 to 30 years

Lunar

Relating to the Moon. See also 'Phases of the Moon', below.

Natal

Literally means 'birth'. In astrology this term is used to distinguish between planetary positions that occurred at the time of a person's birth (natal) and those that are current (transiting). For example, Natal Sun refers to where the Sun was when you were born; transiting Sun refers to where the Sun's position is currently at any given moment – which usually doesn't coincide with your birth, or Natal, Sun.

Out of Bounds

The planets move through the Zodiac at various angles relative to the celestial equator (if you were to draw an imaginary extension of the Earth's equator out into the universe, you would have an illustration of this celestial equator). The Sun – being the most dominant and powerful influence in the Solar system – is the measure astrologers use as a standard. The Sun never goes more than approximately 23 degrees north or south of the celestial equator. At the winter solstice the Sun reaches its maximum southern angle of orbit (declination); at the summer solstice it reaches its maximum northern angle. Any time a planet exceeds this Solar boundary – and occasionally planets do – it is said to be 'out of bounds'. This means that the planet exceeds or trespasses into strange territory – beyond the limits allowed by the Sun, the Ruler of the Solar system. The planet in this condition becomes more emphasized and exceeds its authority, becoming an important influence in the forecast.

Phases of the Moon

After the full Moon, the Moon seems to shrink in size (as perceived from the Earth), gradually growing smaller until it is virtually invisible to the naked eye – at the time of the next new Moon. This is called the waning Moon phase, or the waning Moon.

After the new Moon, the Moon gradually gets bigger in size (as perceived from the Earth) until it reaches its maximum size at the time of the full Moon. This period is called the waxing Moon phase, or waxing Moon.

Retrogrades

The planets move around the Sun at different speeds. Mercury and Venus move much faster than the Earth, while Mars, Jupiter, Saturn, Uranus, Neptune and Pluto move more slowly. Thus there are times when, relative to the Earth, the planets appear to be going backwards. In reality they are always going forward, but relative to our vantage point on Earth they seem to go backwards through the Zodiac for a period of time. This is called 'retrograde' motion and tends to weaken the normal influence of a given planet.

Short-term Planets

The fast-moving planets move so quickly through a Sign that their effects are generally of a short-term nature. They reflect the immediate, day-to-day trends in a Horoscope.

Moon	stays in a Sign for only 2½ days
Mercury	20 to 30 days
Sun	30 days
Venus	approximately 1 month
Mars	approximately 2 months

T-square

A T-square differs from a Grand Square in that it is not a complete square. If you look at the pattern in a chart it appears as 'half a complete square', resembling the T-square tools used by architects and designers. If you cut a complete square in half, diagonally, you have a T-square. Many astrologers consider this more stressful than a Grand Square, as it creates tension that is difficult to resolve. T-squares bring learning experiences.

Transits

This refers to the movements or motions of the planets at any given time. Astrologers use the word 'transit' to make the distinction between a birth or Natal planet (see 'Natal', above) and the planet's current movement in the heavens. For example, if at your birth Saturn was in the Sign of Cancer in your 8th House, but is now moving through your 3rd House, it is said to be 'transiting' your 3rd House. Transits are one of the main tools with which astrologers forecast trends.

Aries

Υ

THE RAM
*Birthdays from
21st March to
20th April*

Personality Profile

ARIES AT A GLANCE

Element – Fire

Ruling Planet – Mars
 Career Planet – Saturn
 Love Planet – Venus
 Money Planet – Venus
 *Planet of Fun, Entertainment, Creativity and
  Speculations* – Sun
 Planet of Health and Work – Mercury
 Planet of Home and Family Life – Moon
 Planet of Spirituality – Neptune
 *Planet of Travel, Education, Religion and
  Philosophy* – Jupiter

Colours – carmine, red, scarlet

ARIES

Colours that promote love, romance and social harmony – green, jade green

Colour that promotes earning power – green

Gem – amethyst

Metals – iron, steel

Scent – honeysuckle

Quality – cardinal (= activity)

Quality most needed for balance – caution

Strongest virtues – abundant physical energy, courage, honesty, independence, self-reliance

Deepest need – action

Characteristics to avoid – haste, impetuousness, over-aggression, rashness

Signs of greatest overall compatibility – Leo, Sagittarius

Signs of greatest overall incompatibility – Cancer, Libra, Capricorn

Sign most helpful to career – Capricorn

Sign most helpful for emotional support – Cancer

Sign most helpful financially – Taurus

Sign best for marriage and/or partnerships – Libra

Sign most helpful for creative projects – Leo

Best Sign to have fun with – Leo

Signs most helpful in spiritual matters – Sagittarius, Pisces

Best day of the week – Tuesday

Understanding an Aries

Aries is the activist *par excellence* of the Zodiac. The Arien need for action is almost an addiction, and those who do not really understand the Arien personality would probably use this hard word to describe it. In reality 'action' is the essence of the Arien psychology – the more direct, blunt and to-the-point the action, the better. When you think about it, this is the ideal psychological makeup for the warrior, the pioneer, the athlete or the manager.

Ariens like to get things done, and in their passion and zeal often lose sight of the consequences for themselves and others. Yes, they often try to be diplomatic and tactful, but it is hard for them. When they do so they feel that they are being dishonest and phony. It is hard for them even to understand the mindset of the diplomat, the consensus builder, the front office executive. These people are involved in endless meetings, discussions, talks and negotiations – all of which seem a great waste of time when there is so much work to be done, so many real achievements to be gained. An Aries can understand, once it is explained, that talks and negotiations – the social graces – lead ultimately to better, more effective actions. The interesting thing is that an Aries is rarely malicious or spiteful – even when waging war. Aries people fight without hate for their opponents. To them it is all good-natured fun, a grand adventure, a game.

When confronted with a problem many people will say 'Well, let's think about it, let's analyse the situation.' But not an Aries. An Aries will think 'Something must be done. Let's get on with it.' Of course neither response is the total answer. Sometimes action is called for, sometimes cool thought. But an Aries tends to err on the side of action.

Action and thought are radically different principles. Physical activity is the use of brute force. Thinking and deliberating require one not to use force – to be still. It is not good for the athlete to be deliberating the next move; this will only slow down his or her reaction time. The athlete must act instinctively and instantly. This is how Aries people tend to behave in life. They are quick, instinctive decision-makers and their decisions tend to be translated into action almost immediately. When their intuition is sharp and well tuned, their actions are powerful and successful. When their intuition is off, their actions can be disastrous.

Do not think this will scare an Aries. Just as a good warrior knows that in the course of combat he or she might acquire a few wounds, so too does an Aries realize – somewhere deep down – that in the course of being true to yourself you might get embroiled in a disaster or two. It is all part of the game. An Aries feels strong enough to weather any storm.

There are many Aries people who are intellectual: Ariens make powerful and creative thinkers. But even in this realm they tend to be pioneers – outspoken and blunt. These types of Ariens tend to elevate (or sublimate) their desire for physical combat in favour of intellectual, mental combat. And they are indeed powerful.

In general, Aries people have a faith in themselves that others could learn from. This basic, rock-bottom faith carries them through the most tumultuous situations of life. Their courage and self-confidence make them natural leaders. Their leadership is more by way of example than by actually controlling others.

Finance

Arien people often excel as builders or estate agents. Money in and of itself is not as important as are other things – action, adventure, sport, etc. They are motivated by the need to support and be well-thought-of by their partners. Money as a way of attaining pleasure is another important motivation. Ariens function best in their own businesses or as managers of their own departments within a large business or corporation. The fewer orders they have to take from higher up, the better. They also function better out in the field rather than behind a desk.

Aries people are hard workers with a lot of endurance; they can earn large sums of money due to the strength of their sheer physical energy.

Venus is their Money Planet, which means that Ariens need to develop more of the social graces in order to realize their full earning potential. Just getting the job done – which is what an Aries excels at – is not enough to create financial success. The co-operation of others needs to be attained. Customers, clients and co-workers need to be made to feel comfortable; many people need to be treated properly in order for success to happen. When Aries people develop these abilities – or hire someone to do this for them – their financial potential is unlimited.

Career and Public Image

One would think that a pioneering type would want to break with the social and political conventions of society. But this is not so with the Aries-born. They are pioneers within conventional limits, in the sense that they like to start their own businesses within an established industry.

Capricorn is on the 10th House (Career) cusp of Aries' Solar Horoscope. Saturn is the planet that rules their life's work and professional aspirations. This tells us some interesting things about the Arien character. First off, it shows that in order for Aries people to reach their full career potential they need to develop some qualities that are a bit alien to their basic nature: They need to become better administrators and organizers; they need to be able to handle details better and to take a long-range view of their projects and their careers in general. No one can beat an Aries when it comes to achieving short-range objectives, but a career is long term, built over time. You cannot take a 'quickie' approach to it.

Some Aries people find it difficult to stick with a project until the end. Since they get bored quickly and are in constant pursuit of new adventures, they prefer to pass an old project or task on to somebody else in order to start something new. Those Ariens who learn how to put off the search for something new until the old is completed will achieve great success in their careers and professional lives.

In general, Aries people like society to judge them on their own merits, on their real and actual achievements. A reputation acquired by 'hype' feels false to them.

Love and Relationships

In marriage and partnerships Ariens like those who are more passive, gentle, tactful and diplomatic – people who have the social grace and skills they sometimes lack. Our partners always represent a hidden part of ourselves – a self that we cannot express personally.

An Aries tends to go after what he or she likes aggressively. The tendency is to jump into relationships and marriages. This is especially true if Venus is in Aries as well as the Sun. If an Aries likes you, he or she will have a hard time taking no for an answer; many attempts will be made to sweep you off your feet.

Though Ariens can be exasperating in relationships – especially if they are not understood by their partners – they are never consciously or wilfully cruel or malicious. It is just that they are so independent and sure of themselves that they find it almost impossible to see somebody else's viewpoint or position. This is why an Aries needs as a partner someone with lots of social grace.

On the plus side, an Aries is honest, someone you can lean on, someone with whom you will always know where you stand. What he or she lacks in diplomacy is made up for in integrity.

Home and Domestic Life

An Aries is of course the ruler at home – the Boss. The male will tend to delegate domestic matters to the female. The female Aries will want to rule the roost. Both tend to be handy round the house. Both like large families and both believe in the sanctity and importance of the family. An Aries is a good family person, although he or she does not especially like being at home a lot, preferring instead to be roaming about.

Considering that they are by nature so combative and wilful, Aries people can be surprisingly soft, gentle and even vulnerable with their children and partners. The Sign of Cancer, ruled by the Moon, is on the cusp of their Solar 4th House (Home and Family). When the Moon is well aspected – under favourable influences – in the birth chart an Aries will be tender towards the family and want a family life that is nurturing and supportive. Ariens like to come home after a hard day on the battlefield of life to the understanding arms of their partner and the unconditional love and support of their family. An Aries feels that there is enough 'war' out in the world – and he or she enjoys participating in that. But when Aries comes home, comfort and nurturing are what's needed.

Horoscope for 2006

General Trends

You've been through a rough few years, Aries, but things improve vastly this year. Things got easier at the beginning of July 2005 when Saturn left Cancer and moved into Leo, replacing a stressful aspect with a harmonious one. Where for two years you felt that 'order' and 'limits' were something antagonistic to you, now you can see their benefits. A good order in your life will make you shine even more. You learned not to waste your time on frivolities, and the Great Orderer of the Universe is rewarding you.

Though you will have a few shocking events – perhaps wake-up calls – overall the year ahead looks very happy. Many of you are still under the influence of the Lunar Eclipse of October 17th 2005, which occurred in your sign. There will be a Solar Eclipse on March 29th in your sign and a Lunar Eclipse on October 30th which impacts on you. These are forcing changes in your self-image, self-concept, personal appearance and relationships. These changes – which few of us undertake unless we are nagged into it – will ultimately be very positive.

The good news this year is that all the major long-term planets are either in harmonious aspect to you or are leaving you alone. This is a year for positive achievement. You can cover more ground this year because you journey under sunny skies with little resistance.

With Jupiter in your 8th House for most of the year ahead, there will be more sexual activity for most of you (depending on your age and stage). Sexual experiences will tend to be happy but there will be challenges if this energy is abused.

Your most important interests in the year ahead are children, creativity, sex, personal transformation, past lives, occult studies, the deeper things of life (until November 24th); religion, metaphysics, higher education, foreign travel (after November 24th); friendships and group activities; spirituality.

Your paths to fulfilment in the year ahead are sex, personal transformation, occult studies, the prospering of other people, paying off debts (until November 24th); religion, metaphysics, higher education, foreign travel (after November 24th); the image, body and appearance (until June 23rd); spirituality (after June 23rd).

Health

(Please note that this is an astrological perspective on health, not a medical one. At one time, both perspectives were identical, but in these times there could be quite a difference. For the medical perspective, please consult your physician or health professional.)

Health is vastly improved this year, Aries. Overall energy is back to the high levels you are used to. And since you are probably more organized with your energy these days (Saturn in Cancer saw to that), health is likely to be good.

We see good health in other ways too. Your 6th House is not a House of Power this year, which shows that you are not paying too much attention to it. You don't need to – you take good health for granted as you should.

You have made much psychological progress in the past two years, and now there's no need to go further. Psychologically you seem where you want to be. Aries is one of the most naturally optimistic signs of the zodiac. For the past two years, however, this was less apparent, but now your natural optimism returns.

Even with overall good health aspects, there will be times in the year when health is 'less easy' than normal. These periods come from the transiting planets and are temporary things, not tendencies for the year. These periods will be January 1st to 19th; June 21st to July 22nd; September 22nd to October 23rd; December 21st to December 31st. It's good to rest and relax as much as you can during those periods to pace yourself better.

With Mercury as your health planet, you can enhance your already good health by paying attention to the arms and shoulders (they can be regularly massaged), the lungs and the small intestine. Since Aries rules the head, you can always benefit from scalp massage and facials (when Aries get stressed they often get migraines).

ARIES

There is a Solar Eclipse in your 6th House of Health on March 14th. Often these can bring up health issues that have long been neglected. In your case, however, since health seems so good, it is most probably showing major and long-term changes to your diet and overall health regime. Many people change their doctors under this kind of event too.

Mercury moves quickly and often erratically. During the course of the year he will move through all the signs and houses of your horoscope. This means that your health needs – the therapies that will be powerful for you – will fluctuate month by month depending on where Mercury is.

Health issues in general will become important for you from July 21st to September 23rd. This is a particularly good time to start an exercise programme or health regime.

The health of parents or parent figures in your life can be enhanced through detox regimes. In many cases, they will have had operations in recent years, and could have them this year as well.

The health of children seems good. They are very interested in good health (more so than you). It is a high priority for them and they will not let problems fester. They can enhance their health by giving more attention to the spine, knees and teeth.

Your lover or spouse is very experimental in health matters this year – this has been going on for a while and will continue for many years to come. It's as if they are throwing out all the rule books and learning how their body functions by trial and error. Orthodox medicine is not for them. They will benefit more from alternative medicine or from newly invented therapies. The feet and the ankles seem important for them. Both should be regularly massaged, and the ankles should be given more support when exercising.

Grandchildren (for those of you at that stage) can also enhance health through detox regimes. Regular neck massage is also good. They seem involved in 'transforming' their bodies and images. Hopefully they will do it by natural means such as yoga, t'ai chi, herbs and diet, but cosmetic surgery wouldn't be a surprise either.

Home, Domestic and Family Issues

Many of you wanted to move house in the past few years and felt blocked. Now the blockages are gone and it is easier to achieve. It doesn't mean that you *must* move, only that the obstructions to it are gone.

Children seem more the focus now than the home or other family members. Learning how to deal with your children (and children in general) is going to be an important challenge for the year ahead. They seem a 'burden' rather than the joy they should be. Of course they are a joy, but you're seeing the price tag attached. Learning how to discipline them – to maintain some semblance of order – seems the major challenge. Also the cosmos, in its wisdom, is reinforcing a certain discipline on you as well. You will have to lead them by example, which is easier said than done. The children are going to force you to make them your number one priority. If they feel that you have other priorities, they will do things to get you back. You have to let them know how important they are to you, but also to set some kind of limit on them.

If you're not giving the children the attention they need, you can expect the cosmos to create all kinds of 'events' that will bring your attention back to them. Mysterious problems or ailments will arise that you'll have to deal with.

Good times for building or remodelling your home are April 14th to June 3rd, and June 21st to July 22nd. If you're beautifying your home by decorating or buying art objects, July 19th to 28th is good.

Older children are moving and profiting from property this year. Perhaps they are buying big items for the home. Parents or parent figures are likely to stay where they are this year, as are siblings (they may have moved in recent years).

Love and Social Life

Your 7th House of Love and Marriage is not a House of Power this year. Thus the cosmos is not pushing you one way or another. You have more freedom and free will in this area this year. This kind of year usually sees little change to the status quo: marrieds tend to stay married and singles tend to stay single.

Free will is a wonderful thing but lack of interest – which the chart is showing – often nullifies the blessing.

In the course of a year there will be social ups and downs. There will be periods where love is more important and less important. But these are temporary things caused by the transiting planets and are not trends for the year. We will deal with these in the monthly reports.

The Solar Eclipse on September 20th occurs very near your 7th House. This eclipse will test your current relationship but need not break it up. For singles it can often mean a change of status in coming months.

Your most active period socially will be from September 8th to October 23rd. You are reaching out to others during this period and going after what you want. Though you can have a few adventures here, seekers tend to get what they want eventually.

Love affairs (outside of marriage) seem stressful. A current one is probably ending. Some of you are going to have flings with older partners, but the 'fire in the heart' seems absent. These affairs can be matters of convenience and not passion. In some cases they are merely career moves.

Venus, your love planet, spends more than two months[1] (an unusually long time) in the sign of Capricorn this year.

[1] *January 1 to March 5.*

23

She also makes one of her rare (once in two years) retro-grades. This means there could be a serious love affair at the office, perhaps with a boss. It seems very complicated, leav-ing both parties confused. I don't think it will end well. It might help your career and finances, but will that be enough to maintain the passion?

For singles, this is a year for being more selective in love, for focusing on quality rather than quantity. A wrong choice seems to have a high price tag attached. Gaining this discern-ment could be harder as this is a very sexually active year.

Aries of childbearing age are much less fertile than usual. Pregnancies seem unlikely. And if they happen there are more complications bringing them to term.

Those of you looking to marry for the second time need to be patient for a while. But from November 24th, major love comes into your life, and this will be marriage material. Jupiter will be in your house of the second marriage well into 2007 – so this could happen next year as well. You may very well meet this person abroad (or they could be a foreigner visiting your country). Church, church functions, educational functions and universities are also likely meet-ing places. This person could be your teacher or mentor.

Those of you looking for a third marriage also find love, but it seems nebulous and uncommitted, drifting this way and that. It is very idealistic as the person seems spiritual but hard to pin down.

Children of marriageable age should perhaps wait before naming the day. There is love, perhaps even serious love, but it is all unsettled. Time is needed to clarify things.

Grandchildren of marriageable age have a status-quo kind of year. Marrieds will probably stay married and singles will stay single.

Many of your friends are having marital (or social) crises this year.

Friendships in general seem more important to you than romance. And, like last year, this area is very exciting. You

24

are mingling with a creative, glamorous crowd – artists, musicians, spiritual types. Like the wind, no one knows where they go or when they come. But they are friends and they are enhancing your spirituality.

Finance and Career

The houses associated with money, career and work are mostly empty this year. This means there will not be major issues in these areas of your life. Of course, you will probably have a job, a career and earnings, but these are not your priorities. I suspect it will be a status-quo year in all these areas. I read this as a good thing. You are more or less satisfied with where you are financially and career-wise, and have no need to make major changes.

Some changes are indicated on the job front, however, shown by two eclipses in your 6th House of Work. There is a Lunar Eclipse on March 14th and a Solar Eclipse on September 22nd. Usually people change jobs under these conditions. Sometimes they change companies or move to a new job within the same company. Working conditions also undergo change, such as new rules or surroundings. Colleagues may leave and supervisors may get shifted. For those of you who employ others, these eclipses show upheavals and changes in the workforce. Perhaps you were satisfied with the status-quo while the Higher Power wanted you to have better, so it shakes things up. It can seem unpleasant while these things are happening, but the end result will be fine.

Your career planet, Saturn, is in your 5th House all year. This is telling us many, many things. First and foremost, you want to enjoy your career. You want it to be fun and creative, and to avoid drudgery at all costs. Nothing wrong with that. Perhaps you will be shown ways to make your existing career more creative and fun. Those just starting out might opt for a glamorous career, such as the entertainment field. There are also other ways to read this. Many of you will opt for a career that deals with children. Many of you will leave your present career and focus on your own children. And even for those who stay in their career, the love for their children will be the motivating factor: 'I've got to succeed so I can do the right thing by my kids.'

Whatever your actual career is, you seem involved with either managing creative people (a great and difficult art) or managing children (another difficult one). Your career success seems to hinge on how well you do these things.

In your Solar Chart (the charts we work with here), Venus serves double duty. She is both the love and financial planet. And since she moves so quickly through the zodiac, financial opportunities will come in many ways and from many sources, depending on where she is at any given time.

Early in the year – from January 1st to March 5th – Venus will make an unusually long transit in Capricorn and your 10th House. This generally shows pay rises and promotions – money that comes from good professional and community standing. So, a lucrative career boost is happening. The only problem here is that Venus will be retrograde much of that time, so this is not a smooth ride. There are delays and challenges to deal with.

Your spouse or partner is having one of the most prosperous periods in their life, and they are generous with you. This is a year when you easily access outside capital. Borrowing is much more straightforward than usual. If you have good ideas there are investors waiting for you. Debts are easily paid or easily refinanced. If you have tax issues with the government there are best-case outcomes. This year you prosper as you help other people prosper, seeing the wisdom of putting other people's financial interests ahead of your own. Of course, you shouldn't ignore your interests, but try to see things from the perspective of others.

Many of you will inherit money this year. Sometimes this comes as actual inheritance; sometimes you are merely named in someone's will; and sometimes there is a trust fund set up. There are many scenarios as to how this can happen – no one need actually die. Many of you will receive big insurance settlements rather than inheritance. But the major money this year comes 'outside' your personal earning power.

When outside money is readily available, and with your line of credit probably increasing, the main challenge is to avoid frivolous, non-constructive debt. The temptations are so great that it is difficult to resist.

Self-improvement

Ever since Uranus moved into your 12th House in 2004, spirituality has become important in your life. It will be important for many years to come. Later this year (November 24th), Jupiter will move into your 9th House of Religion and Philosophy, making this area even more prominent. You are going to be involved in spiritually-oriented groups and organizations, and participate in spiritual-type group activities (perhaps prayer circles, healing circles, charitable functions or altruistic activities).

If you approach things scientifically you will make much faster and deeper progress. You will be in line with your horoscope and with the forces of the cosmos.

Month-by-month Forecasts

January

Best Days Overall: 6, 7, 15, 16, 25, 26

Most Stressful Days Overall: 12, 13, 14, 20, 21, 27, 28

Best Days for Love: 8, 9, 17, 18, 19, 20, 21, 27, 28

Best Days for Money: 3, 4, 8, 9, 12, 13, 17, 18, 19, 22, 23, 27, 28, 31

Monthly Career Peaks: 15, 16, 27, 28

Monthly Personal Pleasure Peaks: 6, 7, 8, 9

Your year begins with 80 per cent of the planets above the horizon. Your 10th House of Career is powerful, while your 4th House of Home and Family is empty (only the Moon will visit there on the 12th, 13th and 14th). Not only are ambitions strong, but you are also in the midst of your yearly career peak. Much progress and career opportunity is happening. It is good that you are focusing here and letting family issues slide for a while.

Your 2nd House of Finance is also strong this month. Mars, your ruler, will be there all month, so this is a very strong financial month as well. You are enjoying your prosperity and your career these days. In fact, the more 'fun' you can bring to these things, the more prosperous and successful you become. There are many challenges in these areas (more on this later) but your relaxed, happy manner will help you to overcome them.

With your career and financial planets retrograde all month, you might not experience full success right away. There are some delays. But you are planting positive seeds that will bear fruit in due course.

This month we have a rare retrograde of Venus, which affects both your love and financial life. Current relationships need reviewing so that you can see what can be improved. Important love decisions – either for marriage or divorce – should not be taken. Important financial decisions should be researched further and avoided if possible. Guaranteed, when Venus starts moving forward (next month) you will have a different financial perspective.

There is a status-quo in your love life this month. Venus will re-stimulate the Solar Eclipse point of October 3rd 2005 from the 11th to the 14th. Very often the re-stimulation of an eclipse point can be as powerful as the actual eclipse. So your love relationship may be tested further. There could be a short-term financial disturbance as well. You may need to make some changes to your thinking and planning.

We have a very unusual Grand Square pattern this month, which will only intensify (more planets will be involved) as the month progresses. In general, something big is manifesting for the world at large. It shows something similar for you personally, but on a smaller scale. You are building something, trying to balance many diverse forces, people and energies. It is delicate work.

Family members are more temperamental on the 6th, 7th, 12th, 13th, 20th, 21st, 27th and 28th. Be more patient with them. Old emotional patterns are surfacing for cleansing. (The Moon is re-stimulating eclipse points on those days.)

For singles, love opportunities come at work or as they pursue their career path. Older, more established people are alluring these days. Singles gravitate to people who can help them financially and career-wise. There is a love opportunity with a boss or supervisor from the 13th to the 15th, but it doesn't seem serious.

This month the lesson is about learning how to handle delay and uncertainty. (In general, Aries is not too good at that.) If you vent frustration you can make matters worse. But you can make delays benefit you by using the time to improve your product and service – and, in the case of love, to improve yourself.

Rest and relax more until the 20th. You can enhance health this month by giving more attention to the thighs and liver (until the 4th); the spine, knees, teeth and skeletal alignment (from the 4th to the 22nd) – back massage is excellent; the ankles (after the 22nd) – massage them and give them more support.

February

Best Days Overall: 2, 3, 11, 12, 21, 22

Most Stressful Days Overall: 9, 10, 16, 17, 23, 24

Best Days for Love: 4, 5, 14, 15, 16, 17, 23, 24

Best Days for Money: 1, 4, 5, 9, 10, 14, 15, 19, 20, 23, 24, 27, 28

Monthly Career Peaks: 11, 12, 23, 24

Monthly Personal Pleasure Peaks: 2, 3, 6, 7

The Grand Square pattern (in the fixed signs) continues until the 18th. So carry on building your projects. The energy of the entire cosmos is helping you in this, but you still need to learn how to harmonize diverse forces and people.

Most of the planets (80 per cent) are still above the horizon. Your 10th House of Career is stronger than your 4th House of Home and Family, so ambitions are strong. Family issues can be safely put aside for a while as you focus on your career and life work.

With Venus (your love and financial planet) prominently placed, love is a high priority. But love is also complicated. Venus will be retrograde until the 3rd. She re-stimulates eclipse points on the 25th and 26th, testing current relationships. Most of your planets (70 per cent) are in the Eastern sector, which can make you self-willed and inflexible, wanting your own way. Perhaps your attitude to love is too 'practical'. But this is a temporary phase. Like last month, we see love opportunities as you pursue your career, perhaps with people at work and above you in status. But where is the passion? The good news is that, with Venus moving forward after the 3rd, you have more clarity in love and relationships.

With your financial planet going forward, many of last month's delays and snags are resolved. Prosperity is strong all month (but especially until the 18th). Not only are the aspects reasonable, but you also have a strong interest in finance – you are willing (and have the energy) to overcome the various obstacles that arise. Professional investors should look at property, building and blue chip companies. Financial opportunities will come from your good professional reputation and pay rises, and from the grace of parents, elders and authority figures. Business people can often gain government contracts under this kind of transit. What I like here is that financial judgement (especially after the 3rd) is very sound – conservative and practical. When you shop or invest, you will get value for money. Venus's re-stimulation of the eclipse points on the 25th and 26th can cause some financial disturbance – perhaps you need to change thinking or strategy – but this is short term.

After the 3rd, 90 per cent of the planets are in forward motion, and 70 per cent are in the East. This is a time for building your life as you desire it to be, for personal initiative and direct action towards your goals.

Health is excellent all month. You can enhance it further by paying more attention to the ankles (until the 9th) and the feet (afterwards). Regular foot and ankle massage will do wonders when you feel tired or under the weather.

Until the 19th, the focus is on friendships (this seems just as important as romance) and group activities. After the 19th, the focus is on spirituality and altruistic interests. This will be a good period to go on spiritually-oriented retreats and get involved in charitable causes.

One of the main challenges of the year is balancing your ideals with the practical day-to-day career. The solution is likely to come after the 19th.

March

Best Days Overall: 1, 2, 10, 11, 12, 20, 21, 29, 30

Most Stressful Days Overall: 8, 9, 15, 16, 17, 23, 24

Best Days for Love: 4, 5, 6, 15, 16, 17, 25, 26

Best Days for Money: 3, 4, 5, 6, 8, 9, 15, 16, 18, 19, 25, 26, 27, 28, 31

Monthly Career Peaks: 10, 23, 24

Monthly Personal Pleasure Peaks: 1, 2, 6, 7, 29, 30

Two T-squares (unusual) and two eclipses this month ensure that this will be an eventful period, both for you and for the world at large. The Lunar Eclipse of March 14th is relatively benign for you, though it won't hurt to reduce your schedule anyway. But the Solar Eclipse of March 29th occurs in your own sign and will have a strong influence on you. Eclipse periods are times to stay close to home, catch up on your reading or, if you are on a spiritual path, to meditate and pray.

The Lunar Eclipse of the 14th is announcing job changes and alterations in workplace conditions. Also, you will probably make long-term changes to your diet and health regime.

The Solar Eclipse in your own sign will cause you to rethink your concept of yourself, to redefine your personality (sometimes this will test a love relationship too) and change your image, appearance and overall demeanour. Sometimes impurities in the physical body come up for cleansing, but this is not sickness as we understand the term. The body just takes the opportunity to get rid of some old stuff. If you eat properly and take care of yourself, this probably won't happen.

Those involved with Aries romantically need to be patient during this period. Your lover might act strangely and be more temperamental, but this is being caused by inner processes.

There are also stresses in the world at large. Apparently immovable objects seem to block progress, and it is the job of the eclipses to blast them away. Perhaps there are things in each of us – mental and emotional conditions – that contribute to these blockages. And these get blasted away too.

With the planets moving ever more eastwards in your chart, giving you increasing independence and freedom of action, the eclipses (especially of the 29th) will blast away obstructions to your personal progress. When the dust settles you will have a new-found freedom, either of mind or body.

Like last month, this is still a very spiritual period. Going on a retreat or spending time in spiritually-oriented activities is a great way to soften the impact of an eclipse.

For the past few months you seemed hard-headed and unsentimental about love. This is about to change on the 6th as Venus leaves Capricorn and moves into Aquarius. The romantic feeling is coming back, especially from the 25th as your love planet starts to travel with Neptune, the most spiritual and idealistic of the planets. Singles will meet glamorous types. Friends might play cupid (or this person could also be a friend). Love opportunities could also happen at meetings of organizations you belong to. Spiritual or meditation retreats are also a likely meeting ground. Your financial intuition will also be pretty incredible during this period.

Enhance health by paying more attention to the feet. Like last month, foot massage is an excellent tonic when you feel low.

Your body and image (and sensual delights) will be a priority from the 20th onwards.

April

Best Days Overall: 7, 8, 17, 18, 25, 26

Most Stressful Days Overall: 4, 5, 12, 13, 19, 20

Best Days for Love: 2, 3, 12, 13, 14, 15, 23, 24

Best Days for Money: 1, 2, 3, 4, 5, 14, 15, 23, 24, 27, 28

Monthly Career Peaks: 7, 19, 20

Monthly Personal Pleasure Peaks: 2, 3, 25, 26

As the month opens, the dust is still settling from last month's eclipse. Let it settle and clarity will come.

The body, image and overall appearance are still a major priority until the 20th.

Like last month, most of the planets are still in your Eastern sector of independence – your favourite sector. Work to design your life as you like it without offending others (or keeping offence to a minimum). Your actions and personal initiative really make a difference now. Your way is best for you. If others don't cooperate you can go it alone.

Most of the planets are still above the horizon, showing ambition and a need for outer achievement and recognition, but this is changing little by little. On the 14th, your 4th House of Home and Family becomes very important as your ruler, Mars, moves there. So, this is a month for balancing home and career. You may be doing repairs or renovations in the home. You become more interested in psychological issues, delving into yourself and your moods. Your personal past seems very interesting too.

Your career planet, Saturn, has been retrograde since the beginning of the year. Of course this didn't stop career progress from happening, but only delayed things or introduced glitches. On the 5th, Saturn will start moving forwards and many of the delays will get resolved.

ARIES

With the Sun in your own sign, this is a month for having fun, for personal pleasure and sensual fulfilment. You will advance your career by pursuing it in fun ways, perhaps through entertaining customers, or by making your work more enjoyable.

Financial intuition was super late last month and that trend continues this month. Venus, the financial planet, moves into spiritual Pisces on the 6th. This is a month for charitable giving and for learning the spiritual laws of affluence. Sudden windfalls (perhaps opportunities) come from the 16th to the 19th. There are also sudden love meetings, totally out of the blue. There could also be an unexpected (and happy) social invitation.

Singles find love opportunities, like last month, in spiritual or altruistic settings. You also gravitate to creative, other-worldly types. Psychics, astrologers and mediums have important information about finance and love. But guidance is also very likely to come in dreams.

Health is excellent this month, but you can enhance it further by paying more attention to the feet (like last month) until the 16th, and then to the scalp and head. Scalp massage and facials become powerful after the 16th.

Your money house becomes powerful after the 20th. With intuition so sharp these days, speculations should be favourable. What is interesting here is that money comes in happy and fun ways. A parent or elder might seem less supportive after the 20th but it is a temporary condition. Perhaps they disapprove of your 'easy money' attitude and want you to be more serious.

Mars, your ruler, is re-stimulating eclipse points from the 2nd to the 5th and on the 29th and 30th. Don't plan any risky or stressful activities for those days.

May

Best Days Overall: 4, 5, 14, 15, 22, 23, 29, 30

Most Stressful Days Overall: 2, 3, 9, 10, 16, 17, 29, 30

Best Days for Love: 3, 9, 10, 14, 15, 22, 23

Best Days for Money: 2, 3, 12, 13, 14, 15, 20, 21, 22, 23, 25, 26, 29, 30

Monthly Career Peaks: 4, 16, 17, 31

Monthly Personal Pleasure Peaks: 2, 3, 22, 23, 29, 30

The planetary power shifts this month from the upper to the lower half of the horoscope. Career and ambition are still important but now the focus is on home and family issues.

There is a rare Grand Square pattern in the heavens (it began last month on the 20th), which will be in effect until the 21st. It shows you are building something big, and that big things are being constructed in the world at large. But remember, in building we follow a rhythm – outer work and inner work. You are in a period of more inner work. Without personal emotional harmony, the building won't get built.

Last month should have been prosperous, but this month will be even more so. You can focus more on feeling good emotionally because love, money and financial opportunity are pursuing you. After the 4th they will find you. There's no need to be gung ho and aggressive now. Just go about your normal business and enjoy your life, and these things will come to you.

Expensive personal items – perhaps clothing, jewellery or accessories – are coming. Objects of beauty are coming too. You look great. Your sense of style is exquisite. The opposite sex takes notice. Singles may have to beat them away with a bat!

ARIES

Most of the planets are still in the East and so you continue to have the power to create your life as you want it to be, especially your personal life.

Mars, your ruler, re-stimulates an eclipse point on the 1st, so avoid risky or stressful activities that day. Also try to steer clear of power struggles or confrontations.

Venus re-stimulates eclipse points on the 11th and 12th. This could test a relationship or make your spouse or lover more temperamental. Be patient with them as this will soon pass. This could also bring some temporary financial disturbance or weird events. You probably need to change your financial thinking and planning. Prosperity is likely to be enhanced because of these disturbances.

Family members will probably be more temperamental on the 2nd, 8th, 9th, 15th, 16th, 21st, 22nd and 28th. Unexpected things may happen in the home, but nothing major. The Moon is re-stimulating eclipse points on those days. Be patient.

Mercury will re-stimulate eclipse points on the 30th and 31st so there could be some disturbances at work, perhaps with colleagues.

Health is still excellent and can be enhanced even more by scalp and facial massage (until the 5th); neck and throat massage (especially the back of the neck) from the 5th to the 19th – cranial-sacral therapy is good during this period; and arm and shoulder massage afterwards. After the 19th give more attention to the lungs. Air purity seems more important then too.

Finance is still a major focus all month, but intellectual pursuits become more interesting after the 21st. This is a good period to take courses in subjects that interest you, and to plan a talk or lecture.

June

Best Days Overall: 1, 2, 10, 11, 19, 20, 28, 29

Most Stressful Days Overall: 5, 6, 12, 13, 25, 26

Best Days for Love: 3, 4, 5, 6, 12, 13, 22

Best Days for Money: 3, 4, 8, 9, 12, 13, 17, 18, 21, 22, 25, 26

Monthly Career Peaks: 1, 12, 13, 28

Monthly Personal Pleasure Peaks: 19, 20, 28, 29

Retrograde activity is increasing this month, Aries. By the 19th, 40 per cent of the planets will be in retrograde motion. Delays in many areas of life seem inevitable – and you, more than most, are uncomfortable with this. This is a period for slow, methodical progress.

The north node of the Moon – a signal for happiness and fulfilment – changes signs on the 23rd. It moves from your own sign into Pisces, your 12th House. Spirituality has been more important of late, but now it becomes even more so. Where you might have struggled in this area in the past, now it is going to bring fulfilment and happiness.

Like last month, most of the planets are in the lower half of the horoscope – the night side. Your 4th House of Home and Family, which was powerful last month, gets even stronger now, so this is a good time to focus on domestic and psychological issues. Interestingly, you might make more progress career-wise by focusing on the home, psychology and emotional harmony, rather than on the outer world. Happy career opportunities are coming from the 13th to the 19th. A cherished career goal may be attained as you are having fun, at a party or entertainment or sporting event. Your feeling of emotional harmony brings it to pass. If you have adult children, they too are likely to be experiencing an exciting career opportunity.

The planets make another important shift this month. Since the beginning of the year, the Eastern sector of your horoscope has been strong. But now the power shifts to the West. By the 21st, 60 per cent of the planets will be there. Next month, the percentage will be even greater, so you are in a less independent period. Personal initiative and direct actions are not as effective as usual. You need the help of other people to attain your ends so this is a time for cultivating social graces.

We have another Grand Square pattern this month showing big manifestation – the building of big things, both personally and in the world. These big building projects are creating opportunities for you, though there are stresses involved. It is the stresses that create the opportunities.

This month, home, family, children, fun and intellectual interests are highlighted. Finances are important but there are some delays involved and you may have to work a little harder than usual. Financial judgement is sound – you seem very down to earth this month – but this practicality could create conflict with your financial intuition. The intuition has a different perspective on what is and is not practical, and you are feeling this. Guess which will prove to be right in the end.

Love, too, is more challenging. You are torn between idealistic love and practical love but this will resolve itself by the 24th. Singles find love opportunities as they pursue their financial goals or with people involved with their finances. Current lovers seem very active – in a personal way – in your finances. Marrieds are experiencing better spousal support. After the 24th, love opportunities happen in educational surroundings, perhaps at a course or seminar you attend. There are also romantic opportunities close to home, perhaps with neighbours. Siblings enjoy playing cupid.

Your health needs more attention than usual after the 21st. Overall energy levels are not as high as normal. You can enhance health through arm and shoulder massage (until the 3rd), and by paying more attention to the lungs and air purity. Being out in the fresh air is a wonderful tonic when you feel low. After the 3rd, enhance health by paying more attention to the stomach and breasts. Diet and nutrition are more important during this period. Emotional health is also very important. If you feel under the weather, it is likely to be coming from some past emotional trauma. Water therapies will be more powerful during this time. After the 28th, enhance health by paying more attention to the heart and the spleen. Also, just being happy is a wonderful tonic. A night out on the town might do as much good as a visit to a health professional.

July

Best Days Overall: 8, 9, 16, 17, 25, 26

Most Stressful Days Overall: 3, 4, 10, 11, 23, 24, 30, 31

Best Days for Love: 3, 4, 12, 13, 22, 23, 30, 31

Best Days for Money: 3, 4, 5, 6, 12, 13, 14, 15, 18, 19, 22, 23, 24

Monthly Career Peaks: 10, 11, 25, 26

Monthly Personal Pleasure Peaks: 16, 17, 27, 28

Retrograde activity reaches a spasmodic peak this month and then slowly starts to ebb to more normal levels. From the 3rd to the 7th, 50 per cent of the planets will be in retrograde motion. This is a huge percentage. From the 7th to the 29th, 40 per cent will be retrograde, which is still a high percentage. After the 29th, only 30 per cent will be retrograde.

The message here for everyone – but especially for gung ho Aries – is patience. Go easy on yourself. Perhaps it's a good thing that all these retrogrades correspond with a strong lower half of the horoscope. You are better off dreaming, visualizing, working in an inner way rather than an outer way.

Delays can be used constructively as well. You can do more planning for the future and figure out improvements in your products or services.

Happily, there are no delays in love and finances. Love is still in the neighbourhood and close to home. Good communication seems important in love. You want to fall in love with a person's mind as much as with the body. On the 19th, Venus will move into Cancer and into your 4th House. This produces another shift in love. Now you want to share feelings. Ideas and mental harmony are not that important. Nurturing and emotional support are what matters. Though you seem very fun-oriented this month (and you should be), romance doesn't need wild nights out on the town. Quiet evenings at home will be just as satisfying, perhaps even more so. Singles might reconnect with old flames in order to resolve unfinished business or old issues.

Your health needs more watching until the 21st. It is a good idea to just rest and relax more. Don't allow yourself to get overtired. Your health planet will be retrograde from the 3rd to the 29th, so this is not a time to make drastic changes to your diet or health regime. Study things carefully during this period and make decisions after the 29th. Job offers at this time also need more study. You can enhance your health by taking better care of the heart and spleen until the 10th. Also, like last month, feeling happy is very important. After the 10th, pay more attention to the stomach and breasts and to emotional health.

Finances are reasonable this month. Sales, marketing and good use of the media seem unusually important. Neighbours and siblings have useful information for you and perhaps bring opportunity. After the 19th, family seems very supportive, especially a parent or parent figure. Financial intuition will be excellent after the 19th. With the financial planet in the moody sign of Cancer, make sure you are in the right mood before making an important financial decision. Financial opportunities can come from family members, family connections and the family business.

August

Best Days Overall: 4, 5, 12, 13, 21, 22, 23, 31

Most Stressful Days Overall: 6, 7, 19, 20, 26, 27

Best Days for Love: 2, 3, 11, 21, 22, 26, 27, 31

Best Days for Money: 2, 3, 10, 11, 14, 15, 19, 20, 21, 22, 29, 30, 31

Monthly Career Peaks: 6, 7, 21, 22

Monthly Personal Pleasure Peaks: 12, 13, 24, 25

The planetary shift to the Western sector of your chart intensifies this month, with 70 to 80 per cent of the planets there. While this limits your independence, it does enable you to practise social skills, have more fun in life and trust in the perfect actions of a Higher Power. Happily, with your ruling planet in Virgo all month, humility comes easier to you.

Most of the planets are still below the horizon, and your 4th House of Home and Family is much stronger than your 10th House of Career. Continue to focus on home and family, especially children, and find your point of emotional harmony. By next month, the planetary power will shift to the upper half of the chart and you will be in a very good psychological position to pursue your career goals.

As we saw last month, many wonderful career opportunities are happening now. Perhaps this is because you are more laid back about your career. It seems like fun. Adult children are also having good career opportunities now and are generally being recognized and honoured.

Home, family, children, fun, creativity, health and work are the dominant interests in the month ahead. You are working hard and being productive, but also playing hard.

Health is wonderful this month and you seem very focused on it. You are deeply into healthy diets, lifestyles and health regimes. You can enhance it even further by paying more attention to the stomach, breasts and overall emotional health until the 11th; to the heart and spleen (and to just feeling happy) until the 28th; to the small intestines after the 28th.

Finances were good last month and should be good again this month. Until the 13th, income and earning opportunities come from family support (probably a parent or parent figure), family connections and businesses. Professional investors should look at property and industries that cater to the home for profit ideas. After the 13th earnings come from personal creativity and as you pursue leisure activities. Money is earned in happy ways. Children can have good wealth ideas and suggestions. Speculations are favourable (but always under intuition and never blindly). A parent or parent figure prospers and is generous with you. Bosses and elders are supportive of financial goals. The main danger now is spending too much as you feel overconfident.

Love is reasonable this month. Until the 13th your love needs are the same as last month. You want emotional support and nurturing. You want to share feelings. You want to 'parent' and be 'parented'. The sensitivities in love are unusually strong this month – both in you and your lover – so be more careful of voice tones and body language. After the 13th, love is about having fun and a good time. You might not feel like getting serious in love, and might be content with just fun-and-games types of relationships. Love opportunities will come in places of leisure and entertainment.

Mars, your ruler, will re-stimulate eclipse points towards the end of the month, from the 29th to the 31st. Try to avoid risky, stressful activities.

September

Best Days Overall: 1, 9, 10, 17, 18, 19, 27, 28, 29

Most Stressful Days Overall: 3, 4, 15, 16, 22, 23, 24, 30

Best Days for Love: 1, 2, 11, 20, 21, 22, 23, 24, 30

Best Days for Money: 1, 2, 7, 8, 11, 12, 15, 16, 20, 21, 25, 26, 30

Monthly Career Peaks: 3, 4, 17, 18, 30

Monthly Personal Pleasure Peaks: 9, 10, 22, 23

Two simultaneous T-squares (one in the fixed and one in the mutable signs) and two eclipses ensure that this will be a tumultuous and eventful month, especially for the world at large. Big changes and dramas are going on. Of course you are affected to some degree, but not as much as most people.

The Lunar Eclipse of the 15th occurs in your 12th House of Spirituality. The effects of this eclipse happen behind the scenes and not that overtly. It brings long-term change to your spiritual life, to your spiritual regime and practice and perhaps with your teachers. For those not on a path, this might be a time to get on one. If you are involved in charitable or spiritual organizations, these kinds of eclipses often bring upheavals, and you might change your relationship with them. This eclipse occurs very near Uranus, your planet of friendship, so friendships could get tested too. Every Lunar Eclipse impacts on the home and family, for the Moon is your family planet. Sometimes hidden flaws in the home are revealed and you're forced to correct them. Often long-standing resentments between family members surface and the air gets cleared.

The Solar Eclipse of September 22nd is an unusual one. It occurs right on the border of your 6th and 7th Houses. Technically it is in the 6th House, but it is so close to the 7th that we must read it as impacting on the 7th as well. So,

44

there will be job changes within your present company or with another one, and general alterations in the conditions at work. You may also make changes to your diet and over-all health regime. Your marriage or current relationship or friendships will be tested.

Singles need not worry. This is a very social month, perhaps the strongest of the year. (Next month will also be strong.) You are out there looking. You are aggressive in love (more so than usual) and your personal popularity has seldom been better. You put other people first, which influences how others feel about you. Opportunities for romance will be found in the usual places, but the workplace also seems a scene of love opportunity, especially after the 6th. The only challenge in love is a tendency to be too critical and too much of a perfectionist (your love planet is in Virgo). Also, with Venus in Virgo, you are more likely to attract partners who are like this.

Keep a lid on your spending until after the 6th. Venus in Virgo is a very good position for finance; ensuring that you are a careful spender, getting the most for your money. With the financial planet in Virgo, earnings come in the normal way – through work.

Job-seekers have had wonderful aspects for the past few months, and this trend continues in September. There seems to be no problem here. Even if the eclipse causes you to change jobs, there are other jobs available – and easily.

Health is good, but rest and relax more after the 23rd. Your intense focus on health is a good sign. You will not let problems fester and you will be alert to your body. Health can be enhanced by paying more attention to the small intestine until the 13th and to the kidneys and hips afterwards. After the 13th, happiness in friendship and love is important (and you seem to have it). Health problems can come from love problems. If you feel low or under the weather, check out your relationships and try to restore harmony. Hip and buttock massage is powerful after the 13th.

October

Best Days Overall: 6, 7, 15, 16, 25, 26

Most Stressful Days Overall: 1, 12, 13, 14, 20, 21, 27, 28

Best Days for Love: 2, 3, 10, 11, 20, 21, 22

Best Days for Money: 2, 3, 4, 5, 8, 9, 10, 11, 12, 13, 14, 21, 22, 23, 24

Monthly Career Peaks: 1, 15, 16, 27, 28

Monthly Personal Pleasure Peaks: 6, 7, 21

The planetary power is now at its maximum Western position. Seventy to eighty per cent of the planets are in the West, and your 7th House of Love, Romance and Social Activities is the strongest in the horoscope. Your 1st House of Self is empty (only the Moon will visit there on the 6th and 7th). Like last month (only more so) there is a need to tone down the ego and your personal needs and to put other people first. You can attain your aims by compromise, consensus and cooperation, not by high-handed actions. Social skills and who you know are more important than who you are and what you can do. Happily, you seem to be able to do this. You are in your yearly social peak until the 23rd.

So, there are many parties and social invitations happening. Singles are dating more and have many romantic opportunities. Again we see love pursuing you, but this time you can't just stay at home – you have to be 'out there'. The social circle is varied – there are athletic types, colleagues, doctors, health professionals and an entertainer or two there. Serious romance happens from the 22nd to the 26th.

Since Venus is both your love and financial planet there is always a strong connection between love and money in your horoscope. But this month the connection is even stronger. Your social success will translate to financial success. Your social connections, friends and romantic partner are helping you to prosper. Those of you who earn your money through sales, marketing and networking should have a successful month. Professional investors should look at the beauty industry as well as confectioners and the copper industry for profit or trading ideas (until the 24th). After the 24th, bonds and the bond market look interesting. This is also a good time to pay off debts and deal with tax issues. Those of you who are doing estate planning would do well to wait until after the 24th to start. In general, prosperity comes by putting the financial interests of others ahead of your own. Marrieds should experience greater spousal support.

Attitudes to love are also interesting this month. Until the 24th it is romance that allures you. But after the 24th, love is more about passion and emotional intensity. Sex is the way you express and receive love.

This month the planets make another important shift from the lower half of the horoscope – the night side – to the upper half, or day side. Career and outer achievement start to become more important than family, domestic or psychological issues. You feel that you can serve your family best by succeeding out in the world, that your success will produce emotional harmony. Your active social life is not only bringing financial increase but also much career opportunity. After the 23rd you might start fine-tuning your career path, making important changes there. Your focus on the prosperity of others might distract you from your own career path so don't ignore it altogether.

Health-wise, this isn't your best month. This doesn't necessarily mean sickness, only that overall energy is not up to its usual standards. Set aside times for rejuvenation. Health can be enhanced by giving more attention to the hips, buttocks and kidneys (until the 2nd) and to the colon, bladder and sexual organs afterwards. Sexual passions run high this month but keep sexual expression in balance. Don't force the body into more than it needs. Your health planet starts to move retrograde on the 28th, so important health decisions should be made before then.

November

Best Days Overall: 3, 11, 12, 21, 22, 30

Most Stressful Days Overall: 9, 10, 16, 17, 23, 24

Best Days for Love: 1, 9, 10, 16, 17, 21, 30

Best Days for Money: 1, 2, 5, 9, 10, 20, 21, 30

Monthly Career Peaks: 11, 12, 23, 24

Monthly Personal Pleasure Peaks: 3, 19, 20, 30

The main headline this month is the awesome power in your 8th House of Transformation and Regeneration. On the mundane level, there is more sexual activity. The deeper things of life also call to you. You want to understand more about life and death, life after death, reincarnation and past lives. As the month progresses, you *will* understand more. The planets in this House are mostly happy ones, so there will probably be no physical deaths, but the cosmos will arrange things so that you confront death in some way, probably on a psychological level. Those who are involved in in-depth psychology will make very important break-throughs now.

Many of you will start behaving like Scorpios this month. You will be bored with superficial, inane conversation. There is a hunger for essence and depth.

This is a very prosperous month for your spouse, partner or beloved. The year in general has been prosperous for them, but this month is especially so, a peak period in a peak year. This prosperity will naturally translate into greater generosity towards you.

Most of you will experience increases in your line of credit. Those of you seeking outside investors or capital will have much success. Debts will be easily paid – but also easily made. Because outside money is so easily available you need to resist the temptation to borrow frivolously.

Those involved in insurance claims will have a happy outcome now.

Your powers of concentration are greatly enhanced now, so it is important that you focus on happy and positive things.

Like last month, love is about sex, passion and emotional intensity. By the 17th, the passions are spent (no one can take that much intensity for too long) and love becomes more light-hearted. Singles will find love opportunities in foreign lands or with foreigners, and also in educational and religious settings. There is a need to be in philosophical and religious harmony with your beloved. Passion alone doesn't satisfy you.

Religion and philosophy are becoming more important in general, not just in love. Jupiter makes an important move on the 24th from your 8th House to your 9th House. So the year ahead is a 'religious' kind of year. You are going to explore the meaning of life in general, but especially the meaning of your own life.

Those of you involved in personal transformation will have an excellent month. You will make much progress here and expand your knowledge.

Health is much improved over last month. Your health planet, Mercury, is retrograde until the 18th, so avoid making major changes to your health regime or diet until then. Really, with health improving, there is no need to do so. Like last month, enhance health by paying more attention to the colon, bladder and sexual organs.

With Mercury retrograde, job-seekers need to do more homework on job offers. Wait until the 18th to decide. The whole job picture will change after that, so present thinking is probably not realistic.

December

Best Days Overall: 1, 8, 9, 10, 18, 19, 27, 28

Most Stressful Days Overall: 6, 7, 13, 14, 15, 21, 22

Best Days for Love: 1, 9, 10, 11, 13, 14, 15, 21, 22, 29, 30

Best Days for Money: 1, 2, 3, 4, 8, 9, 10, 11, 18, 21, 22, 27, 29, 30

Monthly Career Peaks: 9, 10, 11, 21, 22

Monthly Personal Pleasure Peaks: 1, 18, 19, 27, 28

The main headline this month is the power in your 9th House and the sign of Sagittarius. This is a very harmonious situation for you. The Fire element, your native element, is unusually strong with 70 to 80 per cent of the planets either in, or moving through, fire signs. So, not only is health vastly improved, but you have the energy of 10 people.

With more energy, enthusiasm and boundless optimism, prosperity is huge. It's as if the whole universe is conspiring to make you prosper. You catch the lucky breaks. Speculations are favourable. People are receptive to your ideas and financial goals. Your financial goals are larger than life these days – especially until the 11th – and you earn more because of that. We receive what we believe we can receive. You are earning big and spending big, perhaps even recklessly. But no matter – you have caught Jupiter's fever. Overspending is perhaps the main financial danger. It's OK to increase spending, since you have more money, but never lose your sense of proportion. This is the kind of month when you are ready to fly to some exotic location merely to have lunch. After the 11th, when Venus moves into conservative Capricorn, you will tone this down of your own accord. You will manage your money better too. It's probably much safer to do your Christmas shopping after the 11th.

ARIES

Students who are applying to college or university should hear happy news. Many of you will travel this month as there are hosts of opportunities coming. Even non-students will have very happy educational opportunities coming their way.

On a deeper level, this is a month for religious and philosophic revelation. The cosmos is pouring its wisdom down on you, and the receptive ones will get it. You will have a new understanding about the meaning of your life and the meaning of many of the events that have happened. They all had very good (and benevolent) reasons.

Health will be excellent all month. The main danger here is too much of a good thing. With all this fire in your horoscope, you will tend to flit from one activity to the other. The danger here is burnout. Try to schedule in some rest periods as well.

This is also a very powerful career month, a yearly career peak. Venus will cross your Midheaven from the 10th to the 12th. The Sun will cross it from the 21st to the 23rd. Mercury will cross on the 27th. Major career advancement and opportunity is happening.

With Venus in your 10th House after the 11th, you are socializing with the high and the mighty – with people of power, status and prominence. There could even be love opportunities with these kinds of people. Bosses, elders, parents, and even the government, all seem kindly disposed to you. (If you have issues with the government, this is a time to resolve them as I expect a best-case scenario outcome.) Love is more practical these days. You are allured by people who can help you career-wise. There is something comforting about people who take the 'duties' of love seriously. You want to feel secure in love. And people who can make you feel secure are attractive.

Mars, your ruler will re-stimulate eclipse points from the 26th to the 28th. Avoid high-risk or stressful activities during this time.

Taurus

♉

THE BULL
*Birthdays from
21st April to
20th May*

Personality Profile

TAURUS AT A GLANCE

Element – Earth

Ruling Planet – Venus
   Career Planet – Uranus
   Love Planet – Pluto
   Money Planet – Mercury
   Planet of Health and Work – Venus
   Planet of Home and Family Life – Sun
   Planet of Spirituality – Mars
   *Planet of Travel, Education, Religion and
      Philosophy* – Saturn

Colours – earth tones, green, orange, yellow

*Colours that promote love, romance and social
   harmony* – red-violet, violet

TAURUS

Colours that promote earning power – yellow,
yellow-orange

Gems – coral, emerald

Metal – copper

Scents – bitter almond, rose, vanilla, violet

Quality – fixed (= stability)

Quality most needed for balance – flexibility

Strongest virtues – endurance, loyalty, patience,
stability, a harmonious disposition

Deepest needs – comfort, material ease, wealth

Characteristics to avoid – rigidity, stubbornness,
tendency to be overly possessive and
materialistic

Signs of greatest overall compatibility – Virgo,
Capricorn

Signs of greatest overall incompatibility – Leo,
Scorpio, Aquarius

Sign most helpful to career – Aquarius

Sign most helpful for emotional support – Leo

Sign most helpful financially – Gemini

Sign best for marriage and/or partnerships –
Scorpio

Sign most helpful for creative projects – Virgo

Best Sign to have fun with – Virgo

Signs most helpful in spiritual matters – Aries,
Capricorn

Best day of the week – Friday

Understanding a Taurus

Taurus is the most earthy of all the Earth Signs. If you understand that Earth is more than just a physical element, that it is a psychological attitude as well, you will get a better understanding of the Taurus personality.

A Taurus has all the power of action that an Aries has. But Taureans are not satisfied with action for its own sake. Their actions must be productive, practical and wealth-producing. If Taureans cannot see a practical value in an action they will not bother taking it.

Taureans' forte lies in their power to make real their own or other people's ideas. They are generally not very inventive but they can take another's invention and perfect it, making it more practical and useful. The same is true for all projects. Taureans are not especially keen on starting new projects, but once they get involved they bring things to completion. A Taurus carries everything through. Their finishers and will go the distance so long as no unavoidable calamity intervenes.

Many people find Taureans too stubborn, conservative, fixed and immovable. This is understandable, because Taureans dislike change – in their environment or in their routine. Taureans even dislike changing their minds! On the other hand, this is their virtue. It is not good for a wheel's axle to waver. The axle must be fixed, stable and unmovable. Taureans are the axle of society and the heavens. Without their stability and so-called stubbornness, the wheels of the world (and especially the wheels of commerce) would not turn.

Taureans love routine. A routine, if it is good, has many virtues. It is a fixed – and, ideally, perfect – way of taking care of things. Mistakes can happen when spontaneity comes into the equation, and mistakes cause discomfort and uneasiness – something almost unacceptable to a Taurus.

Meddling with Taureans' comfort and security is a sure way to irritate and anger them.

While an Aries loves speed, a Taurus likes things slow. They are slow thinkers – but do not make the mistake of assuming they lack intelligence. On the contrary, Taureans are very intelligent. It is just that they like to chew on ideas, to deliberate and weigh them up. Only after due deliberation is an idea accepted or a decision taken. Taureans are slow to anger – but once aroused, take care!

Finance

Taureans are very money-conscious. Wealth is more important to them than to many other Signs. Wealth to a Taurus means comfort and security. Wealth means stability. Where some Zodiac Signs feel that they are spiritually rich if they have ideas, talents or skills, Taureans only feel their wealth when they can see and touch it. Taurus' way of thinking is 'What good is a talent if it has not been translated into a home, furniture, car and holidays?'

These are all reasons why Taureans excel in estate agency and agricultural industries. Usually a Taurus will end up owning land. They love to feel their connection to the Earth. Material wealth began with agriculture, the tilling of the soil. Owning a piece of land was humanity's earliest form of wealth: Taureans still feel that primeval connection.

It is in the pursuit of wealth that Taureans develop their intellectual and communication abilities. Also, in this pursuit Taureans are forced to develop some flexibility. It is in the quest for wealth that they learn the practical value of the intellect and come to admire it. If it were not for the search for wealth and material things, Taureans might not try to reach a higher intellect.

Some Taureans are 'born-lucky' – the type of people who win any gamble or speculation. This luck is due to other factors in their Horoscope; it is not part of their essential nature. By nature they are not gamblers. They are hard workers and like to earn what they get. Taureans' innate conservatism makes them abhor unnecessary risks in finance and in other areas of their lives.

Career and Public Image

Being essentially down-to-earth people, simple and uncomplicated, Taureans tend to look up to those who are original, unconventional and inventive. Taureans like their bosses to be creative and original – since they themselves are content to perfect their superiors' brain-waves. They admire people who have a wider social or political consciousness and they feel that someday (when they have all the comfort and security they need) they too would like to be involved in these big issues.

In business affairs Taureans can be very shrewd – and that makes them valuable to their employers. They are never lazy; they enjoy working and getting good results. Taureans do not like taking unnecessary risks and do well in positions of authority, which makes them good managers and supervisors. Their managerial skills are reinforced by their natural talents for organization and handling details, their patience and thoroughness. As mentioned, through their connection with the earth, Taureans also do well in farming and agriculture.

In general a Taurus will choose money and earning power over public esteem and prestige. A position that pays more – though it has less prestige – is preferred to a position with a lot of prestige but fewer earnings. Many other Signs do not feel this way, but a Taurus does, especially if there is nothing in his or her personal birth chart that modifies this. Taureans will pursue glory and prestige only if it can be shown that these things have a direct and immediate impact on their wallet.

Love and Relationships

In love, the Taurus-born likes to have and to hold. They are the marrying kind. They like commitment and they like the terms of a relationship to be clearly defined. More importantly, Taureans like to be faithful to one lover, and they expect that lover to reciprocate this fidelity. When this does not happen their whole world comes crashing down. When they are in love Taureans are loyal, but they are also very possessive. They are capable of great fits of jealousy if they are hurt in love.

Taureans are satisfied with the simple things in a relationship. If you are involved romantically with a Taurus there is no need for lavish entertainments and constant courtship. Give them enough love, food and comfortable shelter and they will be quite content to stay home and enjoy your company. They will be loyal to you for life. Make a Taurus feel comfortable and – above all – secure in the relationship, and you will rarely have a problem.

In love, Taureans can sometimes make the mistake of trying to control their partners, which can cause great pain on both sides. The reasoning behind their actions is basically simple: Taureans feel a sense of ownership over their partners and will want to make changes that will increase their own general comfort and security. This attitude is OK when it comes to inanimate, material things – but is dangerous when applied to people. Taureans need to be careful and attentive to this possible trait within themselves.

Home and Domestic Life

Home and family are vitally important to Taureans. They like children. They also like a comfortable and perhaps glamorous home – something they can show off. They tend to buy heavy, ponderous furniture – usually of the best quality. This is because Taureans like a feeling of substance in their environment. Their house is not only their home but their place of creativity and entertainment. The Taureans' home tends to be truly their castle. If they could choose, Taureans would prefer living in the countryside to being city-dwellers. If they cannot do so during their working lives, many Taureans like to holiday in or even retire to the country, away from the city and closer to the land.

At home a Taurus is like a country squire – lord (or lady) of the manor. They love to entertain lavishly, to make others feel secure in their home and to encourage others to derive the same sense of satisfaction as they do from it. If you are invited for dinner at the home of a Taurus you can expect the best food and best entertainment. Be prepared for a tour of the house and expect to see your Taurus friend exhibit a lot of pride and satisfaction in his or her possessions.

Taureans like children but they are usually strict with them. The reason for this is they tend to treat their children – as they do most things in life – as their possessions. The positive side to this is that their children will be well cared for and well supervised. They will get every material thing they need to grow up properly. On the down side, Taureans can get too repressive with their children. If a child dares to upset the daily routine – which Taureans love to follow – he or she will have a problem with a Taurus parent.

Horoscope for 2006

General Trends

This is going to be a bittersweet kind of year. Make no mistake, there are many wonderful happy things going on – especially in love and career – but there is also more resistance to your efforts. With three long-term planets in stressful aspect with you, there are strong headwinds to be overcome. You need to be kinder to yourself – judge yourself less harshly these days. When there are no headwinds, a walker can cover many miles with ease. With headwinds, the same journey can take many days. In a blizzard, taking 10 steps in a day could be considered success. To judge yourself fairly you need to take into account your surrounding conditions, especially the cosmic condition. You will earn your good luck this year – and know that you earned it.

Part of what is happening is that you are attempting big things, so there are more challenges involved. It's the very power of your aspiration that is bringing on many of these challenges. For these things go with the territory – they are part of the league that you play in.

Two eclipses will occur in your 12th House of Spirituality this year – a Solar Eclipse on March 9th and Lunar Eclipse on October 17th. Although spirituality is not a major interest this year (though it should be), these eclipses are showing important and long-term changes here. Those who are already on a spiritual path might change regimes, techniques or teachers. Those not on one might face upheavals in their charitable activities or in the charitable organizations they belong to.

There will also be an eclipse in your 6th House this year. This is showing job and health regime changes, and we will discuss this later on.

Your main interests in the coming year are love (until November 24th); sex, personal transformation, occult studies, past lives and the deeper things of life (all year but even stronger after November 24th); career, friendships and group activities; home, family and psychological issues.

Your paths to greatest fulfilment in the year ahead are love and social activities (until November 24th); sex, personal transformation, occult studies, past lives and the deeper things of life (after November 24th); spirituality and altruistic activities (until June 23rd); friendships, groups, organizations, astrology and scientific interests (after June 23rd).

Health

(Please note that this is an astrological perspective on health, not a medical one. At one time, both perspectives were identical, but in these times there could be quite a difference. For the medical perspective, please consult your physician or health professional.)

This is an area that needs watching this year. And the main danger here – because your 6th House of Health is not strong – is that you will take good health for granted. Thus minor ailments can become major illnesses.

As three long-term planets are in stressful aspect to you, your overall energy level is not as high as usual. If you understand this, you will rest and relax more. Listen to your body.

Alternate different activities, rotating the use of your faculties. If you've been working mentally for a while, switch to something physical – do some exercise. Then do something creative.

With these kinds of aspects on you it is a good idea to rethink your priorities in life. Focus on the important things and let frivolities and distractions go. We are involved in so many things that have little bearing on our true heart's desire. When energy is abundant we can afford the luxury of these distractions. But when energy is lessened, we can't.

If you are taking care of yourself and watching your energy, the Solar Eclipse in your 6th House of Health (September 22nd) will probably bring changes to your overall regime and lead to health improvements. But if you're not taking care of yourself, this eclipse can be a wake-up call.

Since Taurus rules the neck and throat, regular neck massage (especially the back of the neck) will be wonderful.

With Venus as both your personal ruler and health planet, the kidneys, buttocks and hips will need more attention. Buttocks and hips can be regularly massaged. The kidneys can be strengthened by many natural therapies.

Try to wear your healing metals and colours more this year. This will be a big help to the subtle energy levels.

Venus is a fast-moving planet. During the course of the year ahead she will move through all the signs and houses of your horoscope. Health needs and powerful therapies will tend to change with the movements of Venus. We will deal with these short-term trends in the monthly reports.

A parent or parent figure is very health-conscious this year. They are undertaking disciplined regimes and are probably involved in weight-loss projects, and seem to gravitate towards orthodox medicine. Their health can be enhanced through paying more attention to the heart, spine, knees and teeth. Children can benefit from more experimental therapies – the cutting edge of technology. Their health is enhanced by paying more attention to the ankles and feet. Regular foot and ankle massage will do wonders for them. They need to give their ankles more support when they exercise or play sports. The health of your lover or spouse seems to be consistent, although the eclipses of March 29th and October 17th can be wake-up calls. The health of grand-children also seems unchanged.

Home, Domestic and Family Issues

Ever since July 17th 2005, this has been an important and perhaps challenging area of life. Saturn moved into your 4th House of Home and Family and will be there all this year and well into next. Often this brings a feeling of being cramped in the home and there is a desire to move. Yet a move is probably not advisable and may be difficult. (A year or two from now will be much better.) So, you need to become more efficient with the space that you have and reorganize the home.

Sometimes this feeling of tightness is due to a new child or a visiting relative, perhaps someone from a foreign land. You are challenged to maximize what you have, and if you put your mind to it you'll be amazed at how much space you really have. The tightness came from inefficiency.

Often one feels the burden of family under this kind of a transit. Family supports us, and it works both ways. Now it seems you have to be there for them, to pick up the burden and take responsibility. But it's not easy. Career is very important this year. The duties there are also powerful. And so you have to seesaw back and forth between these two obligations. As if this weren't enough – and this is probably the hardest part – you are having a wonderful social life this year, perhaps one of the best of your life, so social urges are also conflicting here. All of this can be handled by giving each area its due. If love is real, your partner will understand your family and career responsibilities.

Saturn moving through the 4th House also has an important psychological impact. The cosmos wants you to get your emotional life in order. You can't let your emotions run wild these days. Non-constructive feelings and emotions will simply have to go. Many of you will have to delve deep, to go back to experiences of early childhood (and maybe even further than that) to track down the origins of these unruly responses, and then clear them. It is definitely a period for psychological progress and breakthroughs. There are no short cuts here, and anyone promising them should be avoided.

Feelings of depression are quite normal under a transit like this, and these are just signals to go deeper into your psychological research. Depression is easily cleared through meditation and spiritual practice. But if you are not on a spiritual path, perhaps a therapist can help. And, sometimes, if this interferes with your 'functionality', medication could help, but this is always the last resort.

If you plan to renovate or extend the home (and it might be a good idea this year – better than moving), June 3rd to August 23rd is a good time. If you're planning to redecorate – beautifying the home in a cosmetic way – August 12th to September 6th is a good time.

A parent or parent figure is moving this year, a happy move to larger and more opulent quarters. They might buy an additional home as well.

Adult children will move later in the year, after November 24th. But it could also happen in 2007.

Love and Social Life

As already mentioned, this is an excellent year socially, perhaps one of the best in your life. It began late October 2005 when Jupiter moved into Scorpio and your 7th House of Love. It will continue for another two years or so. (Next year Jupiter will travel with your love planet in Sagittarius, so the party continues even after Jupiter leaves your 7th House.)

For singles (those working on their first marriage), this is likely to lead to marriage or a very significant relationship. For those with partners, it means more romance within your current relationship. Those of you working on your second marriage will have a happy social life too, but marriage doesn't seem likely. Love affairs are more probable. Those working on their third marriage probably shouldn't marry, even though there are many opportunities. There is too much instability here.

All Taureans will have an expanded social life and social circle. New and very important friends are coming into your life. They seem like money people – well educated, refined, sophisticated. Just the kind of people you love to associate with. Your social life is a real joy this year, a bringer of fulfilment.

Since money is very prominent in this transit (Jupiter rules your 8th House of other people's money), this could also manifest as an important business partnership. In astrology, a business partnership is considered a certain type of 'marriage'.

Though love is very happy, there are still a few challenges. Saturn is making a stressful aspect to Jupiter, and this suggests caution in love. I read this as 'letting love develop as it will', not a good time to rush to the altar. Let time work its perfect magic. Also, there could be a challenge in getting your family to accept this new romance or partnership. This person and the family don't seem to get along. Friendships are also affected. This is not a surprise. You will have a new interest and friends will be relegated to second or third place. Perhaps this new love doesn't get on with some of your friends. Religious differences are playing a role here too, both with friends and family. But true love – and time – will resolve these challenges.

Love is always a transforming experience. It is a death that leads to greater life. And this is especially so for you. You will have a new set of friends and perhaps a new relationship with your family.

Your best social periods (in a great year) will be February 19th to March 20th; June 21st to 22nd; October 23rd to December 21st.

The marriages of children seem unstable and in crisis. If they are single (and of marriageable age), they are better off not marrying this year. They are too experimental and attracting partners who are the same. Nobody seems ready for commitment.

Grandchildren of marriageable age have a status-quo year. Singles will most likely stay single and marrieds will stay married.

Finance and Career

Though finance is always important to you, Taurus, your 2nd House is not a House of Power this year. I read this as contentment with things as they are.

As we saw with Aries, the major prosperity seems to come from the outside, not from personal earning power. Marrieds will get very strong spousal support. There can be an inheritance or trust fund set up for you, or you can be remembered in someone's will. Many of you will have substantial insurance settlements. If you are in a position to collect royalties, you will see them increase.

This is a good year (especially after November 24th) for paying off debts, refinancing existing debts, and attracting outside investors to your projects.

Because outside money is so easy to get hold of, you need to be careful of debt – especially frivolous debt. If you borrow to buy assets that will increase their value over time, you will enhance your wealth. But if you borrow just to take a holiday or to buy clothing you can create problems for yourself.

Fast-moving Mercury is your financial planet. In a given year Mercury will move through all the signs and houses of your horoscope. Thus financial opportunities and earnings will tend to come to you in many ways and through many sources.

Mercury rules sales, marketing and communication, so all these areas (and good use of the media) are especially important to you on the financial level. Basically, you need to get the message out about your product or service.

Mercury goes retrograde three times a year, and these periods always impact on your earnings. They don't stop earnings but can cause delays and glitches. This year these periods are from March 2nd to 25th; July 4th to 29th; October 28th to November 18th.

Although, as we mentioned, you are juggling a full social and family life with your career, your career seems good. Many of you are gravitating to the film, radio and television industry, but the Internet would also fit the bill. You are idealistic in your career and want to work in industries that are changing the world for the better. This idealism is probably complicating things with your family as you feel 'I'm doing things that are *so* important, how can I be bothered with petty family things?' But you will find that the petty, mundane things also have their importance.

Career-wise you have friends in the right places. Your social connections and networking skills are superb. You have a lot of cosmic help here.

The Solar Eclipse of September 22nd is very near your 6th House of work – not exactly there, but close enough to be a factor. This means many of you will have job changes. You might not leave your present company, but will probably have a different job. The conditions at work will also change. If you employ others, there could be upheavals among your employees. Some could leave.

Personal earning power will be strongest from May 5th to June 21st. Career is very strong from January 20th to March 20th.

One of the parents (or parent figures in your life) is greatly prospering. They are taking risks and into glamorous work. Finances are unstable, but when earnings come, they come big time.

Children's income is fairly consistent. Adult grandchildren are experimenting financially, trying out different things, throwing out the rule books and learning about money for themselves. They will learn a lot this way.

Self-improvement

We discussed earlier how the cosmos is going to bring order to your emotional nature. This is the deeper meaning of Saturn's move through your 4th House. Though the experience is not necessarily pleasant, it is a wonderful thing – you will see this in hindsight. Not many people understand that emotional energy *is* energy. These are real forces, as real as electricity or magnetism. Cosmically speaking, people are held accountable for the use or abuse of these forces. There is karma attached to them. If you are not in control of these things, chances are that you are continually creating negative karma on yourself, and this is impacting on your health, finances and relationships, and also on your overall feeling of 'wellness'. It is difficult to study, make decisions or reason properly when we are upset, angry or depressed. Your anger is bringing more anger upon you. Your fear is attracting more fear to you. So, the cosmos is really doing you a favour by helping you to manage these things.

Theoretically, a human has total dominion over the emotional nature, especially the lower emotions. In practice, we find few who are exercising this. Most people are victims of their emotional nature, rather than its master. You might not make it to full mastery over the next two years – this is unrealistic as it is a life-long project – but you will make much progress towards it, and that's wonderful.

Here are a few ways to help neutralize the impact of negative emotions on you. One technique is to write down your feelings on paper. Just allow these feelings expression, but only in writing. 'So and so is a B-; I really despise so and so.' Do this for half an hour and then destroy the paper. Don't reread what you've written – it's considered psychic garbage – just throw out or destroy the paper. Watch how good you feel afterwards. You haven't yet cured the issue, but you've expressed your feelings and taken the pressure off. You don't need to express it on the person and create more negative karma. Another technique is to speak out your feelings in a tape recorder. Rage and rant all you want on tape. Then, when you feel calm, erase the tape. Make a statement that 'these feelings are now gone from me forever'. You still need to explore the origin of these things, as we mentioned earlier, but at least you won't be lashing out at innocent family members as you search for the solution. Your mind will become clear as well.

Month-by-month Forecasts

January

Best Days Overall: 8, 9, 17, 18, 19, 27, 28

Most Stressful Days Overall: 1, 2, 15, 16, 22, 23, 29, 30

Best Days for Love: 7, 8, 9, 16, 17, 18, 19, 22, 23, 26, 27, 28

Best Days for Money: 3, 4, 8, 9, 10, 11, 12, 13, 18, 19, 22, 23, 29, 30, 31

Monthly Career Peaks: 1, 2, 3, 4, 19, 20, 29, 30

Monthly Personal Pleasure Peaks: 8, 9, 27, 28

You begin your year with 70 to 80 per cent of the planets above the horizon. The day side of your horoscope predominates. Day is for doing and achieving in the outer world, for acting on the dreams you have nurtured in the past. And though you can't ignore home and family issues, with your 10th House much stronger (especially after the 20th) than your 4th House, you can safely down-play family interests. Right now you can probably serve the family best by succeeding in your profession. The good news is that family seems supportive of your career. Family members are also succeeding. The family as a whole is elevated in status this month. Probably you will work more from the home. Many will work to make the office more home like and comfortable. The New Moon of the 29th will occur in your 10th House of Career, and this is going to bring clarity and revelation in all things involving work. Any information you need to make a good decision is on its way to you – from the 29th onwards.

This month there is an important shift of planetary power – from the West side of the horoscope to the Eastern side. The shift will be complete by the 22nd. In the meantime you are in a twilight zone – neither totally Western (other-oriented), nor totally Eastern (self-oriented). But as the shift establishes itself, you will find yourself becoming more and more independent.

Your personal planet, Venus, is retrograde all month – a pretty rare event. So this is a good time to gain clarity on what your personal goals are. Once this clarity is achieved, you will make better use of your coming independence.

TAURUS

Aside from career, your 9th House of Religion, Philosophy, Higher Education and Foreign Travel is very strong this month. Many of you will be travelling and have opportunities to travel. Happy educational opportunities are coming. There is much religious and philosophical revelation for those who are receptive.

This is a very strong love year in general. But this month – especially after the 22nd – love gets competition from the career. Love is about sex and passion these days. Aside from sexual harmony there is a need for religious and philosophical harmony as well.

Finances are reasonable for most of the month. Financial judgement is sound, practical and down to earth. With your financial planet moving through the 9th House from the 4th to the 22nd, there is prosperity now. Financial horizons increase, and opportunity can happen in foreign lands or with foreigners. Professional investors should look at property and conservative blue chip types of stock. Your partner or spouse and other family members are prospering and generous with you. Insurance and tax issues will have best-case scenarios (especially before the 20th). After the 22nd there can be a pay rise, promotion or bonus at work. Your good professional reputation leads to referrals and increases income.

Mars will be in your own sign all month. In general (and if used properly) this gives more energy, more libido, and enhances athletic performance. But temper is the main danger.

Health needs watching all month, but especially after the 20th. You are working hard and carrying a big load, but you need to pace yourself better. Enhance health by paying more attention to the spine, knees, teeth and skeletal alignment. With your health planet retrograde all month, avoid making major changes to your regime. Regular visits to the chiropractor seem like a good idea these days.

With a powerful Grand Square pattern happening all month, you are attempting big things, and this taxes the energy.

Venus, your ruler, will re-stimulate eclipse points from the 11th to the 14th.

February

Best Days Overall: 4, 5, 14, 15, 23, 24

Most Stressful Days Overall: 11, 12, 19, 20, 25, 26

Best Days for Love: 3, 4, 5, 12, 14, 15, 19, 20, 22, 23, 24

Best Days for Money: 1, 6, 7, 9, 10, 16, 17, 19, 20, 27, 28

Monthly Career Peaks: 1, 25, 26, 27, 28

Monthly Personal Pleasure Peaks: 4, 5, 23, 24

The Grand Square pattern of last month continues until the 18th. You are working on big things – major projects – and it takes much energy. Health needs watching until the 19th. After the 19th you will be amazed at how much better you feel. In the meantime, continue to enhance health by paying more attention to the spine (back massage is very therapeutic now), the knees, and the overall skeletal alignment. Be more aware of your posture now. The kidneys are always important for you, and these too can impact on the lower back.

The main headline now is the career. Like last month, 70 to 80 per cent of the planets are above the horizon and your 10th House of Career is still very strong. After the 19th, your career planet, Uranus, will receive powerful stimulation, so you are very much into your yearly career peak. You can expect more honour, recognition, pay rises, promotions and, of course, responsibility. Sudden career advancement will happen after the 19th. It might involve relocation as well, but perhaps you can avoid this. This is not a good year for a move.

Like last month, your spouse, partner or current love is prospering in a big way, especially after the 19th. They will, of course, be more generous with you. Like last month, money is earned because of your good professional reputation, as well as through pay rises and promotion. After the 9th, friends and organizations play a big role in earnings, either as clients or customers or through providing financial opportunity. Sudden and unexpected windfalls come from the 13th to the 15th. This could be from parents, but also from other authority figures in your life. More windfalls (or opportunities) come on the 19th and 20th.

Jupiter, the ruler of your 8th House of other people's money, receives powerful stimulation after the 19th. So your line of credit should increase, as should your access to outside capital. Debts will be easily paid and easily made. Avoid the temptation to borrow frivolously merely because credit is easy. If you are involved in insurance and tax issues, these get resolved in positive ways. You can profit from troubled companies, properties and even people. You can see value where others see junk, a very beautiful financial gift.

Mars stays in your own sign for most of the month (until the 18th) so avoid haste, impatience and temper. Even very placid types like you can get more impatient under a Mars transit.

Love is a mixed picture this month for singles. But the overall picture is bright indeed. Love will become much more harmonious next month. In the meantime, solve financial disputes with compromise. Family might have difficulty accepting your current love, and vice versa. Or perhaps this is just a short-term disagreement between them.

Friendships, organizations and group activities become significant this month. They are especially important financially and career-wise – perhaps this is the reason you are so involved here. Business could be calling you to these things.

Venus, your ruler, will re-stimulate eclipse points from the 24th to the 26th. This could bring some disturbance at the workplace or perhaps a health scare, but it doesn't seem serious. It's best to avoid risky types of activity those days, and to take it easy.

March

Best Days Overall: 3, 4, 13, 14, 23, 24, 31

Most Stressful Days Overall: 10, 11, 12, 18, 19, 25, 26

Best Days for Love: 2, 4, 5, 6, 11, 12, 15, 16, 18, 19, 21, 25, 26, 30

Best Days for Money: 6, 7, 8, 9, 18, 19, 27, 28

Monthly Career Peaks: 5, 6, 7, 25, 26, 27, 28

Monthly Personal Pleasure Peaks: 3, 4, 25, 26, 31

Like last month, the planetary power is still overwhelmingly in the upper (day) sector of your chart. Your 10th House of Career is much more powerful than your 4th House of Home and Family. Continue to focus on the career and down-play family and domestic issues. You are still very much in a yearly career peak as Venus, your ruler, crosses your Midheaven on the 5th, 6th and 7th. So you need to make the most of these opportunities. People are looking up to you now.

An important friendship is being made from the 24th to the 27th. You might already know this person, or it might be someone new. This individual seems spiritual and creative. They have important information to impart that relates not just to your career but also to your mission for this life. In general, you are very inspired and creative during this period. The dream life is sure to be overactive and spectacular.

Family members – perhaps a parent or parent figure – are more temperamental on the 1st. Be patient. They are making a dramatic change. Perhaps you are thinking of renovating your house or upgrading it in someway.

By the 6th, the overwhelming majority (60 to 70 per cent) of the planets will be in the independent Eastern sector of your chart. Your ruling planet, Venus, is now moving forwards as well. So this is a time to correct unpleasant personal conditions, to take the bull by the horns and design your life as you want it to be.

Both the planets involved with your love life are retrograde this month. Pluto, your actual love planet, goes retrograde on the 29th. Jupiter (which is in your 7th House of Love) goes retrograde on the 4th. So, though love is good, it might be wise to take stock now, to review your current love situation and see how it might be improved. Focus more on personal happiness – this is where the power is now.

The Grand Square pattern of the last two months has dissipated, but two eclipses this month keep the pot boiling. Never a dull moment for you this year. Neither eclipse seems especially dramatic for you personally, but they will be powerful for the people around you and for the world at large.

The Lunar Eclipse of the 14th occurs in your 5th House of Children and Love Affairs. A current love affair (not marriage) gets tested and could end. Children make important and long-term changes, and your relationship to them will change. Much of this could be very natural, such as a child going off to school, leaving home or marrying.

The Solar Eclipse of the 29th occurs in the 12th House of Spirituality. This could cause people not on a path to seek one. Those already on a path are likely to change their teachers or spiritual regime. If you are involved in charitable organizations or altruistic enterprises, there could be shake-ups here.

Every Solar Eclipse affects the home and family, for the Sun is your family planet. So, flaws in the home could surface that force you into improvement. Family members can be temperamental, so be more patient now.

Health is much improved and you can enhance it further through supporting and massaging the ankles.

Your financial planet, Mercury, goes retrograde from the 2nd to the 25th. Try to avoid making major financial decisions or commitments then. This is a time for study, for resolving doubts and for negotiations.

April

Best Days Overall: 1, 9, 10, 19, 20, 27, 28

Most Stressful Days Overall: 7, 8, 14, 15, 21, 22

Best Days for Love: 2, 3, 8, 14, 15, 18, 23, 24, 26

Best Days for Money: 2, 3, 4, 5, 14, 15, 16, 23, 24, 25, 26, 29, 30

Monthly Career Peaks: 21, 22, 23, 24

Monthly Personal Pleasure Peaks: 19, 20, 23, 24, 27, 28

Like last month, the planetary power remains above the horizon. Career and outer achievement are still more important than home, family and emotional concerns.

The planetary power is still mostly in the East (and getting ever more intensely Eastern). This continues to be a time to follow your star and to take personal responsibility for your happiness.

Again, like last month, the two planets involved in love are retrograde. This is not going to stop love from happening, but it slows things down a bit. More caution in love is called for, especially for singles. Don't try to hurry love, but let it develop as it will. Although your social confidence is probably not up to its usual high standards, this is still a great love year, and many of you will marry. After the 20th, either the family has patched up its dispute with your lover, or you find someone new who is more harmonious with them. Your family, in general, is more supportive of your social goals, and might play cupid. Love opportunities can come through the family or family connections, and also in spiritually-oriented places.

Friendships, group activities, organizations and spirituality are important in the month ahead. Your financial intuition is super, and you will prosper if you follow and trust it. Financial information will come in dreams, ESP experiences, or through spiritual people. Now that your financial planet is moving forwards, financial judgement is very sound. Earnings snags or delays get resolved. You are more generous and charitable during this period. Until the 20th this is a good period to go on spiritually-oriented retreats or to involve yourself in altruistic causes and charities.

Health is excellent this month. You can enhance it further by paying more attention to the ankles until the 6th and then to the feet afterwards. Regular foot massage is a powerful tonic when you feel low. Good health for you, this period, means good career health, good relations with parents and elders, and healthy friendships. Should a health problem occur, the core issue is probably in these areas, so resolve it before running to a health professional.

You seem very vulnerable and sensitive after the 6th, not like your usual self. Your friends, spouse or lover are mystified. Try not to take things too personally. The reason for your sensitivity is that your intuition overall (not just financial) is super. So this is the price we sometimes pay for these spiritual gifts.

Venus, your ruler, will re-stimulate eclipse points on the 27th, 28th and 29th. Try to avoid risky types of activities then.

Mercury, the financial planet, will re-stimulate eclipse points on the 11th and 12th, and then again on the 22nd and 23rd. This could create some financial disturbances, especially if there is a need to change your financial thinking, planning or assumptions. The cosmos sends you a wake-up call. If financial thinking is sound, these re-stimulations can often bring windfalls.

May

Best Days Overall: 7, 8, 16, 17, 25, 26

Most Stressful Days Overall: 4, 5, 12, 13, 18, 19, 31

Best Days for Love: 3, 5, 12, 13, 14, 15, 22, 23, 31

Best Days for Money: 2, 3, 5, 6, 12, 13, 17, 20, 21, 27, 28, 29, 30

Monthly Career Peaks: 18, 19, 20, 21

Monthly Personal Pleasure Peaks: 22, 23, 25, 26

Another Grand Square pattern formed on the 20th of last month, and it will be in effect until the 29th of this month. So you've got a powerful inner squabble going on. This inner project must be handled with great delicacy. If you can succeed in this, it brings great power and success.

The Grand Square also shows that big things are being developed in the world at large and you are impacted by these things.

These big projects you are involved with take up much of your time and energy, so health needs more watching. Enhance health, until the 4th, by paying more attention to the feet. After the 4th, give more attention to the head and scalp.

As in the past few months, most of the planets are in the East. Your 1st House of the self is very powerful, and stronger than your 7th House of other people (the 7th House, though, is still strong). And, since your love planets are still retrograde, and love is slowing down, you may as well please yourself and do the things that make you happy. Take charge of your own affairs and design your life as you want it to be. Others will eventually come around to your point of view.

The planetary power shifts this month. For many months, the upper, day, side of your horoscope was dominant. Now, especially from the 5th onwards, the lower, night, side is of equal power. So, this is a time for juggling your home and your career. Family is both a boon and a burden this month.

Spirituality continues to be important, and this is still a good month for going on spiritually-oriented retreats. But the body and image is also important. Sensual desires are ardent and they will be fulfilled. Expensive items for the home are coming. Financial windfalls are happening. Financial opportunity is seeking you out, and after the 5th it will find you. Speculations are more favourable. A non-serious love opportunity pursues you. Perhaps this is some-one involved in your financial life.

Venus, your ruler, re-stimulates eclipse points on the 11th and 12th, so take it easy. Do what you must do, but avoid taking undue risks.

The financial planet, Mercury, will re-stimulate eclipse points on the 30th and 31st, so avoid risky financial behaviour then. Important and perhaps long-term financial changes will be made. In general, this will be a strong finan-cial month, especially after the 21st. This is a month when you learn the importance of self-esteem on earnings. If you want to earn more you have to be more. And self-esteem is stronger now earnings naturally increase. Your personal appearance and overall demeanour play a big role in finance this month, especially until the 29th. Perhaps this is why you are investing in yourself, in clothing and appearance.

June

Best Days Overall: 3, 4, 12, 13, 21, 22, 30

Most Stressful Days Overall: 1, 2, 8, 9, 14, 15, 28, 29

Best Days for Love: 2, 3, 4, 8, 9, 11, 12, 13, 20, 22, 29

Best Days for Money: 8, 9, 17, 18, 23, 24, 25, 26, 27

Monthly Career Peaks: 14, 15, 17, 18

Monthly Personal Pleasure Peaks: 21, 22, 23

This month the planetary shift to the lower half of your horoscope is established. The two planets most involved with your career are retrograde. (Neptune began to move retrograde in your 10th House last month, and Uranus, your career planet, goes retrograde on the 19th.) Your 4th House of Home and Family grows ever stronger, and by the 28th, contains 40 per cent of the planets. The message is very clear: your career can be down-played now. Not much is happening there anyway, and career issues will need time to sort themselves out. You can safely focus on building a stable domestic base, maintaining family harmony, and finding your personal point of emotional balance.

In spite of the lull in the career (and many nice things are happening behind the scenes, but with a delayed reaction), prosperity seems intact. In fact, you are in one of the strongest financial periods of your year. Family is supportive, especially a parent or parent figure, and family connections play a big role in earnings too. There is profit from property, and perhaps you are spending in that department as well. Sales, marketing, buying, selling, trading, and good use of the media are also important. You will find financial opportunity right in your back yard. Perhaps neighbours are customers or clients. Siblings are prospering and seem supportive of you too.

A spiritual person comes visiting after the 3rd. Perhaps a charity function or religious meeting is held then as well. Religion and spirituality are being brought into the home. Family in general seems more involved in these things, and this is a long-term trend.

Friendships and group activities have been important to you for many years. Often it was a struggle. But now, on the 23rd, the north node of the Moon makes a rare move from your 12th House to your 11th House. This whole area is going to get a lot happier.

Intellectual interests are important this month. This is a wonderful period to take courses in subjects that interest you, and also for teaching and giving seminars in your areas of expertise. Catch up on your letter-writing and make those calls you should have made weeks ago.

For many months the planetary power has been mostly in the Eastern sector of Self, but this power is shifting now. By the end of the month, the Eastern and Western halves of your chart will be equally balanced. By next month, the power will be in the West. So, right now, you are in transition. Sometimes you will be more independent and sometimes more dependent on others.

The planets involved in your love life are still retrograde, so this is a time for more caution in love, especially for singles. Of course this won't stop your social life; it only slows things down. You seem out of synch with your current love or spouse this period – you see things from opposite perspectives. Compromise is the key but this will be easier to achieve later on in the month. Early in the month you seem very self-willed.

Your spouse or partner is prospering but their financial planet is retrograde, so they need to do a lot more homework in financial matters these days. Perhaps earnings have slowed. They are still good, but slower than they have been. This is a good time for them to review and perfect their products and services.

Your financial planet, Mercury, will re-stimulate eclipse points on the 1st and again from the 8th to the 10th. This could bring important and probably necessary financial changes and shifts in strategy and thinking. On these days a love affair (not a marriage) could be tested. Children could be more temperamental as well. Be patient.

July

Best Days Overall: 1, 10, 11, 18, 19, 27, 28, 29

Most Stressful Days Overall: 5, 6, 12, 13, 25, 26

Best Days for Love: 3, 4, 5, 6, 9, 12, 13, 17, 22, 23, 26

Best Days for Money: 5, 6, 7, 8, 14, 15, 20, 21, 23, 24

Monthly Career Peaks: 12, 13, 14, 15

Monthly Personal Pleasure Peaks: 18, 19, 23

By the 21st, the planetary shift to the Western half of your horoscope will be established. This power will grow in coming months. So, you are in a period when you need to be more adaptable – not one of Taurus's strong points. Getting your way will be more difficult, and perhaps not even desirable, as your way might not be best over the long haul. Others have important perspectives. This shift will force you to cultivate your social skills, and will definitely improve your love life or current relationship.

Like last month, the planetary power is firmly below the horizon. Your 4th House of Home and Family is the most powerful in the chart this month with 40 to 50 per cent of the planets either there or moving through it. The planets involved with your career are still retrograde. So continue to get the home base and, more importantly, your emotional life in order. This will pay big dividends career-wise (and in other ways) later on. Nice career opportunities are still happening all month, but if they violate your emotional harmony or disrupt the family situation you should pass.

In most things you seem dependent on others, but in financial matters you are still master of your own destiny. Personal appearance plays a big role in earnings these days. Investments in yourself are probably the best investments. You are dressing expensively and for success. Finances are complicated this month by the retrograde of Mercury, your financial planet, from the 3rd to the 29th. This won't stop earnings, of course, but slows things down and creates delays. Financial expansion has to happen methodically and gradually. All the details need to be right. This is also a good time to perfect your product or service. Avoid major purchases or investments until after the 29th, as you are guaranteed to see things in a different way by then. Also, events happen – new offers, new products, new upgrades – that also change your whole perspective.

A parent or parent figure is prospering financially by being very aggressive and taking risks. Your lover or spouse still needs to be more cautious with their finances. Overall prosperity is intact, but more homework is needed for pending deals. Financial uncertainty could affect their support.

Love is definitely improving this month. Jupiter starts moving forward again in your 7th House of Love. A serious relationship makes progress, or you may be ready to let go of something old and get ready for the new. Important love decisions are being made now. Your social confidence is getting stronger, and your family seems more supportive of your love life these days.

Intellectual and creative interests are more important. You are also into fun, sports and entertainment. Children seem more athletic. Children of appropriate age are experimenting sexually and are, in general, more prone to passion and temper.

Venus, your ruler, re-stimulates eclipse points from the 25th to the 27th. Avoid risky activities then, doing only what is necessary.

There is a lot of overall retrograde activity this month. For most of the month, 40 per cent of the planets are retrograde, and from the 3rd to the 7th, 50 per cent. Be patient and philosophical with the delays you see around you. This is just cosmic weather.

August

Best Days Overall: 6, 7, 14, 15, 24, 25

Most Stressful Days Overall: 2, 3, 8, 9, 21, 22, 23, 29, 30

Best Days for Love: 2, 3, 5, 11, 13, 21, 22, 23, 29, 20, 31

Best Days for Money: 2, 3, 10, 11, 12, 17, 18, 19, 20, 22, 23, 29, 30

Monthly Career Peaks: 8, 9, 10, 11

Monthly Personal Pleasure Peaks: 14, 15, 21, 22

Like last month, the planetary power is mostly below the horizon. Your two career planets are still retrograde. Your 4th House of Home and Family is the most powerful in the horoscope (40 to 50 per cent of the planets). So this is still a period for cultivating emotional harmony, for dealing with psychological issues – especially root causes of depressed feelings – and for getting the home base in order.

Most of the planets are still in the West, and the power there is growing. By the 13th, two more planets will be in the Western sector, so this is a time to down-play the self. You can shine but, like the sun, shine silently. Allow things to happen rather than trying to force them. Put other people first and cultivate social skills. Your good comes through others rather than by personal effort. Though you are skilled and intelligent, if others don't like you it will impede progress. This doesn't mean that you should make no effort. Do what is possible and then relax and enjoy your day.

This is a wonderful month for entertaining from home, redecorating, or buying art objects for the home (after the 13th). It's also a good time to review your past and digest some of the lessons from your present vantage point. The cosmos will arrange this anyway by bringing people from your past into the picture or re-creating, in a new form, some of your earliest experiences.

Health in general needs more watching, especially until the 23rd. Rest and relax more and listen to your body. Give the stomach, breasts and heart more attention during this period. Emotional health takes on greater importance too, as discussed above.

Intellectual interests, fun, joy and creativity are important this month. When the cosmos says this is play time, it's best to listen. The feeling of joy will not only have positive health effects, but will also benefit other areas of life, such as your spirituality and finances. This is also a good month for dealing with children and for getting in touch with your own inner child.

Love is stormy this month. There will be a crisis in a current relationship or marriage at the end of the month. Will it be a healing crisis or a break-up? Much depends on the nature of the relationship. True love will survive and get even better. Impure love probably won't make it. Either way, the love life, overall, is still wonderful.

If you are involved in charitable, altruistic or spiritual organizations, there are crises there from the 29th to the 31st. Those on the spiritual path will make important changes to their regimes – probably suddenly and abruptly.

Finances are reasonable this month. Prosperity is especially strong until the 11th as your financial planet receives wonderful aspects from Jupiter. Spousal support seems strong. Your partner is prospering more, now that Jupiter is moving forward too. Perhaps earnings come from insurance claims or royalties. There is good access to outside capital.

After the 11th you are spending more on the home and family, and they in turn are more supportive of you. Family connections are important financially. Overspending can be a danger from the 11th to the 28th. After the 28th money is earned through work, but speculations are also favourable.

September

Best Days Overall: 3, 4, 11, 12, 20, 21, 30

Most Stressful Days Overall: 5, 6, 17, 18, 19, 25, 26

Best Days for Love: 1, 2, 10, 11, 18, 19, 20, 21, 25, 26, 28, 29, 30

Best Days for Money: 3, 4, 7, 8, 12, 13, 14, 15, 16, 22, 23, 25, 26

Monthly Career Peaks: 5, 6, 7, 8

Monthly Personal Pleasure Peaks: 11, 12, 20, 21

Two stressful T-squares (one of them in your native fixed signs) and two eclipses this month show a turbulent and eventful month ahead, both personally and for the world at large. Although the effect of these eclipses is not as strong on you as on other signs, it won't hurt to reduce your schedule during these periods.

The Lunar Eclipse takes place on September 7th in your 11th House. This will test friendships and your relationship to certain organizations to which you belong. Shake-ups could change the dynamics of these organizations. Friends could be having personal dramas too. Since this eclipse occurs very near to Uranus – your career planet – dramatic changes are happening on that front as well over the next six months. A drama with a parent or parent figure wouldn't be a surprise either.

The Solar Eclipse of September 22nd is an unusual one. It occurs right on the border of two houses – the 5th and 6th houses. Technically, it is in your 5th House, but it is so close to the cusp of your 6th that we must read it as an event there as well. So this eclipse is affecting two areas of life. Children are making dramatic changes. A love affair will be tested. Creative people will make long-term changes to their creativity. The most likely scenario involves changes of jobs and workplace conditions. Employers will have upheavals with their employees, and the workforce seems more unstable these days. Many of you will make important changes to your diet and health regime in the next six months (especially when this point gets re-stimulated by other planets).

Love is becoming more harmonious and happier day by day. On the 4th, your love planet, Pluto, which has been retrograde for many months, starts moving forwards again. Your other love planet this year, Jupiter, is also moving forwards. Your social life is greatly clarified. You know where you're going, one way or another. You have confidence, and your social judgement is good. Romantic opportunities are plentiful, especially after the 23rd. Temptations to infidelity after the 6th will certainly not sit well with a current love, so avoid these things unless you want to break up with this person. Financial disputes could test love until the 13th, but these are short-term things and seem easily resolved.

Money is earned in happy ways until the 13th. You are also spending on pleasure. After the 13th, money is earned in the normal way, through work. But social connections are also playing a big role.

Like last month, home and family are more important than career, but this is soon to change. This is still a time to down-play the self and to focus on other people. Your good comes through others.

Health is much improved over last month, and you can enhance it further by paying more attention to the heart (until the 6th) and to the small intestine afterwards. Diet, after the 6th, is more of an issue now.

October

Best Days Overall: 1, 8, 9, 17, 18, 19, 27, 28

Most Stressful Days Overall: 2, 3, 15, 16, 22, 23, 24, 29, 30

Best Days for Love: 2, 3, 7, 10, 11, 16, 21, 22, 23, 24, 26

Best Days for Money: 4, 5, 10, 11, 12, 13, 14, 22, 23, 24

Monthly Career Peaks: 2, 3, 4, 5, 29, 30

Monthly Personal Pleasure Peaks: 8, 9, 20, 21

The planets make an important shift this month, from the lower, night, side of the horoscope to the upper, day, side. This represents an important psychological shift for you. By now, after these many months, you have found your point of emotional harmony and are ready for outer achievement and career focus. One of your career planets (Neptune in your 10th House) will start moving forwards again on the 29th. So, you can safely down-play the home and start focusing on your outer, worldly goals. This shift will be complete by the 23rd. On the 24th, it will be even stronger as your ruler moves over the horizon.

Like last month, the planetary power is still in the West, and about to enter maximum Western position. Your 7th House of Love becomes awesomely powerful after the 24th as 50 to 60 per cent of the planets will either be there or moving through there. So this is a social month, and a month for enjoying romantic opportunities. Wedding bells (or engagements) can very well ring for many of you now. Business partnerships, mergers and joint ventures could also happen. You are entering one of the happiest, most active social periods of your life. You are having what are called 'peak experiences'. Enjoy.

Health and work also seem important. You are working hard and are productive and serious. Job-seekers are having success, as are those who employ others. There are happy social experiences at work as well. Health regimes are interesting and successful. It seems to me there is a vanity component here. Good health for you means looking good – and with the social life as wonderful as it is, this is understandable. It's as if you want to give the gift of beauty to your beloved and to friends.

Your increased social life is also bringing – almost as a side-effect – new and wonderful career opportunities. Though your abilities are good, it certainly doesn't hurt to know the right people.

Money comes from work until the 2nd. But afterwards it comes (again) from social connections, your spouse, partner or current relationship. Try to make important purchases, investments or financial commitments before the 28th, when your financial planet starts to move retrograde.

Health needs watching more carefully after the 23rd. Don't allow social euphoria to overtax your body. Enhance health by paying more attention to the kidneys and hips (until the 24th) and to the colon and sexual organs afterwards. Hips (and buttocks) should be regularly massaged. This will strengthen the kidneys and lower back. Detox regimes are beneficial after the 24th. There will be increased sexual activity this month for those of you of appropriate age, but be careful of overdoing things. Safe sex becomes more important these days as well.

November

Best Days Overall: 5, 13, 14, 15, 23, 24

Most Stressful Days Overall: 11, 12, 19, 20, 26, 27

Best Days for Love: 1, 3, 9, 10, 12, 19, 20, 21, 22, 30

Best Days for Money: 1, 2, 7, 8, 9, 10, 19, 20, 28, 29, 30

Monthly Career Peaks: 1, 26, 27, 28, 29

Monthly Personal Pleasure Peaks: 5, 21, 22

The social bliss continues in full swing this month. Most of the planets are in the West, and your 7th House of Love is packed with planets – 50 to 60 per cent of the planets are either there or move through there. This is wonderful not only for love, but for friendships as well. The social sphere is expanding rapidly. Continue to take a low profile and focus on others. Good luck comes to you easily and effortlessly through the good graces of others, and not from your personal actions. With your ruling planet, Venus, in your 7th House until the 17th, you don't have much of a problem doing these things.

Your career is getting better and stronger day by day. Most of the planets are established above the horizon now.

Your career planet, Uranus, starts moving forwards (after many months of retrograde motion) on the 20th. Now both career planets are moving forwards. Like last month, your social contacts are bringing career opportunities. You can safely down-play domestic and family concerns and focus on outer achievement. There is much progress happening.

Putting other people first pays dividends not only socially, but financially as well. Your focus should be on the prosperity of others, on their financial interests. As you help them prosper, your own prosperity manifests easily and effortlessly. Your financial planet is retrograde until the 18th, so avoid making major investments or purchases during that period. This is a time to review pending deals and the overall financial life in general, but not for acting on these things. Financial delays are probably working to your advantage now. Your financial perspective will be very different after the 18th.

Your spouse, partner or lover is really prospering these days. Their prosperity and generosity towards you will get even stronger after the 24th. This is a time for paying off or refinancing debt, and for attracting outside investors or capital. Tax or insurance matters seem fortunate as well.

Your 8th House of Transformation and Regeneration becomes an important interest from the 17th. This is a wonderful period to lose weight, detox the body, and to rid yourself of old emotional and mental baggage. It's also a good time to get rid of excess possessions, to clear the decks so that the new and the better can come in.

Venus will re-stimulate eclipse points on the 29th and 30th. Avoid risky activities or behaviour at this time.

Your health needs watching until the 22nd. Much of what was said last month still applies. Sexual activity should be kept in balance and not overdone. Detox regimes are good. The colon and bladder should be given more attention. After the 17th, health can be enhanced through paying more attention to the liver and thighs (thighs can be regularly massaged) and through metaphysical types of therapy such as prayer.

December

Best Days Overall: 2, 3, 11, 12, 21, 22, 29, 30

Most Stressful Days Overall: 8, 9, 10, 16, 17, 23, 24

Best Days for Love: 1, 9, 10, 11, 16, 17, 19, 21, 22, 28, 29, 30

Best Days for Money: 4, 5, 8, 18, 27, 31

Monthly Career Peaks: 23, 24, 25, 26

Monthly Personal Pleasure Peaks: 2, 3, 21, 22, 29, 30

Although your 7th House is weaker than last month, your social life is still going strong (it will be strong in 2007 as well). This is because your love planet, Pluto, is receiving intense and positive stimulation from 60 to 70 per cent of the planets. Sexual activity increased during the past few months, and the trend continues this month.

Like last month, most of the planets are still in the West, so refer to the discussion for November.

Aside from sex, there are other strong urges for personal transformation. Sixty to seventy per cent of the planets are in your 8th House or moving through there, which is highly unusual. Many of you are involved in these kinds of projects and you should see amazing – and quick – progress this month. Your understanding of life, death, life after death, past lives and occultism in general is greatly expanded this month.

Your spouse, lover or partner is prospering big time now. Important windfalls and other opportunities are manifesting now. Spousal support is very strong. Like last month, this is a good time to resolve insurance and tax issues. Those of you looking for outside capital or investors will also have good fortune. If you have good ideas investors will just throw money at you.

But this will also be a turbulent month. Many sudden and abrupt changes are happening. Often the good that comes to us can be just as disruptive as the difficult things. Many adjustments have to be made for the new condition. Fifty per cent of the planets will be re-stimulating eclipse points this month, and this is very unusual. This will also impact the world at large.

Mars will re-stimulate eclipse points from the 26th to the 28th. For you this is showing spiritual changes and disruptions. For the world it can show increased violence, the intensification of wars, more terrorism and the like.

Venus, your ruler, will re-stimulate eclipse points from the 9th to the 12th, and this has a more personal impact. You will probably make important changes to your image and appearance. It is best to avoid risky types of activity during that period.

Mercury, your financial planet, will re-stimulate eclipse points from the 17th to the 19th and from the 26th to the 28th. This could bring important changes in financial thinking and planning.

The Sun will re-stimulate eclipse points from the 6th to the 8th and on the 21st and 22nd. Family members will be more temperamental then so be more patient with them. (This is also strong for the world at large. Sometimes it brings down governments; sometimes it just puts them in crisis.)

Health is much improved over last month. You can enhance it further by paying more attention to the liver and thighs (until the 11th) and to the spine, knees, teeth and skeletal alignment afterwards. Thigh massage is beneficial until the 11th, and back massage afterwards.

Gemini

⛢

THE TWINS
Birthdays from
21st May to
20th June

Personality Profile

GEMINI AT A GLANCE

Element – Air

Ruling Planet – Mercury
   Career Planet – Neptune
   Love Planet – Jupiter
   Money Planet – Moon
   Planet of Health and Work – Pluto
   Planet of Home and Family Life – Mercury

Colours – blue, yellow, yellow-orange

Colour that promotes love, romance and social
   harmony – sky blue

Colours that promote earning power – grey, silver

Gems – agate, aquamarine

Metal – quicksilver

Scents – lavender, lilac, lily of the valley, storax

Quality – mutable (= flexibility)

Quality most needed for balance – thought that is deep rather than superficial

Strongest virtues – great communication skills, quickness and agility of thought, ability to learn quickly

Deepest need – communication

Characteristics to avoid – gossiping, hurting others with harsh speech, superficiality, using words to mislead or misinform

Signs of greatest overall compatibility – Libra, Aquarius

Signs of greatest overall incompatibility – Virgo, Sagittarius, Pisces

Sign most helpful to career – Pisces

Sign most helpful for emotional support – Virgo

Sign most helpful financially – Cancer

Sign best for marriage and/or partnerships – Sagittarius

Sign most helpful for creative projects – Libra

Best Sign to have fun with – Libra

Signs most helpful in spiritual matters – Taurus, Aquarius

Best day of the week – Wednesday

Understanding a Gemini

Gemini is to society what the nervous system is to the body. It does not introduce any new information but is a vital transmitter of impulses from the senses to the brain and vice versa. The nervous system does not judge or weigh these impulses – it only conveys information. And does so perfectly.

This analogy should give you an indication of a Gemini's role in society. Geminis are the communicators and conveyors of information. To Geminis the truth or falsehood of information is irrelevant, they only transmit what they see, hear or read about. Thus they are capable of spreading the most outrageous rumours as well as conveying truth and light. Geminis sometimes tend to be unscrupulous in their communications and can do great good or great evil with their power. This is why the Sign of Gemini is called the Sign of the Twins: Geminis have a dual nature.

Their ability to convey a message – to communicate with such ease – makes Geminis ideal teachers, writers and media and marketing people. This is helped by the fact that Mercury, the Ruling Planet of Gemini, also rules these activities.

Geminis have the gift of the gab. And what a gift this is! They can make conversation about anything, anywhere, at any time. There is almost nothing that is more fun to Geminis than a good conversation – especially if they can learn something new as well. They love to learn and they love to teach. To deprive a Gemini of conversation, or of books and magazines, is cruel and unusual punishment.

Geminis are almost always excellent students and take well to education. Their minds are generally stocked with all kinds of information, trivia, anecdotes, stories, news items, rarities, facts and statistics. Thus they can support any intellectual position that they care to take. They are awesome debaters and, if involved in politics, make good orators.

Geminis are so verbally smooth that even if they do not know what they are talking about, they can make you think that they do. They will always dazzle you with their brilliance.

Finance

Geminis tend to be more concerned with the wealth of learning and ideas than with actual material wealth. As mentioned they excel in professions that involve writing, teaching, sales and journalism – and not all of these professions pay very well. But to sacrifice intellectual needs merely for money is unthinkable to a Gemini. Geminis strive to combine the two.

Cancer is on Gemini's Solar 2nd House (of Money) cusp, which indicates that Geminis can earn extra income (in a harmonious and natural way) from investments in residential property, restaurants and hotels. Given their verbal skills, Geminis love to bargain and negotiate in any situation, but especially when it has to do with money.

The Moon rules Gemini's 2nd Solar House. The Moon is not only the fastest-moving planet in the Zodiac but actually moves through every Sign and House every 28 days. No other heavenly body matches the Moon for swiftness or the ability to change quickly. An analysis of the Moon – and lunar phenomena in general – describes Gemini's financial attitudes very well. Geminis are financially versatile and flexible. They can earn money in many different ways. Their financial attitudes and needs seem to change daily. Their feelings about money change also: sometimes they are very enthusiastic about it, at other times they could not care less.

For a Gemini, financial goals and money are often seen only as means of supporting a family; these things have little meaning otherwise.

The Moon, as Gemini's Money Planet, has another important message for Gemini financially: in order for Geminis to realize their financial potential they need to develop more of an understanding of the emotional side of life. They need to combine their awesome powers of logic with an understanding of human psychology. Feelings have their own logic; Geminis need to learn this and apply it to financial matters.

Career and Public Image

Geminis know that they have been given the gift of communication for a reason, that it is a power that can achieve great good or cause unthinkable distress. They long to put this power at the service of the highest and most transcendental truths. This is their primary goal, to communicate the eternal verities and prove them logically. They look up to people who can transcend the intellect – to poets, artists, musicians and mystics. They may be awed by stories of religious saints and martyrs. A Gemini's highest achievement is to teach the truth, whether it is scientific, inspirational or historical. Those who can transcend the intellect are Gemini's natural superiors – and a Gemini realizes this.

The Sign of Pisces is in Gemini's Solar 10th House of Career. Neptune, the Planet of Spirituality and Altruism, is Gemini's Career Planet. If Geminis are to realize their highest career potential they need to develop their transcendental – their spiritual and altruistic – side. They need to understand the larger cosmic picture, the vast flow of human evolution – where it came from and where it is heading. Only then can a Gemini's intellectual powers take their true position and he or she can become the 'messenger of the gods'. Geminis need to cultivate a facility for 'inspiration', which is something that does not originate in the intellect but which comes through the intellect. This will further enrich and empower a Gemini's mind.

Love and Relationships

Geminis bring their natural garrulousness and brilliance into their love life and social life as well. A good talk or a verbal joust is an interesting prelude to romance. Their only problem in love is that their intellect is too cool and passionless to incite ardour in others. Emotions sometimes disturb them, and their partners tend to complain about this. If you are in love with a Gemini you must understand why this is so. Geminis avoid deep passions because these would interfere with their ability to think and communicate. If they are cool towards you, understand that this is their nature.

Nevertheless, Geminis must understand that it is one thing to talk about love and another actually to love – to feel it and radiate it. Talking about love glibly will get them nowhere. They need to feel it and act on it. Love is not of the intellect but of the heart. If you want to know how a Gemini feels about love you should not listen to what he or she says but rather observe what he or she does. Geminis can be quite generous to those they love.

Geminis like their partners to be refined, well educated and well travelled. If their partners are more wealthy than they, that is all the better. If you are in love with a Gemini you had better be a good listener as well.

The ideal relationship for the Gemini is a relationship of the mind. They enjoy the physical and emotional aspects, of course, but if the intellectual communion is not there they will suffer.

Home and Domestic Life

At home the Gemini can be uncharacteristically neat and meticulous. They tend to want their children and partner to live up to their idealistic standards. When these standards are not met they moan and criticize. However, Geminis are good family people and like to serve their families in practical and useful ways.

The Gemini home is comfortable and pleasant. They like to invite people over and they make great hosts. Geminis are also good at repairs and improvements around the house – all fuelled by their need to stay active and occupied with something they like to do. Geminis have many hobbies and interests that keep them busy when they are home alone.

Geminis understand and get along well with their children, mainly because they are very youthful people themselves. As great communicators, Geminis know how to explain things to children; in this way they gain their children's love and respect. Geminis also encourage children to be creative and talkative, just like they are.

Horoscope for 2006

General Trends

The past few years have been very difficult, but things have been getting progressively easier. Many of you are experiencing some discomfort as the stirrings of dramatic change are being felt. Many of you – especially those born early in the sign – have already experienced dramatic change. For those of you born later in the sign, change is happening this year or over the next few years.

Work and career were the main interests of 2005 and this will continue in the year ahead. Love, which has been turbulent for many years, is going to get very happy later on this year as Jupiter moves into your 7th House of Love and Marriage. We'll discuss these things later on.

Communication is always a big interest for you, and this year you will refine and hone your skills even more.

Your paths of greatest fulfilment in the year ahead will be health and work (especially until November 24th); love, romance and social activities (all year but especially after November 24th); friendships, group activities, organizations, astrology, astronomy and science (until June 23rd); career (after June 23rd).

Health

(Please note that this is an astrological perspective on health, not a medical one. At one time, both perspectives were identical, but in these times there could be quite a difference. For the medical perspective, please consult your physician or health professional.)

Health looks reasonable this year. Sure, you have two (and after November 24th, three) long-term planets in stressful aspect, but you also have a great interest in health. Your 6th House is a House of Power. This interest, this drive for good health, will enable you to overcome the various challenges that arise. You are more inclined to watch your diet and to embrace health regimes. Many of you are learning more about health in an intellectual way but the cosmos wants you to go deeper this year, to learn about the true origins of health and disease.

With Jupiter in your 6th House for most of the year, the metaphysical aspects of healing will become more apparent to you. Prayer therapy and affirmations will be particularly powerful and beneficial.

In general, Pluto is your health planet. Your health is therefore generally enhanced by paying more attention to the sexual organs, the colon and the bladder. Sexual activity needs to be kept in balance. Safe sex is more important for you than for most people. Since Pluto rules detox regimes that eliminate impurities from the body, these are beneficial for you.

The liver and thighs are also very important in the year ahead. Pluto rules your health from the sign of Sagittarius, which rules these organs. Jupiter, the planetary ruler of these organs, is in your 6th House – a very strong connection. Thighs can be regularly massaged, and there are all kinds of reflex points in the thighs that strengthen the colon and lower back. There are many natural ways to strengthen the liver, colon, sexual organs and bladder.

It also helps to wear the colours, gems and metals of your sign. This strengthens you in subtle ways.

Your interest in health will be strong all year but especially from October 2nd onwards.

There is a very powerful connection between love and health this year – it's been there for many years, but is even stronger now. This means that love issues could impact on health. If health problems occur, check your relationships and try to bring some harmony there.

Parents or parent figures can enhance their health by paying more attention to the heart, ankles and feet. Regular foot and ankle massage will do wonders for them. This applies to children too. The health of grandchildren can be enhanced by good nutrition and by paying more attention to the stomach and breasts. Their health seems good this year. Your spouse or partner also seems to be in reasonable health. They can improve things by paying more attention to the neck and throat.

Home, Domestic and Family Issues

Your 4th House of Home and Family is not a House of Power this year, so it isn't a major focus. You are probably content where you are and in your present situation. Career seems much more important than the domestic life this year.

Yet, because the career is so frenetic, this is bound to impact on the home and family situation indirectly. You can be transferred to another city or even country! This could force moves even though you are content where you are.

Also there are two eclipses in your 4th House this year – a Lunar Eclipse on March 14th and a Solar Eclipse on September 22nd. These often bring up hidden flaws and imperfections in the home so that you can correct them.

Family members tend to be more temperamental under these conditions as well.

A parent or parent figure is undergoing great personal change. Perhaps their marriage is in crisis, or merely undergoing evolution. This parent is also moving around a lot and exploring their freedom. They are also probably experimenting with their image and appearance. You feel as if you are dealing with a new, unpredictable person. Also this person is probably more emotionally volatile these days. The best policy is to give them as much emotional and mental freedom as you can, so long as it isn't destructive.

One of the parents (or parent figures) will move, either late this year or in 2007.

The domestic life of the children seems stable, but a move could happen in 2007.

Mercury is both your personal ruler and your family planet. Since Mercury is such a fast-moving planet – it moves through all the signs and houses of your horoscope in a given year – the family situation tends to fluctuate from month to month. So it's best to consult the monthly reports for a discussion of these issues.

If you're planning heavy construction in the home – a major renovation or remodelling project – July 21st to September 8th is a good time. If you want to beautify the home in a cosmetic way or buy art objects, September 6th to 30th is good.

Love and Social Life

Pluto has been in your 7th House of Love for many years now. Love life and love attitudes are being transformed. New love ideals are being born. Many of you have been divorced over this period. Many have been widowed. Many have seen the actual death of friends or experienced the death of friendships.

Pluto is the planet of death, but every death brings resurrection. Pluto is revealing the deeper mysteries of life, but in the realm of your love situation. So this has been the story of your love life – deaths and resurrections, over and over. He wants to make sure you get the message.

This year things are about to change. Jupiter, your love planet, is moving into your 7th House of Love and Marriage. This will happen on November 24th, and Jupiter will stay there well into 2007. For singles (those working on their first marriage), this means a marriage or a committed relationship. In the meantime you (and your future lover) are getting prepared. You could pass your soul mate on the street many times and not recognize this person – until the timing is right. The timing is soon to be right.

All Geminis, married or unmarried, will experience an expanded social life. Your social charm and grace will grow too, and you will express love to others more easily. You will become more popular and will attract new and high-calibre friends.

Two issues are playing a role in your love life now – your interest in health and work. Love opportunities can come from either place, perhaps the nutritionist's office, the gym, the yoga studio, the health-food store or that health lecture. Perhaps at that prayer circle too. You also have the aspects for the classic office romance. Health and work are not just about money and wellness – this is where the social action is.

Those working on their second marriage will also have a happy love life – but marriage seems more questionable. Both of you seem interested in your freedom and space.

Those working on their third marriage have a status-quo year. You will have romance but it will be tested pretty thoroughly.

As mentioned, the marriage of parents (or parent figures) seems in crisis. Unless each gives the other a *lot* of freedom, I don't think it can work. Children of marriageable age have a stable year – marrieds will stay married, singles will probably stay single. Adult grandchildren will probably not marry this year. Those who are married are having their marriages tested. Siblings have love this year, probably with glamorous types.

Of course you don't have to wait until November 24th to have fun and romantic opportunities. Your social life looks happy and active from February 19th to March 20th; June 21st to July 22nd and from October 23rd onwards. But the real and important activity will be after November 24th.

There is a Solar Eclipse in your 11th House of Friends on March 29th. Before then, your friendships are still being influenced by the Lunar Eclipse of October 17th 2005. So friendships are getting tested well into September, the duration of the March 29th eclipse's effect, though this doesn't affect romance.

Finance and Career

Your 2nd House of Finance is not a House of Power this year, so money doesn't seem like a big issue. Professional status and career satisfaction seem more important than the bottom line.

There is prosperity this year, but you don't make a big deal about it. Your finances are probably where you want them to be and you have no need to focus overly on them.

Job-seekers have an outstanding year. There are great jobs out there for you – dream jobs – and you will find them. You are also learning how to be a more productive employee, and that too will help earnings. Job-seekers should check their social connections for jobs. The most important thing now is to love what you do – to have a passion for it.

Those already in careers will also have an exciting time. Perhaps you are travelling to foreign lands on business. Perhaps you are involved in new and exciting industries or business ventures. Your communication skills and natural gift for media is going to play a big role here.

With aspects like these (Uranus moving through your 10th House of Career), many people don't want to be tied down to just one line of work. Sometimes, this need for freedom and change makes people choose the freelance life. Where many people fear career change and insecurity, you seem to thrive on it. You have the confidence – you know something will always turn up.

The cosmos wants to show you that there are many ways to get to your dreams. It wants you to launch out into the deeper waters of life – into the unknown.

Aside from having Uranus in your House of Career – a guarantee for change – there is also a Lunar Eclipse in your 10th House on September 7th. If you haven't made the appropriate changes by then, the eclipse will force it on you.

As with Taurus, idealism is very important for you career-wise. You want a career that helps the world as a whole. It's not just about personal success for you.

The Moon – the fastest-moving planet in the horoscope – is your financial planet. And she matches your mentality to a tee. She is quick and agile, moving through all the signs and houses of your chart in one month, so financial needs and opportunities tend to fluctuate day by day.

The Moon will be eclipsed twice this year – on March 14th and September 7th. During these periods you get a chance to review and change financial strategies and thinking. Flaws and imperfections come to the surface. By now you are a pro at these things as they happen very often.

In general, your earning power is stronger when the Moon waxes than when she wanes, and you should schedule yourself accordingly.

Your spouse or partner has a status-quo financial year, as do parents. Children and grandchildren are prospering, although the children's prosperity is more stable. The grandchildren can have wild ups and downs, but they are also having more fun.

Self-improvement

In July of last year, Saturn moved into your 3rd House of Communication. He will stay here for another two years. The cosmos wants you to bring order to your thought processes and communication. It's almost as if it wants you to limit, refine and restructure your thought process and the way you communicate. At first glance, this seems one of the great ironies of the universe. You Geminis are the golden-tongued ones, the natural orators and teachers of the world. Where others mangle names and can hardly string two thoughts together, you just open your mouth and the words come out like well-trained army regiments – orderly and beautifully formed. You inhale information the way others inhale air. You are never at a loss for facts.

So what's going on here? Why would the cosmos want to limit such a great gift? Only one reason – to make it even better. It wants to add depth to your thought. It wants you to eliminate ideas or conclusions that are in error. It wants to purify your mental body. Let's face it – you can be very indiscriminate in the facts and knowledge you take in. You basically devour everything – true or untrue. Information is good for its own sake, whether it is useful or not. Now you need to sift through all these things. If it's true, hold on to it. If not, discard it. Error in the mind is a very serious thing. It leads to bad judgement and bad decisions – and these can be painful enough. Worse, over time, error will manifest in the physical body as some condition. So you want to be just as hygienic with your mind as you are with your body. There is a mental detox going on now. You won't be able to get away with a quick remark or offhand brilliance. People will come into your life who will demand rigorous and clear thinking. And, if you don't do your homework before talking, they will nail you.

Also, this is a good period to learn the power of mental silence. Silence is indeed golden. Silence will not deprive you of speech or thought, but the reverse. All great thoughts, all eloquence, is born in the silence. It's OK, Gemini, to be silent sometimes.

Month-by-month Forecasts

January

Best Days Overall: 1, 2, 10, 11, 20, 21, 29, 30

Most Stressful Days Overall: 3, 4, 17, 18, 19, 25, 26, 31

Best Days for Love: 3, 4, 8, 9, 12, 13, 17, 18, 19, 22, 23, 25, 26, 27, 28, 31

Best Days for Money: 3, 4, 8, 9, 12, 13, 14, 18, 19, 20, 22, 23, 29, 30, 31

Monthly Career Peaks: 1, 2, 3, 4, 29, 30, 31

Monthly Personal Pleasure Peaks: 10, 11, 29, 30

Your year begins with 70 to 80 per cent of the planets above the horizon. Your 10th House of Career is stronger than your 4th House of Home and Family – the 4th House is basically empty (only the Moon will visit there on the 17th, 18th and 19th). Your career planet is moving forwards and receiving powerful stimulation. The message is clear: focus on the career and your outer goals and down-play home and family issues. This seems easy to do now as your family seems supportive of your career. There is much career progress and success this month, especially towards the end. Enjoy.

Most of the planets are in the Western sector this month. This is a period of adapting to situations rather than trying to change them (something you are very good at), of putting other people first, and of down-playing personal interests and self-will. The grace and goodwill of other people will do more for you than personal effort or abilities.

Finances don't seem a big issue this month. Your 2nd House is basically empty (only the Moon will visit there on the 12th, 13th and 14th), so you will probably have a status-quo kind of month. However, there are many bumps on the road, changes and adjustments to your financial planning and thinking as the Moon, the financial planet, re-stimulates eclipse points on the 6th, 7th, 12th, 13th, 14th, 20th, 21st, 27th and 28th. Many nice things can happen on those days through making adjustments in your financial thinking. And there is no one in the zodiac who can adjust better than a Gemini. For sure, you are more interested in prestige, status and professional reputation than in mere pounds and pence. This is the kind of a period when you would take a high-status job for less money over a low-status job that paid more. Overall, financial power is strongest from the 1st to the 14th and from the 29th onwards – as the Moon waxes.

Job-seekers, in general, are having a good year, but after the 20th they need more patience. Don't settle for something second-rate now out of panic. There are beautiful, dream jobs out there if you are patient.

Love is reasonable until the 20th. After that it seems more challenging. You and your lover don't see eye to eye. They are having more emotional issues (perhaps stemming from family relationships) after the 20th, and seem more temperamental. They also seem out of sorts with one of your friends. Perhaps they resent any attention given to your friends. Your current relationship will get a testing now. (The retrograde of Venus, the generic planet of love, is not helping matters either.) True love will always survive.

There is a rare Grand Square pattern this month in the fixed signs. Big projects are going on in the world and in your environment. These could affect you after the 22nd, and perhaps the family or the home is affected too.

Health is excellent this month, especially after the 20th. You have lots of energy. Self-esteem could be better though. But have no fear: honours and recognition are coming late this month and early next month. Since your health planet is a long-term planet (Pluto), health needs rarely change throughout the year. Enhance health through detox regimes and paying more attention to the liver, thighs, colon, bladder and sexual organs.

Mercury, your ruler, re-stimulates eclipse points on the 10th and 11th and from the 18th to the 20th. Avoid risky, stressful activities during these periods. Family members can be more temperamental on those days as well.

February

Best Days Overall: 6, 7, 16, 17, 25, 26

Most Stressful Days Overall: 1, 14, 15, 21, 22, 27, 28

Best Days for Love: 1, 4, 5, 9, 10, 14, 15, 19, 20, 21, 22, 23, 24, 27, 28

Best Days for Money: 1, 6, 7, 9, 10, 17, 18, 19, 20, 27, 28

Monthly Career Peaks: 1, 8, 9, 18, 19, 20, 25, 26, 27, 28

Monthly Personal Pleasure Peaks: 6, 7, 27, 28

Like last month, most of the planets are above the horizon. Your 10th House of Career becomes very powerful after the 19th. Forty per cent of the planetary power will either be there or move through there this month. Your 4th House of Family, by contrast, is mostly empty (only the Moon will move through there on the 14th and 15th). You are now in your yearly career peak and it is best to make the most of it. Pay rises and promotions are likely. Beautiful job offers are coming after the 19th. There is career-related travel – happy travel too. But aside from the recognition you receive for professional achievement, we see personal recognition and honour on the 1st and 2nd, and again after the 19th.

The family as a whole is elevated now too. Family members are also enjoying career success on an individual level, so down-playing your day-to-day domestic life is not a big hardship now. This is a month when you are trying to merge the career with the home – to make your office more homely and comfortable, less corporate. Some of you will make your home more like an office and work more from home. You feel (and the family feels) that you can best serve them by succeeding in the outer world.

A sudden opportunity for travel and/or education comes from the 13th to the 15th. This could be on a personal level or for a family member as well. A career opportunity could force an important change in the home, but you might decline it. We don't see a move in your chart. Those on a spiritual path receive important religious and philosophical revelation during that period as well. Many of you will experiment with your appearance then too. Perhaps you are buying high-tech personal accessories.

Like last month, finance doesn't seem a big deal. Your 2nd House is mostly empty (except for the Moon's visit on the 9th and 10th). However, the Moon's re-stimulation of eclipse points (on the 2nd, 3rd, 9th, 10th, 16th, 17th, 23rd and 24th) might force needed changes and adjustments. Overall, financial power and enthusiasm is strongest from the 1st to the 12th and from the 27th onwards – when the Moon waxes.

As the month begins, most of the planets are still in the West. There is a need to cultivate your social skills, to down-play the self and personal interests, and adapt to existing situations. Personal initiative is less important than the good grace of others. But after the 19th, the planetary power shifts. East and West are balanced. Slowly you are becoming more independent.

Health needs more watching after the 19th. Your career focus taxes your energies so try to schedule in more time for rest and rejuvenation. Continue to enhance your health through detox regimes, and paying more attention to the liver, thighs, sexual organs, colon and bladder. Mars will move into your own sign after the 18th, so vigorous exercise will be both fun and healthful.

Love is much improved after the 10th. Either the current crisis is resolved or you are meeting new people. Love opportunities are plentiful. As has been the pattern for the year, these happen at the office or as you pursue health goals.

March

Best Days Overall: 6, 7, 15, 16, 17, 25, 26

Most Stressful Days Overall: 13, 14, 20, 21, 27, 28

Best Days for Love: 4, 5, 6, 8, 9, 15, 16, 18, 19, 20, 21, 25, 26, 27, 28

Best Days for Money: 8, 9, 18, 19, 20, 27, 28, 29, 30

Monthly Career Peaks: 25, 26, 27, 28

Monthly Personal Pleasure Peaks: 6, 7, 27, 28

You are still in your yearly career peak. Most of the planets remain above the horizon, and your 10th House of Career is the strongest in the horoscope until the 20th. You are right to down-play the home and family situation and to focus on your career. However, if you have been overly ignoring these things (understandable), a Lunar Eclipse on the 14th is going to get your attention. If there are flaws in the home, needed repairs you've been putting off, or seething issues within the family, they will now come up and you'll have to deal with them. Perhaps some of you will decide to move (you will embrace the career opportunity of last month and take the plunge). Emotions at home will be volatile and it is best to let the dust settle before making important decisions. This eclipse is stressful on you, so reduce your schedule a few days before the eclipse and for about a day after.

There is a Solar Eclipse on the 29th that seems more benign. It occurs in your 11th House of Friends and will probably test a friendship (not a romantic relationship). It could also bring increased dramas with friends – shocking or surprising things happen to them, and they might need you. If you belong to a social or professional organization, there can be shake-ups that may affect your relationship to it. Every Solar Eclipse will test your communication equipment. Often it will test the car as well.

Mercury, your ruler, goes retrograde from the 2nd to the 25th. This often weakens self-confidence and causes you to review your personal interests. Since this is happening in the 10th House, I read it as a review of recent career offers and perhaps a change of heart with them. Another career opportunity is coming at the end of the month (perhaps a repeat of a previous one). This retrograde period is not a good time to make drastic changes to your image or to buy personal items and accessories, especially expensive ones.

Not only is your ruler retrograde, but the love planet goes retrograde as well (on the 4th). This doesn't stop love or social activities; it only slows things down a bit. Love still seems happy, but singles need to let it develop slowly.

Health improves after the 20th. In the meantime, continue to exercise (without overdoing it) and enhance health in the ways described last month. The important thing is to keep your energy levels high until the 20th.

As has been the case in the past few months, the 2nd House of Money is empty (only the Moon passes through on the 8th and 9th). Finances are not a big issue with you. Status and prestige are much more important. You seem content here. Financial power will be stronger from the 1st to the 14th and from the 29th onwards – the days when the Moon waxes – and you can schedule yourself accordingly. If you need to make adjustments to finances, the Moon's re-stimulation of eclipse points on the 24th and 28th will provide opportunity.

April

Best Days Overall: 2, 3, 12, 13, 21, 11, 29, 30

Most Stressful Days Overall: 9, 10, 17, 18, 23, 24

Best Days for Love: 2, 3, 4, 5, 14, 15, 17, 18, 23, 24

Best Days for Money: 4, 5, 7, 8, 14, 15, 18, 23, 24, 27, 28

Monthly Career Peaks: 5, 6, 7, 21, 22, 23, 24

Monthly Personal Pleasure Peaks: 2, 3, 25, 26, 29, 30

Hopefully you used the delays of last month (the retrograde of your ruler) to gain clarity about the conditions you would like to create in your life, especially your personal life. The planets are now shifting to the Eastern sector of your horoscope (by the 6th, 60 to 70 per cent will be there), so you will be in a good position to implement your plans. You are becoming ever more independent. You can start to have things your way, and your personal initiative and actions begin to matter. Personal independence will get even stronger after the 16th when your ruler moves into dynamic Aries.

Like last month, most of the planets are above the horizon, and your 10th House of Career is much, much stronger than your 4th House of Home and Family. Ambitions are still very strong. Domestic issues can be down-played and de-emphasized. Your family is still supportive of your career goals, and family members are also succeeding these days – especially a parent or parent figure and adult children. With the ruler of your spiritual 12th House moving into your House of Career on the 6th, there is more idealism in the career. You can further your career through involvement with charities and altruistic causes. Spiritual people have important career guidance for you. Dreams will also guide the career. The presence of your spiritual planet in your 10th House shows that you are getting revelation about your true mission in life – much more important for your wellbeing than just the career. You probably won't get a complete revelation, but you will increase your understanding here.

Job-seekers have great fortune this month, as do those who employ others. But there could be delayed reactions here, such as an offer coming but being stalled by bureaucrats. Also make sure that a dream job offer is really what it is.

The 2nd House of Finance (which has been basically empty all year) becomes more powerful after the 14th. Mars moves in there and stays for the rest of the month. This shows you are taking aggressive, perhaps even risky, financial actions. You want to make wealth happen rather than just allow it to happen. Since Mars receives beautiful aspects, your bold moves will pay off. Friends are very helpful in finances and are likely to create opportunity. Perhaps you are using new technology to enhance financial skills. Perhaps you are involved in a new invention that is bringing earnings. You want quick money and it will probably happen.

Though your love planet remains retrograde, love still seems happy. The retrograde doesn't stop love, only slows it down. Caution in love is a good thing these days. Friends play cupid. There are love opportunities at group meetings and activities. Try to enjoy these things for what they are without projecting too far into the future. A friend gets involved in a serious romance this month, and this advice can apply to them as well. A parent or parent figure, if single, has a strong romantic opportunity. In general, parents are more sociable.

Health is reasonable. With Mars in your own sign and with your new independence, the main danger is overactivity. Your health planet is retrograde all month, so it is not a good idea to make drastic changes to your diet or health regime without a lot of research.

Mercury, your ruler, re-stimulates eclipse points on the 11th, 12th, 22nd and 23rd. Avoid risky activities then.

GEMINI

May

Best Days Overall: 9, 10, 18, 19, 27, 28

Most Stressful Days Overall: 7, 8, 14, 15, 20, 21

Best Days for Love: 2, 3, 12, 13, 14, 15, 20, 21, 22, 23, 29, 30

Best Days for Money: 2, 3, 7, 8, 12, 13, 16, 17, 20, 21, 27, 28, 29, 30

Monthly Career Peaks: 18, 19, 20, 21

Monthly Personal Pleasure Peaks: 20, 21, 22, 27, 28

Try to wrap up career projects before the 21st. After that your career planet, Neptune, starts to move retrograde, and the planetary power begins to shift towards the lower half (the night side) of the horoscope. This tends to weaken ambition and changes the focus from career to a need for feeling good and emotional harmony. Also, important career decisions shouldn't be made when Neptune is retrograde.

The planetary power will be equally distributed between the upper (day) side and lower (night) side of the horoscope after the 21st. Home and emotional issues become just as important as outer achievement, and you find yourself alternating between the two interests. The trend, however, is moving away from the career.

Like last month, the planetary power is now mostly in the East – but even more so. Your 1st House of Self becomes very powerful after the 21st (two out of three of the most important planets will be there). The planets involved with social activities, by contrast, will be retrograde. So you can safely down-play social interests and pursue personal fulfilment.

Of course, you will still have a social life this month. Love continues to be happy and there are plenty of love opportunities – at the workplace, as you pursue career and health goals, in educational settings and through friends. But the lust for relationships seems lessened. You want your own space and your own interests. Love and relationships need more review and thought. At times like these you realize that a relationship in itself can't really make you happy. Happiness is up to you, a personal choice.

The financial trends mentioned last month are still very much in effect. Dynamic, macho Mars occupies your 2nd House all month. It is part of a beautiful and rare Grand Trine in the Water Signs. This is a prosperous month. You make it happen through bold and aggressive moves. Friends and organizations are helpful, as are social contacts. But really, you prosper through your own action and initiative.

Health is excellent this month. You can enhance it further by paying more attention to the liver, thighs, colon, bladder and sexual organs. It won't hurt to give the stomach and breasts more attention as well.

Mercury, your ruler, will re-stimulate eclipse points on the 30th and 31st. Take it easy on those days. Do what needs to be done, but avoid high-risk activities. Be more patient with family members and parent figures then.

June

Best Days Overall: 5, 6, 14, 15, 23, 24

Most Stressful Days Overall: 3, 4, 10, 11, 17, 18, 30

Best Days for Love: 3, 4, 8, 9, 10, 11, 12, 13, 17, 18, 22, 25, 26

Best Days for Money: 5, 6, 8, 9, 14, 15, 17, 18, 25, 26

Monthly Career Peaks: 14, 15, 17, 18

Monthly Personal Pleasure Peaks: 23, 24, 26, 27

The lower, night side of your horoscope is now stronger than the upper, day side. Two out of the three most important planets (the Sun and your ruler, Mercury) are below the horizon, and the other important planet (the Moon) will spend half the month below the horizon. The two planets involved with your career will also be retrograde. Neptune, your career planet, went retrograde last month, and Uranus, in your 10th House, begins to move retrograde on the 19th. The message now is very clear: your career will need development time. It can safely be down-played while your focus is on recharging your emotional batteries, finding (and functioning from) your emotional comfort zone. Feeling good is more important than doing good. You haven't lost your ambition; you are going to pursue it in a different way – an inner way. You are building the psychological foundations of future career success.

Like last month, the Eastern sector of the horoscope is stronger than the Western sector. Your 1st House of Self is stronger than your 7th House of Others. This is still a time for pursuing and manifesting personal happiness, for sensual fulfilment and personal pleasure, for having things your way and doing the things that really make you happy. As you pursue your path of personal happiness (so long as it isn't destructive) you will find that others consent to it.

Though your career is on hold for a while, bottom-line issues are important. This is another month of prosperity. Your 2nd House of Finance, which was strong during the last two months, becomes even stronger this month. Early in the year you were more concerned with status and prestige than with mere money. Now the situation is reversed. Money is more important than status and glory. Part of being emotionally comfortable is being financially comfortable. Now, a job of lesser status that pays well will be more attractive than a job of great prestige that pays less. Job-seekers have many opportunities now, only they need to do more research and homework. Your skills are in demand now and there are plenty of fish in the sea. Money is earned through your native strengths – communication, marketing, sales, networking, trading. Good use of the media is important. Your personal appearance and overall demeanour is another big factor in earnings, and many of you are spending on yourselves because of this. Your interest in finance is intense, and with interest comes success. Your family also seems supportive.

Your 3rd House of Communication also becomes more important this month. This is always an important area in your life, but now it's even more prominent. So you will be going on many short trips and taking courses in subjects that interest you. Health-wise you need to be careful not to let the mind get over-stimulated these days and now more so. Avoid arguments where possible. Through meditation and disciplines such as yoga, you can learn to turn the mind off when not in use. Enhance health in the ways mentioned for previous months by paying more attention to the liver, thighs, colon, bladder and sexual organs. If you feel low, a good detox might be in order.

Mercury, your ruler, will re-stimulate eclipse points on the 1st, 8th, 9th and 10th. Avoid risky behaviour on those days. Be more patient with family members (especially parents or parent figures) as they are apt to be more temperamental.

July

Best Days Overall: 3, 4, 12, 13, 20, 21, 30, 31

Most Stressful Days Overall: 1, 8, 9, 14, 15, 27, 28, 29

Best Days for Love: 3, 4, 5, 6, 8, 9, 12, 13, 14, 15, 22, 23, 24

Best Days for Money: 5, 6, 14, 15, 23, 24, 25, 26

Monthly Career Peaks: 12, 13, 14, 15

Monthly Personal Pleasure Peaks: 20, 21, 23, 24

GEMINI

Many of the trends mentioned last month are continuing now. Most of the planets are still below the horizon (the night side) of your horoscope. Your two career planets, Neptune and Uranus, remain retrograde. This means that emotional and family issues continue to be more important than career. Many wonderful career opportunities are happening now but these are in development and might be behind the scenes, not in your conscious awareness.

Finances remain important, and you are still in your yearly financial peak. Communication, marketing, media, sales and trading – all the things you do best – are bringing in money and earnings opportunity. On the 19th, Venus (your planet of intuition, your spiritual planet) will move into your money house. Generally, you Geminis are logical and matter-of-fact, but now intuition – which transcends even brilliant logic such as yours – comes into the picture. It's best to listen to it.

With the spiritual planet in the money house you are more generous and charitable this month. This will help you to prosper in very subtle ways. Systematic charitable giving is one of the best financial medicines available.

Like last month, most of the planets are still in the East, so continue to pursue your personal path of happiness. Please yourself and you will find that others are pleased (so long as you are not destructive about it).

Many planets in the East do not usually bode well for love. By definition, love is partnership and mutual dependence. But here we see an exception. Your love planet, Jupiter, is moving forwards on the 7th after many months of retrograde motion. Not only that, but it is receiving fabulous aspects from the other planets – it is part of a beautiful Grand Trine in Water. There are many happy love opportunities. Could it be that your happy demeanour is the actual cause? A current relationship starts moving forwards again. Your social confidence is stronger. Love opportunities come as you pursue your financial goals. You have more self-love and thus are more able to love others. Love opportunities also come at the office or workplace and as you pursue health goals. Your love life is going to get better and better over the next few months too.

Your ruler, Mercury, goes retrograde from the 3rd to the 29th. This is a good time to review personal goals and your image and personal appearance. It's not wise at this time to make drastic changes to your image or invest heavily in clothes and accessories. These things all need more study, and when Mercury starts moving forwards on the 29th, you will have a totally different perspective on these things.

Cars and communication equipment get tested on the 1st and 2nd as the Sun re-stimulates eclipse points. Children can be more temperamental from the 25th to the 27th as Venus re-stimulates eclipse points. You might hear of weird love problems from friends at this time too.

August

Best Days Overall: 8, 9, 17, 18, 26, 27

Most Stressful Days Overall: 4, 5, 10, 11, 24, 25, 31

Best Days for Love: 2, 3, 4, 5, 10, 11, 19, 20, 21, 22, 29, 30, 31

Best Days for Money: 2, 3, 4, 5, 10, 11, 12, 13, 19, 20, 22, 23, 29, 30

Monthly Career Peaks: 8, 9, 10, 11

Monthly Personal Pleasure Peaks: 17, 18, 22, 23

The planets are making an important shift from the East (self) to the West (others) this month. By the 23rd, 60 to 70 per cent of the planets will be in the West. The time for 'my way' is over. Now it's time to put other people first, to understand and tend to their interests ahead of your own. This Western shift will also enhance your already wonderful love life. By becoming more other-oriented, you become more popular and socially magnetic.

Love is bittersweet this month. There is opportunity, but also some conflict with your beloved. But by the time the Western shift is completed, these conflicts will resolve. Love opportunities can still be found at work and as you pursue financial goals, but intellectual interests conflict with them.

Finances continue to be good this month, but your interest in these things is waning. By the 13th, your 2nd House of Finance will be empty again (only the Moon will pass through on the 21st, 22nd and 23rd). I read this as the attainment of financial goals and the desire to move on to more interesting things. Intuition continues to be important here, especially until the 13th. Communication, marketing, sales and media also remain significant. Donning the image of wealth is again important. Your family continues to be supportive.

As for the past few months, most of the planets are below the horizon (the night side of the chart), and the 4th House of Home and Family becomes very powerful, especially after the 23rd. Both of your career planets continue to be retrograde. This is a time to focus on building a happy and stable home base. Down-play your career and give attention to the family and to your own emotional needs. It is a good month for reviewing your past – perhaps your early childhood – to find the origin of your emotional patterns and states. There is much psychological progress to be made this month. Tempers in the family could run high, and this will be useful as you can see what's beneath the pattern. A lot of this temper is coming from religious and philosophical differences, not just old traumas, and you should look into this as well. Seems like you are installing high-tech gadgets in the home, and it is more complicated than you thought.

There are dramas with friends (or among your friends) from the 12th to the 15th. There could be temporary fallings out here. There is some major disruption in an organization you belong to as well.

Health is basically good, but you need to rest and relax more after the 23rd. Emotional volatility can tax the energies. Emotional health is unusually important for physical health this period. Health problems are likely to be coming from old traumas or family discord. Pay more attention to the stomach and breasts, as well as the liver, thighs, colon and sexual organs.

September

Best Days Overall: 5, 6, 13, 14, 22, 23, 24

Most Stressful Days Overall: 1, 7, 8, 20, 21, 27, 28, 29

Best Days for Love: 1, 2, 7, 8, 11, 15, 16, 20, 21, 25, 26, 27, 28, 29, 30

Best Days for Money: 3, 4, 7, 8, 11, 12, 15, 16, 22, 23, 25, 26

Monthly Career Peaks: 5, 6, 7, 8

Monthly Personal Pleasure Peaks: 13, 14, 22, 23

A tumultuous and eventful month, Gemini, so try to rest and relax more. There are two eclipses this period, and both have a strong effect on you. The Lunar Eclipse of the 7th seems strongest for most of you. It occurs in your 10th House of Career and impacts on Uranus, the ruler of your 9th House. This is bringing major career and financial changes. These are necessary and probably should have been made long ago. Your personal philosophy of life and your personal religion (and we all have one) will get some testing too. You will make big adjustments to your understanding of the meaning of life and the meaning of your own life. There could be dramas with a parent or parent figure. There are shake-ups within your industry and within your corporate hierarchy as well. A new (and better) career pattern is forming for you.

GEMINI

The Solar Eclipse of September 22nd will be strongest on those of you born late in the sign of Gemini (from June 15th to 20th). If you are one of these, do try to reduce your schedule a few days before and a day after this period. This eclipse will affect two areas of life as it occurs right on the border of the 4th and 5th houses. Long-term changes are happening within the family and the family pattern. Flaws in the home (and in the family relationship) are forced to the surface so that you can correct them. There could be more dramas with a parent or parent figure. Emotions at home run high, like last month. There is more personal emotional volatility as well, and a general clearing of the air within the family. Children are making important and long-term changes, and perhaps your relationship to them is affected. The career changes of the previous eclipse seem to be impacting on your domestic life. This is not at all unusual as one goes with the other.

A love affair will get tested and could end. Serious, committed loves seem unaffected here.

Health is still delicate until the 23rd. Like last month, continue to focus on emotional health, the liver, thighs, colon and bladder.

As the dust settles from the eclipses, take a positive approach. If there are constructive things to be done, do them. But if not, go out and enjoy your day. Fun is very important after the 23rd.

Finances are stable this month. Your 2nd House is basically empty (only the Moon will visit there on the 15th and 16th) so you seem content in your financial life. Earning power will tend to be stronger from the 1st to the 15th and from the 22nd onwards, the periods when the Moon waxes.

October

Best Days Overall: 2, 3, 10, 11, 20, 21, 29, 30

Most Stressful Days Overall: 4, 5, 17, 18, 19, 25, 26

Best Days for Love: 2, 3, 4, 5, 10, 11, 12, 13, 14, 21, 22, 23, 24, 25, 26

Best Days for Money: 2, 3, 4, 5, 10, 11, 12, 13, 14, 21, 22, 23, 24

Monthly Career Peaks: 2, 3, 4, 5, 29, 30

Monthly Personal Pleasure Peaks: 10, 11, 22, 23, 24

A much quieter and easier month than September, Gemini. Health is vastly improved. Energy is high. You can enhance it further by paying more attention to the liver, thighs, colon, bladder and sexual organs. Keeping the harmony in love and with friends will also do much to improve overall health. Your 6th House of Health gets packed with planets after the 23rd. This shows your great interest in health, health regimes and preventive medicine, and in taking a holistic approach. Good health these days means more than just the absence of symptoms – it means good mental, social, romantic and spiritual health. It also means looking good. With your love life sparkling these days, it is understandable that you want to look your best.

This is a period for R&R – for fun, leisure and creative pursuits. With 40 to 50 per cent of the planets in your 5th House, you see that life is to be enjoyed. This is a wonderful period for exploring creative hobbies and for dealing with children. Geminis of childbearing age are more fertile this month. A good period for connecting with your inner child, the part of you that knows how to have fun.

Work is also important but that happens later in the month, after the 23rd. You will work with renewed enthusiasm when the time comes and will be much more productive.

Job-seekers have great success all month, but especially after the 23rd. A real dream job awaits. Employers are increasing their staff then too.

Finances are stable. Your 2nd House of Finance is still empty (except when the Moon visits on the 12th, 13th and 14th). Earning power will be strongest (overall) from the 1st to the 7th and from the 22nd onwards, the periods when the Moon waxes. Financial enthusiasm will also be stronger during those periods.

The lower (night) side of your horoscope is still stronger than the upper (day) side, so family and emotional issues are more important than the career. In spite of your seeming lack of ambition, all kinds of wonderful career opportunities are coming. But now you might be more selective as these will have to be harmonious and non-disruptive to your emotional life. Both your career planets are still retrograde so many of these opportunities can come with a delay – many are happening behind the scenes and you might be unaware of it.

Love is really the main headline now. You are entering your yearly social and romantic peak. Until the 23rd, you just want a good time so non-commitment suits you fine. But afterwards you will be more serious and love is certainly there. Wedding bells or engagements could happen now and over the next few months. Serious love is happening for singles.

November

Best Days Overall: 7, 8, 16, 17, 26, 27

Most Stressful Days Overall: 1, 13, 14, 15, 21, 22, 28, 29

Best Days for Love: 1, 2, 9, 10, 20, 21, 22, 30

Best Days for Money: 1, 2, 9, 10, 19, 20, 30

Monthly Career Peaks: 1, 26, 27, 28, 29

Monthly Personal Pleasure Peaks: 7, 8, 19, 20

Your ruler, Mercury, is retrograde from the 1st to the 18th. In a way this is a good thing. You are less likely to be self-assertive or self-centred, which could hinder romance. This is not a good time to make drastic changes to your image or appearance. Wait until Mercury moves forwards when you will have a different (and more realistic) perspective on things.

Love, health and work are the main headlines of the coming month. As has been the case all year, the workplace and health interests are where love tends to happen. The job has not been just a job this year – it's been a social centre. Health interests focus on looking good. You want good health because it makes you more attractive.

Your love planet, Jupiter, makes a major move into your 7th House of Love and Marriage on the 24th. It will be in this house well into 2007. Serious romance is happening, especially for singles. For marrieds, there will be a general increase in social life, and more romance within the marriage. With the move of the love planet the social scene will also change. Now love opportunities will come in more conventional ways – at parties, weddings, social gatherings and the like. Romance can bloom in foreign countries and with foreigners. Those already involved in romance might make the relationship stronger by going on trips to exotic locales. Romance can bloom at the church, synagogue, ashram or mosque. Also at university. Geminis are not especially religious people but they like religious qualities in a partner. Devout people are alluring to them. This is the kind of person you are involved with these days. They also seem wealthy, or live an opulent sort of lifestyle. Love with a teacher or mentor is also more likely.

The planets are moving from the lower (night) side of the horoscope, to the upper (day) side. Further, the planets involved in your career are now moving forwards. Neptune, your career planet, moved forwards at the end of last month. Uranus (the occupant of your 10th House) starts moving forwards on the 20th, just about when the planets make their shift. The timing here is uncanny! Hopefully by now you have found your point of emotional harmony and are solidly established there. (You still have until the 23rd to do this.) After the 23rd your vision is on the outer world and career heights. First off, you will have more interest in your career, more passion and drive. Second, with the career planets moving forwards, you will have a clear plan. Also, many pending career opportunities and developments start to make progress again.

Finance is again stable. The 2nd House is empty, except when the Moon passes through on the 9th and 10th. Love, work, health and professional status are all more important than mere money. In general, earning power is stronger from the 1st to the 5th and from the 20th onwards.

December

Best Days Overall: 4, 5, 13, 14, 15, 23, 24

Most Stressful Days Overall: 11, 12, 18, 19, 25, 26

Best Days for Love: 1, 4, 8, 9, 10, 11, 18, 19, 21, 22, 27, 29, 30

Best Days for Money: 1, 4, 6, 7, 8, 9, 18, 19, 20, 27, 29

Monthly Career Peaks: 23, 24, 25, 26

Monthly Personal Pleasure Peaks: 4, 5, 18, 19, 31

You are not only in a yearly social peak right now, but perhaps in a lifetime peak. Amazing social and romantic experiences are happening. Seventy per cent of the planets are either in or moving through your 7th House of Love and Marriage. The social life is the centre of almost all activity in your life this month.

With Mercury, your ruler, also in this House (from the 8th to the 27th), you are definitely focused here, going out of your way to please others and your lover or partner. Popularity is probably at an all-time high. If there are still some of you who haven't yet found that special someone, the choices and opportunities are bewildering right now.

All this social activity can tax your energy so be sure to schedule in some rest and relaxation time. You can enhance health further by paying more attention to the liver, thighs, colon, bladder and sexual organs. Detox regimes are still beneficial.

At times like this you can easily see the power of non-action. There's no need for mental or psychological manipulation now – this will only slow things down.

Not surprisingly, sexual activity should increase this month (for those of you of appropriate age). Nothing wrong with that, only don't overdo a good thing. The sexual organs are unusually important for overall health. Whatever your age and stage, libido will be stronger than usual, especially after the 22nd.

Personal finance, as in the past few months, is not a big issue for you. Your 2nd House is again empty (only the Moon will make a brief visit on the 6th and 7th). You seem financially content. Earning power is strongest from the 1st to the 5th and from the 20th onwards – as the Moon waxes. Other people's prosperity seems much more important to you than your own. You prosper as you help others to prosper. Outside money is easily available after the 22nd. Debts are easily paid (and also easily made). Money can come from spousal support or the generosity of your current lover. If you are involved with insurance or estate issues you should see good progress later in the month, but do more homework with these things.

Mercury is going to re-stimulate eclipse points from the 17th to the 19th and from the 26th to the 28th. Avoid risky behaviour on those days. Also be more patient with family members.

Cancer

♋

THE CRAB

Birthdays from
21st June to
20th July

Personality Profile

CANCER AT A GLANCE

Element – Water

Ruling Planet – Moon
  Career Planet – Mars
  Love Planet – Saturn
  Money Planet – Sun
  Planet of Fun and Games – Pluto
  Planet of Good Fortune – Neptune
  Planet of Health and Work – Jupiter
  Planet of Home and Family Life – Venus
  Planet of Spirituality – Mercury

Colours – blue, puce, silver

Colours that promote love, romance and social
  harmony – black, indigo

Colours that promote earning power – gold, orange

Gems – moonstone, pearl

Metal – silver

Scents – jasmine, sandalwood

Quality – cardinal (= activity)

Quality most needed for balance – mood control

Strongest virtues – emotional sensitivity, tenacity, the urge to nurture

Deepest need – a harmonious home and family life

Characteristics to avoid – over-sensitivity, negative moods

Signs of greatest overall compatibility – Scorpio, Pisces

Signs of greatest overall incompatibility – Aries, Libra, Capricorn

Sign most helpful to career – Aries

Sign most helpful for emotional support – Libra

Sign most helpful financially – Leo

Sign best for marriage and/or partnerships – Capricorn

Sign most helpful for creative projects – Scorpio

Best Sign to have fun with – Scorpio

Signs most helpful in spiritual matters – Gemini, Pisces

Best day of the week – Monday

Understanding a Cancer

In the Sign of Cancer the heavens are developing the feeling side of things. This is what a true Cancerian is all about – feelings. Where Aries will tend to err on the side of action, Taurus on the side of inaction and Gemini on the side of thought, Cancer will tend to err on the side of feeling.

Cancerians tend to mistrust logic. Perhaps rightfully so. For them it is not enough for an argument or a project to be logical – it must feel right as well. If it does not feel right a Cancerian will reject it or chafe against it. The phrase 'follow your heart' could have been coined by a Cancerian, because it describes exactly the Cancerian attitude to life.

The power to feel is a more direct – more immediate – method of knowing than thinking is. Thinking is indirect. Thinking about a thing never touches the thing itself. Feeling is a faculty that touches directly the thing or issue in question. We actually experience it. Emotional feeling is almost like another sense which humans possess – a psychic sense. Since the realities that we come in contact with during our lifetime are often painful and even destructive, it is not surprising that the Cancerian chooses to erect barriers – a shell – to protect his or her vulnerable, sensitive nature. To a Cancerian this is only common sense.

If Cancerians are in the presence of people they do not know, or find themselves in a hostile environment, up goes the shell and they feel protected. Other people often complain about this, but one must question these other people's motives. Why does this shell disturb them? Is it perhaps because they would like to sting, and feel frustrated that they cannot? If your intentions are honourable and you are patient, have no fear. The shell will open up and you will be accepted as part of the Cancerian's circle of family and friends.

Thought-processes are generally analytic and dissociating. In order to think clearly we must make distinctions, comparisons and the like. But feeling is unifying and integrative.

To think clearly about something you have to distance yourself from it. To feel something you must get close to it. Once a Cancerian has accepted you as a friend he or she will hang on. You have to be really bad to lose the friendship of a Cancerian. If you are related to Cancerians they will never let you go no matter what you do. They will always try to maintain some kind of connection even in the most extreme circumstances.

Finance

The Cancer-born has a deep sense of what other people feel about things and why they feel as they do. This faculty is a great asset in the workplace and in the business world. Of course it is also indispensable in raising a family and building a home, but it also has its uses in business. Cancerians often attain great wealth in a family type of business. Even if the business is not a family operation, they will treat it as one. If the Cancerian works for somebody else, then the boss is the parental figure and the co-workers are brothers and sisters. If a Cancerian is the boss, then all the workers are his or her children. Cancerians like the feeling of being providers for others. They enjoy knowing that others derive their sustenance because of what they do. It is another form of nurturing.

With Leo on their Solar 2nd House (of Money) cusp, Cancerians are often lucky speculators, especially with residential property or hotels and restaurants. Resort hotels and nightclubs are also profitable for the Cancerian. Waterside properties allure them. Though they are basically conventional people, they sometimes like to earn their livelihood in glamorous ways.

The Sun, Cancer's Money Planet, represents an important financial message: in financial matters Cancerians need to be less moody, more stable and fixed. They cannot allow their moods – which are here today and gone tomorrow – to get in the way of their business lives. They need to develop their self-esteem and feelings of self-worth if they are to realize their greatest financial potential.

Career and Public Image

Aries rules the 10th Solar House (of Career) cusp of Cancer, which indicates that Cancerians long to start their own business, to be more active publicly and politically and to be more independent. Family responsibilities and a fear of hurting other people's feelings – or getting hurt themselves – often inhibit them from attaining these goals. However, this is what they want and long to do.

Cancerians like their bosses and leaders to act freely and to be a bit self-willed. They can deal with that in a superior. Cancerians expect their leaders to be fierce on their behalf.

When the Cancerian is in the position of boss or superior he or she behaves very much like a 'warlord'. Of course the wars they wage are not egocentric but in defence of those under their care. If they lack some of this fighting instinct – independence and pioneering spirit – Cancerians will have extreme difficulty in attaining their highest career goals. They will be hampered in their attempts to lead others.

Since they are so parental, Cancerians like to work with children and make great educators and teachers.

Love and Relationships

Like Taurus, Cancer likes committed relationships. Cancerians function best when the relationship is clearly defined and everyone knows his or her role. When they marry it is usually for life. They are extremely loyal to their beloved. But there is a deep little secret that most Cancerians will never admit to: commitment or partnership is really a chore and a duty to them. They enter into it because they know of no other way to create the family that they desire. Union is just a way – a means to an end – rather than an end in itself. The family is the ultimate end for them.

If you are in love with a Cancerian you must tread lightly on his or her feelings. It will take you a good deal of time to realize how deep and sensitive Cancerians can be. The smallest negativity upsets them. Your tone of voice, your irritation, a look in your eye or an expression on your face can cause great distress for the Cancerian. Your slightest gesture is registered by them and reacted to. This can be hard to get used to, but stick by your love – Cancerians make great partners once you learn how to deal with them. Your Cancerian lover will react not so much to what you say but to the way you are actually feeling at the moment.

Home and Domestic Life

This is where Cancerians really excel. The home environment and the family are their personal works of art. They strive to make things of beauty that will outlast them. Very often they succeed.

Cancerians feel very close to their family, their relatives and especially their mothers. These bonds last throughout their lives and mature as they grow older. They are very fond of those members of their family who become successful, and they are also quite attached to family heirlooms and mementos. Cancerians also love children and like to provide them with all the things they need and want. With their nurturing, feeling nature, Cancerians make very good parents – especially the Cancerian woman, who is the mother par excellence of the Zodiac.

As a parent the Cancerian's attitude is 'my children right or wrong.' Unconditional devotion is the order of the day. No matter what a family member does, the Cancerian will eventually forgive him or her, because 'you are, after all, family'. The preservation of the institution – the tradition – of the family is one of the Cancerian's main reasons for living. They have many lessons to teach others about this.

Being so family-orientated, the Cancerian's home is always clean, orderly and comfortable. They like old-fashioned furnishings but they also like to have all the modern comforts. Cancerians love to have family and friends over, to organize parties and to entertain at home – they make great hosts.

Horoscope for 2006

General Trends

The years 2003–2005 were difficult for you, Cancer. These were character-building years when you took on – and handled – greater responsibility, when you didn't shirk your true duties but laboured bravely under them. The worst is over. The lessons that needed to be learned are learned. Ever since July 2005, things are much easier. This year, almost like a reward for all you've been through, you have a cosmic holiday – a party year. And, when the cosmos schedules a party, it also supplies all the wherewithal for it. So enjoy.

Many of you married in the past few years. Many of you moved. So, now you can rest and enjoy yourselves.

Of course there are some challenges in the year ahead, probably in the financial area. We'll discuss this very important area of life later on.

Health seems much improved this year too.

Religion and philosophy – also higher education – have been important since 2004, when Uranus moved into your 9th House. This seems an exciting area of life now. Foreign trips could happen out of the blue. Exciting educational opportunities are coming – not run-of-the-mill things either.

Your most important interests in the year ahead will be finance; children, fun, creativity and leisure pursuits (until November 24th); health and work (after November 24th); personal transformation, sex, occult studies, the deeper things of life; religion, philosophy and higher education.

Health

(Please note that this is an astrological perspective on health, not a medical one. At one time, both perspectives were identical, but in these times there could be quite a difference. For the medical perspective, please consult your physician or health professional.)

Your health should have improved vastly over the past two years, now that Saturn has left your sign. All the other long-term planets are either in harmonious aspect or leaving you alone. Overall, energy is much increased.

Sure there will be times in the year when energy is not as high as usual. These phenomena come from the transits and are not trends for the year. When the transits pass, your health reverts to its normal level. These more stressful times are January 1st to 19th; March 20th to April 19th; September 22nd to October 23rd; December 21st to 31st. These are times to pace yourself and rest and relax more.

Also helping matters is that your 6th House is strong this year, as it has been for many years now. But it will get even stronger after November 24th. This shows a strong interest in health and in maintaining health, in diet, exercise and healthy lifestyles. Health regimes for you are not burdens but fun. Also, you are unlikely to let little problems fester into big ones.

Jupiter is your health planet. In the physical body, Jupiter rules the liver and thighs. Thus these organs should always be given more attention, but especially this year.

Jupiter will be in the sign of Scorpio for most of the year ahead. Scorpio rules the sexual organs, colon, rectum and bladder. (Pluto, the generic ruler of these organs, is in your 6th House of Health, where it has been for many years.) More attention needs to be given to these organs. Sexual activity should be kept in balance. Safe sex is very important as well. Detoxing your liver and colon periodically would also be powerful.

With the health planet in the 5th House most of the year, we get many other messages. You learn the healing power of joy. If problems come up, go out on the town and have fun. Watch some slapstick comedy. Go to a party. The joy will heal.

Being a Cancer, diet is always an issue. Cancer rules the stomach. Right nutrition will not only help the stomach but the colon and bladder as well.

The health of parents and parent figures seems reasonable this year. One of them can benefit from regular foot and ankle massage. Ankles in general should be given more support, especially when exercising. Feet should be kept warm in the winter. The health of children also looks good, though two eclipses in their 6th House of Health could either be wake-up calls or force changes in their health regime. They benefit from vigorous exercise and thermal therapies. Grandchildren might be taking too many risks with the physical body, testing its limits, and this could pose a danger. They need to take better care of the spine, knees, teeth and heart. Your spouse's health seems reasonable.

Home, Domestic and Family Issues

The major home and family project seems to have occurred last year, when Jupiter moved through your 4th House. By now things seem settled. And though Cancerians will always consider the home and family important, this year there is less emphasis on this area.

Your 4th House is basically empty for most of the year. You have more personal freedom to shape this area as you desire it to be. But with nothing goading you, chances are things will be stable. Your home is pretty much the way you want it to be.

Children seem a big issue this year, both making them and raising them. Cancerians of childbearing age are very fertile. Pregnancies and/or new births are very likely. Cancerians of a certain age are likely to become grandparents too. It all seems happy and goes smoothly, though it does create some financial stress.

Until March you are still under the influence of last year's Solar Eclipse of October 3rd, which occurred in your 4th House. Every month, the Moon will make aspects to this point, and this could bring minor upheavals in the home. Perhaps emotions run high. Perhaps some flaws are discovered in the home, but nothing of a major or serious nature.

Another Solar Eclipse on September 22nd sideswipes your 4th House. This too could bring up hidden flaws in the home and force corrections.

A Solar Eclipse on March 14th occurs in your 10th House. Most probably it will bring career changes, but it can also bring some dramas with a parent or parent figure. Long-term change will happen with that person. (This doesn't have to happen exactly on March 14th – it could happen in the six-month period following it.)

With fast-moving Venus as your family planet, the home and family situation tends to be dynamic and rapidly changing.

Older children could be moving many times in the coming year. Children are also getting high-tech entertainment equipment. Grandchildren also seem very nomadic.

If you're planning to do construction in the home, September 8th to October 23rd seems like a good time. (A parent or parent figure might be staying with you and can probably help out, supervise or even do the work.) If you're redecorating in a cosmetic way, September 30th to October 24th is good. This will also be a good time to entertain from home.

CANCER

Love and Social Life

Now that your love planet has left your own sign (July 17th 2005) and your 7th House of Love is pretty much empty, your social life is not a big priority or interest this year. Oh sure, you will socialize (short-term planets will move through your 7th House, and the love planet will periodically get stimulated), but the driving urge is not there as compared to other things.

I read this as the achievement of social or love goals in past years and so now there's no need to pay too much attention here. Many of you have married in the past two years. Many are involved in significant relationships that are like a marriage. You seem content with the status quo. Those of you who are still single also seem content about it.

Your love planet is now in the sign of Leo for two years. So this is about enjoying your present relationship. Love is about fun, sex and making babies. Relationships need to be fun. When someone shows you a good time, you feel loved. And you show your love by giving your beloved a good time.

Your love planet is also in the 2nd House of Finance, and this has many messages for us. Love is shown by practical, material support. Material gifts are romantic turn-ons. Also, this is showing a business partnership for many of you.

For singles there are love opportunities as you pursue your financial goals. A normal visit to the bank or broker's office can turn out to be more than that. There are important romantic opportunities with people involved in your financial life – the accounting firm, clients, financial advisors, money managers and the like.

Those of you who managed to stay single over these past few years can still walk down the aisle this year or next year – but after November 24th. This looks like an office-type romance.

For marrieds, your spouse or partner seems heavily involved in your financial life. They seem committed to your prosperity. Although they might be over-controlling here, their motives seem good. More on this later.

Those into their second marriage are facing crisis in the relationship. True love will conquer all – but boy, what a ride! Those looking to marry for the second time are better off staying uncommitted. Enjoy the many love opportunities that are available, but sit loose. Affections seem unstable here.

Those into, or working on, the third marriage have a status-quo year. Singles will tend to stay single; marrieds will tend to stay married. For singles working on the third marriage there is a love affair happening from January 1st to March 5th. This has marriage potential, but it's a very complicated situation. Don't rush into anything here.

Your happiest and most socially active periods this year will be from January 1st to 19th; March 20th to April 19th; July 23rd to August 22nd; November 22nd to December 31st.

Your most stressful love periods will be from January 20th to February 18th; April 20th to May 20th and October 23rd to November 21st. These are times to be more patient with your friends, spouse or lover.

Siblings are facing crisis in their marriage or important relationship. Single siblings probably shouldn't marry this year. Children of marriageable age are having a good year overall, but love is status-quo for them. Singles will stay single; marrieds will probably stay married. Grandchildren of marriageable age also shouldn't marry this year. They need to explore their freedom more.

Finance and Career

Your 2nd House of Finance has become important since July 17th 2005, when Saturn moved in there. It will be important this year and well into 2007. This is probably the most important area of life this year.

CANCER

There's much to say here. In general, Saturn in the money house shows a financial reorganization, a need to bring order and system to this area. Though this can be unpleasant to some (especially if you've been neglectful or irresponsible) the ultimate result will be good.

So this is a year to get spending and investing under control. Good budgets that allow for everything necessary are useful tools. The laws of long-term wealth – which is how you should be thinking now – should be studied. Real wealth (from Saturn's perspective) is an evolution, a gradual enfoldment over time. Saturn abhors quick money. It comes from real and practical service given to others.

Earnings don't seem to be the issue this year. The focus is on managing the income and wealth that you do have; on making good use of it; and allowing enough for regular and systematic saving while avoiding waste or non-essentials.

What complicates Saturn's job here is Jupiter in your 5th House. Jupiter, of course, has the opposite perspective to Saturn. He believes in quick and easy money and can be quite the speculator, especially in the 5th House. So these two urges are at war this year. Curiously, both of them are right at certain times, but you will probably be wavering between these two positions. The answer is somewhere in the middle.

For sure you deserve fun this year. No question about it. The cosmos has provided for it, and perhaps you need to cut spending in other areas. If you speculate, make sure it is a calculated risk. Calculated risks are rewarded this year, but not the wild casino-type risks.

Your career doesn't seem a big priority for most of the year – you're more in the mood for fun than work. However, job-seekers will have good fortune after November 24th and well into 2007. Those who employ others will increase their staff during that period as well.

Your 10th House is empty. I read this as a good thing too. You seem content with your career and professional status as it is. You don't have any compelling urge to make important efforts or changes here. However, if you ignore this area too much, a Solar Eclipse in your 10th House on March 29th will shake things up. It will be the goad that forces needed change. It could also show shake-ups in your corporate hierarchy.

Self-improvement

Ever since Uranus moved into your 9th House in 2004, religion and philosophy have become major interests. So you are in a period when you are breaking down old religious or philosophical ideas and bringing in the new. You are dramatically changing your metaphysical and philosophical perspective on life.

Few people realize how important the 9th House is. It rules our 'upper mind', our higher thought process. It is in the upper mind that we interpret the meaning of events, the meaning of our lives and work, and the meaning of life in general.

Right now you seem very rebellious – you are into breaking with the religion of your parents. Many of you will convert to other religions. Many of you will merely experiment and flit from one to the other, taking bits from each. The good news here is that you're subjecting these religious ideas to scientific inquiry. You are concerned with truth. The only problem is that your science might not be adequate for the job at hand. Religion deals with things that secular science (not real, spiritual science) can't weigh or measure. However, it is good to adapt the scientific method to your religious experiences. What you are really looking to do – beneath all your rebellion – is to find a 'scientific religion', and you will eventually.

Month-by-month Forecasts

January

Best Days Overall: 3, 4, 12, 13, 14, 22, 23, 31

Most Stressful Days Overall: 6, 7, 20, 21, 27, 28

Best Days for Love: 6, 8, 9, 15, 17, 18, 19, 25, 27, 28

Best Days for Money: 3, 4, 8, 9, 12, 13, 15, 16, 18, 19, 20, 22, 23, 29, 30, 31

Monthly Career Peaks: 6, 7, 8, 9

Monthly Personal Pleasure Peaks: 12, 13, 14, 27, 28, 29

You begin your year in a strong social peak. Seventy to eighty per cent of the planets are in the Western sector of your horoscope, and your 7th House will contain thirty to forty per cent of the planets. This makes it one of the strongest houses of the horoscope this month. Your 1st House of Self, by contrast, is mostly empty (only the Moon will visit on the 12th, 13th and 14th). This is a month to down-play the ego, self-interest and its concerns, and focus on other people. So cultivate the social graces, put other people first, attain goals through consensus and compromise, adapt to situations as best you can, and all will be well. And you will be much more popular as well. The time for independence and self-assertion will come soon enough.

Home and family are always dominant interests for you, but last year (December) the planetary power started shifting to the upper (day) side of your horoscope. This shift is even stronger this month. After the 4th (when Mercury crosses over to the day side), 60 to 70 per cent of the planets will be there. Of course, you will never ignore your family or home, but you can best serve them now by succeeding in the outer world, by attaining career goals, by being the good provider. In the end, family will understand. Also, with your family planet, Venus, retrograde all month, many family issues or tangles will not be resolved now anyway. Only time will resolve them so you might as well focus on business.

Finances are stressful now. You have to work a lot harder for earnings than usual. Though your spouse or partner is supportive, there seems to be some financial hesitation there. It's as if you are developing financial muscles – it is the overcoming of the stresses that builds the muscles. The good news here is that finance is important to you, and you have the drive and determination to overcome the various obstacles that arise. Progress is slow and methodical, but it happens. Never give up.

Singles are socially active and have many opportunities, but with the two love planets in the horoscope retrograde this month (Venus, the generic love planet and Saturn, the actual one) no important love decisions should be made one way or another. There are plenty of opportunities for frivolous love affairs, but even one of these will get tested after the 20th.

Health needs more watching until the 20th. The most important thing is to rest and relax more, and to maintain good energy levels. Health can also be enhanced by paying more attention to the liver, thighs, colon, bladder and sexual organs. Avoid depression by any means at your disposal.

The Moon, your ruler, will re-stimulate eclipse points on the 6th, 7th, 12th, 13th, 14th, 20th, 21st, 27th and 28th. Avoid risky behaviour or activities on those days.

February

Best Days Overall: 1, 9, 10, 19, 20, 27, 28

Most Stressful Days Overall: 2, 3, 16, 17, 23, 24

Best Days for Love: 2, 4, 5, 11, 14, 15, 21, 23, 24

CANCER

Best Days for Money: 1, 6, 7, 9, 10, 14, 15, 16, 17, 19, 20, 27, 28

Monthly Career Peaks: 2, 3, 4, 5

Monthly Personal Pleasure Peaks: 9, 10, 23, 24, 27

Like last month, most of the planets are still in the Western, social side of your horoscope (70 to 80 per cent), and your 7th House of Others is much stronger than your 1st House of Self (which is basically empty, except for a brief visit by the Moon on the 9th and 10th). So you are still in a period when you can attain ends through the good graces of others. Who you know is sometimes more important than who you are and what you can do, and this is one of those times. Adapt to situations rather than try to change them.

Your love and social situation is becoming a bit clearer this month as one of your love planets, Venus, starts to move forwards on the 3rd. But caution in love is still called for, especially serious love. Saturn, your actual love planet, is still retrograde all month. Avoid hasty love decisions one way or another. This is a good time to review your present love situation and see where you can improve things. Of course, the retrograde of your love planet will not stop love from happening. You will still have a social life, but it slows things down somewhat. Love affairs, like last month, seem plentiful – especially after the 19th.

Like last month, the planetary power is mostly in the upper (day) side of the chart, so career and outer achieve-ment are important now. You haven't yet hit your career peak for the year, but you are approaching it. Career is furthered through social contacts, involvement with organi-zations and associations and through charitable activities (after the 18th). Finances are still stressful until the 19th, but if you hang in there, your faith and perseverance will pay off. Things get a lot easier after the 19th, plus your financial muscles will be a lot stronger. Until then, focus on the prosperity of other people. You feel (and it is true) that your job is to make other people rich. When we help others to prosper, we inevitably prosper ourselves, and when we prosper, others will also naturally prosper. The only difference is the emphasis.

Financial intuition is excellent on the 5th and 6th but can arouse opposition from your spouse, lover or partner. It is more difficult to follow this intuition (though you should). Earning opportunities come in foreign lands or with foreigners after the 19th. A debt is miraculously paid on the 27th and 28th. Perhaps a windfall comes from your spouse, partner or an insurance claim. The line of credit increases then too.

Job-seekers have good fortune after the 19th as well. There's a dream job waiting for you.

Health is much improved now, and by the 19th becomes super. Energy and vitality are high. Health can be further enhanced in the ways described last month – these are trends for the entire year.

The Moon re-stimulates eclipse points on the 2nd, 3rd, 9th, 10th, 16th, 17th, 23rd and 24th. Do what needs to be done, have fun and enjoy life, but there's no need for daredevil stunts on those days. People in general are more temperamental then as well.

March

Best Days Overall: 8, 9, 18, 19, 20, 27, 28

Most Stressful Days Overall: 1, 2, 15, 16, 17, 23, 24, 29, 30

Best Days for Love: 1, 4, 5, 6, 10, 15, 16, 20, 23, 24, 25, 26, 29

Best Days for Money: 8, 9, 10, 11, 12, 18, 19, 20, 27, 28, 29, 30

CANCER

Monthly Career Peaks: 1, 2, 6, 7, 29, 30

Monthly Personal Pleasure Peaks: 8, 9, 18, 19, 25, 26

Like last month, most of the planets are still above the horizon, in the upper (day) side of your chart. Your 10th House of Career becomes very powerful after the 20th, while your 4th House of Home and Family is basically empty (except for the Moon's brief visit on the 13th and 14th). So outer, career interests are dominating family and emotional concerns. This is as it should be. You are entering (around the 19th) your yearly career peak. There is much action happening here, including a Solar Eclipse on the 29th. This seems an eventful and powerful eclipse, so do reduce your schedule where possible.

This eclipse is bringing important and long-term career changes. It often produces shake-ups in the corporate hierarchy where you work. (On a worldly level, it often shows the fall of governments and leaders, or crises with them.) There will be dramas with parents or parent figures. The cosmos is installing a new and happier pattern in your life and in the world, but first the wrecking crews have to come in and prepare the way. This is the function of an eclipse.

Since the Sun is your financial planet, the Solar Eclipse also brings important and long-term financial changes. Financial thinking and strategy will change. If thinking has been unrealistic, events will happen – disruptive kinds of things – that will show it to you. Then you can make adjustments.

There is another, less dramatic Lunar Eclipse on the 14th. This happens in your 3rd House. For students (especially below college level), this shows important educational changes. Perhaps there is a shake-up at school. Perhaps you change schools. There are dramas with siblings and neighbours. And since the Moon is your ruler, every Lunar Eclipse brings changes to your image, appearance and personality. An eclipse in the 3rd House often tests communication equipment and cars, so it's a good idea to have these things checked out beforehand. But if your equipment can survive this, it is probably of good quality.

Like last month, most of the planets are still in the Western, social sector of your chart. So continue to cultivate social graces and attain aims through consensus and compromise. Adapt to situations as best you can. Your good comes through others. Your love planet is still retrograde this month, so serious love needs patience. Current relationships, whether happy or not so happy, just need more review. Important love decisions shouldn't be made now.

Health needs more watching this month, especially after the 20th. With the health planet going retrograde on the 6th, avoid making drastic changes to your diet or health regime. Health is enhanced in the ways mentioned in previous months, but most importantly through keeping energy levels high.

April

Best Days Overall: 4, 5, 14, 15, 23, 24

Most Stressful Days Overall: 12, 13, 19, 20, 25, 26

Best Days for Love: 2, 3, 7, 14, 15, 17, 19, 20, 23, 24, 25

Best Days for Money: 4, 5, 7, 8, 14, 15, 18, 23, 24, 27, 28

Monthly Career Peaks: 2, 3, 25, 26

Monthly Personal Pleasure Peaks: 4, 5, 14, 15, 23, 24, 27

You are well into your yearly career peak. Most of the planets are still above the horizon, and your 10th House of Career is still powerful. Further, your career planet, Mars, makes an important move into your own sign on the 14th, intensifying ambitions even more. You are seen as very ambitious by others, a rising star. Younger Cancerians will dress above their level, according to their aspiration rather

146

than their current status. All of this is good and will enhance the career.

Success and advancement will come with all this interest. Pay rises and promotions are more likely now. A boss or elder takes a personal interest in you. The down side here is that you feel 'owned' by the company. There is more connection with a parent or parent figure too. Perhaps they are staying in your home. There may be a crisis with them (perhaps surgery), which is why you are more involved.

Like last month, continue to enhance your career through involvement with charities and altruistic causes. Psychics, astrologers, ministers and mediums all have important career guidance for you.

Health still needs watching this month, especially until the 20th. With dynamic Mars in your own sign (and with the Sun in Aries), the danger is overactivity. And while you will achieve much the danger is that you will push the body beyond its capacity, so schedule in some rest time. Your health planet is still retrograde so avoid making drastic changes to your diet or health regime now. With Mars in your own sign, you look good and are magnetic and charismatic, but perhaps hot tempered and rash. You excel in exercise regimes and sports.

The love situation is slowly getting ready to change. Your love planet will start to move forwards (after being retrograde all year) on the 5th. Clarity will start to come in a current relationship and in your overall social situation. A relationship should start moving forwards again. The planets are also starting to shift to the East. They are not there yet and the West is still stronger, but not as strong as it has been in previous months. Greater independence, slowly but surely, is coming to you. With Mars in your own sign you probably feel very independent even now (after the 14th), but you need to tone this down for a while.

Your lover, partner or spouse is prospering this month and will be more generous. Parents or parent figures prosper.

Job-seekers need to research job offers better and see if reality lives up to all the hype. But this research is probably more important for those who hire others. Both job-seekers and employers have many, many opportunities, but they should be slow and methodical here.

Finances seem stronger than last month. Money comes from the career (pay rises or promotions), your good professional reputation (you get recommended because of it), the grace and support of elders and bosses and perhaps government contracts. After the 20th, money comes through social contacts, friends and organizations you belong to. Professional investors should look at property, copper or agricultural commodities for profit ideas. In general, earning power is strongest from the 1st to the 13th and from the 27th to the 30th, as the Moon waxes.

The Moon, your ruler, will re-stimulate eclipse points on the 3rd, 4th, 10th, 12th, 18th, 19th, 24th, 25th and 30th. Enjoy your life and do what needs to be done, but avoid risky behaviour (you will be sorely tempted this month).

May

Best Days Overall: 2, 3, 12, 13, 20, 21, 29, 30

Most Stressful Days Overall: 9, 10, 16, 17, 22, 23

Best Days for Love: 3, 4, 14, 15, 16, 17, 22, 23, 31

Best Days for Money: 2, 3, 4, 5, 7, 8, 12, 13, 16, 17, 20, 21, 27, 28, 29, 30, 31

Monthly Career Peaks: 2, 3, 22, 23, 29, 30

Monthly Personal Pleasure Peaks: 2, 3, 12, 13, 22, 23, 27

The planets make an important shift from the Western, social sector of your chart to the Eastern, personal sector. This shift, which began last month, is established by the 4th, when Venus crosses over from the West to the East. This is a time for having your way in life. Not only is the Eastern sector of the chart strong, but dynamic Mars is still in your own sign all month. This is a time for direct action to change things.

Most of the planets are still above the horizon. Your 10th House of Career is still much stronger than your 4th House of Home and Family. And your career planet is not only prominently placed (in your own sign) but is also part of a beautiful Grand Trine pattern in the Water signs. With all this positive career energy, it would be foolish of you to ignore it. Serve your family by being successful now. Right actions will lead, eventually, to right feeling and emotional harmony. You are still in a yearly career peak, a time for opportunities and advancement.

Much of what was said last month about the career still applies now. You look ambitious. In fact, you work to create that 'look', dressing for status and success. It's a good idea to accessorize with reds this month. You are still very personally involved with a boss, elder or parent – someone above you in status. Your personal appearance and overall demeanour is a big factor in whether you get that promotion or not.

Finances are more stressful until the 21st. Although earnings will come and you won't want for any necessities, you will have to work harder. You are building financial muscles and achieving better financial health. Your spouse, partner or current love is supportive but perhaps controlling, and you are not in agreement financially. They will be more supportive after the 21st. Love, too, is more stressful until the 21st. Both you and your lover are juggling many areas of life and it's hard to keep the balance and give the relationship the attention it needs. Singles might find themselves too busy to do much dating until the 21st, but this will change afterwards.

In general, earning power will be strongest from the 1st to the 13th and from the 27th to the 31st, when the Moon waxes.

Platonic friendships, group activities and spirituality seem important this month. Charitable activities not only help your career but are also interesting in their own right. After the 21st, it is a good period for going on a spiritual retreat and spending more time in seclusion.

The Moon will re-stimulate eclipse points on the 2nd, 8th, 9th, 15th, 16th, 21st, 22nd and 28th. Go ahead and enjoy your life by all means, but do you really need to go bungee jumping on those days?

June

Best Days Overall: 8, 9, 17, 18, 25, 26

Most Stressful Days Overall: 5, 6, 12, 13, 19, 20

Best Days for Love: 1, 2, 3, 4, 10, 12, 13, 19, 22, 28, 29

Best Days for Money: 1, 2, 5, 6, 8, 9, 14, 15, 17, 18, 25, 26, 28, 29

Monthly Career Peaks: 19, 20, 28, 29

Monthly Personal Pleasure Peaks: 8, 9, 21, 22, 25, 26

Like last month, the planetary power is mostly in the Eastern, personal sector of the horoscope. Your 1st House of Self was powerful for a few months and will be even more powerful later in the month. Your 7th House of Others, by contrast, is empty (only the Moon visits there, briefly, on the 12th and 13th). A very clear message: this is a period for taking care of number one. Your happiness is just as important as the happiness of others. Pamper yourself. Create the conditions that will make you happy. Your way is the best way now. If others disagree, go it alone.

An important planetary shift is happening this month. The lower (night) side – your favourite side – of the horoscope is going to become stronger than the upper (day) side. This shift is established on the 21st when 60 to 70 per cent of the planets will be below the horizon. You can safely start to down-play the career now. Career opportunities will come, but if they violate your emotional harmony or disrupt your family situation, you should pass. This shift doesn't kill ambition altogether, but means you pursue it in a different way through building the psychology that will support your goals. It is a time for dreaming and visualizing future career successes.

We see other things that also shift the focus away from the career. The north node of the Moon (an indicator of happiness and fulfilment) will make an important move out of your 10th House into your 9th House. Religious, educational and philosophical interests bring happiness and fulfilment now. The 9th House also rules higher education so many of you may want to go back to college and get some more qualifications.

Your 12th House and 2nd House will also be strong this month, so spirituality is important. This is still an excellent time to go on spiritually-oriented retreats as well. The important thing is to clear the mental and emotional decks so you can start your astrological new year (your birthday) on the right footing.

Though you are still building up your financial muscles and you need to be proportionate in your spending and investing, this is a prosperous month. Parents or elders are supportive. Your good professional reputation leads to referrals and opportunities. A government contract could come after the 3rd. Your spouse or partner is still supportive, though their income slows a bit this month. Beginning on the 19th, your partner needs to do more homework on financial deals, major purchases or investments. The retrograde of their financial planet will not stop earnings, but there is a need for a review here.

Love is improving. You are getting your way and your spouse or partner is on your side. Singles find romantic opportunity as they pursue financial goals or with people involved in their finances. Wealth and material gifts are a great romantic turn-on for you. You are mingling with people of power and status these days. Romance blooms with these kinds of people.

Health is good this month but continue to avoid making drastic changes to your diet and health regime. When your health planet goes forwards next month, you will certainly have a different perspective on these things.

July

Best Days Overall: 5, 6, 14, 15, 23, 24

Most Stressful Days Overall: 3, 4, 10, 11, 16, 17, 30, 31

Best Days for Love: 3, 4, 8, 9, 10, 11, 12, 13, 16, 17, 22, 23, 25, 26

Best Days for Money: 5, 6, 14, 15, 23, 24, 25, 26

Monthly Career Peaks: 16, 17, 27, 28

Monthly Personal Pleasure Peaks: 5, 6, 23, 24, 25

Like last month, most of the planets are still in the East. Your 1st House of Self is very strong (40 per cent of the planets are either there or move through there), while your 7th House of Others is empty (only the Moon will visit on the 10th and the 11th). Continue to exercise your independence and personal initiative. Follow your own road to happiness. This attitude is not usually good for love, but this month it might actually enhance love. You are getting your way here as well.

The fact that most of the planets are now below the horizon reinforces the above. Emotional harmony is now the main thrust of your life. Cultivate being in 'right state' and right actions will naturally follow.

With your 1st House so strong this month, you are in a yearly personal pleasure peak. This is a time for pampering the body and treating it right, a time when sensual fantasies get fulfilled. You are looking good these days. Energy is high and so is personal magnetism. Venus's move into your own sign on the 19th further enhances your personal glamour. This will be a wonderful time to buy clothing, jewellery or personal accessories as your sense of style and beauty is unusually good. (You might not have to buy them – they can come to you in other ways.) In a man's chart, this transit brings contact with young women. In a woman's chart, it enhances her natural beauty.

Though your 7th House of Love is basically empty, there is still much love opportunity. Your love planet is getting a lot of stimulation. There will be many romantic meetings and opportunities. These occur (like last month) as you pursue your financial goals or with people involved in them. Financial and material support is what turns you on in love. You feel loved when you get it, and this is how you like to show love too.

Health is excellent. You can enhance it further by paying more attention to the liver, thighs, colon, bladder and sexual organs (the important organs for the year). On the 7th, your health planet starts moving forwards after many months of retrograde motion. Now, if you like, you can make those changes to the diet, doctor or health regime that you've been contemplating.

Prosperity is also very strong this month. You are well into your yearly financial peak. Sure, you've got to budget and manage your money better, but now you have more to manage. Bottom-line issues are more important than status or prestige.

If your financial thinking has been unrealistic, you'll find out about it on the 1st and 2nd as your financial planet re-stimulates eclipse points.

The Moon, your ruler, will re-stimulate eclipse points on the 2nd, 3rd, 9th, 10th, 15th, 16th, 22nd, 23rd, 29th and 30th. No need for risky types of activity on those days.

August

Best Days Overall: 2, 3, 10, 11, 19, 20, 29, 30

Most Stressful Days Overall: 6, 7, 12, 13, 26, 27

Best Days for Love: 2, 3, 4, 5, 6, 7, 11, 12, 13, 21, 22, 23, 31

Best Days for Money: 2, 3, 4, 5, 10, 11, 12, 13, 19, 20, 21, 22, 23, 29, 30

Monthly Career Peaks: 12, 13, 24, 25

Monthly Personal Pleasure Peaks: 2, 3, 19, 20, 21, 22, 23

Most of the planets are still below the horizon, so continue to focus on the family, on feeling good, on right inner state and on the stability of the home base. You can safely downplay the career now. Of course you can't ignore the career completely. If you do, the career planet's (Mars) re-stimulation of eclipse points on the 29th, 30th and 31st will create some disturbance and force you to correct the balance. There could be some dramas with a parent or parent figure during that period as well. But for the most part, your heart is with the family as it should be.

Most of the planets are still in the Eastern, personal sector of the horoscope. Your 1st House of Self is still strong (until the 13th), while your 7th House of Others is empty – only the Moon makes a brief visit there on the 6th and 7th. So this is still a time of independence, of the pursuit of personal happiness, of building the conditions that make you happy.

You are still in a yearly personal pleasure and financial peak. This is another month for the fulfilment of sensual desires and fantasies. Peak financial experiences are happening. Earnings can come from many sources – your lover, spouse or partner, social connections, friends and organizations, new technologies or inventions, family support, intuition (very important after the 11th), sales, marketing, communication and good use of the media. Many people seem supportive of financial goals.

Job-seekers need a little more patience this month. There are jobs available but you don't like the pay. Job-seeking will be easier and more fortunate after the 23rd.

Love is still wonderful. You look good, you are magnetic, and the opposite sex notices. For singles, very happy love experiences are happening from the 20th to the 26th. A friend might become more than that. A spiritual person – perhaps a creative person – comes into your life. These things happen as you pursue your normal financial goals. Perhaps these people are involved in your finances or want to be involved.

Your spouse, lover or partner still needs to do more homework on finances, especially important purchases, investments or commitments. There is a need to rethink and review the whole financial strategy. It is also a good time for your partner to perfect their product or service. Earnings are still happening but more slowly than usual. Financial confidence could be better too, and financial intuition needs verification these days.

The Moon, your ruler, will re-stimulate eclipse points on the 5th, 6th, 11th, 12th, 18th, 19th, 25th and 26th. As usual, avoid high-risk activities on those days.

Health is excellent and can be enhanced further in the ways described in past months. Pay more attention to the liver, thighs, colon, bladder and sexual organs. Detox regimes are good if you feel low.

September

Best Days Overall: 7, 8, 15, 16, 25, 26

Most Stressful Days Overall: 3, 4, 9, 10, 22, 23, 24, 30

Best Days for Love: 1, 2, 3, 4, 9, 10, 11, 18, 19, 20, 21, 28, 29, 30

Best Days for Money: 3, 4, 7, 8, 11, 12, 15, 16, 17, 18, 19, 22, 23, 25, 26

Monthly Career Peaks: 9, 10, 22, 23

Monthly Personal Pleasure Peaks: 15, 16, 20, 21, 25, 26

Though health needs more watching after the 23rd, this month is basically Cancerian heaven. Seventy to eighty per cent of the planets are below the horizon, and your 4th House of Home and Family becomes one of the strongest in the horoscope, especially after the 23rd. You get to do what you most like to do – be involved with the family, nourish and nurture. A parent or parent figure is coming to stay. Your family is supportive financially, and you are spending on them and on the home. This is a very good month, from the 8th onwards, for doing heavy renovation or construction in the home. Tempers seem volatile these days. This is a month for psychological progress, for reviewing your past – especially your early life – from your present perspective. This brings much growth and understanding.

A Solar Eclipse on the 22nd adds spice to the above. It occurs right on the border of your 3rd and 4th Houses, and will probably impact on both of them. Important changes are happening with the family and family relationships. But your intense focus here is positive, and you will handle these changes with ease. This eclipse also brings dramas with siblings and neighbours. Cars and communication equipment will get tested. If there are flaws in these things, the eclipse will bring them up and you'll be able to correct them. Those of you born early in the sign of Cancer (from June 21st to 25th) will feel this eclipse the strongest. Those of you born later in the sign will feel the eclipse more with your siblings, neighbours and neighbourhood than in the home.

A Lunar Eclipse on the 7th seems much milder on you. But every Lunar Eclipse affects your body, image, appearance and personality – so they are never weak. You will make important and long-term changes to your image, perhaps changing your hairstyle, hair colour or the way you dress. More importantly, you redefine your personality – who you are, how you think of yourself.

This eclipse occurs in your 9th House of Religion, Philosophy, Higher Education, Metaphysics and Foreign Travel. Students will often change their subject of study under such an eclipse – sometimes they even change college. There could be upheavals in your church, synagogue, mosque or university that change your relationship to these institutions. People often change their church or pastor under these eclipses. On a deeper level, this eclipse will test your personal beliefs. Flaws in these things will be revealed and you will make positive adjustments, all to your long-term benefit.

This eclipse occurs very near Uranus, the lord of your 8th House of Death. Now this doesn't mean literal death (sometimes it does, sometimes it brings near-death experiences – close calls). The cosmos will arrange things so that you confront this psychologically and come to terms with it on a deeper, philosophical level. Under these kinds of eclipses people inherit money or are remembered in a will. Your partner will have some financial upheaval to force corrections in their planning or thinking.

Rest and relax more this month but especially after the 23rd.

October

Best Days Overall: 4, 5, 12, 13, 14, 22, 23, 24

Most Stressful Days Overall: 1, 6, 7, 20, 21, 27, 28

Best Days for Love: 1, 2, 3, 7, 10, 11, 16, 21, 22, 26, 27, 28

Best Days for Money: 2, 3, 4, 5, 10, 11, 12, 13, 14, 15, 16, 21, 22, 23, 24

Monthly Career Peaks: 6, 7, 21

Monthly Personal Pleasure Peaks: 12, 13, 14, 20, 21, 22, 23, 24

The planets make an important shift this month – from the Eastern, personal sector to the Western, social sector. This represents an important psychological shift in you as well. Personal independence is lessened, and is in fact unnecessary. This is a time for putting other people first and for attaining goals through compromise, consensus and the grace of others, rather than by direct action. In general now, your social life is becoming ever more important.

Most of the planets are still below the horizon. Your 4th House of Home and Family is easily the most powerful in the horoscope as 40 to 50 per cent of the planets are either there or moving through there this month. By contrast, your 10th House of Career is empty (only the Moon visits there on the 6th and 7th, making those days monthly career peaks). Even your career planet spends much of the month in the 4th House. So your favourite interest is what is important now. You can safely down-play the career in favour of home and family responsibilities. If career responsibilities get too intense, you might offer to do more work at home.

Though marriage is not indicated, there is still serious romance for singles. This is close to home as well. Family members or family connections might play cupid. But the pursuit of financial goals is still the major scene of romantic activity. Love can get more stressful later in the month. Perhaps you have other opportunities that stress your lover out. A current relationship can be in crisis after the 24th. Infidelity (or the perception of infidelity) could be the cause. Your lover might be in conflict with a parent or parent figure as well. True love will always survive.

CANCER

Aside from home and family, the 5th House is also important. After the 24th it becomes even stronger than the 4th House with 60 per cent of the planets (an amazing percentage) either there or moving through there. Thus this will be a time for enjoyment, fun and leisure activities. Children are always interesting to you, and this month more so. Cancerians of childbearing age are much more fertile now – they have been fertile all year, but this month especially so. You get on with children in a different way than usual. (Usually you are the parent.) Now you can relate to them as equals. You are more in contact with your own inner child, which understands them perfectly.

Job-seekers have great fortune after the 23rd. Dream jobs are manifesting. Those who employ others have no problem finding good quality workers.

One of the problems with all this fun is that it might stress you financially. But you can figure out ways to enjoy yourself that don't bust your budget. You will be tempted into easy money, perhaps speculations (a very 5th House interest). It's best to avoid it. If you must, calculate your risks and hedge yourself.

Here we also see one of the problems with a current relationship. You want to have fun; your partner wants to tend to business and be serious. You might want children; they don't. There are some major clashes happening.

Health is excellent.

The Moon re-stimulates eclipse points on the 4th, 5th, 13th, 14th, 18th, 19th, 25th and 26th. Reschedule high-risk activities for another time.

November

Best Days Overall: 1, 9, 10, 19, 20, 28, 29

Most Stressful Days Overall: 3, 16, 17, 23, 24, 30

Best Days for Love: 1, 3, 9, 10, 11, 12, 21, 22, 23, 24, 30

Best Days for Money: 1, 2, 9, 10, 11, 12, 19, 20, 30

Monthly Career Peaks: 3, 19, 20, 30

Monthly Personal Pleasure Peaks: 9, 10, 20, 21

Health, work and leisure are the main headlines of the coming month. You are working hard but also playing hard, alternating from one to the other. But as the month progresses, you become more serious and get down to work.

The fertility of the Cancerian was discussed last month, and it seems even stronger now. Fifty to sixty per cent of the planets are either in the 5th House or moving through there this month. This is an awesome percentage. Those of you not of childbearing age might be thinking of adopting these days.

Personal creativity in general is at an all-time high. Many of you are professional artists and this will be an exceptional month. You will have no trouble selling your creations.

With the financial planet in the 5th House, speculative tendencies will be very strong. The lure of easy money is also difficult to resist. True, you will earn money in more fun ways, but speculations need to be well-hedged. Job-seekers still have good fortune, and the jobs and the pay look wonderful. Employers will have no problem finding good workers or expanding their staff. Financial and job opportunities come as you are having fun, indulging in sports, at a party or at a club. (Looks like some very nice pay days are happening from the 19th to the 22nd.) After the 22nd, money is earned in the normal ways, through work. Your work planet, Jupiter, will move into your 6th House of Work on November 24th. Many of you are going to be shown how to become more productive workers. And, with greater productivity, you can expect more earnings.

Health is wonderful all month. Many interesting trends are happening. Your health planet is receiving intense stimulation (for the most part positive), so many of you will be hearing very good news about a long-standing health problem. Miraculous healings this period would not be a surprise. You have a great interest in healthy diets, daily regimes and lifestyles. This interest will continue well into 2007. On November 24th, your health planet, Jupiter, makes a major move from your 5th House to your 6th House, entering its own sign and house. This is also good for health. The liver and thighs (which have been important all year) are still important after November 24th. The colon, bladder and sexual organs become less important.

Love is still stressful until the 22nd. Your playful, fun-loving attitude perhaps doesn't sit well with a current love or your spouse. Like last month, there could be disputes about children. For singles, your attitude is too fun-loving to think about committed love. But all of this will change after the 24th. Jupiter will move into Sagittarius and into beautiful aspect with Saturn, your love planet. The love planet will receive intense and positive stimulation from other beneficial planets as well. Love is definitely in the air, and this love seems more serious. Marriage for singles is a definite possibility now.

December

Best Days Overall: 6, 7, 16, 17, 25, 26

Most Stressful Days Overall: 1, 13, 14, 15, 21, 22, 27, 28

Best Days for Love: 1, 9, 10, 11, 19, 21, 22, 28, 29, 30

Best Days for Money: 1, 4, 8, 9, 10, 18, 19, 20, 27, 29

Monthly Career Peaks: 1, 18, 27, 28

Monthly Personal Pleasure Peaks: 6, 7, 18, 21, 22

The main headline this month is the awesome and unusual power in the sign of Sagittarius and your 6th House. Sixty to seventy per cent of the planets will either be there or move through there this month, making this a work-oriented period.

The intense interest in health that began last month becomes even stronger now. This is a period for 'miraculous'-type healings when you discover more of your own innate healing abilities. Younger Cancerians might even consider the health field as a career. Your knowledge and understanding of health is greatly expanded. And though you need to rest and relax more after the 22nd, there are no real health dangers these days. Health is enhanced through paying more attention to the liver and thighs, a trend that will continue for most of 2007 as well. Regular thigh massage will do wonders if you feel low.

With your health planet now in a Fire sign (it was in a Water sign almost all year), you respond better to heat-oriented therapies. Too much cold weather is not good for you. If you feel low, eat more hot and spicy kinds of food.

Though you are working and serious, love is blooming. The workplace itself can be the source of romance. Marrieds are enjoying more harmony with their partner. Singles are meeting the special someone. Wedding bells can ring in the year ahead (although it's not advisable to make those decisions this month as your love planet goes retrograde on the 6th). You are well into your yearly social peak and are having wonderful romantic experiences.

Finances are expanding in the old-fashioned way: slowly, methodically, through work. But growth is happening. You are seeing the results of your work. For marrieds, there is wonderful spousal support all month. Social connections are important financially, and friends seem very supportive as well.

Leo

♌

THE LION
Birthdays from
21st July to
21st August

Personality Profile

LEO AT A GLANCE

Element – Fire

Ruling Planet – Sun
  Career Planet – Venus
  Love Planet – Uranus
  Money Planet – Mercury
  Planet of Health and Work – Saturn
  Planet of Home and Family Life – Pluto

Colours – gold, orange, red

Colours that promote love, romance and social harmony – black, indigo, ultramarine blue

Colours that promote earning power – yellow, yellow-orange

Gems – amber, chrysolite, yellow diamond

Metal – gold

Scents – bergamot, frankincense, musk, neroli

Quality – fixed (= stability)

Quality most needed for balance – humility

Strongest virtues – leadership ability, self-esteem and confidence, generosity, creativity, love of joy

Deepest needs – fun, elation, the need to shine

Characteristics to avoid – arrogance, vanity, bossiness

Signs of greatest overall compatibility – Aries, Sagittarius

Signs of greatest overall incompatibility – Taurus, Scorpio, Aquarius

Sign most helpful to career – Taurus

Sign most helpful for emotional support – Scorpio

Sign most helpful financially – Virgo

Sign best for marriage and/or partnerships – Aquarius

Sign most helpful for creative projects – Sagittarius

Best Sign to have fun with – Sagittarius

Signs most helpful in spiritual matters – Aries, Cancer

Best day of the week – Sunday

LEO

Understanding a Leo

When you think of Leo, think of royalty – then you'll get the idea of what the Leo character is all about and why Leos are the way they are. It is true that, for various reasons, some Leo-born do not always express this quality – but even if not they should like to do so.

A monarch rules not by example (as does Aries) nor by consensus (as do Capricorn and Aquarius) but by personal will. Will is law. Personal taste becomes the style that is imitated by all subjects. A monarch is somehow larger than life. This is how a Leo desires to be.

When you dispute the personal will of a Leo it is serious business. He or she takes it as a personal affront, an insult. Leos will let you know that their will carries authority and that to disobey is demeaning and disrespectful.

A Leo is king (or queen) of his or her personal domain. Subordinates, friends and family are the loyal and trusted subjects. Leos rule with benevolent grace and in the best interests of others. They have a powerful presence; indeed, they are powerful people. They seem to attract attention in any social gathering. They stand out because they are stars in their domain. Leos feel that, like the Sun, they are made to shine and rule. Leos feel that they were born to special privilege and royal prerogatives – and most of them attain this status, at least to some degree.

The Sun is the Ruler of this Sign, and when you think of sunshine it is very difficult to feel unhealthy or depressed. Somehow the light of the Sun is the very antithesis of illness and apathy. Leos love life. They also love to have fun; they love drama, music, the theatre and amusements of all sorts. These are the things that give joy to life. If – even in their best interests – you try to deprive Leos of their pleasures, good food, drink and entertainment, you run the serious risk of depriving them of the will to live. To them life without joy is no life at all.

Leos epitomize humanity's will to power. But power in and of itself – regardless of what some people say – is neither good nor evil. Only when power is abused does it become evil. Without power even good things cannot come to pass. Leos realize this and are uniquely qualified to wield power. Of all the Signs, they do it most naturally. Capricorn, the other power Sign of the Zodiac, is a better manager and administrator than Leo – much better. But Leo outshines Capricorn in personal grace and presence. Leo loves power, where Capricorn assumes power out of a sense of duty.

Finance

Leos are great leaders but not necessarily good managers. They are better at handling the overall picture than the nitty-gritty details of business. If they have good managers working for them they can become exceptional executives. They have vision and a lot of creativity.

Leos love wealth for the pleasures it can bring. They love an opulent lifestyle, pomp and glamour. Even when they are not wealthy they live as if they are. This is why many fall into debt, from which it is sometimes difficult to emerge.

Leos, like Pisceans, are generous to a fault. Very often they want to acquire wealth solely so that they can help others economically. Wealth to Leo buys services and managerial ability. It creates jobs for others and improves the general well-being of those around them. Therefore – to a Leo – wealth is good. Wealth is to be enjoyed to the fullest. Money is not to be left to gather dust in a mouldy bank vault but to be enjoyed, spread around, used. So Leos can be quite reckless in their spending.

With the Sign of Virgo on Leo's 2nd House (of Money) cusp, Leo needs to develop some of Virgo's traits of analysis, discrimination and purity when it comes to money matters.

They must learn to be more careful with the details of finance (or to hire people to do this for them). They have to be more cost-conscious in their spending habits. Generally, they need to manage their money better. Leos tend to chafe under financial constraints, yet these constraints can help Leos to reach their highest financial potential.

Leos like it when their friends and family know that they can depend on them for financial support. They do not mind – even enjoy – lending money, but they are careful that they are not taken advantage of. From their 'regal throne' Leos like to bestow gifts upon their family and friends and then enjoy the good feelings these gifts bring to everybody. Leos love financial speculations and – when the celestial influences are right – are often lucky.

Career and Public Image

Leos like to be perceived as wealthy, for in today's world wealth often equals power. When they attain wealth they love having a large house with lots of land and animals.

At their jobs Leos excel in positions of authority and power. They are good at making decisions – on a grand level – but they prefer to leave the details to others. Leos are well respected by their colleagues and subordinates, mainly because they have a knack for understanding and relating to those around them. Leos usually strive for the top positions even if they have to start at the bottom and work hard to get there. As might be expected of such a charismatic Sign, Leos are always trying to improve their work situation. They do so in order to have a better chance of advancing to the top.

On the other hand, Leos do not like to be bossed around or told what to do. Perhaps this is why they aspire so for the top – where they can be the decision-makers and need not take orders from others.

Leos never doubt their success and focus all their attention and efforts on achieving it. Another great Leo characteristic is that – just like good monarchs – they do not attempt to abuse the power or success they achieve. If they do so this is not wilful or intentional. Usually they like to share their wealth and try to make everyone around them join in their success.

Leos are – and like to be perceived as – hard-working, well-established individuals. It is definitely true that they are capable of hard work and often manage great things. But do not forget that, deep down inside, Leos really are fun-lovers.

Love and Relationships

Generally, Leos are not the marrying kind. To them relationships are good while they are pleasurable. When the relationship ceases to be pleasurable a true Leo will want out. They always want to have the freedom to leave. That is why Leos excel at love affairs rather than commitment. Once married, however, Leo is faithful – even if some Leos have a tendency to marry more than once in their lifetime. If you are in love with a Leo, just show him or her a good time. Travel, go to casinos and clubs, the theatre and discos. Wine and dine your Leo love – it is expensive but worth it and you will have fun.

Leos generally have an active love life and are demonstrative in their affections. They love to be with other optimistic and fun-loving types like themselves, but wind up settling with someone more serious, intellectual and unconventional. The partner of a Leo tends to be more political and socially conscious than he or she is, and more libertarian. When you marry a Leo, mastering the freedom-loving tendencies of your partner will definitely become a life-long challenge – and be careful that Leo does not master you.

Aquarius sits on Leo's 7th House (of Love) cusp. Thus if Leos want to realize their highest love and social potential they need to develop a more egalitarian, Aquarian perspective on others. This is not easy for Leo, for 'the king' finds his equals only among other 'kings'. But perhaps this is the solution to Leo's social challenge – to be 'a king among kings'. It is all right to be royal, but recognize the nobility in others.

Home and Domestic Life

Although Leos are great entertainers and love having people over, sometimes this is all show. Only very few close friends will get to see the real side of a Leo's day-to-day life. To a Leo the home is a place of comfort, recreation and transformation; a secret, private retreat – a castle. Leos like to spend money, show off a bit, entertain and have fun. They enjoy the latest furnishings, clothes and gadgets – all things fit for kings.

Leos are fiercely loyal to their family and of course expect the same from them. They love their children almost to a fault; they have to be careful not to spoil them too much. They also must try to avoid attempting to make individual family members over in their own image. Leos should keep in mind that others also have the need to be their own people. That is why Leos have to be extra careful about being over-bossy or over-domineering in the home.

Horoscope for 2006

General Trends

This is what we call a character-building year. Saturn, which moved into your sign on July 17th 2005, is going to teach you many things now – deep things, wonderful things, true things. You might not like the methods as they can be stern – but they work. Sure we should enjoy life, but we should enjoy all aspects of life – the parties as well as our legitimate responsibilities. It is said that medicine 'ain't supposed to taste good', but once we get past the taste, the result is surely beneficial. Resistance, carrying burdens, walking uphill – all serve to build the spiritual and mental muscles you will need to fulfil your life's mission and purpose. Embrace it all with joy.

Yes, this is a serious kind of year. A work year. A year for taking a low profile and letting other people shine as well (not so easy for a Leo). But it will not be unrelenting challenge. Fun and joy will start happening after November 24th. The cosmos is going to reward your effort. But don't wait around for November 24th. Enjoy your life now, with all the burdens. Make sure you smile as you walk up the mountain.

Love and social activities have been important for many years, and this trend continues again.

Home and family is a major (and happy) focus this year too.

Your paths of greatest fulfilment are home, family and domestic interests (until November 24th); children, joy and creativity (after November 24th); religion, philosophy, higher education and foreign travel (until June 23rd); personal transformation, sex, occult studies, depth psychology, the deeper things of life (after June 23rd).

Health

(Please note that this is an astrological perspective on health, not a medical one. At one time, both perspectives were identical, but in these times there could be quite a difference. For the medical perspective, please consult your physician or health professional.)

Health needs more watching this year. Three long-term planets (including Saturn) are in stressful aspect to you. The good news is that you are on the case here. Saturn, your health planet, is very prominently placed in your own sign

LEO

(on your Solar Ascendant). You are interested in health regimes, diets and healthy lifestyles. You willingly undertake disciplined (and even harsh) health regimes.

With Saturn in your own sign, good health for you also means looking good, so this is a great year for dieting, weight-loss regimes and generally improving your personal appearance. No one loves the good life more than Leo, but this year (and next) you are more Spartan and strict with yourself. Right now you are probably paying the price for excesses of the good life in years past. So a wonderful adjustment is happening now.

There are many ways you can enhance your health this year. Difficult aspects don't necessarily mean disease if precautions are taken.

The first line of defence against any disease is your energy level. A person with high energy is immune to most diseases. And, since energy is not up to its usually high standards, this is something you need to monitor. See if you can organize your activities more efficiently – you seem good at that this year. With a little planning you can do more with less energy.

With Saturn as your health planet, you can enhance health by paying more attention to the spine, knees and teeth. Being a Leo, and with your health planet also in the sign of Leo, the heart needs more attention than usual.

Though you are in a serious year, this doesn't mean that you have to walk around depressed. There is a great difference between the two. Learning to be joyful inside as you handle your work and responsibilities is one of the great lessons we can learn in life.

The herbs, aromas and flowers of Saturn are all natural health tonics this year. Lead is a nice metal to have on your person (never take it internally). Darker colours, such as indigo and black, are healing for you. Ginkgo and magnolia are beneficial herbs, and magnolia will also work as an aroma. Wearing the gems, metals and aromas of your sign will also strengthen you in subtle ways.

The health of a parent or parent figure can be enhanced through paying more attention to the feet and ankles. Regular foot and ankle massage would be very powerful for them. Also, you seem very orthodox and traditional when it comes to health and healing, whereas this person is totally experimental – so don't try to impose your ways on them. The health of children seems reasonable. Grandchildren's health also seems reasonable, though two eclipses – on March 14th and September 22nd – impact on them. They will probably change their health regimes this year. Your lover or spouse has fairly good, status-quo health this year.

Home, Domestic and Family Issues

With Jupiter in your 4th House of Home and Family for most of the year (until November 24th), this is an important area of life in the year ahead. It is also a happy area.

Normally, when someone has Saturn moving over their sign there is depression. But here we see modifying factors. Jupiter in your 4th House suggests happy emotions and a happy home life. Also, Leos by nature are not depressive kinds of people. Depression can happen, but they shrug it off quickly.

Jupiter in the 4th House usually brings moves – happy moves – to larger and more opulent quarters. It can mean a major upgrade of the domestic situation, or expensive items for the home. Money is made through the fortunate purchase or sale of a home. People often buy second homes and additional properties under this transit. All the above could happen here but there could be delays involved.

The family circle generally expands when Jupiter moves through the 4th House. This happens either through births (very likely) or marriages. Often you meet new people who are like family to you.

Since Jupiter is the Ruler of your 5th House of Children, Fun and Creativity, this transit has other meanings too. You are getting entertainment or sporting equipment for the home, making it a place of entertainment as well as somewhere to live. Many of you (of appropriate age) are getting pregnant and giving birth. Both male and female Leos are more fertile these days.

Children are spending more time in your home. This could be other people's children as well as your own. Some of you could be boarding foreign children – exchange students or visitors. Many are thinking of adopting a child.

In general, there is more family support this year. Family members are generous financially and in emotional terms.

A parent or parent figure is prospering this year (and this could be the cause of the generosity). They could be moving to larger quarters too. In general, this person seems to be leading the good life, eating in good restaurants, travelling more, buying better clothing and accessories and things of this nature. A foreign trip (or educational project) needs a lot more homework and planning from January 1st to March 5th. Children of appropriate age could make multiple moves this year.

The whole year is good for remodelling, construction and renovation, but October 23rd to December 6th looks like an excellent time. This is a beneficial year for entertaining from the home, particularly October 24th to November 17th.

Love and Social Life

This has been an important area of life for many years now, and the trend continues this year. Many, many changes have occurred here over the years. It is doubtful whether any long-term relationship survived. Though this instability still exists, you seem more serious about love and commitment this year. For years you were very infatuated with the 'glamour crowd'. A run-of-the-mill kind of person – whatever their virtues – just didn't interest you. But this year we see a bit of a change.

Your previous interests are still there, but a more stable type of person is coming into your life. This person might not be glamorous and is probably a good deal older than you, but they are dutiful and devoted. Perhaps this is a business person, a corporate type. But a doctor, health professional or colleague would also fit the bill. This could lead to marriage for singles, especially if you are working on your first marriage. Though this person can seem over-controlling – they feel that you need to get organized – these things are coming from love and not from a need for power.

There's nothing you need to do to attract this person – they are coming to you (it might have happened late last year too). You just need to show up.

It will be interesting to watch this relationship for you certainly have other romantic opportunities. None of them offers any stability though. Family members and children are not especially thrilled with any of your opportunities. Gaining their acceptance will take time, but this 'Saturn' type we have been discussing is patient and has lots of time.

You also seem allured by money people. And this person would fit that bill as well.

This year, many of you are faced with a classic romantic problem. Do you do the sensible thing – go with your head – or the romantic thing – go with your heart? You might waver back and forth.

A Lunar Eclipse on September 7th could knock some competitors out of the picture and leave the way clear for Mr or Miss Saturn. It's going to clarify your love life by first throwing it into disarray.

On the friendship level, things are more or less status-quo. The Solar Eclipse on March 29th occurs in your 11th House of Friends, which probably tests a current friendship. Though friendships are not prominent, you should make an effort to improve this area. The Moon's North Node occupies your House of Friends until June 23rd, showing that there is great fulfilment to be had here. Also, you have more free will in this area.

Those of you into your second marriage will have the relationship tested by a Solar Eclipse on March 29th. (It is still being tested by the Lunar Eclipse of October 17th 2005.) If you are single, these eclipses might spur you to change your single condition. Those working on their second or third marriage have more or less free will in that department. (Romance has been difficult for quite a few years, but it improves this year.)

Children of marriageable age are prospering and probably travelling late in the year, but marriage doesn't seem in the picture. The same is true of adult grandchildren.

Your happiest and most active social periods this year will be from January 20th to March 20th; June 21st to July 22nd; October 23rd to November 21st.

Your most stressful social periods will be from May 20th to June 21st; August 23rd to September 22nd; November 22nd to December 21st. These are periods to be more patient with both yourself and your lover and friends.

Finance and Career

Neither your 2nd House of Finance nor your 10th House of Career are houses of power this year, Leo, so this is not an especially important financial or career year. Home, family, children, love, romance and health are the main issues for you this year. This doesn't mean you won't have earnings or a profession but these will probably be status-quo.

There will also be times (even during an off-year such as this) when you are more ambitious and career-driven than usual. Finances will seem very important at times as well. But these urges are coming from the transiting planets and are not trends for the year. When the transits pass, your interests flow elsewhere.

The lack of emphasis on finance and career means you have more freedom in moulding and shaping this area. But can free will overcome lack of interest? In certain charts (those of you born with a strong 10th and 2nd House) the free will we see here *will* translate to greater prosperity and professional status. But for those who were not born that way, it probably won't.

Your strongest and most active financial period will be from July 21st to September 30th. Many short-term planets are moving through your 2nd House that period, activating your financial interest and boosting earning power.

Your strongest and most active career periods will be from January 1st to February 17th and from March 5th to June 24th. Many short-term planets are moving through your 10th House of Career, your yearly career peak.

Work seems the main interest in the year ahead. And here things seem fortunate. Jobs and work opportunities are coming to you. You just have to sit tight and they will find you. You will probably be able to pick and choose between offers. Those of you who hire others will probably have a similar experience. Employees will come to you effortlessly.

Parents or parent figures are enjoying great prosperity and are supportive of you. Married Leos are going to have very generous spousal support, for the partner is prospering as well. This support can be erratic, as there will be wild ups and downs here. Your spouse seems involved in some media, film or internet enterprise.

Siblings are having an excellent financial year. Communication or transportation seems the source. Children will start prospering after November 24th. Next year also looks like a particularly good financial year for them. The income of grandchildren is status-quo.

Mercury, your financial planet, is very fast-moving and sometimes erratic. Sometimes he is very speedy, sometimes slow, and sometimes he goes backwards. And this is pretty much a picture of your financial life. Because his movements are short-term, these things will be discussed in the monthly reports. Also, Mercury will be retrograde three times in the year ahead – from March 2nd to 25th; July 4th to 29th; and October 28th to November 18th. These are times when you need to do more homework on investments or major purchases. Avoid these things during those periods if you can, but if you can't you just need to do more research. Financial judgement is not up to its usually high standards.

Self-improvement

With Saturn in your own sign, your renowned pride and self-esteem will get a reality check. If it is overly inflated, it will be brought down. If it is unrealistically low, it will be raised. In other words, there are adjustments going on. Self-esteem is a wonderful thing, but the psychological community places too much emphasis on it. The body and personality certainly have their place in our lives, but they are not who we are. And, all too often, the body's urge for self-esteem – its false sense of identity – gets in the way of a higher and truer self-esteem, the self-esteem of the true being you are. This is beyond all material conditions and circumstances. Often – and there are many documented stories about this – it is precisely when the 'body ego' is most crestfallen, feels weakest, and is lowest in its self-esteem that this higher self-esteem comes in. 'My strength is made perfect in your weakness.' So as your body ego – your personality, the person with the history and story – is getting its adjustments this year, it is good to remember that you are much more than that. And many of you will attain the realization of this – for the conditions are perfect.

Month-by-month Forecasts

January

Best Days Overall: 6, 7, 15, 16, 25, 26

Most Stressful Days Overall: 1, 2, 8, 9, 22, 23, 29, 30

Best Days for Love: 1, 2, 3, 4, 8, 9, 12, 13, 17, 18, 19, 22, 23, 27, 28, 29, 30, 31

Best Days for Money: 3, 4, 8, 9, 12, 13, 17, 18, 19, 22, 23, 29, 30, 31

Monthly Career Peaks: 8, 9, 13, 14, 27, 28

Monthly Personal Pleasure Peaks: 13, 14, 15, 16, 29

You begin your year with 70 to 80 per cent of the planets in the Western, social sector of your chart. Though your 1st House of Self is strong, your 7th House of Others will be even stronger. So you are in your yearly social peak, having wonderful social and romantic experiences. Put other people first and attain ends through compromise and consensus. Your ability to change conditions is lessened this period so adapt yourself as best you can.

The 6th House of Health, Work and Service is prominent this month. Thirty to forty per cent of the planets will either be there or move through there. The ruler of your 6th House is prominent by placement – it is in your own sign of Leo. So this month (and probably all year) you are learning one of the most important lessons of kingship. Rulership itself – good leadership – is also a form of service.

Health is good, but after the 20th you need to rest and relax more. Keeping energy levels high is probably the most important thing. Happily, health is a priority for you, and you are unlikely to let small problems fester. Pay more

178

attention to the heart, spine, knees, teeth and overall bone structure and skeletal alignment.

Most of the planets are below the horizon, and your career planet, Venus, will be retrograde all month. Though you are working hard, career issues need some time to resolve. Inner, subjective processes are going on. It's best to focus more energy on the home, family and attaining emotional harmony. You won't be able to ignore your career completely, but you can de-emphasize it in subtle ways.

Finances don't seem a big issue this month. Your 2nd House is basically empty – only the Moon will visit there on the 17th, 18th and 19th. I read this as financial contentment. Money is earned easily and happily until the 4th. Speculations seem favourable then (but always under intuition and never blindly). From the 4th to the 22nd, money comes through work. Investors should look at property and traditional blue-chip companies. Financial judgement is very sound this period. After the 22nd, money comes from your spouse or lover, or through social connections. Financial opportunities happen at parties and social gatherings as well. Job-seekers have many opportunities this month, but all these offers need more study and research. Your work planet, Saturn, is retrograde so job descriptions might not match the reality of the job. There is probably more travelling involved with the career this month, but perhaps you will be able to minimize it. Your duty to children (or a current lover) might be affected by this.

February

Best Days Overall: 2, 3, 11, 12, 21, 22

Most Stressful Days Overall: 4, 5, 19, 20, 25, 26

Best Days for Love: 1, 4, 5, 9, 10, 14, 15, 19, 20, 23, 24, 25, 26, 27, 28

Best Days for Money: 1, 6, 7, 9, 10, 14, 15, 16, 17, 19, 20, 27, 28

Monthly Career Peaks: 4, 5, 23, 24

Monthly Personal Pleasure Peaks: 11, 12, 27

A powerful and rare Grand Square pattern shows that you are building something big. It takes much of your energy so your health needs to be watched. (You might not be building something for yourself as such, but involved in a big project.) Enhance health in the ways discussed last month. But, more importantly, keep energy levels as high as possible.

The planets have shifted this month. Now the upper (day) side and lower (night) side of the horoscope are equally powerful. Neither one nor the other dominates. So you are equally involved with career and with the home and family. You alternate between the two. Now you lean one way and now another. This situation will change next month as the upper half becomes more dominant. In the meantime you are in this twilight zone.

Most of the planets are still in the Western sector, and your 7th House of Others is very strong until the 19th. You continue to be well into your yearly social peak – it is in full swing. Personal interests take a back seat to the interests of others. With the Sun, your ruling planet, also in the 7th House, you are able to do this more easily. In fact, you are going out of your way to please others in general, or your current love or spouse in particular. Your personal popularity is at a yearly high now. Love is blooming but there are many distractions from work, children and family (and perhaps from other, less serious lovers). You are still in a period of adaptability. Personal independence will not get you very far but the willing co-operation of others will. Social skills are more important than personal gifts or high self-esteem.

LEO

Like last month, money is not a big issue. Your 2nd House is mostly empty – except for the Moon's quick visit on the 14th and 15th. You seem financially content. Whatever you lack in personal earning power is more than made up for by good support from your spouse, friends and social connections. Money, like most of the other good in your life, comes through and from others and not so much through personal effort. This is a month when you prosper by helping others to prosper, by putting their financial interests ahead of your own. Professional investors should look at the high-tech industry (until the 9th) and energy, oil, natural gas and water utilities afterwards. Bonds and the bond market also look interesting after the 9th. There is good fortune for those of you involved with insurance claims, tax issues or estates from the 18th to the 20th. Other kinds of windfalls could come that period too. Speculations seem very favourable then.

Interesting ESP experiences happen on the 5th and 6th. There is also a passionate love meeting. Those looking for outside investors have good fortune on those days. Sudden love (perhaps an unexpected social invitation) happens at the end of the month.

March

Best Days Overall: 1, 2, 10, 11, 12, 20, 21, 29, 30

Most Stressful Days Overall: 3, 4, 18, 19, 25, 26, 31

Best Days for Love: 4, 5, 6, 8, 9, 15, 16, 18, 19, 25, 26, 27, 28

Best Days for Money: 8, 9, 13, 14, 18, 19, 27, 28

Monthly Career Peaks: 3, 4, 25, 26, 31

Monthly Personal Pleasure Peaks: 10, 11, 12

On the 6th, the dominance of power in the upper (day) side of the horoscope is established. Though home and family issues will be important all year and you can't ignore them completely (nor do you want to), now is a good time to shift your emphasis to the career and to your objectives in the outer world. This is probably the best way to serve the family as well. The two planets involved with family and emotional issues are going retrograde this month – Jupiter on the 4th and Pluto on the 29th. Many pending family issues will need time to resolve. There are no quick fixes so you might as well focus on your career.

There are two eclipses this period, a Lunar Eclipse on the 14th and a Solar Eclipse on the 29th. The Solar Eclipse is the more powerful one for you as the Sun is your ruling planet. It's good to take a reduced schedule during both eclipse periods, but especially around the Solar Eclipse.

Your 2nd House of Finance has not been strong since the beginning of the year. Money hasn't been a big issue for you, and this trend continues this month. But if you have been ignoring finance unduly – not giving it the respect it deserves – the Lunar Eclipse of the 14th will be a wake-up call as it occurs in your money house. This will bring important and long-term financial changes. If planning, thinking or strategy has been awry, now is when you find out about it. We seldom make needed changes unless we are pushed into it, and now the cosmos supplies the push. It will be exactly what you need, no more and no less. (Since your financial planet will be retrograde that period, try to enact the changes after the 25th when it moves forwards again.)

The Lunar Eclipses also bring spiritual changes, and this one is no different. Revelation will come that will cause you to change your spiritual regime, path or teachers. Sometimes the eclipse brings shake-ups in a spiritual or charitable organization you belong to. The dream life will be hyperactive around this eclipse, but don't give too much weight to it. Much of it is emotional flotsam stirred up by the eclipse.

The Solar Eclipse of the 29th occurs in your 9th House of Religion, Philosophy, Higher Education and Metaphysics. It involves your personal religion, your philosophy of life. This gets tested now. False beliefs or attitudes will be revealed for what they are and you can correct your belief system. Often there is a crisis of faith under these kinds of eclipses. People may change pastors or churches. There may be a crisis or shake-up in the church, synagogue, mosque or place of worship. Changes in personal philosophy – 9th House activities – have a very profound (but unsung) effect on the entire life. It has a much greater impact than psychological issues. Students often experience disruptions under these kinds of eclipses. Perhaps the college they wanted doesn't accept them, but a different one does. Often they will change subjects or even colleges under this eclipse. Legal issues will take a dramatic turn and will start to resolve themselves one way or another. Since the Sun is your ruling planet, this is a period when you redefine your personality, fine-tune and upgrade it. Important and long-term changes will happen to your personal appearance and overall demeanour. People often change their hair colour or style under these kinds of eclipses. They also change the way they dress and accessorize, adopting a new look.

Love seems especially exciting on the 1st.

April

Best Days Overall: 7, 8, 17, 18, 25, 26

Most Stressful Days Overall: 1, 14, 15, 21, 22, 27, 28

Best Days for Love: 2, 3, 4, 5, 14, 15, 21, 22, 23, 24

Best Days for Money: 4, 5, 9, 10, 14, 15, 16, 23, 24, 25, 26

Monthly Career Peaks: 19, 20, 27, 28

Monthly Personal Pleasure Peaks: 7, 8, 27

Like last month, most of the planets are above the horizon, in the upper (day) side of the horoscope. But this month your 10th House becomes very strong – after the 20th – and you are entering your yearly career peak. Family is important, as are emotional issues and relations with children. But you can best serve them now by succeeding in the outer world. Until the 6th you can advance your career through your social connections. Your spouse or partner is supportive. Attending parties – the right ones – and social gatherings, perhaps even throwing some yourself, will advance your career.

After the 6th, you need to do 'detox' on your career goals, plans and urges. Choose one or two main goals and just focus on those. There is sudden career advancement (or important opportunity) from the 17th to the 20th. (This also brings romantic opportunity with someone involved in your career or above you in status). More important career happenings occur from the 19th to the 21st, as the Sun crosses the Midheaven of your chart. There is also more personal honour, glory and recognition – not so much for your professional achievements, but for who you are. You are very elevated these days. A pay rise or promotion wouldn't be a surprise.

Now that your financial planet is moving forwards (since the 25th of last month), and the dust has probably settled from last month's eclipse, finances are straightening out. They are still not that important to you. Your 2nd House is still empty (except when the Moon visits on the 9th and the 10th) and you're not paying too much attention here. But financial judgement is sound. Until the 16th, like last month, you prosper by helping others to prosper – partners and shareholders and the like. If you are looking for outside capital, the quest is fortunate. It's good to pay off or refinance debt this period. After the 16th, financial opportunities come through educational organizations, foreign countries or foreign lands. In general, there should be more prosperity and you take it for granted. Your financial planet will re-stimulate eclipse points on the 11th, 12th, 22nd and 23rd. Thus if you have not yet made the financial changes you should have made last month, you will get another cosmic nudge.

Like last month, most of the planets are still in the West. This continues to be a time for attaining ends through consensus, co-operation and compromise rather than direct action.

Your love life still seems happy, but you appear more interested in career and education this month. It's as if you are pulling away from the current love, not breaking up but creating a little space. Love is where you want it to be and you are off to explore other interests.

Health is excellent until the 20th, but after that you will need to rest and relax more. A Grand Square pattern (which happened a few months ago) is again manifesting from the 20th onwards. This shows your involvement in major projects, either on a personal level or for others. There is much achievement happening, but it taxes the energy. Build, but build in a rhythmic way.

Avoid unnecessary foreign travel from the 2nd to the 5th and from the 29th to the 30th.

May

Best Days Overall: 4, 5, 14, 15, 22, 23, 29, 30

Most Stressful Days Overall: 12, 13, 18, 19, 25, 26

Best Days for Love: 2, 3, 12, 13, 14, 15, 18, 19, 20, 21, 22, 23, 29, 30

Best Days for Money: 2, 3, 5, 6, 7, 8, 12, 13, 17, 20, 21, 27, 28, 29, 30

Monthly Career Peaks: 25, 26

Monthly Personal Pleasure Peaks: 4, 5, 27, 31

Most of the planets are still above the horizon and your 10th House of Career is still very strong. The planets involved with the home and family, Jupiter and Pluto, are both retrograde. Not much can be done with pending family issues anyway, so you might as well focus on your career. You are still very much in your yearly career peak and enjoying great career experiences (these are not lifetime peaks, but relevant only to this year). After the 5th there is more career-related travel. On the 11th and 12th, when your career planet re-stimulates eclipse points, there could be some dramas in your corporate hierarchy – shake-ups, power struggles and the like. There are also dramas with a parent or parent figure. Stay calm. Your career is still very much intact.

Neither the Eastern nor Western side of the horoscope is dominant this month, so personal independence is growing but not yet fully established.

The Grand Square pattern that began last month is still very much in effect. Big projects are happening, both for you and for the world. You are creating a new order in your life. Your health still needs watching: continue to enhance health in the ways mentioned in the yearly report. Most importantly, like last month, monitor your energy levels.

The project you are involved with is big enough to make you forego many of life's pleasures – highly unusual for a Leo. But don't give up fun altogether.

Aside from career, friendships and group activities are important. It is a social period but more with friends than with romance. There is romantic opportunity for singles – especially until the 21st – but nothing serious. Love is more stressful after the 21st. You and your lover don't see eye to eye, and perhaps this is why you seek out friends more than romance. Another scenario is that there is friction with your lover because of the attention you give to your friends. This is a short-term problem and will soon pass.

Higher education also seems important this month. Perhaps the company is sending you off for more training. Education seems career related.

As we have seen almost all year, your 2nd House of Finance is basically empty. Status and prestige are more important than mere money. Finances become more important to you from the 5th onwards as your financial planet moves into your 10th House of Career. This is a good financial aspect (though you will earn every penny). It shows pay rises, money from parents or parent figures, sometimes from government contracts or programmes or from people involved in government. Your good professional reputation leads to referrals and other opportunities. The problem is that all the money focus cramps your joyous lifestyle, forcing you to go without many pleasures. Important financial changes will happen on the 30th and 31st as your financial planet re-stimulates eclipse points.

June

Best Days Overall: 1, 2, 10, 11, 19, 20, 28, 29

Most Stressful Days Overall: 8, 9, 14, 15, 21, 22

Best Days for Love: 3, 4, 8, 9, 12, 13, 14, 15, 17, 18, 22, 25, 26

Best Days for Money: 3, 4, 8, 9, 17, 18, 25, 26, 27, 30

Monthly Career Peaks: 21, 22

Monthly Personal Pleasure Peaks: 1, 2, 25, 28, 29

This month the planets finally make their shift from the West to East. East, the sector of self and personal interests, becomes dominant over the West. Dominance is not over-powering – between 50 to 60 per cent of the planets – but it is still in effect. Your 1st House of Self will become very strong after the 3rd, stronger than your 7th House of Others.

Also, the planets involved with love are retrograde this month (Neptune started to move retrograde last month and Uranus goes retrograde on the 19th). So your social life, in general, is starting to slow down, and you may as well please yourself, following the path of your own bliss. Other people are still important to you, but you know what's right for you better than anyone else.

Most of the planets are still above the horizon, and your 10th House is still strong (Venus, the career planet, is there until the 14th). So continue to pursue your outer world goals. Doing right will lead to feeling right. As in the past few months, both the planets involved with the home and family are retrograde, so important family and domestic decisions need more study and research.

The retrograde of your love planets will not stop your love and social life. It will only slow things down. Perhaps your social confidence will not be as strong as usual. Your social judgement is also not up to its usually high standards, so it is good to go slow in love. Important love decisions, such as marriage or divorce, shouldn't be made after the 19th. This is a good period for introspection, for reviewing your relationships and seeing where things can be improved. For singles, it is a time for considering your real needs in love. Love opportunities will come at spiritually-oriented retreats and gatherings, charitable functions or as you pursue altruistic goals.

The Grand Square pattern that has been in effect for the past two months continues until the 14th but is weaker. Health is improved, but still needs watching. Mars moves into your sign on the 3rd and brings much extra energy and magnetism, but sometimes Mars pushes the body beyond its capacity so maintain awareness of your body. You excel in exercise regimes, sports and athletics during this period. Health is enhanced through vigorous exercise and in the ways discussed in the yearly report. Thermal therapies are better now than they've been all year.

LEO

Your 2nd House of Finance is still empty – only the Moon will visit there on the 2nd, 4th and 30th – so you don't seem to care much about these things. In spite of this, the month is prosperous and you are getting your way in finance. Financial opportunities are running after you these days, and after the 28th they will find you. From the 23rd to the 28th your financial intuition is super. Mercury will re-stimulate eclipse points on the 1st and from the 8th to the 10th. These will be times when you get pushed to make the financial changes that should have been made long ago.

The Sun will re-stimulate eclipse points this month as well. This is powerful for the world at large as it tends to re-create the conditions of the original eclipse. But it is especially powerful for you as the Sun is your ruler. You are certainly a risk-taker this month (Mars is in your own sign) but avoid it on the 1st, 8th, 9th and 10th.

July

Best Days Overall: 8, 9, 16, 17, 25, 26

Most Stressful Days Overall: 5, 6, 12, 13, 18, 19

Best Days for Love: 3, 4, 5, 6, 12, 13, 14, 15, 22, 23, 24

Best Days for Money: 1, 5, 6, 7, 8, 14, 15, 23, 24, 27, 28, 29

Monthly Career Peaks: 18, 19, 23

Monthly Personal Pleasure Peaks: 20, 21, 25, 26

This month's horoscope, like life itself, is filled with contradictions. Most of the planets are in the East and your 1st House is very powerful. This shows independence and making things happen by direct action. Yet we have many planets retrograde, as much as 50 per cent (from the 3rd to the 7th), and these counsel caution. Active Fire is the dominant element this month. This also gives independence and a desire to do everything in a hurry. Yet all those retrogrades slow everything down and advise patience. Saturn, the planet of caution and patience, also gets much stimulation. So design your life, exercise your independence, have things your way, but be patient. The results of your action might come through a delayed reaction.

In spite of the delays (which give you a lesson in patience) this is a time for having things your way, for having life on your terms. And as long as you're not destructive to others, why not?

With both of your love planets still retrograde, you may as well pursue your own bliss – do the things that make you happy.

You are entering your yearly personal pleasure peak, Leo, so enjoy. This is a period for fulfilling sensual desires, for pampering the body and treating it well. With Saturn still in your own sign it is unlikely that you will overdo it.

Though your love planets are retrograde, there are still many love opportunities for singles this month. The spiritual arena – retreats, meditation seminars, prayer gatherings, charity functions – seems the place of romantic opportunity now. Enjoy your romantic experiences but don't try to rush them or make them into something they're not. Those on a spiritual path will have greater realization of Divine Love – unconditional and impersonal love – this month.

Health is excellent this month. You have lots of energy and magnetism, and you look great. You excel in exercise and sports, and you are dynamic. Saturn, the health planet, is getting lots of positive stimulation so miraculous (so-called) healing of any health problems is likely. Also, you will find that your personal healing abilities are much greater than usual.

In finance we see more of the contradictions we spoke of earlier. On the one hand, dynamic Mars will move into your money house on the 21st. This shows a desire to make wealth happen, for quick money, a rashness and impatience in finances. Yet your financial planet, Mercury, is retrograde from the 3rd to the 29th, almost the whole month. This counsels caution and reflection, doing more homework and resolving doubts. This will be a difficult contradiction to resolve.

The Sun, your ruler, re-stimulates eclipse points on the 1st and 2nd. No need for bungee-jumping contests on those days.

August

Best Days Overall: 4, 5, 12, 13, 21, 22, 23, 31

Most Stressful Days Overall: 2, 3, 8, 9, 14, 15, 29, 30

Best Days for Love: 2, 3, 8, 9, 10, 11, 19, 20, 21, 22, 29, 30, 31

Best Days for Money: 2, 3, 10, 11, 12, 19, 20, 22, 23, 24, 25, 29, 30

Monthly Career Peaks: 12, 13, 14, 15

Monthly Personal Pleasure Peaks: 12, 13, 21, 22, 23

The same contradictions we saw last month are still mostly in effect now. Most of the planets remain in the independent East. The independent 1st House is much stronger than the 7th House of Others, so this is still a time for having your way in life and for following your personal bliss.

Both the love planets are still retrograde and love seems stressed. There could be financial disagreements with the beloved or current relationship. Perhaps you and your spouse are in a financial competition. Or singles might find they are too busy making money to socialize. Some months (and even some years) are not especially social. This is part of the rhythm of nature.

You are still very much in your yearly personal pleasure peak. So continue to enjoy yourself and treat yourself well.

The month ahead seems very prosperous – you are entering a yearly financial peak too. So, the wherewithal for this pampering will be there.

This is a month when you invest in yourself, in your body, your health, your image and personal appearance. You are taking a direct and personal role in finance, not delegating it to others. Expensive personal items are coming to you.

This should be a very prosperous month. Mercury, your financial planet, is now moving forwards, so speculations are much safer than they were last month. With Mars in your money house all month, financial progress should be rapid. Quick money is attainable now, but keep it honest. From the 13th to the 28th, financial opportunity seeks you out. But there are also financial opportunities in foreign lands and with foreigners. Academics, publishers, travel companies and higher education also seem to play a role here. Perhaps they are clients or customers.

Job-seekers have excellent and effortless success this month.

For the past two months, the planets have shifted to the lower (night) side of the horoscope, so worldly ambitions are not that important now (money is, but not status or prestige). So, this is a time for stabilizing the home base and cultivating emotional harmony and peace. Curiously, in spite of your lack of interest, career opportunities (as well as financial) are pursuing you after the 13th. Also, you seem more ambitious than you really are. (Perhaps you dress this way or give this impression.) These days, if you had to choose between family and the career, you would choose family. Seems like you will be more choosy about these career opportunities. Your emotional harmony and your family situation will play a bigger role in which opportunities you take or let pass.

Health is still excellent. Miraculous healings remain likely. Personal healing ability is greatly increased.

LEO

September

Best Days Overall: 1, 9, 10, 17, 18, 19, 27, 28, 29

Most Stressful Days Overall: 5, 6, 11, 12, 25, 26

Best Days for Love: 1, 2, 5, 6, 7, 8, 11, 15, 16, 20, 21, 25, 26, 30

Best Days for Money: 3, 4, 7, 8, 12, 13, 15, 16, 20, 21, 22, 23, 25, 26

Monthly Career Peaks: 11, 12

Monthly Personal Pleasure Peaks: 17, 18, 19

Retrograde activity is greatly reduced this month. By the 4th, 80 per cent of the planets will be in forward motion. And, with most of the planets in the independent East, personal projects you started in the past few months start moving forwards again. Also, your personal initiative and direct actions will have quicker results. Continue to follow the path of your bliss.

Career opportunities are still seeking you, but you are more choosy now. With most of the planets below the horizon, in the night side of your chart, your family and emotional harmony is most important. This is the time to advance your career by more subjective methods – by dreaming and visualizing, reviewing and digesting, resting and recharging the career faculties. You are building the psychological foundations for future success.

The Lunar Eclipse on the 7th seems mild, but it won't hurt to reduce your schedule anyway. This eclipse occurs in your 8th House and seems to affect the income of your spouse, lover or partner more than your own. They will be making dramatic financial changes in the next six months as flaws in financial thinking or planning are revealed. Since this eclipse occurs very near your love planet, Uranus, a current relationship or marriage will get tested as well. True love will survive and thrive, but the other kinds will probably not make it. Since Uranus is retrograde, this testing could be delayed and might not happen around the eclipse. Eclipses in the 8th House tend to bring confrontations with death. This need not be a literal death, but could be a psychological confrontation with it. People sometimes report having dreams of death or near-death experiences under these aspects. Sometimes they dream of their own death or the death of someone close to them. There is a need to understand this on a deeper level, to replace fear with understanding. If you are involved in property, insurance or tax issues, this eclipse will mark a turning point and events will start to move forwards.

The Solar Eclipse of the 22nd will probably have a stronger effect on you. This eclipse occurs right on the border of the 2nd and 3rd houses, and will probably impact on both of them. Changes in your partner's income (from the Lunar Eclipse) might force changes in your own financial strategy and thinking too. Many people change their banks, brokers, financial planners and investments under these kinds of aspects. Overall, in spite of the eclipse, this is a very prosperous month – you are having peak financial experiences these days.

There could be dramas with siblings and neighbours. Children may have dramas at school, perhaps with a teacher. Sometimes there are upheavals in the school itself rather than something personal. Cars and communication equipment will get tested as well.

Health is good but try to reduce your schedule around the eclipse periods.

October

Best Days Overall: 6, 7, 15, 16, 25, 26

Most Stressful Days Overall: 2, 3, 8, 9, 22, 23, 24, 29, 30

LEO

Best Days for Love: 2, 3, 4, 5, 10, 11, 12, 13, 14, 21, 22, 23, 24, 29, 30

Best Days for Money: 4, 5, 12, 13, 14, 17, 18, 19, 22, 23, 24

Monthly Career Peaks: 8, 9, 24, 25, 26, 27

Monthly Personal Pleasure Peaks: 15, 16, 22, 24, 25, 26, 27

If there is any situation or condition that still needs changing, now is the time to do it. Very soon, by the 23rd, the planetary power will shift to the West, making you more dependent on others and less able to change things. This shift gives you the opportunity to develop your social skills. The social life in general becomes more active and important.

Most of the planets are below the horizon and at the nadir (midnight point, the lowest point) in the horoscope. Your 4th House becomes packed with planets after the 23rd (60 per cent of the planets are either there or moving through there), so this is the main headline for the month. Home, family and children are where your heart is. Your 10th House of Career, by contrast, is empty (except when the Moon visits on the 8th and 9th – this will be the monthly career peak). So you can down-play career and pay attention to the family. This is also a period when you can make accelerated psychological progress. You are in touch with the past, and your memory is super sharp these days.

The ruler of your 5th House of Children gets super stimulation this month. This means that Leos of childbearing age are ultra-fertile. Pregnancies – especially after the 23rd – are likely. Even if you are not of childbearing age, you will be dealing more with children and perhaps thinking of adopting.

Whatever your age and stage, libido is much stronger than the norm.

Last month's eclipse provoked a crisis in love. Some relationships have broken up. But have no fear: your love life is starting to straighten out and get more exciting. First off, one of the love planets (Neptune in your 7th House) starts moving forwards on the 29th. Your actual love planet, Uranus, will start moving forwards next month. After the 23rd, Uranus will also be super stimulated (by 60 per cent of the heavenly powers!), so serious love is happening now. Your new feeling of emotional harmony is helping out. Family connections are also helping. The psychological progress you're making – your ability to contact and cleanse your past – is also beneficial. It is easy to get into the mood for love these days.

Health needs watching more closely after the 23rd. Rest and relax more. Pace yourself. Keep energy levels as high as possible. Enhance health in the ways mentioned in the yearly report.

Finances are so-so this month. You have just come through a very strong financial period and probably feel sated and content. Family support is strong – and it works both ways. Your financial planet, Mercury, goes retrograde on the 28th. This won't stop earnings but slows things down a bit. As usual, avoid major purchases, investments or financial commitments after the 28th. Many of you are tempted to spend on the home now. This is basically a good idea, but try to wrap these things up before the 28th. Otherwise wait until November 18th when Mercury goes forwards.

November

Best Days Overall: 3, 11, 12, 21, 22, 30

Most Stressful Days Overall: 5, 19, 20, 26, 27

Best Days for Love: 1, 9, 10, 19, 20, 21, 26, 27, 28, 29, 30

Best Days for Money: 1, 2, 9, 10, 13, 14, 15, 19, 20, 28, 29, 30

LEO

Monthly Career Peaks: 5, 14, 15, 16

Monthly Personal Pleasure Peaks: 11, 12, 21, 22, 23

Seventy to eighty per cent of the planets are in stressful aspect to you this month, so take more care of your health. There is probably nothing organically wrong, but when energy drops it can certainly feel that way. The solution is to rest more. Keep your focus on the priorities of your life – on essence issues – and drop the frivolous things.

This is a good month to get massages, reiki treatments, acupuncture, acupressure and chiropractic adjustments. Any therapy that increases your energy is good.

Watch how much better you feel after the 22nd. It will be like magic, as if a switch were thrown in some cosmic generator and your energy is back.

Happily, with your strong focus on feeling good (most of the planets are below the horizon and your 4th House is the strongest in the horoscope until the 23rd), you will probably be more attentive to health issues. Career-wise, do the minimum now. Don't get fired from your job or anything like that. Do what needs to be done, but shift focus to the home and the emotional life, and also to health.

If you can maintain decent energy levels, the month ahead is basically happy. Love continues to improve. Your love planet goes forwards on the 20th, and by then both love planets will be moving forwards. Most of the planets are in the West and so your social life in general becomes more important. Love is blooming and clarifying. Stuck relationships are moving forwards. Singles have many new opportunities, probably close to home, through family connections or people who are like family to you. Perhaps there is a nostalgic feeling for an old flame.

Children and fun are important all month, but these interests are even stronger after the 22nd. These are always important to Leo, but this month (and in 2007) they are even more so. Creative hobbies are also interesting, and if you don't have one yet, this is a good month to start. The unusual fertility of last month continues this month.

The financial planet is still retrograde until the 18th, so wait until after that to make major purchases or investments. Family support and connections seem the path to earnings. Investments in the home, though called for now, are best left until after the 18th as well. When Mercury goes forwards you will have a whole new perspective on these things.

December

Best Days Overall: 1, 8, 9, 10, 18, 19, 27, 28

Most Stressful Days Overall: 2, 3, 16, 17, 23, 24, 29, 30

Best Days for Love: 1, 6, 7, 9, 10, 11, 16, 17, 21, 22, 23, 24, 25, 26, 29, 30

Best Days for Money: 4, 7, 8, 11, 12, 18, 19, 27, 29

Monthly Career Peaks: 2, 3, 21, 22, 29, 30

Monthly Personal Pleasure Peaks: 8, 9, 10, 20

What a turnaround from last month when 70 to 80 per cent of the planets were in stressful aspect to you. Now the situation is exactly opposite – 70 to 80 per cent of them are in harmonious aspect. First you will feel this health-wise. Energy levels are naturally high; sickness and disease flee far from you. Many of you with long-standing health problems will experience 'miraculous' healings (a trend we also saw last month) and your own healing abilities are again vastly increased. Those of you in the healing professions will heal by your mere presence, by your touch. (Many of you who are not professionals will also discover this ability.) You can walk into a room of sad and depressed people and lift them up just by your presence. Now you have the energy to achieve any goal you set for yourself.

LEO

The only health danger this month is burnout. The Fire element is so strong – 70 to 80 per cent of the planets are in Fire signs – that you can push the body beyond its capacity without even realizing it. Also, it is a hyperactive month. There is a need to be more aware of the body.

Leos are natural 5th House people. They are fun-loving and creative people, even if their 5th House in the chart is weak. So now we have to ask ourselves what they will be like with 60 to 70 per cent of the planets in the 5th House this month! This is not just a long party but a real 'blowout'.

Now you experience what it is like to be in the flow of life. Life becomes a total joy. The many parties and entertainments that happen this month are merely manifestations of the joy you carry within.

Personal fertility (for those of childbearing age) is increased even further (it was strong for the past few months anyway). Your already strong libido is even stronger.

Curiously, this fun and joy could negatively impact on serious romance. You seem happy to be non-committed, playing the field. Also, as there are many, many love opportunities available, there's no need to get serious. People of the opposite sex are throwing themselves at you, and this will test a current relationship.

This is a very prosperous month. Speculations are favourable, and money comes in easy and happy ways. Artists and artisans have no trouble selling their creativity.

By the 22nd you will get a bit more serious, productive and work-oriented. If you've overdone the partying, now you will get more into diet and health regimes and bring things back into balance. The most important thing, though, is that you caught a glimpse of what life can and should be like. Eventually you will manifest more and more of it.

The Sun, your ruler, will re-stimulate eclipse points from the 6th to the 8th and on the 21st and 22nd. Have fun but avoid risky activities. These days will also be significant for the world at large.

Virgo

♍

THE VIRGIN
Birthdays from
22nd August to
22nd September

Personality Profile

VIRGO AT A GLANCE

Element – Earth

Ruling Planet – Mercury
  Career Planet – Mercury
  Love Planet – Neptune
  Money Planet – Venus
  Planet of Home and Family Life – Jupiter
  Planet of Health and Work – Uranus
  Planet of Pleasure – Saturn
  Planet of Sexuality – Mars

Colours – earth tones, ochre, orange, yellow

Colour that promotes love, romance and social
  harmony – aqua blue

VIRGO

Colour that promotes earning power – jade green

Gems – agate, hyacinth

Metal – quicksilver

Scents – lavender, lilac, lily of the valley, storax

Quality – mutable (= flexibility)

Quality most needed for balance – a broader perspective

Strongest virtues – mental agility, analytical skills, ability to pay attention to detail, healing powers

Deepest needs – to be useful and productive

Characteristic to avoid – destructive criticism

Signs of greatest overall compatibility – Taurus, Capricorn

Signs of greatest overall incompatibility – Gemini, Sagittarius, Pisces

Sign most helpful to career – Gemini

Sign most helpful for emotional support – Sagittarius

Sign most helpful financially – Libra

Sign best for marriage and/or partnerships – Pisces

Sign most helpful for creative projects – Capricorn

Best Sign to have fun with – Capricorn

Signs most helpful in spiritual matters – Taurus, Leo

Best day of the week – Wednesday

Understanding a Virgo

The virgin is a particularly fitting symbol for those born under the Sign of Virgo. If you meditate on the image of the virgin you will get a good understanding of the essence of the Virgo type. The virgin is, of course, a symbol of purity and innocence – not naïve, but pure. A virginal object has not been touched. A virgin field is land that is true to itself, the way it has always been. The same is true of virgin forest: it is pristine, unaltered.

Apply the idea of purity to the thought processes, emotional life, physical body, and activities and projects of the everyday world, and you can see how Virgos approach life. Virgos desire the pure expression of the ideal in their mind, body and affairs. If they find impurities they will attempt to clear them away.

Impurities are the beginning of disorder, unhappiness and uneasiness. The job of the Virgo is to eject all impurities and keep only that which the body and mind can use and assimilate.

The secrets of good health are here revealed: 90 per cent of the art of staying well is maintaining a pure mind, a pure body and pure emotions. When you introduce more impurities than your mind and body can deal with, you will have what is known as 'dis-ease'. It is no wonder that Virgos make great doctors, nurses, healers and dietitians. They have an innate understanding of good health and they realize that good health is more than just physical. In all aspects of life, if you want a project to be successful it must be kept as pure as possible. It must be protected against the adverse elements that will try to undermine it. This is the secret behind Virgo's awesome technical proficiency.

One could talk about Virgo's analytical powers – which are formidable. One could talk about their perfectionism and their almost superhuman attention to detail. But this would be to miss the point. All of these virtues are manifestations of a Virgo's desire for purity and perfection – a world without Virgos would have ruined itself long ago.

A vice is nothing more than a virtue turned inside out, misapplied or used in the wrong context. Virgos' apparent vices come from their inherent virtue. Their analytical powers, which should be used for healing, helping or perfecting a project in the world, sometimes get misapplied and turned against people. Their critical faculties, which should be used constructively to perfect a strategy or proposal, can sometimes be used destructively to harm or wound. Their urge to perfection can turn into worry and lack of confidence; their natural humility can become self-denial and self-abasement. When Virgos turn negative they are apt to turn their devastating criticism on themselves, sowing the seeds of self-destruction.

Finance

Virgos have all the attitudes that create wealth. They are hard-working, industrious, efficient, organized, thrifty, productive and eager to serve. A developed Virgo is every employer's dream. But until Virgos master some of the social graces of Libra they will not even come close to fulfilling their financial potential. Purity and perfectionism, if not handled correctly or gracefully, can be very trying to others. Friction in human relationships can be devastating not only to your pet projects but – indirectly – to your wallet as well.

Virgos are quite interested in their financial security. Being hard-working, they know the true value of money. They do not like to take risks with their money, preferring to save for their retirement or for a rainy day. Virgos usually make prudent, calculated investments that involve a minimum of risk. These investments and savings usually work out well, helping Virgos to achieve the financial security they seek. The rich or even not-so-rich Virgo also likes to help his or her friends in need.

Career and Public Image

Virgos reach their full potential when they can communicate their knowledge in such a way that others can understand it. In order to get their ideas across better, Virgos need to develop greater verbal skills and fewer judgemental ways of expressing themselves. Virgos look up to teachers and communicators; they like their bosses to be good communicators. Virgos will probably not respect a superior who is not their intellectual equal – no matter how much money or power that superior has. Virgos themselves like to be perceived by others as being educated and intellectual.

The natural humility of Virgos often inhibits them from fulfilling their great ambitions, from acquiring name and fame. Virgos should indulge in a little more self-promotion if they are going to reach their career goals. They need to push themselves with the same ardour that they would use to foster others.

At work Virgos like to stay active. They are willing to learn any type of job as long as it serves their ultimate goal of financial security. Virgos may change occupations several times during their professional lives, until they find the one they really enjoy. Virgos work well with other people, are not afraid to work hard and always fulfil their responsibilities.

Love and Relationships

If you are an analyst or a critic you must, out of necessity, narrow your scope. You have to focus on a part and not the whole; this can create a temporary narrow-mindedness. Virgos do not like this kind of person. They like their partners to be broad-minded, with depth and vision. Virgos seek to get this broad-minded quality from their partners, since they sometimes lack it themselves.

Virgos are perfectionists in love just as they are in other areas of life. They need partners who are tolerant, open-minded and easy-going. If you are in love with a Virgo do not waste time on impractical romantic gestures. Do practical and useful things for him or her – this is what will be appreciated and what will be done for you.

Virgos express their love through pragmatic and useful gestures, so do not be put off because your Virgo partner does not say 'I love you' day-in and day-out. Virgos are not that type. If they love you, they will demonstrate it in practical ways. They will always be there for you; they will show an interest in your health and finances; they will fix your sink or repair your video recorder. Virgos deem these actions to be superior to sending flowers, chocolates or St Valentine's cards.

In love affairs Virgos are not particularly passionate or spontaneous. If you are in love with a Virgo, do not take this personally. It does not mean that you are not alluring enough or that your Virgo partner does not love or like you. It is just the way Virgos are. What they lack in passion they make up for in dedication and loyalty.

Home and Domestic Life

It goes without saying that the home of a Virgo will be spotless, sanitized and orderly. Everything will be in its proper place – and don't you dare move anything about! For Virgos to find domestic bliss they need to ease up a bit in the home, to allow their partner and kids more freedom and to be more generous and open-minded. Family members are not to be analysed under a microscope, they are individuals with their own virtues to express.

With these small difficulties resolved, Virgos like to stay in and entertain at home. They make good hosts and they like to keep their friends and families happy and entertained at family and social gatherings. Virgos love children, but they are strict with them – at times – since they want to make sure their children are brought up with the correct sense of family and values.

Horoscope for 2006

General Trends

As has been the case for some years now, the year ahead (and next few years) is about learning to deal with dramatic change and the insecurities that come with it. It's as if your highest dreams and ideals are right there for you – you can touch them and feel them in your imagination – but in order to attain them you need to take the next, bold step. Figuratively speaking, you must jump into an abyss – the unknown. Some of you might even have been pushed into this abyss. Surrender to it wholly, and watch yourself grow wings. It is your fear that has kept you from your dreams. When you take the plunge, there could be a few crashes, but they can never have the impact you imagine. And there will be sweet successes too ...

The insecurities you are dealing with centre around love and your concept of yourself. We will deal with this later on.

The theme of 2005 was your finances, and by now these issues have been settled. This year the focus is on intellectual and mental expansion.

For many years there has been an emotional separation from family, and these trends continue in 2006. We will deal with them later.

Health and work are always important to you. They are the mainstays of your life. This year is no exception.

Ever since Saturn moved into your 12th House on July 17th 2005, spirituality has become very important. This trend will be even more intense this year. Many will begin their spiritual journeys in a serious way. Those already on it will renew their commitment and go much deeper. More on this later.

Your paths to greatest fulfilment in the year ahead are intellectual and educational interests, communication (until November 24th); home, family and psychological issues (all year but especially after November 24th); personal transformation, sex, past lives, occult studies, the deeper things of life (until June 23rd); love and romance (after July 23rd).

Health

(Please note that this is an astrological perspective on health, not a medical one. At one time, both perspectives were identical, but in these times there could be quite a difference. For the medical perspective, please consult your physician or health professional.)

Health is reasonable most of the year as only two long-term planets are in stressful alignment with you. But later on in the year – after November 24th – Jupiter will also be in stressful aspect and you will need to take more care.

The good news is that Virgos don't need lectures from astrologers about taking care of their health (they can give *us* lectures). With your 6th House of Health strong, and with your natural Virgo interests always in play, you will be on the case. The least little symptom will be jumped on and dealt with.

Uranus, your health planet, rules the ankles, so these always need special attention. They should be regularly massaged and given more support, especially when exercising.

Uranus rules your health from the sign of Pisces, which rules the feet. Neptune, the planet that rules the feet, is in your 6th House of Health, showing that the feet need special attention. Shoes should be sensible. Feet should be kept warm in the winter. Foot massage, foot baths and foot hydro-spas are powerful and beneficial.

Uranus recently moved from an Air sign to a Water sign – from Aquarius to Pisces. This shows that water-oriented therapies are particularly powerful and beneficial for you. Air therapies – fresh air, air purity, breathing exercises, air baths – are still very good but now water is also helpful.

The spiritual dimension of healing is also of particular importance to you – this year and for many years to come. Your knowledge of this area is going to increase vastly. Spiritual healing is all over your chart. The health planet is in the most spiritual of the signs, Pisces. Neptune, the most spiritual of all the planets, is in your 6th House of Health.

Your health planet is in your 7th House of Love and Romance (it will be there for many years to come), and this shows a strong connection between love and health. First, it shows that you are involved in the health of your partner – not a surprise. You feel that good health also means healthy relationships and a healthy love life. And, if health problems arise, chances are that their origin is in the love life. Best to clear up any disharmonies there before running to a health professional.

Energy becomes a major issue after November 24th. You need to maintain high energy levels. So the sensible thing to do is rest when tired and focus your available energies on things that are really important to you.

A parent or parent figure may have had surgery recently, or perhaps it is being contemplated this year. Let them get a second opinion. There could be other ways to deal with this issue. Parents can enhance their health by paying more attention to the neck, throat, kidneys, hips, sexual organs, colon and bladder. Children's health seems status-quo, but they can enhance it by paying more attention to the arms, shoulders, lungs and small intestine. Mental health is also very important for them. Grandchildren can optimize their health by paying more attention to the kidneys and hips.

Love issues can impact on their health as well, and any disharmonies should be cleared up. Your spouse or lover needs to be more careful health-wise. They are taking on a disciplined health regime. What is interesting here is that their perspective on health is opposite to yours. He or she is traditional and orthodox while you are alternative and experimental. Let them have their way on this – though you want to be helpful, you don't want to force even a good thing on someone. Your partner needs to pay more attention to the heart, spine, knees, teeth and overall skeletal alignment.

Home, Domestic and Family Issues

This has been an important area for many years and will continue to be important for some years to come. This year, after November 24th, it becomes one of the most powerful interests of your year (Jupiter joins Pluto in your 4th House of Home and Family).

Two important trends are happening here. The first is the deep psychological cleansing and transformation that has been going on for many years. It is as if your psyche has died and been reborn many times over the years. Many of you have had literal deaths in your family. Others have experienced only psychological deaths of the family and domestic patterns. Many of you are discovering who your true family is – and it might not be the biological one. Your emotional nature is being transformed in wonderful ways. Old emotional wounds and traumas are being brought to the surface too. Some of this could even be from past lives. No matter. They are on their way out. Real emotional health is being born in you.

Many of you have physically separated from your family. Others have separated only on a psychological level. Whether the separation was physical or psychological, it won't last long. You will reconnect on a better and more conscious level.

When deep psychological processing is happening, we usually see the outer results in the actual physical home. Deep repairs happen. The pipes get ripped out and new and better ones get installed. Walls are sometimes torn down and the physical structure of the house is rearranged. This is Pluto's normal action. Your personal underworld is revealed to you, as is the underworld of the physical house.

You deserve a lot of credit for sticking things out all these years. You have insights that few will ever attain in this life – and you paid the price for them. But now, especially after November 24th, you start experiencing some of the pleasant side of home and domestic matters. Your home will be made more spacious, either through renovation, a move or through buying additional homes. Your moods will become more optimistic and upbeat, reflecting the higher qualities of your nature. Expensive items will come to the home. The home will be a place of happiness and pleasantness. Your family circle will expand either through births or marriage. You start to meet people who are like family to you. Perhaps they are even better than family – they are your spiritual family. Further, you are going to lay the psychological groundwork for future prosperity and career success.

Building and remodelling projects are good all year but especially after December 6th. If you're redecorating in a cosmetic way or buying curtains, carpets or art objects for the home, November 17th to December 11th seems good. If you're buying or selling a home, the best time is after November 24th.

Parent or parent figures are probably moving – perhaps a few times. They also seem to be constantly upgrading the home. The same is true of siblings, though in their case children could be the reason for this. Adult children have a forced move caused by the Solar Eclipse of March 29th. Grown-up grandchildren should stay where they are, even though they feel cramped. They should make better use of the space available.

Love and Social Life

Your 7th House of Love and Romance started becoming a House of Power in 2004, a trend that continues this year. This is a very important and exciting area of life but you need a strong stomach to handle it. Nothing here is predictable.

You are attracting partners who are in transition – in experimental mode. They are not settled in their lives or with themselves. You fell in love with person X, but after a while person X becomes person Y, and that is not whom you loved. The reverse is also happening. Person X thought you were the divine ideal, but person Y doesn't think so and wants to find greener pastures.

Married Virgos (especially those on their first marriage) will have their relationship tested. Perhaps the only way to save the marriage is to allow maximum freedom, as long as it isn't destructive.

The winds of dramatic change are storming and blustering their way through your social life. Hold on to your hat!

Single Virgos (those working on their first marriage) probably shouldn't marry for a while. Enjoy each love experience for what it is without trying to project too far into the future. Don't resist change. When one love leaves, there will be another, and in unexpected places and ways. This is a time for gaining love experiences and experimenting.

Run-of-the-mill people (though there's nothing wrong with them) don't seem to interest you. You like out of the ordinary genius types, media and creative types, the glamour crowd. Healers and doctors – especially those involved in cutting-edge therapies – are alluring. Astrologers, astronomers, high-tech people and inventors are also attractive. But the very unconventionality of these people is what makes them unstable in love.

The good thing about all this is that your love adventures – and there will be many – will lead you to rethink who you are. Each experience is leading you closer to your ideal.

Virgos in or working on their second or third marriages will have a status-quo year. Singles will tend to stay single, and marrieds will tend to stay married.

Love opportunities can happen for you at any time and in any place. But the workplace seems the most likely area. Love opportunities can also happen as you pursue health goals, or with people involved in your health. You are very much a love-at-first-sight person this year and for many years to come.

You want perfection in everything – but especially in love. You have this trait naturally, but now it is even stronger because of the planetary influences. It may be wonderful to analyse your love relationships with the intention of improving them, but don't do it at a romantic moment or you'll kill the magic. Wait a day or two and then analyse. Also, when trying to make an improvement in love, read your lover's signals. They might not be in the right frame of mind to process what you have to say. Phrase your statements in constructive rather than hurtful ways. If nothing constructive can be done, do nothing and stay silent. A time will come when you can do something.

Love will be active all year but especially from February 19th to March 20th and from April 6th to May 5th.

Finance and Career

Neither your 2nd (finance) or 10th (career) Houses are strong this year. For the most part they are empty. This doesn't mean that you won't have a profession, career or earnings – of course you will – only that these areas are not so important in the scheme of things. Some years are not intended to be career years. We have other, more interesting things on our plate. For you, these are the home, family, intellectual, mental and social sides of life.

Most of you have just experienced a very strong financial year. Earnings rose, assets you owned increased in value, and you probably achieved your major financial goals. Many of you are seeing that mere money-making is way overblown. You feel you have enough and now want to develop your mind.

There is probably a general feeling of contentment both in career and in finance, and you have no need to pay too much attention to these areas.

The work front is a much more interesting and active area of life. These days you are the true blue Virgo. You feel that work is good for its own sake. It's not so much about money, status or professional prestige – it's about service, being useful. But work is even more than that lately. It's also the centre of your social life. Jobseekers are very conscious of this when they apply for a job. More than the money or the prestige, the Virgo will check out the social possibilities of any job offer. Multiple job changes in the year ahead wouldn't be a surprise. You tend to work in companies where the workforce is in a permanent state of flux. There are always new people to meet at work, and this is part of the charm. When it comes to love, you will do better at the office than at the club, disco or bar.

In any given year there will be times when finance is more important than at other times. For you, this period will be from September 8th to October 23rd.

Your career will be active and happy from May 20th to June 21st. You will probably be more ambitious in a worldly sense during that period as well.

Siblings are having an excellent financial year. They are also travelling and enjoying the sensual pleasures and delights of life. A parent or parent figure comes into prosperity after November 24th. Children are highly speculative and take risks. They can hit it big this year but can also have major reverses. They are going for gold but should hedge themselves better. Grandchildren and their partners have a status-quo year, though we do see some important financial changes being created by the Solar Eclipse of March 29th.

Venus is your financial planet. A fast-moving planet, she will move through your entire horoscope in any given year. This means that money and earning opportunities will come from various places, people and situations during the year.

Self-improvement

Saturn moved into your 12th House of Spirituality on July 17th 2005, a major, long-term transit that will last for another two years. This is a time to bring order to your inner life. For those of you not yet on a spiritual path, this is a period when you might embark on it. You might be faced with unknown fears and blockages which can't be addressed by standard therapies. You might rail at this, but it is a gift from the cosmos. It will force you to go deeper – to the spirit, to the Divine, to your true and eternal self.

For those of you already on a spiritual path, this is a time for applying system, order and organization to it. More discipline and regularity is needed in your practice. It will become part of your daily regime, like brushing your teeth and bathing. The inner journey is long and sometimes arduous, and you need to learn to enjoy every step of the way. This is also a time for verifying your intuition and inner faculties. They will be subjected to reality checks – sometimes harshly. This will force you to be more careful when you 'tune in' or express what you have received. It will make you learn to interpret what you receive in a better way. You will be forced to live your spiritual ideals – to apply them to the practical affairs of life. And this is wonderful, though not always comfortable. Spirit must become as real to you as the ground beneath your feet. All of this will happen as a process, and not all at once, but you can cooperate with it.

Month-by-month Forecasts

January

Best Days Overall: 8, 9, 17, 18, 19, 27, 28

Most Stressful Days Overall: 3, 4, 10, 11, 25, 26, 31

Best Days for Love: 1, 2, 3, 4, 8, 9, 10, 11, 17, 18, 19, 20, 21, 27, 28, 29, 30, 31

Best Days for Money: 3, 4, 8, 9, 12, 13, 17, 18, 19, 20, 21, 22, 23, 27, 28, 31

Monthly Career Peaks: 10, 11, 17, 18, 26, 27

Monthly Personal Pleasure Peaks: 17, 18, 26, 27

You begin your year with most of the planetary power below the horizon – the night side of the horoscope. Your 4th House of Home and Family is strong, while your 10th House of Career is basically empty (only the Moon will visit there on the 10th and 11th, and this will be your monthly career peak). So the message is clear: you are in 'night mode'. You further your career by cultivating emotional harmony and by subjective processes – dreaming, visualizing, reviewing and digesting. This is more a period for setting goals than for actually achieving them. But this is just as important, for achievement won't happen without it. Focus on the home and family and down-play the career. Attending your child's soccer game might be more important in the scheme of things than another humdrum deal or overtime at the office. When night comes we should surrender to it. Then the activities of the day (which is going to happen shortly) will go much better.

Family members seem to need your attention. A parent or parent figure could be having surgery or some other drama. There is tension in the home – perhaps conflict –

and this needs your focus. A major repair might be underway as well.

Most of the planets are in the West this month – and this will be a trend for a few months into the future. This is a time to adapt to conditions as best you can and to cultivate your social skills. Ego and self-interest should be downplayed and the focus given to others. The cosmos is not at war with your ego, but the ego merely needs to know its place. There are times and situations when it is qualified to set policy, and times when it is not. There are larger ideas of good that are beyond its imagination – and this is one of those times. Your ways – your ideas – are probably not the best ways. See and understand the perspectives of others and their interests. Gain your objectives through consensus and co-operation and not by direct, arbitrary actions. Who you know is now more important than who you are.

All in all, though, this is a happy month. Your 5th House of Fun and Creativity is strong until the 20th. After that, your 6th House of Health and Work gets strong. For most people, power in the 6th House is not considered fun – but for a Virgo it is as you enjoy work for its own sake. Jobseekers have success and there are social opportunities at the workplace, especially later in the month.

Your 2nd House of Finance is basically empty – only the Moon will visit there on the 10th and 21st – so finances are not a big issue for you these days. Your financial planet is in a very rare (once every two years) retrograde. This doesn't stop earnings, but slows things down a bit, so this is not a time to make major purchases or investments. Rather, this is a time for studying and reviewing these things, for financial planning rather than doing. You can take action after February 3rd when Venus starts moving forwards again. Finances are slower but they are status-quo. (Venus will re-stimulate eclipse points from the 11th to the 14th – this will show the financial changes that need to be made, but wait until next month to make them.)

Health is excellent and your interest here will probably enhance it further. Continue to optimize health by paying more attention to the ankles and feet.

February

Best Days Overall: 4, 5, 14, 15, 23, 24

Most Stressful Days Overall: 1, 6, 7, 21, 22, 27, 28

Best Days for Love: 1, 4, 5, 6, 7, 14, 15, 16, 17, 23, 24, 25, 26, 27, 28

Best Days for Money: 1, 4, 5, 9, 10, 14, 15, 16, 17, 19, 20, 23, 24, 27, 28

Monthly Career Peaks: 6, 7, 18, 27, 28

Monthly Personal Pleasure Peaks: 14, 15, 27, 28

The planets start shifting to the upper half of the horoscope this month. Mars will enter your 10th House of Career on the 18th. While you still can't ignore family or emotional concerns, the outer world is calling to you. Your career duties are intense. You need to work hard to maintain your professional status as rivals have their eyes on what you have. Heads could be rolling in your company. But family responsibilities are also strong. A parent or parent figure seems especially difficult. They are impatient and hot tempered, which could be caused partly by health issues.

With the Lord of the 8th House in your 10th House all month, this is a time to 'detox' the career and your attitudes towards it. Eliminate the side issues here and focus on essence – what you want to do, be and achieve.

Most of the planets are still in the West, the social sector of your chart. This month they move into their maximum Western position. Your 7th House of Love becomes very strong after the 19th (40 per cent of the planets are either there or move through there), while your 1st House of Self is empty (only the Moon visits there on the 14th and 15th). Continue to down-play personal interests and focus on others. Mercury, your ruler, enters your 7th House on the 9th, so all of this comes naturally. You are into your yearly social and romantic peak now. The workplace is still the scene of romance, but it could also happen as you pursue your health goals. You seem just as concerned with, and actively involved in, the health of your lover, spouse or friends as you are with your own health. There are many out-of-the-blue romantic meetings and social invitations. Love happens instantly for singles. But stability in love is the great difficulty.

Now that Venus is moving forwards (after the 3rd), finances are better than last month, but they are still not a big issue. Your 2nd House remains, for the most part, empty. Speculations are more favourable this month. Money is earned in happy ways. You are spending on children and leisure as well. Professional investors should look at traditional, blue chip companies and property. Conservative investments seem best. You are always a good shopper, but this month you get real value for money. Your financial judgement is sound and down to earth. You have a good instinct for what things will be worth far into the future.

Venus, your financial planet, re-stimulates eclipse points on the 24th and 26th. This will test your financial thinking and planning and show where changes need to be made.

Health is basically good, but needs more watching after the 19th. Your priority should be keeping energy levels high. Also, enhance your health through foot and ankle massage. Harmonious relationships with your friends, lover or spouse are also very important health-wise.

March

Best Days Overall: 3, 4, 13, 14, 23, 24, 31

Most Stressful Days Overall: 6, 7, 20, 21, 27, 28

VIRGO

Best Days for Love: 4, 5, 6, 7, 15, 16, 25, 26, 27, 28

Best Days for Money: 4, 5, 6, 8, 9, 15, 16, 17, 18, 19, 25, 26, 27, 28

Monthly Career Peaks: 6, 7, 27, 28

Monthly Personal Pleasure Peaks: 13, 27, 28

Fifty to sixty per cent of the planets are in stressful aspect to you this month. And there are two eclipses – one of which has a very strong effect on you. Watch your health and energy levels. Career, family and love pull you in different directions. Don't let them pull you apart. Give each their due and maintain harmony as best you can. You can also enhance health through foot and ankle massage.

The Lunar Eclipse of the 14th occurs in your own sign and seems strong. Reduce your schedule and avoid needless risks. The eclipse will cause you to redefine your personality – a good thing. Impurities in the body can come up for cleansing. As you redefine your personality you will change your image. With Mercury, your ruler, retrograde from the 6th to the 25th, wait a few days before making drastic changes. Since the Moon is your planet of friends, every Lunar Eclipse tends to test and purify friendships, and this one is no different. There could also be dramatic events with your friends and shake-ups in an organization you belong to.

The Solar Eclipse of the 29th is more benign, but it won't hurt to reduce your schedule anyway. These eclipses are usually powerful on a worldly level. In your case, it occurs in the 8th House, bringing dramatic changes in your part-ner's income. These changes probably needed to be made for a long time, and the eclipse supplies the impetus. Finances will have to be reshuffled and reorganized. This eclipse also impacts on the normal level of support you receive from your spouse. On a psychological level, many of you will have to confront death and gain a deeper understanding of it. No-one need literally die – though that can happen – but many people report dreams of death under these eclipses. If you are involved in estate, tax or insurance issues, there is a dramatic turn one way or another, and things start getting resolved.

The social life is still very active and you are having peak social experiences now. Stability in your love life is still the biggest problem. Although singles have opportunities this month, marriage doesn't seem advisable.

Personal finances are still stable. Your financial planet moves into your 6th House on the 6th, showing that money comes in the normal ways, through work. You are probably spending more on health this month – a good thing – and you can also earn from this field. Colleagues have interesting financial ideas. Uncles and aunts seem more supportive.

April

Best Days Overall: 1, 9, 10, 19, 20, 27, 28

Most Stressful Days Overall: 2, 3, 17, 18, 23, 24, 29, 30

Best Days for Love: 2, 3, 12, 13, 14, 15, 21, 22, 23, 24, 29, 30

Best Days for Money: 2, 3, 4, 5, 12, 13, 14, 15, 23, 24

Monthly Career Peaks: 2, 3, 25, 26, 29, 30

Monthly Personal Pleasure Peaks: 9, 10, 25, 26

Like last month, the Western, social sector of the horoscope is stronger than the Eastern, personal sector. Your 7th House of Others is much stronger than your 1st House of Self (which is basically empty except on the 9th and 10th, when the Moon passes through). Continue to adapt to situations, to play down the ego and personal interests, and to focus on other people and your social life in general. Avoid power struggles and undue self-assertion.

VIRGO

You are still well in to your yearly social peak. Venus, the generic ruler of love and romance, enters your 7th House of Love on the 6th. Mercury, your ruler, is there until the 16th. Your personal popularity is at a yearly peak now. You are still going out of your way to please others. Anyone romantically involved with a Virgo these days is getting royal treatment. A business partnership could be in the works.

This month the planets shift from the lower, night side of the chart to the upper, day side. This shift began in February but now it is fully established. By the 6th, 60 to 70 per cent of the planets will be above the horizon. The two planets involved with home and family are retrograde all month to boot. Thus, there is little that can be done with the home and family right now and you may as well focus on your career. With Mars still in the 10th House, it is still very active. The demands are great, and you advance through bold actions and hard work. The pace will slow a bit after the 14th, but your interest in outer achievement is still strong. Though you have to take strong actions this month, you can also enhance your career through social means, by attending or hosting parties and gatherings. You have a good knack for knowing the right people who can help you.

Mars will re-stimulate eclipse points from the 2nd to the 5th and on the 29th and 30th. This is a very dynamic transit for the world at large. Personally, try to avoid risky activities. Also, avoid high-risk activities on the 11th, 12th, 22nd and 23rd, as Mercury, your ruler, re-stimulates eclipse points then too.

Your health still needs watching but is much improved over last month. You can enhance your health in the ways mentioned in previous months.

Happy financial surprises happen from the 17th to the 19th. Money and financial opportunities come from your lover, spouse or partner. You seem very involved in their finances after the 16th. Social connections in general are important financially (just as they are with the career) but money itself is not a big interest. You seem more interested in helping other people to prosper.

With your 8th House strong all month, this is a good time to pay off or refinance debt. It's also good for detox regimes in general, and for getting rid of old and needless possessions, character traits and emotional patterns. Many of you are involved in personal transformation, and this will be an excellent month for this.

May

Best Days Overall: 7, 8, 16, 17, 25, 26

Most Stressful Days Overall: 14, 15, 20, 21, 27, 28

Best Days for Love: 3, 9, 10, 14, 15, 18, 19, 20, 21, 22, 23, 27, 28

Best Days for Money: 2, 3, 9, 10, 12, 13, 14, 15, 20, 21, 22, 23, 29, 30

Monthly Career Peaks: 18, 19, 27, 28

Monthly Personal Pleasure Peaks: 7, 8, 18, 19

Both planets involved with home and family issues are still retrograde. Most of the planets are above the horizon, and your 10th House of Career gets powerful from the 19th onwards. You can safely down-play home and family and focus on the career. From the 19th, you are entering your yearly career peak and you should take advantage of it. Not only is there career success and advancement now, but also more personal honour and recognition. You are almost like a celebrity this month. Many of you will be interested in politics or community affairs. You may be exercising more power and authority too, which is a mixed blessing.

You can also advance your career through involvement with charities and altruistic causes. Psychics, astrologers and ministers have important career guidance for you. Dreams might also be guiding the career.

Your spiritual planet, the Sun, is in the 10th House this month, so deeper things are going on than just worldly success (nothing wrong with that). This month you learn more about your spiritual mission for this life – the reason you were born. This is the true career.

The planets are shifting from the Western, social side of the horoscope to the Eastern, personal side. The shift is not yet complete, but by the 21st you will start feeling more independent again.

Your 8th House is strong again this month. Like last month, prosperity comes as you help others to prosper. This is still a good time to pay off or refinance debt, and to deal with tax and estate issues – indeed, many a financial decision is being influenced by these matters. It is also a good month to 'detox' your financial life by getting rid of waste and needless expense. Venus will re-stimulate eclipse points on the 11th and 12th, revealing any financial changes that need to be made.

Mercury re-stimulates eclipse points on the 30th and 31st, and Mars on the 1st, so avoid unnecessary risks on those days.

Your health needs watching more carefully after the 19th. Keep in mind our discussions in previous months.

Love opportunities come as you pursue career goals this month – bosses and elders enjoy playing cupid. There could be romantic opportunities with bosses too (this has been a trend for the year, but this month it is more pronounced). Your ambition and achievement are attracting romantic opportunities now. But with your love planet going retrograde on the 22nd, there's no need to rush love or make any important decisions here.

June

Best Days Overall: 3, 4, 12, 13, 21, 22, 30

Most Stressful Days Overall: 10, 11, 17, 18, 23, 24

Best Days for Love: 3, 4, 5, 6, 12, 13, 14, 15, 17, 18, 22, 23, 24

Best Days for Money: 3, 4, 5, 6, 8, 9, 12, 13, 17, 18, 22, 25, 26

Monthly Career Peaks: 23, 24

Monthly Personal Pleasure Peaks: 3, 4, 30

Both of the love planets are retrograde this month, and the planetary power is mostly in the independent East. Other people and your social life are important of course, but you are in an independent phase of the year. You've been people pleasing and adapting to others for most of the year, and now it's time to have your own way in life.

Like last month, most of the planets are still above the horizon. Your 10th House of Career is very strong, and you are still in your yearly career peak. And the planets involved with home and family are both retrograde. So, like last month, leave family issues be – there's not much you can do about certain things anyway – and take advantage of the career opportunities that are opening now. Much of what was said last month applies now as well. You can further your career through charitable and altruistic activities. You are learning more about your spiritual mission in life – perhaps the most important thing we can ever know. Career gets a further boost on the 24th when Venus moves into the 10th House. Since Venus is the financial planet, this will often show pay rises at work. It also indicates more career-related travel, and perhaps the company sends you off on training. There are happy educational opportunities happening.

With the financial planet crossing the Midheaven on the 24th and then becoming the most elevated planet in the horoscope, money is important these days. You revere and respect rich people (also highly educated and learned people), and aspire to be like them. A parent will be generous and supportive. Bosses at work also seem supportive. Money can come through government contracts, grants or government employees who are customers. If you are in need of favours from the government, or have issues pending here, try to resolve them after the 24th. Your good professional reputation also pays off this month.

With both the love planets retrograde (Neptune, the actual love planet, is retrograde all month; Uranus in your 7th House of Love goes retrograde on the 19th), love is slowing down. Your social life won't stop dead of course, but you need more caution here. Social judgement is affected by the retrogrades so it's not wise to make important love decisions after the 19th. However, it is a good time to review your love life or your current relationship and see what can be done to improve and perfect them. Singles have love opportunities at work, through friends and organizations, and as they pursue health-related goals.

Mercury, your ruler, re-stimulates eclipse points on the 1st and from the 8th to the 10th so reschedule risky activities. Be more patient with parents or parent figures those days as well, as they can be more temperamental.

July

Best Days Overall: 1, 10, 11, 18, 19, 27, 28, 29

Most Stressful Days Overall: 8, 9, 14, 15, 20, 21

Best Days for Love: 3, 4, 12, 13, 14, 15, 20, 21, 22, 23

Best Days for Money: 3, 4, 5, 6, 12, 13, 14, 15, 22, 23, 24, 30, 31

Monthly Career Peaks: 17, 18, 19, 20, 21, 23, 24

Monthly Personal Pleasure Peaks: 1, 17, 18, 19, 27, 28

Passions seem to be running high at home. Tempers are flaring. Perhaps there are repairs or construction going on. The health of a family member may be a concern (looks like a parent or parent figure or a sibling). These things will require some attention, but continue to focus on your career. Most of the planets are still above the horizon, and your 10th House of Career is strong until the 19th. Deal with any household emergencies that arise but keep your eyes on your career prize. Education will enhance the career this month, so take any opportunities that arise. Social gifts and cultivating the right people will also enhance the career. This is another good month to invest in your career and image.

The planets, like last month, are mostly in the Eastern, personal sector of your chart. On the 21st, dynamic Mars will move into your 1st House. Personal independence has rarely been stronger. The only complication to this is that your ruler, Mercury, will be retrograde from the 3rd to the 29th. With Mars in your own sign, you will be tempted to leap into actions, but Mercury's retrograde suggests caution. This is a time for reviewing the design of your life and planning improvements. Take action after the 29th. Mercury's retrograde also complicates the career. It doesn't stop career, only slows things down. Career offers should be studied more carefully from the 3rd to the 29th. Next month you are guaranteed to have a different perspective on things. The retrograde of the career planet and Venus's move out of your 10th House on the 19th is signalling a soon-to-come psychological shift. Home and family are soon to become more important than career – but not quite yet.

Health is much improved over last month. The retrograde of your health planet for some months cautions against making radical changes to your diet or overall health regime. And this is reinforced by Mercury's retrograde mentioned earlier. Mercury is the generic ruler of health. Continue to enhance health in the ways you've been doing all year – through foot and ankle massage. After the 21st, add some vigorous exercise to the mix (remember to support the ankles as you do so).

Mars in your own sign brings enhanced charisma and personal magnetism. You are more energetic and excel more than usual at sports and exercise. You get things done quickly. Libido and sex appeal are enhanced. Temper, impatience and rashness are the main dangers to watch out for.

With your financial planet still the most elevated in the horoscope all month, finances are a high priority. You want to earn in prestigious and honorable ways, to be known and respected for your financial acumen as well as your education and refinement. And your financial abilities *do* get more recognition this month. Like last month, money can come from a parent or parent figure or government connections. Pay rises often happen under this aspect. After the 19th, money comes through social connections, friends and involvement with organizations and trade associations. Good use of high-tech equipment also enhances earnings. After the 19th, with your financial planet in Cancer, moods play a big role in spending and earning. Avoid making important financial decisions when you feel sad, angry or anxious. Financial intuition – when you are at peace – will be awesome.

Your two love planets are still retrograde so love is slowing down. This is a good period for making internal improvements in this area.

August

Best Days Overall: 6, 7, 14, 15, 24, 25

Most Stressful Days Overall: 4, 5, 10, 11, 17, 18, 31

Best Days for Love: 2, 3, 8, 9, 10, 11, 17, 18, 21, 22, 26, 27, 31

Best Days for Money: 2, 3, 10, 11, 19, 20, 21, 22, 26, 27, 29, 30, 31

Monthly Career Peaks: 17, 18, 21, 22

Monthly Personal Pleasure Peaks: 21, 22, 23, 24, 25

If there ever was a time when personal initiative and direct action were powerful, it is now. Your ruler, Mercury, is moving forwards. Mars is in your own sign. Your 1st House of the Self becomes very strong after the 23rd. And, 60 to 70 per cent of the planets are in the independent East. By now you should be much clearer about your goals and what brings you personal happiness – and mental clarity leads to powerful actions.

This new-found independence and clarity can cause changes at work and in your love life. It will certainly test a current relationship. But with both love planets retrograde, it is not wise to make any major love decision just yet.

This is a time for learning to enjoy the company of the most interesting and fascinating person you know – yourself. It is a good month for going on spiritual retreats, meditation seminars and lectures, and for expanding your inner life. Charitable and altruistic activities are also interesting (especially until the 23rd).

This month, the planetary power shifts to the lower, night side of the horoscope. This happens on the 23rd and becomes established on the 28th. Your 10th House of Career is basically empty this month (except when the Moon visits on the 17th and 18th), while your 4th House of Home and Family is strong. It is time to de-emphasize outer objectives and start focusing on building a stable home base, on strengthening the family relationship and getting back to your personal point of emotional harmony. Feeling right will get you further (though more indirectly) than doing right.

Career opportunities are pursuing you, so there is no need to pay too much attention to this area. After the 28th, they will find you. But now you will be more selective. Opportunities that disturb your family or emotional harmony are best left alone.

This is a month for cultivating financial intuition. It is strong all month. Until the 13th, money and financial opportunity come from family, friends, social connections and involvement with groups, clubs or associations. Good use of high technology also enhances earnings. After the 13th, you become more charitable and philanthropic. This giving opens the channels of financial opportunity even further. Financial guidance will come to you in dreams, hunches or through psychics, astrologers, ministers and the like.

Health is excellent this month. Your personal charisma, magnetism and sex appeal are even stronger than last month. Continue to avoid haste, temper tantrums and impatience. Reschedule any risky activities on the 29th, 30th and 31st when Mars is re-stimulating eclipse points.

September

Best Days Overall: 3, 4, 11, 12, 20, 21, 30

Most Stressful Days Overall: 1, 7, 8, 13, 14, 27, 28, 29

Best Days for Love: 1, 2, 5, 6, 7, 8, 11, 13, 14, 20, 21, 22, 23, 24, 30

Best Days for Money: 1, 2, 7, 8, 11, 15, 16, 20, 21, 22, 23, 24, 25, 26, 30

Monthly Career Peaks: 1, 13, 14, 22, 23, 24

Monthly Personal Pleasure Peaks: 1, 5, 6, 20, 21, 22, 23, 24

For the world at large, the month ahead seems turbulent and eventful. Two simultaneous T-squares and two eclipses are roiling the waters now. Though you need to watch your health – especially around the eclipse periods – your health and energy will be better than for the other mutable signs – Gemini, Sagittarius and Pisces.

The Lunar Eclipse of the 7th occurs in your 7th House of Love and Romance. This will test a current relationship. If the motivations behind this relationship are not pure, it will probably dissolve. True love and commitment will weather the storm. This eclipse also occurs very near your health and work planet, Uranus. This shows job changes in the next six months. You will probably make long-term changes to your diet and health regime over the coming months. Those of you who employ others can expect some upheavals with your staff. There can be dramatic events with aunts, uncles and friends too. Organizations you belong to can also be shaken up. Definitely try to reduce your schedule during this period – a few days before and for a day after.

The Solar Eclipse of the 22nd occurs right on the border of your sign and Libra – the cusp of your 1st and 2nd House. In all probability, the affairs of both houses will be affected. Thus you are making important (and long needed) financial changes, motivated by a wake-up call from the cosmos. Like the last eclipse in your sign in March, your body, image and self-concept will change. You will redefine your personality (basically a good thing), and reflect this in the changes you make to your appearance.

Health-wise you are reasonable this month. Many planets in your own sign enhance your energy and vitality. But with so much turbulence around, you might overdo things, pushing your body beyond its capacity. This is especially likely until the 8th, as Mars is still in your sign. Continue to enhance your health in the ways described in previous months.

Finances are active and basically happy this month. The eclipse on the 22nd will shake things up, but prosperity is still strong. Financial opportunities are running after you from the 6th. You will be purchasing expensive personal items – and this is probably a good investment. Your appearance is a big factor in earnings now. The 2nd House of Finance becomes very strong after the 23rd. If you are married, there is good support from your spouse. Your line of credit will probably increase. Money can come from insurance, estate or tax issues. Outside investors – and outside capital – are much easier to obtain now. Financial intuition has been important for some months now and the trend continues. Continue your charitable giving.

Love is turbulent and stressful. But out of this chaos, order and beauty will eventually come. Your sense of independence is unusually strong – basically a good thing – but you are not in the mood for compromise, and neither is your partner or lover. The love situation should start to clarify after the 23rd.

Like last month, most of the planets are below the horizon, and the other family planet, Pluto in your 4th House, starts moving forwards on the 4th. The family situation becomes clearer and things can get resolved now. Pay more attention here and less emphasis to the career.

October

Best Days Overall: 1, 8, 9, 17, 18, 19, 27, 28

Most Stressful Days Overall: 4, 5, 10, 11, 25, 26

Best Days for Love: 2, 3, 4, 5, 10, 11, 20, 21, 22, 29, 30

Best Days for Money: 2, 3, 4, 5, 10, 11, 12, 13, 14, 20, 21, 22, 23, 24

Monthly Career Peaks: 10, 11, 20, 21, 22, 23, 30, 31

Monthly Personal Pleasure Peaks: 17, 18, 19, 20, 21, 22, 23, 30, 31

Finance and intellectual interests are the main headlines this month. You are in your yearly financial peak, which began on September 23rd. Forty to fifty per cent of the planets are either in or moving through your money house – awesome power and energy. Earning power, and your personal interest in finance, is unusually strong. Financial intuition is still very powerful, especially until the 23rd. Psychics, mystics, astrologers and ministers have important financial guidance for you. Support from spouses remains strong. Borrowing power is good. Outside investors are there if you have need (and good ideas). You seem more of a risk-taker than usual this period, but as long as you calculate your risks, you should be OK. Financial success could happen suddenly and quickly this month.

After the 24th, your financial planet moves into your 3rd House and the sign of Scorpio. Thus sales, marketing and communication also become important to earnings. Getting the word out about your product or service becomes important, and it looks like you will be able to do this successfully. Many of you are acquiring new computers, phones, cars or communication equipment.

After the 23rd it is good to expand your mind, to take courses in subjects that interest you, and for teaching or lecturing in your own area of expertise. You could also use this period to catch up on your correspondence and make those phone calls you need to make. Try to do all these things before the 28th, when Mercury (the generic ruler of these things) starts to move retrograde.

Like last month, most of the planets are below the horizon, in the night side of your horoscope. Your 10th House of Career is basically empty (only the Moon visits there on the 10th and 11th, your monthly career peak). So, though you don't need to quit your job or ignore the career completely, it is wise to shift more emphasis to the home and family. This seems active and basically happy this month. A move, renovation or redecoration could happen now – after the 23rd. A sibling is prospering and can be a bit brash these days. A parent or parent figure is more temperamental, as are children. Emotions can run high at home, and it will be useful to look at the origin of these passions as they tend to have their roots in old childhood memories. This is a good month for psychological progress (as are the next few months).

Health is wonderful now, but will get even better after the 23rd. You can enhance it further in the ways described in the yearly report.

Love is improving this month. Either your current relationship survived the past few months and is now more harmonious, or you have moved on to something new and better. Your love planet starts moving forwards (after many months of retrograde motion) on the 23rd, and this will be a turning point. Love opportunities come as you pursue financial goals and intellectual interests.

Most of the planets are still in the East so continue to create your life as you desire it to be.

November

Best Days Overall: 5, 13, 14, 15, 23, 24

Most Stressful Days Overall: 1, 7, 8, 21, 22, 28, 29

Best Days for Love: 1, 7, 8, 9, 10, 16, 17, 21, 26, 27, 28, 29, 30

Best Days for Money: 1, 2, 9, 10, 16, 17, 20, 21, 30

Monthly Career Peaks: 7, 8, 9, 19, 20

Monthly Personal Pleasure Peaks: 7, 8, 9, 13, 14, 15

The main headline this month is the unusual power in your 3rd and 4th Houses. The 3rd House of Communication and Intellectual Interests is the strongest in the horoscope. Sixty per cent of the planets are either there or moving through there. This greatly enhances your communication abilities and intellectual power. However, with Mercury retrograde

233

until the 18th, it's best to initiate lectures or marketing projects afterwards. Students should do better in school as learning requires less effort. This is still a great period for taking courses in subjects that interest you.

The 4th House of Home and Family will have 50 per cent of the planets either there or moving through. Also, 70 to 80 per cent of the planets are below the horizon, further intensifying your interest in family and emotional harmony. Jupiter will move into your 4th House on the 24th and stay there well into 2007. Like last month, moves could happen now – happy moves. Your present home increases in value. Expensive items come for the home. Your family circle is expanding. Financial opportunity comes from the family or family connections – and you are spending on the family and the home. There is great optimism and joy here. There will probably be family gatherings, perhaps celebrations that bring everyone together. Your ability to dream and visualize is stronger, and you can use this ability to enhance your career.

Health is excellent until the 24th, but then you need to watch it more carefully. After the 24th, 50 per cent of the planets will be in difficult aspect with you. This doesn't mean sickness, but with less energy you become more vulnerable. During this period, enhance your health through foot and ankle massage, but also pay more attention to the heart. Of course, the most important thing is to rest when tired and keep your energy levels high.

Finances are not that important this month. The money house is empty – only the Moon will visit on the 16th and 17th. You have probably attained financial goals in the past few months and now you are sated. Sales, marketing and media activities are still important until the 17th. After that, family members and connections are the source of earnings or opportunities. Your financial planet will re-stimulate eclipse points on the 29th and 30th, and these could be days when the cosmos reminds you that important changes need to be made. Looks like there are job changes after the 22nd.

Love is improving. It's far from perfect, but nothing you can't handle. Your other love planet, Uranus in your 7th House, starts moving forwards on the 20th, and from then on both love planets are in forward motion. Social judgement and confidence are back to normal levels. The main challenge in love is instability.

December

Best Days Overall: 2, 3, 11, 12, 21, 22, 29, 30

Most Stressful Days Overall: 4, 5, 18, 19, 25, 26, 31

Best Days for Love: 1, 4, 5, 9, 10, 11, 13, 14, 21, 22, 23, 24, 25, 26, 29, 30

Best Days for Money: 1, 4, 8, 9, 10, 11, 13, 14, 15, 18, 21, 22, 27, 29, 30

Monthly Career Peaks: 4, 5, 10, 18, 19

Monthly Personal Pleasure Peaks: 10, 11, 12

You've really got to watch your health now Virgo. Seventy to eighty per cent of the planets are in stressful alignment with you. Rarely, in your life, have you ever faced this kind of thing (most people never face it). If you are able to go on holiday for a while, that would be best – a healing spa would be wonderful. But if you can't, you will have to minimize activities. Do what needs to be done and then rest and rejuvenate. Pay more attention to the heart (like last month) and to the feet and ankles. Regular massages or reflexology treatments would also be wonderful. Don't judge yourself by lack of career or financial progress either. This month is not about making millions or becoming a celebrity – it's about getting through.

Health will improve dramatically after the 22nd, but still needs some watching.

As you take steps to improve your health and energy, you will also attract romance into your life.

Home, family and domestic issues are still the major headline this month. Career can be down-played. Moves, renovations and major family gatherings are happening now (more so than the usual holiday gatherings). Family matters are happy but probably taxing on your energy. Many core emotional issues will come up this month – a wonderful thing as you can observe and correct them.

The planets make an important shift this month, moving to the West after many months in the East. Personal independence is lessened. Now the cosmos wants you to develop your social skills and gifts.

Many planets are re-stimulating eclipse points this month. This has a great impact on the world at large. It also highlights the need for a holiday, time off or a reduction of your schedule.

For you, the days to be most watchful are the 17th to the 19th and the 26th to the 28th – when Mercury, your ruler, re-stimulates eclipse points. Finances can get more turbulent from the 9th to the 12th, when your financial planet re-stimulates eclipse points. If financial thinking is not right, you will find out about it on these days.

Libra

♎

THE SCALES
*Birthdays from
23rd September to
22nd October*

Personality Profile

LIBRA AT A GLANCE

Element – Air

Ruling Planet – Venus
   Career Planet – Moon
   Love Planet – Mars
   Money Planet – Pluto
   Planet of Communications – Jupiter
   Planet of Health and Work – Neptune
   Planet of Home and Family Life – Saturn
   Planet of Spirituality and Good Fortune –
   Mercury

Colours – blue, jade green

*Colours that promote love, romance and social
   harmony* – carmine, red, scarlet

Colours that promote earning power –
burgundy, red-violet, violet

Gems – carnelian, chrysolite, coral, emerald,
jade, opal, quartz, white marble

Metal – copper

Scents – almond, rose, vanilla, violet

Quality – cardinal (= activity)

Qualities most needed for balance – a sense of
self, self-reliance, independence

Strongest virtues – social grace, charm, tact,
diplomacy

Deepest needs – love, romance, social harmony

Characteristic to avoid – violating what is right
in order to be socially accepted

Signs of greatest overall compatibility – Gemini,
Aquarius

Signs of greatest overall incompatibility – Aries,
Cancer, Capricorn

Sign most helpful to career – Cancer

Sign most helpful for emotional support – Capricorn

Sign most helpful financially – Scorpio

Sign best for marriage and/or partnerships – Aries

Sign most helpful for creative projects – Aquarius

Best Sign to have fun with – Aquarius

Signs most helpful in spiritual matters – Gemini,
Virgo

Best day of the week – Friday

Understanding a Libra

In the Sign of Libra the universal mind – the soul – expresses its genius for relationships, that is, its power to harmonize diverse elements in a unified, organic way. Libra is the soul's power to express beauty in all of its forms. And where is beauty if not within relationships? Beauty does not exist in isolation. Beauty arises out of comparison – out of the just relationship between different parts. Without a fair and harmonious relationship there is no beauty, whether it be in art, manners, ideas or the social or political forum.

There are two faculties humans have that exalt them above the animal kingdom: their rational faculty (expressed in the Signs of Gemini and Aquarius) and their aesthetic faculty, exemplified by Libra. Without an aesthetic sense we would be little more than intelligent barbarians. Libra is the civilizing instinct or urge of the soul.

Beauty is the essence of what Librans are all about. They are here to beautify the world. One could discuss Librans' social grace, their sense of balance and fair play, their ability to see and love another person's point of view – but this would be to miss their central asset: their desire for beauty.

No one – no matter how alone he or she seems to be – exists in isolation. The universe is one vast collaboration of beings. Librans, more than most, understand this and understand the spiritual laws that make relationships bearable and enjoyable.

A Libra is always the unconscious (and in some cases conscious) civilizer, harmonizer and artist. This is a Libra's deepest urge and greatest genius. Librans love instinctively to bring people together, and they are uniquely qualified to do so. They have a knack for seeing what unites people – the things that attract and bind rather than separate individuals.

Finance

In financial matters Librans can seem frivolous and illogical to others. This is because Librans appear to be more concerned with earning money for others than for themselves. But there is a logic to this financial attitude. Librans know that everything and everyone is connected and that it is impossible to help another to prosper without also prospering yourself. Since enhancing their partner's income and position tends to strengthen their relationship, Librans choose to do so. What could be more fun than building a relationship? You will rarely find a Libra enriching him- or herself at someone else's expense.

Scorpio is the Ruler of Libra's Solar 2nd House of Money, giving Libra unusual insight into financial matters – and the power to focus on these matters in a way that disguises a seeming indifference. In fact, many other Signs come to Librans for financial advice and guidance.

Given their social grace, Librans often spend great sums of money on entertaining and organizing social events. They also like to help others when they are in need. Librans would go out of their way to help a friend in dire straits, even if they have to borrow from others to do so. However, Librans are also very careful to pay back any debts they owe, and like to make sure they never have to be reminded to do so.

Career and Public Image

Publicly, Librans like to appear as nurturers. Their friends and acquaintances are their family and they wield political power in parental ways. They also like bosses who are paternal or maternal.

The Sign of Cancer is on Libra's 10th House (of Career) cusp; the Moon is Libra's Career Planet. The Moon is by far the speediest, most changeable planet in the Horoscope. It alone among all the planets travels through the entire Zodiac – all 12 Signs and Houses – every month. This is an important key to the way in which Librans approach their careers, and also to what they need to do to maximize their career potential. The Moon is the Planet of Moods and Feelings – Librans need a career in which their emotions can have free expression. This is why so many Librans are involved in the creative arts. Libra's ambitions wax and wane with the Moon. They tend to wield power according to their mood.

The Moon 'rules' the masses – and that is why Libra's highest goal is to achieve a mass kind of acclaim and popularity. Librans who achieve fame cultivate the public as other people cultivate a lover or friend. Librans can be very flexible – and often fickle – in their career and ambitions. On the other hand, they can achieve their ends in a great variety of ways. They are not stuck in one attitude or with one way of doing things.

Love and Relationships

Librans express their true genius in love. In love you could not find a partner more romantic, more seductive or more fair. If there is one thing that is sure to destroy a relationship – sure to block your love from flowing – it is injustice or imbalance between lover and beloved. If one party is giving too much or taking too much, resentment is sure to surface at some time or other. Librans are careful about this. If anything, Librans might err on the side of giving more, but never giving less.

If you are in love with a Libra make sure you keep the aura of romance alive. Do all the little things – candle-lit dinners, travel to exotic locales, flowers and small gifts. Give things that are beautiful, not necessarily expensive. Send cards. Ring regularly even if you have nothing in particular to say. The niceties are very important to a Libra. Your relationship is a work of art: make it beautiful and your Libra lover will appreciate it. If you are creative about it, he or she will appreciate it even more; for this is how your Libra will behave towards you.

Librans like their partners to be aggressive and even a bit self-willed. They know that these are qualities they sometimes lack and so they like their partners to have them. In relationships, however, Librans can be very aggressive – but always in a subtle and charming way! Librans are determined in their efforts to charm the object of their desire – and this determination can be very pleasant if you are on the receiving end.

Home and Domestic Life

Since Librans are such social creatures, they do not particularly like mundane domestic duties. They like a well-organized home – clean and neat with everything needful present – but housework is a chore and a burden, one of the unpleasant tasks in life that must be done, the quicker the better. If a Libra has enough money – and sometimes even if not – he or she will prefer to pay someone else to take care of the daily household chores. However, Librans like gardening; they love to have flowers and plants in the home.

A Libra's home is modern, and furnished in excellent taste. You will find many paintings and sculptures there. Since Librans like to be with friends and family, they enjoy entertaining at home and they make great hosts.

Capricorn is on the cusp of Libra's 4th Solar House of Home and Family. Saturn, the Planet of Law, Order, Limits and Discipline, rules Libra's domestic affairs. If Librans want their home life to be supportive and happy they need to develop some of the virtues of Saturn – order, organization and discipline. Librans, being so creative and so intensely in need of harmony, can tend to be too lax in the home and too permissive with their children. Too much of this is not always good; children need freedom but they also need limits.

Horoscope for 2006

General Trends

Although 2005 had some difficulties, it turned out to be a prosperous year. This prosperity continues in the year ahead too.

Personal creativity was extraordinary – inspired – in 2005, and this will continue in 2006.

Now that Saturn has moved away from its stressful aspect to you (on July 17th 2005), you feel as if weights have dropped from your shoulders, burdens and fetters removed. You have more strength, more energy, and you are ready to soar.

The stern, character-building lessons you've been getting over the past two years are over. The planetary genies have done their job. You're a stronger, more disciplined, more secure person now. Prosperity will come and you will handle it properly. (Many people can't handle it, and when it comes it actually leaves them worse off than before – but this is not the case with you.) You are ready for new expansions of your horizons.

Your most important areas of interest in the year ahead will be finance (until November 24th); intellectual interests and communication (all year, but especially after November 24th); children, creativity and fun; health and work; friendships, groups and group activities.

Your paths to greatest fulfilment in the year ahead are finance (until November 24th; intellectual interests and communication (after November 24th); love and romance (until June 23rd); health and work (after June 23rd).

Health

(Please note that this is an astrological perspective on health, not a medical one. At one time, both perspectives were identical, but in these times there could be quite a difference. For the medical perspective, please consult your physician or health professional.)

Personal health is much improved over the past two years. Saturn in the sign of Cancer from 2003 to 2005 was stressing you out. Now Saturn is making harmonious aspects to you, as are most of the other long-term planets.

When energy levels are naturally high, disease flees far away. And this is the situation now. The habits of efficiency you learned in the past two years will further increase your energy levels. You will be able to achieve any goal you set for yourself.

What's interesting here is that your 6th House of Health is very strong. And, after June 23rd, the 6th House and its affairs becomes a path of fulfilment for you. Though your health is good, you enjoy health regimes and a healthy lifestyle for their own sake and because you feel they will prevent problems in the future.

There is an amazing connection between your health and fun/joy this year. The Lord of the 5th House (fun) is in your 6th House of Health. The Lord of the 6th House (Health) is in your 5th House of Fun. This is highly unusual.

But there are also other messages here. Many of you will be involved not in your own health but in healing others, especially children (5th House). And practising this healing will bring great fulfilment.

The 5th House also rules creativity, something with which you are naturally endowed. So, a creative hobby will also enhance your already good health. (Blocked creativity could also be the source of health problems these days – another good reason to indulge.)

If health problems arise, check out your relationship with the children – this could also be a cause. If you clear that up, chances are the health problem will dissolve by itself. (The children seem rebellious these days.)

Exercises that involve music and dancing – perhaps like aerobics – also seem powerful.

The health of a parent or parent figure seems delicate this year. Perhaps they are having surgery – but a good detox regime might do just as well. They need to give special attention to the sexual organs, colon, bladder, liver and thighs. The health of siblings seems stable. Children's health – though you seem concerned – appears good. They benefit from experimental and cutting-edge therapies. The health of grandchildren is vastly improved over previous years. If there have been problems in the past, you should hear good news this year.

Home, Domestic and Family Issues

Your 4th House of Home and Family hasn't been a house of power for many years – neither is it this year. The cosmos is pushing you neither one way nor another. Home and family issues seem status-quo. You will probably stay in your present home under the same kind of arrangement and circumstance.

Last year (July 17th) your family planet, Saturn, made a very important move from your 10th House into your 11th. It will be there for the next two years. This is suggesting many things. You are probably installing high-tech gadgetry in the home. Your attitude to family members is friendlier and more detached, and you are giving them more space. Perhaps the home is becoming more democratic. Probably the most important thing you are doing is building a team spirit at home. You will be experimenting in other ways as well. All of this should be educational in the long run.

A parent or parent figure has this attitude with you as well – you're not their child but a pal, an associate, a peer and an equal.

With slow-moving Saturn as your family planet, these are long-term trends.

If you're doing construction work in the home, June 3rd to August 23rd is a good time. If you're decorating, February 3rd to March 5th and August 12th to September 6th are good times. These are also good periods for entertaining from home.

A parent or parent figure faces some disruption – perhaps a major repair – in the home early in the year. A move wouldn't be a surprise either. Siblings could have multiple moves this year and seem rebellious with the rest of the family. The home and family life of adult children and grandchildren is stable. (Grandchildren could have moved in 2004.)

Love and Social Life

Your 7th House of Love and Romance is not a house of power this year, Libra, so though you have a natural interest in these things, this year it will be less so. There are many ways to read this. One (and the most obvious) is that you are more or less content with your relationships as they are and have no need to make extraordinary efforts here. Since most of you are born with a strong interest in this department, this can easily translate to social success and happiness in the year ahead. Also, the Moon's North Node in your 7th House (until June 23rd) shows that this is an area of great fulfilment in your life. So, though interest is less than in most years, it's still good to exercise your free will here.

A current relationship is being tested for the early part of the year. Until March 29th you are still under the influence of the Lunar Eclipse of October 17th 2005 (which occurred in your 7th House of Love). On March 29th, there is a Solar

Eclipse in your 7th House, which will be in effect for about six months. I doubt whether this will cause a marital break-up but the relationship is adjusting, getting purified. True love will always survive these things but impure love might not. An eclipse in the 7th House often signals discontent with the current status. A current relationship must either go forwards or end.

Singles are shown the reasons for their single status so that they can correct them. Uncommitted love affairs seem much more interesting than serious relationships. And there will be plenty of opportunities in the year ahead. These seem to happen at the workplace, with colleagues, bosses or employees. Also, as you pursue your health goals or perhaps with people involved in your health.

Your most active and happy social periods in the year ahead will be from March 20th to April 19th, from May 5th to 29th, and from September 8th to November 25th. This latter period brings an important opportunity for those working on their first marriage. The question is whether you will take the opportunity. This person is pursuing you ardently and tries to sweep you off your feet.

Those in or working on the second marriage have a status-quo year. Marrieds will tend to stay married and singles will tend to stay single. Those working on the third marriage need more patience for the next few years. Love is there – looks like someone older and more established than you – but this needs a lot of time to develop. Rushing romance or marriage is not advisable. This seems to be a 'head' kind of relationship rather than a 'heart' one. But will your romantic ideals be satisfied?

Children of marriageable age shouldn't marry this year. They need to get real about what they want in love. In general, their social lives seem more restricted. The cosmos wants them to focus on the quality rather than the quantity of their relationships. Grandchildren of marriageable age could marry this year or next. A very serious relationship begins to manifest itself after November 24th. Siblings have a stable year socially. The marriage of the parents or parent figures in your life is status-quo.

With Mars as your love planet, romantic opportunities will tend to come in various ways over the course of a year.

Finance and Career

Your social life might be slower this year but the action is now in finance and the attainment of wealth.

Your 2nd House of Finance has been strong and important since October 27th 2005 when benevolent Jupiter moved into this house. With Jupiter, everything is larger than life. Thus the financial goals this year are huge. You are not thinking about survival, earning your living, your daily bread – oh no! You want BIG wealth and you want it now. And you will make very important progress towards this goal in the year ahead.

Not only is Jupiter in your money house, but Jupiter and your financial planet, Pluto, are in 'mutual reception' – guests in each other's houses and signs and co-operating very well with each other. This shows an inheritance or trust fund, an ability to attract outside investors to your projects, and easy access to outside capital. It shows a good instinct for the bond market and an especially good instinct for profiting from troubled, even bankrupt, companies, distressed properties or situations.

Communication, writing, sales, marketing and media are also very important on the financial level this year. This has been the case for many years now (as Pluto, your financial planet, has been in your 3rd House) but this year even more so. For Jupiter, besides being the planet of abundance, is also the Lord of your 3rd House of Communication. Many of you will profit with your mind rather than your body. Many will teach and lecture. Many will write. Many will be involved with the journalistic media. If you have a product, the important thing now is to get the word out about it. Siblings and neighbours seem very co-operative and supportive financially. Financial opportunities happen locally and can also be found in educational settings.

Married Librans should get good financial support from their spouse.

When Jupiter is in the money house, wealth often comes without effort. Assets you own start increasing in value. Your house is suddenly worth more. Your portfolio increases in value though you did nothing in particular to make it happen.

Professional investors should look at telecommunications, transportation, media companies, bonds and travel companies. Investments in foreign companies also look interesting.

Jobseekers have some instability this year. There could be multiple job changes. Also, your workplace is like a game of musical chairs with employees coming and going. Those who employ others are learning lessons in employee change this year.

The main attraction for jobseekers is the fun aspect of the job. And this could be the reason for the many job changes we see. You will take the more enjoyable job rather than the highest paying or more prestigious one.

Career and professional status don't seem like big issues. You are more bottom-line oriented. Glory is wonderful, but you'll take the cash. (Hopefully you'll be able to have both.)

Adult children are prospering – and sometimes in a BIG way – but there is great instability. They are taking enormous risks. They will have a few failures, but when they hit, it will be big. Grandchildren of appropriate age have a status-quo financial year. The income of the spouse and parents seems stable as well. Siblings start to prosper more than usual after November 24th.

Self-improvement

As mentioned earlier, the joy of the job is an important factor for you this year – and also for many years in the future. In many cases this will lead to fun types of jobs, and there's nothing wrong with that. But from the perspective of self-improvement, there is something deeper to be learned here. It's about bringing inner joy to your work, whatever it happens to be. Since joy is an impersonal force – always available to everyone – spiritually speaking our job is to put joy into life, into the world. It's not about getting it from the world. Attaining joy and happiness is a spiritual choice. You are like a pipe – you allow joy in from the Divine, and let it flow through you into the world. When you can do this, you are causing the world – and especially your job and workplace – to be more joyful, and by the karmic law, joy will come back to you. So the cosmic message for you is this: never mind the actual nature of your job, bring joy into it, make it fun. This is true creativity. You become ever more independent of conditions.

Saturn, the stern but loving teacher, is bringing order to your friendships this year. No question, there is a need for this in your life now. He knows how to do this. Medicine doesn't usually taste good, but its effect is beneficial. You might have some disappointments with friends. Perhaps they let you down, are not there for you when you need them. Perhaps some are jealous about your financial success. It can be painful at times to confront this but the stern teacher is applying tough love here. You probably thought that just having lots of friends was a good thing. Libra tends to think so. But Saturn is saying it's not how many you have, but the quality of the friendship that matters. So this is a year where you learn this lesson. Saturn is going to help you weed out the true from the false and the warm from the lukewarm. Saturn is going to show you that a few really good friendships are better than hordes of lukewarm ones.

He will also teach you the art of true forgiveness, which can come only from understanding. Only when we understand why so-and-so behaved a certain way can we truly forgive – in a deep and organic way. Forgiveness with the mouth means very little. It has to be deeper than that.

Month-by-month Forecasts

January

Best Days Overall: 1, 2, 10, 11, 20, 21, 29, 30

Most Stressful Days Overall: 6, 7, 12, 13, 14, 27, 28

Best Days for Love: 6, 7, 8, 9, 17, 18, 19, 27, 28

Best Days for Money: 3, 4, 7, 12, 13, 15, 22, 23, 25, 31

Monthly Career Peaks: 12, 13, 14, 29

Monthly Personal Pleasure Peaks: 13, 14, 15, 20, 21, 27, 28

The planets began shifting to the Western, social sector of your horoscope last month. By the 4th of this month, the shift is established with 60 to 70 per cent of the planets in the West. So this is a time to practise and develop your favourite gift – social skills. It is time to live with the conditions you created during the past six months. Later on, in about six months, you will be able to make corrections.

Further weakening your sense of independence is the rare retrograde of your ruler all month. This is a good month to review personal goals – especially issues involving the body, image and personal appearance – and see where improvements can be made. Avoid making drastic or expensive changes to your image this month. Wait until next month when, guaranteed, you will have a different perspective.

The year begins with most of the planets below the horizon, in the night side of your horoscope. Your 10th House of Career is basically empty (only the Moon visits there on the 12th, 13th and 14th), while your 4th House of Home and Family is a house of power. So the message is clear: downplay the career and focus on the home and family.

You are in a very powerful financial year overall, and prosperity is strong this month. As we have seen for a long time, the communication, sales, marketing and media fields seem most powerful. This month, financial opportunities come from the family, parents or parent figures, and people who are like family to you. Finances become a bit more stressful after the 20th – prosperity is still intact, but you are working harder for it. You will definitely see the fruits of your labours.

Although health is generally good this year, try to rest and relax more until the 20th. After that, energy and vitality zoom to new highs. Enhance health by paying more attention to the heart (until the 20th) and to the feet and ankles (all month).

Though your spouse or a current love seems at odds with a sibling, you don't seem personally affected. Your partner is very involved in finance this month. There is good financial co-operation between you. The Grand Square pattern we see all month seems to involve your spouse or partner more than you. They are involved in a major project that is stressful but fulfilling. They need to watch their health more after the 20th, and maintaining energy levels is important.

Singles can find love opportunities in weird places this month – at funerals, wakes, the surgeon's or broker's office. Love is about passion. After the 20th, you are in a more playful and free mood. Singles have lots of unserious opportunities, which could stress a current relationship.

Venus, your ruler, will re-stimulate eclipse points from the 11th to the 14th. There's no need to indulge in risky behaviour during this period.

LIBRA

February

Best Days Overall: 6, 7, 16, 17, 25, 26

Most Stressful Days Overall: 2, 3, 9, 10, 23, 24

Best Days for Love: 2, 3, 4, 5, 14, 15, 23, 24, 25

Best Days for Money: 1, 2, 9, 10, 11, 19, 20, 21, 27, 28

Monthly Career Peaks: 9, 10, 27

Monthly Personal Pleasure Peaks: 16, 17, 23, 24

Like last month, most of the planets are still in the West, and the thrust of the month is other people and getting on with them. This period is an opportunity for you to sharpen your already strong social skills.

Personal confidence is coming back after the 3rd as Venus, your ruler, starts moving forwards again, so after the 4th is a better time to make drastic changes to your image.

Like last month, most of the planets are still in the night side (lower half) of the horoscope. Your 10th House of Career is, for the most part, empty. Only the Moon will make a brief visit there on the 9th and 10th – and this will be a monthly career peak. Your 4th House of Home and Family, by contrast, is very strong as your ruler is there all month. So the focus should continue to be on the home front, on feeling good, and on establishing and strengthening your home base.

Prosperity is still happening but, like last month, you are working harder for it. But with your money house very strong, you have the drive and the interest to succeed. Jobseekers have success all month. Social connections are a good source of work.

Love still seems stressful and unstable. Singles will have a hard time making long-term social plans. There could be major dramas and upheavals in love towards the end of the month. Love is still about passion and emotional intensity

253

until the 18th. Physical magnetism and sexual attraction seem most important for singles. But after the 18th you seem more interested in mental and philosophical harmony with the beloved. A person's education will be a big factor for singles. Foreigners or people of different cultures have greater allure, as do mentor types, such as teachers and professors. Love opportunities (after the 18th) can come in foreign lands or in educational or religious surroundings.

Your spouse or present love is still out of harmony with siblings or neighbours – finances could be at the root of this dispute. This discord could explode if they don't tone things down.

Health is good this month. You are likely to get involved in healthy diets, health regimes and lifestyles, not because of sickness. You're just interested.

Librans are always creative people, and this month even more so. The many artists among you are having an exceptional month. It is also more of a fun month – a month for working to be sure, but also for playing.

March

Best Days Overall: 6, 7, 15, 16, 17, 25, 26

Most Stressful Days Overall: 1, 2, 8, 9, 23, 24, 29, 30

Best Days for Love: 1, 2, 4, 5, 6, 7, 15, 16, 17, 25, 26, 29, 30

Best Days for Money: 2, 8, 9, 11, 12, 18, 19, 21, 27, 28, 29

Monthly Career Peaks: 8, 9

Monthly Personal Pleasure Peaks: 15, 16, 17, 25, 26

An eventful and turbulent month ahead, Libra. Love, friendships, finance and career are the main areas concerned.

A Solar Eclipse on the 29th occurs in your 7th House of Love. Mars, the love planet, is in stressful aspect with

Uranus, the planet of sudden change, from the 10th to the 13th, and receiving a very stressful aspect from Pluto, the planet of death and transformation, towards the end of the month. A current love relationship could survive, but it will have a 'near death' experience. True love and real commitment will survive any crisis, but anything less is in danger.

Health needs more watching after the 20th, but especially around the period of the Solar Eclipse on the 29th. Definitely reduce your schedule during that period – a few days before and for a day after. Enhance health through foot and ankle massage and taking better care of the heart (after the 20th).

The Solar Eclipse of the 29th also tests friendships. It can bring dramas in the lives of friends as well. It can also bring much-needed disruption to organizations you belong to. These are all preludes to long-term change.

The Lunar Eclipse of the 14th has a more benign effect on you, but it won't hurt to reduce your commitments anyway. Every Lunar Eclipse brings career change, and this one is no different. And, since the planets are getting ready to shift to the upper, day side of your horoscope (they're not quite there yet) this eclipse is probably announcing a new attitude towards the career – you are going to start becoming more ambitious. These kinds of eclipses often show reshuffles in the corporate hierarchy at work. And since this eclipse is impacting on Pluto, your financial planet, you are being forced to make long-needed financial changes. If you are involved in estate or insurance issues, this eclipse marks an important turning point.

This eclipse occurs in your 12th House of Spirituality. For those of you on a spiritual path, it shows changes in your guru, meditation practice or overall spiritual regime. Those of you not on a path might embark on one these days.

April

Best Days Overall: 2, 3, 11, 12, 13, 21, 29, 30

Most Stressful Days Overall: 4, 5, 19, 20, 25, 26

Best Days for Love: 2, 3, 13, 14, 15, 23, 24, 25, 26

Best Days for Money: 4, 5, 8, 14, 15, 18, 23, 24, 26

Monthly Career Peaks: 4, 5, 27

Monthly Personal Pleasure Peaks: 12, 13, 18, 23, 24, 29

Though most of the planets are still below the horizon, your career is becoming ever more important. First off, the power in the night side is lessened, as two planets have moved above the horizon. Second, your 10th House of Career gets powerful after the 14th as Mars moves there. So, home, family and emotional harmony are still important but you will be juggling more with the career.

Most of the planets are still in the Western, social sector, and your 7th House of Love is very strong. Also, the love planet has been the most elevated planet in the horoscope for some time now, but this month it reaches its culmination. Love and social activities are the main headline this month. You are in your yearly social peak. If a current love relationship survived last month, it will probably survive the crisis of the 5th to the 9th. But if not, there are plenty of happy social opportunities in the offing.

With the love planet so elevated now, you value relationships more than usual, and this will help a current relationship survive. Those who are currently uninvolved can find love opportunities in the usual places. Love can also be found as you pursue career goals (after the 14th). You are mingling with people of power and prestige these days, and there are love opportunities with these kinds of people. If you are married, your spouse is very ambitious and is perhaps receiving career recognition. They are supportive of your own career too. However, they want you to look up to them. You seem more able to do this after the 6th.

Your ruler, Venus, moves into the spiritual and hypersensitive sign of Pisces on the 6th. Your love feelings are very tender and idealistic. The only problem here is that this sensitivity brings more pain.

But this sensitivity also brings good things. Personal healing power is expanded. You are more service-oriented and more interested in diet, exercise, health regimes and healthy lifestyles because they make you look better. This interest is good because health does need more watching this month, at least until the 20th.

There can be job changes this month, and sudden opportunities will happen. Finances are strong, but the two planets involved with finance are retrograde, slowing things down a bit. More homework needs to be done in your financial life, especially regarding investments or major purchases. Prosperity, however, is still intact.

May

Best Days Overall: 9, 10, 18, 19, 27, 28

Most Stressful Days Overall: 2, 3, 16, 17, 22, 23, 29, 30

Best Days for Love: 2, 3, 12, 13, 14, 15, 20, 21, 22, 23, 29, 30

Best Days for Money: 2, 3, 5, 12, 13, 15, 20, 21, 23, 29, 30, 31

Monthly Career Peaks: 2, 3, 27, 29, 30

Monthly Personal Pleasure Peaks: 9, 10, 22, 23

Career becomes ever more important now. It is important in its own right and it is the centre of your social life these days. On the 4th, your ruler, Venus, crosses from the lower, night side of the horoscope to the upper, day side. Now the upper side dominates both in quantity (50 to 60 per cent of the planets are there) and in quality (the most important planets in the horoscope are there). Your 10th House of Career is strong, while your 4th House of Home and Family is basically empty – only the Moon visits there briefly on the 16th and 17th. So this is a career-oriented month.

Most of the planets are still in the West, the social sector of your chart. Venus, your ruler, is in your 7th House from the 4th onwards. Another very social month. Like last month, romantic opportunities come as you pursue your career goals and with people involved in your career. Those of you already married or in a relationship will find that your spouse or lover is supporting your career (though they have different ideas about it to you!). Singles will have love opportunities with bosses and people above them in status.

In general, you are much more aggressive in love these days. If you like someone, that person will know it.

You further your career through social means and contacts. Attending the right parties as well as hosting them (for the right people) also enhances the career.

The financial picture is mixed this month. Both planets involved in finances are still retrograde and they receive stressful aspects. This won't stop prosperity but increases the work and the effort involved. Continue to study major investments or purchases carefully.

Your 8th and 9th Houses are very active this month as well, thus your line of credit should increase. If you are not clear about what to invest in, why not use any surplus cash to reduce debt? Bonds look interesting for professional investors. Outside capital is easier to attract now. Tax and tax issues (perhaps estate planning as well) are influencing many a financial decision. This is also a month for getting rid of excess possessions, for breaking addictions and changing old emotional and mental patterns. Many of you are involved in personal transformation.

LIBRA

The 9th House gets strong after the 21st bringing an interest in foreign travel and higher education. Also, it is a month for religious and philosophical revelation.

Health is reasonable. Continue to enhance it in the ways described in the yearly report.

June

Best Days Overall: 5, 6, 14, 15, 23, 24

Most Stressful Days Overall: 12, 13, 19, 20, 25, 26

Best Days for Love: 3, 4, 10, 12, 13, 19, 20, 22, 28, 29

Best Days for Money: 2, 8, 9, 11, 17, 18, 20, 25, 26, 29

Monthly Career Peaks: 2, 3, 19, 20, 21, 25, 26,

Monthly Personal Pleasure Peaks: 5, 6, 21, 22

Like last month, most of the planets are above the horizon, in the day side of your chart. Your 10th House becomes very powerful from the 21st onwards. You are entering your yearly career peak. So you can de-emphasize the family and domestic life for a while. Strike while the iron is hot.

By the 21st, the planetary power will once again shift to the Eastern – independent and personal – side of your chart. Dealing with this is more difficult for the typical Libra. Now is a time to do things solo, to have things your own way and to be willing to go it alone if there is no consensus. It is time to pursue personal happiness even if it seems to make you temporarily unpopular. Really it won't – these fears are only in your mind.

Continue to enhance your career through social means. Being involved in groups, organizations or trade associations also helps. Career is also advanced through involvement in charitable and altruistic activities, and through intuition. Education also enhances the career. There could be more foreign travel involved with the career as well.

Librans are not known as workers. But now, with the North Node of the Moon moving into your 6th House, the cosmos wants you to appreciate the joy of work for its own sake.

Both your financial planets are still retrograde so prosperity is happening slowly. Don't rush in to financial decisions or feel that you must 'make' things happen. Finances are undergoing deep subjective processes, both with you and in others. Until the 14th, you are involved in helping others to prosper – your partner, spouse, lover or shareholders. Outside capital and credit still comes easy.

Issues involving personal transformation remain important until the 14th. Religion, philosophy, higher education and foreign travel are important all month. Religious and philosophical revelation is still there for those who want it.

Health needs watching more carefully after the 21st. Pay more attention to the heart and to the ankles and feet.

The Sun's re-stimulation of eclipse points from the 14th to the 16th and on the 30th creates upheavals in the world. For you it can bring dramas with friends, either in your relationship or in their lives.

Avoid unnecessary foreign travel (though you are sorely tempted) on the 1st and from the 8th to the 10th.

July

Best Days Overall: 3, 4, 12, 13, 20, 21, 30, 31

Most Stressful Days Overall: 10, 11, 16, 17, 23, 24

Best Days for Love: 3, 4, 8, 9, 12, 13, 16, 17, 22, 23, 27

Best Days for Money: 5, 6, 9, 14, 15, 17, 23, 24, 26

Monthly Career Peaks: 18, 19, 20, 23, 24, 25

Monthly Personal Pleasure Peaks: 3, 4, 18, 19, 23, 30, 31

You are still very much into your yearly career peak. Like last month, most of the planets are above the horizon, and your 10th House of Career is strong (30 to 40 per cent of the planets are either in this house or moving through there, as are the two most important planets in the horoscope, the Sun and the Lord of the Horoscope). So this is still a time to focus on the career and take advantage of the many opportunities that are happening. From the 18th to the 24th, we see personal honour and recognition coming to you. You are exercising more power and authority, and seem exalted above all others in the month ahead. (This is a double-edged sword – it feels good, but you also become a target for certain people.)

Like last month, the planets are mostly in the independent East. After the 19th, when your ruler, Venus, crosses over to the East, the percentage is increased. So this is a time for developing some independence – not your strong point.

Love is reasonable this month. With your 7th House basically empty this month (only the Moon visits there on the 16th and 17th), it is less of an interest than usual. The 16th and 17th will mark your monthly social peak. Friendships and group activities seem more important than romance. Your love planet will be in your 11th House of Friends until the 21st. For singles, this means that love opportunities come through friends or as you involve yourself in group activities. Even your needs in love are tinged by the influence of the 11th House. You want friendship with your lover as much as you want romance. Equality is a big issue these days. This 11th House influence is not a good aspect for marriage as the tendency is to want freedom and non-commitment. After the 21st, the love planet moves into your spiritual 12th House. Love will become more idealistic. You want perfect and ideal love. The spiritual connection with the beloved becomes very important. After the 21st, singles shouldn't waste their time at bars and clubs looking for love. Love is found at spiritual retreats, meditation seminars, charity functions, prayer groups or as you involve yourself in altruistic activities.

Your career is furthered by social means, as it has been for the past few months. Knowing the right people opens up all kinds of doors. Attending or hosting parties is also useful.

The two planets involved with travel are retrograde this month. Jupiter, the ruler of foreign travel, is retrograde until the 7th. Mercury, which rules local travel, will be retrograde from the 3rd to the 29th. From the 3rd to the 7th, both of these planets are retrograde simultaneously so try to avoid travelling during that period.

Prosperity is still strong, but it's not a free ride. You are working hard for it, but you will see the results of your hard work.

Health will improve dramatically after the 21st. In the meantime, rest when tired and pace yourself as best as you can. Pay more attention to the heart, feet and ankles.

August

Best Days Overall: 8, 9, 17, 18, 26, 27

Most Stressful Days Overall: 6, 7, 12, 13, 19, 20

Best Days for Love: 2, 3, 6, 7, 11, 12, 13, 14, 15, 21, 22, 24, 25, 31

Best Days for Money: 2, 3, 5, 10, 11, 13, 19, 20, 22, 23, 29, 30, 31

Monthly Career Peaks: 19, 20, 23

Monthly Personal Pleasure Peaks: 21, 22, 26, 27

A huge percentage of planets – 70 to 80 per cent – are in the independent Eastern side of your chart. Many of the trends written about earlier are still in effect so this continues to be a time to develop more independence and personal initiative, to design your life according to your personal specifications. You have the power to do it now.

LIBRA

Most of the planets are still above the horizon, in the day side of your chart. Your 10th House of Career is strong until the 13th and you are coming to the end of a yearly career peak. Family issues were important last month and they are still active this month, but the thrust of your attention should be on the career. Take advantage of the opportunities happening.

Venus, your ruler, resides (until the 13th) at the upper-most part of the chart. Like last month, you are exalted above others, and some will not like it. You are honoured and respected, and seem in charge of things. Mercury, your religious and spiritual planet, is also very elevated this month. And, with your 12th House of Spirituality also very strong, this is a month for spiritually-oriented, altruistic activities. Under these aspects some people like to go on fasts. Introspection is normal now.

The 11th House of Friends is also very strong this month. Like last month, friendships seem more important than romance. Group activities and involvement with organizations are important.

Though you might not see anything obvious, romance is developing in secret. Love is starting to pursue you. You do have free will and can say no – but the love will come anyway. Your love planet will re-stimulate eclipse points from the 29th to the 31st. This is going to bring changes to your love life – perhaps disruptive ones – to make room for the new pattern.

You are still working hard, but financial clarity is getting stronger. Jupiter, in your money house, started moving forward last month and will be forward all of this month. Your hard work and effort is creating luck and opportunity, and not the other way around.

Health is excellent this month. You can enhance it further by paying more attention to the ankles and feet.

September

Best Days Overall: 5, 6, 13, 14, 22, 23, 24

Most Stressful Days Overall: 3, 4, 9, 10, 15, 16, 30

Best Days for Love: 1, 2, 3, 4, 9, 10, 11, 13, 20, 21, 22, 23, 30

Best Days for Money: 1, 7, 8, 10, 15, 16, 18, 19, 25, 26, 28, 29

Monthly Career Peaks: 15, 16

Monthly Personal Pleasure Peaks: 12, 13, 21, 23

This month the planets make an important shift from the day side (upper half) of the chart to the night side (lower half). By the 23rd, 70 to 80 per cent of the planets will be below the horizon. By now career goals have been attained. It is time to attend to the family, the home base and your emotional life.

The Eastern, independent sector of the chart is much more dominant than the Western, social sector of the chart, even more so than last month. Your own sign becomes very powerful after the 3rd. Independence and personal initiative will be much easier to express as Mars will be in your own sign and in your 1st House. Indeed, you find that the world is adapting to you rather than vice versa. It's fun having your own way for a change, especially after many months of adapting to others. Continue to create conditions as you like them.

This is a good month health-wise too. Energy is greatly increased, and you have more charisma and personal magnetism. With Mars in your own sign you get things done in a hurry. Sex appeal and libido in general are increased. This is a wonderful month for exercise and sports, though make sure you support the ankles.

Socially, too, you are having things your way. Love and romance pursue you, as do friendships. Friends and your current love are going out of their way to please you.

For the past few months, love has been spiritual, idealistic, even 'otherworldly'. But now it is physical and tangible. There is more touching, hugging and physical contact, as well as more sex. Physical attraction seems the most important ingredient in love these days.

There are two eclipses this month. The first is a Lunar Eclipse on the 7th that occurs in your 6th House. This eclipse is announcing both job and career changes in the next six months. The other is a Solar Eclipse on the 22nd that occurs right on the border of your 12th and 1st Houses, and will probably impact on both. Thus there will be important changes in your spirituality and spiritual regime. Your self-concept and image will also change.

Finances continue to improve. This month your financial planet, Pluto, starts moving forward again (on the 4th). Financial judgement is sound, and decision making will be good. Oh, you're still working hard for earnings, but that will ease up after the 23rd. Pretty soon now you will enter your yearly (and perhaps lifetime) financial peak. Keep going the extra mile for earnings.

October

Best Days Overall: 2, 3, 10, 11, 20, 21, 29, 30

Most Stressful Days Overall: 1, 6, 7, 12, 13, 14, 27, 28

Best Days for Love: 2, 3, 6, 7, 10, 11, 21, 22

Best Days for Money: 4, 5, 7, 12, 13, 14, 16, 22, 23, 24, 26

Monthly Career Peaks: 12, 13, 14, 22

Monthly Personal Pleasure Peaks: 1, 20, 21

The career and job shake-ups brought on by last month's eclipse certainly seem positive! Prosperity is unbelievably strong after the 23rd. You worked hard this past year, but now wealth seems effortless.

Of course, you will be spending more this month too. This is only natural. But so long as you keep things in proportion, all will work out. Major windfalls and opportunities are happening. You are having peak financial experiences.

Like last month, most of the planets are still in the independent East and your own sign is very strong – 40 to 50 per cent of the planets are either in Libra or moving through there. Mars remains in your sign until the 23rd. You find it easier to be independent and have things your way. You look great too! (Mars and Venus are in your own sign.) You always have a sense of style, but it's even more the case at the moment. This is a good month for buying clothing and personal accessories – not only can you afford it, but your choices will be good too. Love and friendship are still pursuing you – almost a dream-like situation. Your lover and friends are going out of their way to please you. Sensual fantasies are being fulfilled. There are times to pamper the body and times to be more stern with it – this is a time for pampering, for treating it right.

Health is excellent. You have the energy of 10 people. With increased energy comes increased opportunity. These things were always there but perhaps you felt you couldn't take them. Now you can. You have the energy to achieve any goal you choose.

Like last month, most of the planets are below the horizon, in the night side of the horoscope. Finances are important, but career, professional status and reputation don't seem a big deal. The bottom line is much more important than glory and prestige. You just want to be happy now – to feel good. Career opportunities will undoubtedly come, but if they violate your family situation or your personal harmony, you can let them pass.

Money and personal pleasure will dominate the month ahead.

LIBRA

November

The main headline this month is the awesome power in your money house. Fifty to sixty per cent of the planets are either there or moving through there. With so much power here, wealth is increasing in a variety of ways: through the help of your partner and friends; through sales, marketing, communication and trading activities; through personal creativity; through intuition (especially after the 18th); through foreign investments or foreigners; through lucrative business partnerships; through outside investors, inheritance, trust funds, spousal support, insurance claims and perhaps royalties. Like last month, speculations are favourable. Money continues to come easily and effortlessly.

By the 24th, financial goals will have been attained and the emphasis will shift to intellectual interests and communication. Travel will become interesting – probably domestic travel, but foreign travel could also happen. Prosperity is happening after the 24th as well, and you can expect more windfalls and opportunities, but your interest is waning here. This is a great period to enjoy the fruits of prosperity, which is self-development. Money buys free time which we can use to develop other sides of ourselves. This is a wonderful period for pursuing educational goals, for catching up on your reading, for taking courses in subjects that interest you, and for feeding the mental body.

Many of you will buy new cars now and high-tech

communication equipment – computers, the latest fancy mobile phone, and the like.

Health is still excellent all month. You can enhance it further in the ways described all year.

For singles, love opportunities come as you pursue financial goals or with people involved in your finances. Those already in relationships will find that their spouse or lover is deeply involved in their finances.

With all this prosperity, jobseekers are probably not doing much seeking. And some of you will not need to work.

Your focus on finances can stress out parents or parent figures – perhaps they feel neglected. So make sure you give them the attention they deserve. Like last month, you can down-play the career and focus on the family and personal, emotional issues.

Venus, your ruler, will re-stimulate eclipse points on the 29th and 30th, so avoid risky types of activity then.

December

Best Days Overall: 4, 5, 13, 14, 15, 23, 24

Most Stressful Days Overall: 1, 6, 7, 21, 22, 27, 28

Best Days for Love: 1, 8, 9, 10, 11, 18, 19, 21, 22, 27, 28, 29, 30

Best Days for Money: 1, 4, 8, 9, 16, 17, 18, 19, 27, 28

Monthly Career Peaks: 6, 7, 20

Monthly Personal Pleasure Peaks: 13, 14, 15

Like last month, the main interest and power is in the 3rd House of Communication and Intellectual Interests. Sixty to seventy per cent of the planets are either there or will move through there this month. So, this is still a time for taking courses in subjects that interest you and pursuing intellectual interests. It is a time for enjoying the fruits of your prosperity. Students are going to have a good month. The mind is highly energized and you learn easily and quickly. You have a wonderful sense of short-term trends and how to profit from them. Traders in the markets should do exceptionally well because of this. Retailing might be lucrative.

You may find yourself making many short trips. You are more involved with siblings and neighbours – they too are prospering these days. Siblings are getting their way in love as well. You are going out of your way to please the siblings too.

Even though your money house empties out by the 8th, prosperity is still incredibly strong. Writers, journalists and teachers will have an exceptional month. Communication ability is strong and profitable to boot.

This is a month when many of you learn that wealth need not consist of physical and tangible things. There is such a thing as mental wealth – intellectual property is wealth.

Most of the planets are still in the night side of your chart, and your 4th House of Home and Family becomes very strong after the 22nd. So continue to focus more on family and down-play the career. Happily, the family situation seems more harmonious this month. A parent or parent figure is feeling much better – in a better mood and better health-wise as well. Pursue your career through dreaming and visualizing – preparing the psychological ground for success.

The love planet, Mars, will re-stimulate eclipse points from the 26th to the 28th so be more patient with your spouse or current love as he or she is apt to be more temperamental. Perhaps they experience a dramatic event. Things in the world will be more turbulent those days as well.

For singles, love opportunities happen locally or with neighbours and in educational settings.

The Sun will re-stimulate eclipse points from the 6th to the 8th and on the 21st and 22nd. Be more patient with friends on those days – they are likely to be more temperamental. Perhaps they too have dramatic experiences.

Venus, your ruler, re-stimulates eclipse points from the 9th to the 12th, so reschedule risky activities if you can.

Scorpio

♏

THE SCORPION

Birthdays from
23rd October to
22nd November

Personality Profile

SCORPIO AT A GLANCE

Element – Water

Ruling Planet – Pluto
  Co-ruling Planet – Mars
  Career Planet – Sun
  Love Planet – Venus
  Money Planet – Jupiter
  Planet of Health and Work – Mars
  Planet of Home and Family Life – Uranus

Colour – red-violet

Colour that promotes love, romance and social
  harmony – green

Colour that promotes earning power – blue

270

SCORPIO

Gems – bloodstone, malachite, topaz

Metals – iron, radium, steel

Scents – cherry blossom, coconut, sandalwood, watermelon

Quality – fixed (= stability)

Quality most needed for balance – a wider view of things

Strongest virtues – loyalty, concentration, determination, courage, depth

Deepest needs – to penetrate and transform

Characteristics to avoid – jealousy, vindictiveness, fanaticism

Signs of greatest overall compatibility – Cancer, Pisces

Signs of greatest overall incompatibility – Taurus, Leo, Aquarius

Sign most helpful to career – Leo

Sign most helpful for emotional support – Aquarius

Sign most helpful financially – Sagittarius

Sign best for marriage and/or partnerships – Taurus

Sign most helpful for creative projects – Pisces

Best Sign to have fun with – Pisces

Signs most helpful in spiritual matters – Cancer, Libra

Best day of the week – Tuesday

271

Understanding a Scorpio

One symbol of the Sign of Scorpio is the phoenix. If you meditate upon the legend of the phoenix you will begin to understand the Scorpio character – his or her powers and abilities, interests and deepest urges.

The phoenix of mythology was a bird that could recreate and reproduce itself. It did so in a most intriguing way: it would seek a fire – usually in a religious temple – fly into it, consume itself in the flames and then emerge a new bird. If this is not the ultimate, most profound transformation, then what is?

Transformation is what Scorpios are all about – in their minds, bodies, affairs and relationships (Scorpios are also society's transformers). To change something in a natural, not an artificial way, involves a transformation from within. This type of change is a radical change as opposed to a mere cosmetic make-over. Some people think that change means altering just their appearance, but this is not the kind of change that interests a Scorpio. Scorpios seek deep, funda-mental change. Since real change always proceeds from within, a Scorpio is very interested in – and usually accus-tomed to – the inner, intimate and philosophical side of life.

Scorpios are people of depth and intellect. If you want to interest them you must present them with more than just a superficial image. You and your interests, projects or busi-ness deals must have real substance to them in order to stimulate a Scorpio. If they haven't, he or she will find you out – and that will be the end of the story.

If we observe life – the processes of growth and decay – we see the transformational powers of Scorpio at work all the time. The caterpillar changes itself into a butterfly, the infant grows into a child and then an adult. To Scorpios this definite and perpetual transformation is not something to be feared. They see it as a normal part of life. This acceptance of transformation gives Scorpios the key to understanding the true meaning of life.

Scorpios' understanding of life (including life's weaknesses) makes them powerful warriors – in all senses of the word. Add to this their depth, patience and endurance and you have a powerful personality. Scorpios have good, long memories and can at times be quite vindictive – they can wait years to get their revenge. As a friend, though, there is no one more loyal and true than a Scorpio. Few are willing to make the sacrifices that a Scorpio will make for a true friend.

The results of a transformation are quite obvious, although the process of transformation is invisible and secret. This is why Scorpios are considered secretive in nature. A seed will not grow properly if you keep digging it up and exposing it to the light of day. It must stay buried – invisible – until it starts to grow. In the same manner, Scorpios fear revealing too much about themselves or their hopes to other people. However, they will be more than happy to let you see the finished product – but only when it is completely wrapped up. On the other hand, Scorpios like knowing everyone else's secrets as much as they dislike anyone knowing theirs.

Finance

Love, birth, life as well as death are Nature's most potent transformations; Scorpios are interested in all of these. In our society, money is a transforming power, too, and a Scorpio is interested in money for that reason. To a Scorpio money is power, money causes change, money controls. It is the power of money that fascinates them. But Scorpios can be too materialistic if they are not careful. They can be overly awed by the power of money, to a point where they think that money rules the world.

Even the term plutocrat comes from Pluto, the ruler of the Sign of Scorpio. Scorpios will – in one way or another –

achieve the financial status they strive for. When they do so they are careful in the way they handle their wealth. Part of this financial carefulness is really a kind of honesty, for Scorpios are usually involved with other people's money – as accountants, lawyers, stockbrokers or corporate managers – and when you handle other people's money you have to be more cautious than when you handle your own.

In order to fulfil their financial goals, Scorpios have important lessons to learn. They need to develop qualities that do not come naturally to them, such as breadth of vision, optimism, faith, trust and, above all, generosity. They need to see the wealth in Nature and in life, as well as in its more obvious forms of money and power. When they develop generosity their financial potential reaches great heights, for Jupiter, the Lord of Opulence and Good Fortune, is Scorpio's Money Planet.

Career and Public Image

Scorpio's greatest aspiration in life is to be considered by society as a source of light and life. They want to be leaders, to be stars. But they follow a very different road than do Leos, the other stars of the Zodiac. A Scorpio arrives at the goal secretly, without ostentation; a Leo pursues it openly. Scorpios seek the glamour and fun of the rich and famous in a restrained, discreet way.

Scorpios are by nature introverted and tend to avoid the limelight. But if they want to attain their highest career goals they need to open up a bit and to express themselves more. They need to stop hiding their light under a bushel and let it shine. Above all, they need to let go of any vindictiveness and small-mindedness. All their gifts and insights were given to them for one important reason – to serve life and to increase the joy of living for others.

SCORPIO

Love and Relationships

Scorpio is another Zodiac Sign that likes committed, clearly defined, structured relationships. They are cautious about marriage, but when they do commit to a relationship they tend to be faithful – and heaven help the mate caught or even suspected of infidelity! The jealousy of the Scorpio is legendary. They can be so intense in their jealousy that even the thought or intention of infidelity will be detected and is likely to cause as much of a storm as if the deed had actually been done.

Scorpios tend to settle down with those who are wealthier than they are. They usually have enough intensity for two, so in their partners they seek someone pleasant, hard-working, amiable, stable and easy-going. They want someone they can lean on, someone loyal behind them as they fight the battles of life. To a Scorpio a partner, be it a lover or a friend, is a real partner – not an adversary. Most of all a Scorpio is looking for an ally, not a competitor.

If you are in love with a Scorpio you will need a lot of patience. It takes a long time to get to know Scorpios, because they do not reveal themselves readily. But if you persist and your motives are honourable, you will gradually be allowed into a Scorpio's inner chambers of the mind and heart.

Home and Domestic Life

Uranus is ruler of Scorpio's 4th Solar House of Home and Family. Uranus is the planet of science, technology, changes and democracy. This tells us a lot about a Scorpio's conduct in the home and what he or she needs in order to have a happy, harmonious home life.

Scorpios can sometimes bring their passion, intensity and wilfulness into the home and family, which is not always the place for these qualities. These traits are good for the warrior and the transformer, but not so good for the nurturer and family member. Because of this (and also because of their need for change and transformation) the Scorpio may be prone to sudden changes of residence. If not carefully constrained, the sometimes inflexible Scorpio can produce turmoil and sudden upheavals within the family.

Scorpios need to develop some of the virtues of Aquarius in order to cope better with domestic matters. There is a need to build a team spirit at home, to treat family activities as truly group activities – family members should all have a say in what does and does not get done. For at times a Scorpio can be most dictatorial. When a Scorpio gets dictatorial it is much worse than if a Leo or Capricorn (the two other power Signs in the Zodiac) does. For the dictatorship of a Scorpio is applied with more zeal, passion, intensity and concentration than is true of either a Leo or Capricorn. Obviously this can be unbearable to family members – especially if they are sensitive types.

In order for a Scorpio to get the full benefit of the emotional support that a family can give, he or she needs to let go of conservatism and be a bit more experimental, to explore new techniques in child-rearing, be more democratic with family members and to try to manage things by consensus rather than by autocratic edict.

Horoscope for 2006

General Trends

Last year was a time for spiritual expansion and development. Success came to you secretly, inwardly, rather than in your outer life. This year you are going to see the physical results of this inner expansion. Your personal horizons are expanded. You have greater self-esteem and self-confidence;

you believe in yourself more and are generally happier. This happiness is going to manifest as living the good life and increased prosperity. More on this later.

Saturn moved into your 10th House of Career on July 17th 2005, making an inharmonious and stressful aspect to you. Yes, many wonderful and prosperous things are happening now, but you are earning them. In a way this is a good thing. If you weren't working for these things, the jealousy and malice of others would be difficult to deal with. Your hard work is neutralizing much of this effect.

Finance and career matters will be strong and successful in the year ahead. Love, on the other hand, seems on the backburner. Some years are like that. There will be more about this later.

Home and family issues have been important for many years, and the trend continues in the year ahead. Whereas this area has been very stressful in past years, now it is easier. (I won't say easy, but easier than it has been – there is progress happening here.) Again, there is more to be said on this later.

Health is mixed. Two long-term planets are in stressful aspect and two are in harmonious aspect. This area is reasonable in the year ahead.

Your paths to greatest fulfilment in the year ahead are the body, the image and sensual desires; finance; health and work (until June 23rd); children, fun and creativity (after June 23rd).

The major challenges in the year ahead will be in the career and in dealing with elders, authorities, parents and governments.

Health

(Please note that this is an astrological perspective on health, not a medical one. At one time, both perspectives were identical, but in these times there could be quite a difference. For the medical perspective, please consult your physician or health professional.)

As mentioned earlier, this is a mixed picture. Overall energy is not what it should be, but it's not dangerously low and likely to cause disease. Your 6th House of Health is empty so you don't have a big interest in health and diet issues this year – but you should get more involved, especially until June 23rd. Secret happiness and fulfilment will come from these things. More involvement in the healing of other people can bring great joy.

Mars is your health planet. So, as a general rule, you can enhance your health by vigorous exercise, keeping the muscles strong and toned, and paying more attention to the sexual organs, bladder, colon and adrenal glands. Since health problems, should they occur, would most likely begin in these areas, keeping these organs healthy and fit is good preventive medicine.

Keeping their ultra-strong sexuality in balance is a major challenge for Scorpio. Along with Leo, Scorpio is the most highly sexed of all the signs. Still, though your needs are greater than most, it is important not to go overboard. Awareness of your body will be the key. The natural and normal desires of the body should be fulfilled. But are some of your desires of the mind, something you have cultivated mentally? Psychological issues could be forcing you to over- or under-express this area. Safe sex is more important for you than most.

Mars will move through eight signs and houses of your horoscope in the coming year. Thus, depending on where Mars is, different therapies and approaches to health will be called for. These things will be discussed in the monthly reports.

Scorpios always benefit more than most from detox regimes. Colon cleansings are wonderful.

Mars is a fiery planet so thermal (heat) therapies are good. It's important for you to stay warm in the winter or spend more time in sunny climes.

SCORPIO

A Solar Eclipse on March 29th is announcing important changes in your diet, health regime and among the people involved in your health. These events could even be happening sooner as you are still under the influence of the last Lunar Eclipse (October 17th 2005), which also occurred in your 6th House of Health.

With beneficent Jupiter in your own sign most of the year (until November 24th) the main health danger comes from overdoing the good life, from sensual excess, over-eating and the like. Enjoy the best foods, wines and restaurants but only in moderation.

The health of parents or parent figures is status-quo. One of them is embarking on a major weight-loss regime and it looks successful. You and this parent seem opposite. You are enjoying the good life while the parent is being Spartan and disciplined. The health of your spouse or lover is stable. Children's health can be enhanced by experimental and cutting-edge therapies. Grandchildren can optimize their health by detox regimes and better care of the liver and thighs.

Home, Domestic and Family Issues

As mentioned earlier, this has been an important area of life for many years now. It has been important on the physical dimension – the home itself and relations with family members – and on the psychological level.

Dealing with unpredictable and volatile emotions has been the main challenge. These emotional swings could have been personal, or they could have occurred in family members. Moods swings have been sudden and abrupt. These trends continue, but to a reduced degree.

There could have been many moves over the past seven years or so. If not actual moves, there may have been renovations, many changes in the home. There is the feeling of a constant upgrading of the home going on. As soon as you

279

get it the way you want it, you have a new and better idea. If you can afford this tinkering, it's a harmless pastime. But if you can't afford it, this has been difficult.

The overall family pattern has changed many times over the past seven years. Things are easier now and you're becoming adjusted, but changes are still happening. There could have been actual breaks with the family or with family ties and obligations.

Now the changes going on in the home seem to centre around children. Scorpios of childbearing age still seem very fertile. New arrivals are certainly going to force changes and rearrangements in the home. Pregnancies can happen suddenly and unexpectedly.

You are also making the home more fun – a place of entertainment. Perhaps you are installing state-of-the-art entertainment equipment. Sports equipment also seems likely, and of course, toys.

A parent or parent figure is moving this year – a happy move to bigger and larger quarters. Perhaps you are involved physically or financially. Siblings could have unexpected repairs to do in the home. Adult children and grandchildren have a stable year on the home front.

If you're doing heavy construction or renovation in the home, June 3rd to July 21st is a good time. If you're redecorating, or buying art objects for the home, March 5th to April 6th, August 2nd to September 6th and October 24th to November 17th are good times. These are also good periods for entertaining from home and for family get-togethers.

Love and Social Life

Socially, this is not one of your important years. Your 7th House of Love and Romance and your 11th House of Friends are basically empty (no long-term planets there). This doesn't mean you won't have a social or romantic life, but it doesn't seem to be the focus. I expect that most of you will have a status-quo year. Married Scorpios will tend to stay married and singles will tend to stay single.

Most of you seem content with your current marriage, relationship or single status and have no need to make extraordinary efforts to change things. In a horoscope, lack of interest in this particular area is often an indicator of good news. Social goals, in most cases, have already been attained.

There is also another kind of love relationship – the love affair. This is not serious, and more in the nature of entertainment than love. These affairs are abundant this year – abundant and exciting. They always tend to be unstable, but will be even more so this year. None of them seems to have any long-term potential. All the parties involved want to be free and uncommitted. These affairs can come suddenly and end suddenly. Affections can change at the drop of a hat.

Even during an off-year, there will be periods when your social life is more active, prominent and happy than at other times. For you this will happen from April 20th to May 20th, May 29th to June 24th and October 24th to November 17th.

Those in or working on their second or third marriage will have a status-quo year too. Scorpios working on their fourth marriage will have important love this year and perhaps a marriage.

The marriage of parents or parent figures is in crisis. It doesn't mean it will dissolve, but there is a need for much forgiveness, and they will be making efforts here. Children of marriageable age probably shouldn't marry this year as they seem too unsettled. The need for personal freedom is almost obsessive and they will probably have serial love affairs. Grandchildren of marriageable age have a status-quo year.

Finance and Career

This is where the focus will be in the coming year. It's going to be a major financial and career year, but there are some challenges to face.

Jupiter, the planet of abundance, is in your own sign until November 24th. After that it will move into your money house and stay there for another year. In 2007 it will travel with your ruling planet, Pluto. Jupiter also happens to be your financial planet, and he is acting very strongly in this area. The message is clear: this will be a year of great prosperity and the beginning of an 'era of prosperity'; this is not a one-year event, but the start of a long-term process.

Finance has been important to you for many years now. Pluto, your ruling planet, has been in your money house for many years. And it will be there for many years to come. This shows your personal involvement and interest in finance. But now that Jupiter is entering the picture, we get a sense of the big payoff – the reaping of what has been sown for many years.

Jupiter, the financial planet, and Pluto, your ruler, are in 'mutual reception' until November 24th. There is great co-operation between these two planets. It shows that you are in harmony with the money people in your life, and they with you. They are happy to support your financial goals, and you in turn are enjoying the process of money-making.

These aspects also show other things. You invest in yourself – your body, your image, your personal appearance. You are donning the image of wealth. This, of course, puts you in different social circles, and attracts different opportunities. People treat you differently. (The tendency these days will be to overspend on these things – but no matter, you can afford it.)

Your body, your image, your overall demeanour is a major factor in earnings these days too. Perhaps this is the reason for these investments. You have the kinds of aspects we often see in models, athletes, media and marketing people, whose livelihood is based on the impression they make on others or their physical prowess or beauty.

Expensive personal items are coming to you. These could be clothing, jewellery, accessories and the like.

You are travelling more, living like a jetsetter. Your body is being pampered and you are experiencing the fulfilment of sensual fantasies. Self-esteem and self-confidence are high. Assets you own will increase in value and you are very lucky in speculations. And best of all, financial opportunities are running after you, rather than vice versa.

Career, though, seems more challenging. Sure, you are prospering personally, living the happy-go-lucky life, but professional status and prestige are more difficult to attain this year. Saturn in your 10th House of Career is showing that honour and recognition will have to be earned. Mere money will not bring it to you.

Many of you will have a stern and demanding boss who will push you to the limit – and maybe beyond. Those who are self-employed will experience this in different ways – perhaps the government is obstructive to them. Siblings and neighbours may be disrespectful or critical.

Money will come easily. You'll catch the lucky breaks. But career success will have to be earned.

Self-improvement

Though you are succeeding on many levels, one of the main challenges this year is dealing with volatile emotions. This can be difficult both for yourself and for the people around you. Emotional instability can disrupt entire lives – careers, homes and marriages. So there is a need to develop equilibrium here. How do you go about it?

Well, one way is to express pent-up emotion (especially if it is negative) by writing down an overpowering feeling or mood. Write, write, write. Let it pour out of you on to the paper. When you feel you have expressed it – there is nothing left to say and you feel emotionally spent – take the paper and throw it out. If you like, you can say a little prayer. Some people prefer talking out their feelings into a tape recorder. Talk, talk, talk, until you feel emotionally spent. Then, saying a prayer or making a statement, erase the tape. Make a ceremony out of it. Some people like to go to the seashore and write their negative feelings right in the sand – then they cover them over with sand.

The important thing is to express these energies in harmless ways – not to take them out on yourself or the people around you. Your life will become more stable. In addition, a creative hobby seems like a healthy thing. We all have positive, lofty feelings that get pent up – there is no outlet for them. And a creative hobby will give you that outlet. This hobby should be something you do just for fun. In your case, you might enjoy scientific and mathematical pursuits, computer programming, computer games, logic problems, video and film production, photography. Music and dance might also be very enjoyable.

Month-by-month Forecasts

January

Best Days Overall: 3, 4, 12, 13, 14, 22, 23, 31

Most Stressful Days Overall: 1, 2, 8, 9, 15, 16, 29, 30

Best Days for Love: 8, 9, 17, 18, 19, 27, 28

Best Days for Money: 3, 4, 12, 13, 22, 23, 25, 26, 31

Monthly Career Peaks: 15, 16, 29

Monthly Personal Pleasure Peaks: 22, 23, 25, 26

A rare Grand Square pattern in the fixed signs is the main headline this month. As you are a fixed sign, it has a particularly strong effect on you, and will gather strength after the 20th. Sixty per cent (sometimes seventy per cent) of the planets will be involved. You are building something big,

involved in a major project. This could be personal or for
others. There are many difficulties involved and many
diverse forces need to be kept in balance. It's as if you have
four (and after the 20th, six) self-willed and unruly children
at home, each wanting to do something different. Your job is
to make them co-operate with each other, rather than fight.
Your health needs watching more carefully, especially after
the 20th. Enhance your health by paying more attention to
the neck, throat, bladder, colon, adrenal glands and sexual
organs. Exercise is beneficial but keep the workouts light.
Neck massage is also very helpful in avoiding a build-up of
stress there. Maintaining social harmony is also important
health-wise. You seem very involved in the health of your
spouse, lover or friends. Of course, the most important thing
is to maintain high energy levels. You are very active this
month, so it is important to make the actions count, to make
them efficient and to rest when tired.

The planets are shifting from the East to the West this
month. (Previously the dominance was in the East.) By the
22nd, the Eastern and Western sectors will be in balance.
You need to steer a middle course between independence
and dependence; between getting your way by direct action
and through consensus and compromise.

Most of the planets are below the horizon, in the night
side of the chart. Though your 10th House of Career is
strong, your 4th House of Home and Family will be even
stronger after the 20th. So, career demands will be intense
and you won't be able to ignore them, but shift more attention to the home and family where possible.

The year ahead is very prosperous, as is this month, especially until the 20th. But there is a price tag attached to this
prosperity – much work and many challenges to be overcome. Family, social or health issues could stress your
finances.

You seem active socially, but serious love is a mixed
picture. Your love planet is retrograde all month so important

love decisions shouldn't be made now. Mars in your 7th House could show a power struggle in a current relationship. It could also show that while your current love is thinking things over, you are off to new romantic adventures. Your tendency is to rush into love these days, but the retrograde of Venus suggests that you shouldn't.

February

Best Days Overall: 1, 9, 10, 19, 20, 27, 28

Most Stressful Days Overall: 4, 5, 11, 12, 25, 26

Best Days for Love: 4, 5, 14, 15, 23, 24

Best Days for Money: 1, 9, 10, 19, 20, 21, 27, 28

Monthly Career Peaks: 5, 6, 7, 11, 12, 27

Monthly Personal Pleasure Peaks: 19, 20, 21, 22

The Grand Square pattern of last month is in effect until the 18th. This means there is much achievement happening now, but also more stress and effort. Health still needs careful watching, especially until the 18th. (You will see a dramatic improvement after the 19th when the Sun moves into harmonious aspect with you.) Enhance your health in the ways described last month. Pay more attention to the arms, shoulders and lungs after the 18th. Detox regimes are always good for you, but especially after the 18th. Mental health becomes very important then too.

The Eastern and Western sectors of the chart are still in equilibrium. Neither one nor the other dominates – it's rare for something like this to last so long. So you are balancing personal interests with the interests of others.

Most of the planets (70 to 80 per cent) are still below the horizon, the night side of the horoscope. Your career planet, the Sun, is in the 4th House of Home and Family. So, like last month, shift focus and attention to the family and to your emotional life. Also we see you trying to merge the home and the office. Either you are working more from home, or trying to make your office more like your home – more comfortable and casual.

Finances are much improved over last month, especially after the 19th. Until then you still need to work harder for earnings, to overcome many hurdles and challenges and develop your financial muscles. A financial disagreement with a parent, boss or elder is resolved after the 19th. Your spouse or lover becomes more supportive then too. Money will be earned in happy ways, perhaps as you pursue leisure activities. Speculations are favourable, but always under intuition and never blindly. Artists and creative people have a good financial month. Children can have excellent financial ideas after the 19th, and perhaps inspire you.

With Venus, your love planet, moving forwards on the 3rd, love is straightening out. Your social confidence is much improved over the past two months. Singles find love opportunities locally or with neighbours. Educational settings are also likely scenes for romance. You want to fall in love with a person's thought process as much as with their body. The sharing of ideas seems important in love. But most of you seem in a fun-loving mood this month, and serious committed love might not be appealing. Your love planet will re-stimulate eclipse points from the 24th to the 26th, so be more patient with lovers and friends then as they are likely to be more temperamental. Current relationships can get tested on those days.

March

Best Days Overall: 8, 9, 18, 19, 20, 27, 28

Most Stressful Days Overall: 3, 4, 10, 11, 12, 25, 26, 31

Best Days for Love: 3, 4, 5, 6, 15, 16, 25, 26, 31

Best Days for Money: 8, 9, 18, 19, 20, 21, 27, 28

Monthly Career Peaks: 1, 10, 11, 12

Monthly Personal Pleasure Peaks: 18, 19, 20, 21

Two eclipses shake up the world and the people around you this month, but you seem relatively unscathed. Still, with the world in uproar, it won't hurt to reduce your schedule on those days anyway.

The Lunar Eclipse of the 14th occurs in your 11th House and will probably test a friendship or your relationship with an organization. These things often bring disruptive events in the lives of friends – you might not be personally involved here – or with the internal structure of these organizations. Since the Moon is the ruler of your 9th House, every Lunar Eclipse affects students and their education. Important education changes are made. Religious beliefs and the personal philosophy of life get tested, fine-tuned and upgraded over the next six months. Changes in your religious beliefs will have a dramatic, though indirect, impact on your overall life.

The Solar Eclipse of the 29th occurs in your 6th House of Work. And since the Sun, your career planet, is involved here, the message is clear: important job and career changes are happening. Sometimes it shows upheavals in the corporate hierarchy where you work, impacting on your job and career situation. Often it will lead to advancement – but through some disruption. It is very important to see disruptions and upheavals as opportunities rather than disasters. These are signs of much needed change, and ultimately they are good.

With most of the planets still below the horizon and with your 4th House of Home and Family still very strong, it is likely that the career changes being made now will allow more time for family and for emotional harmony. Another scenario is that your internal visualizing and dreaming is now creating the conditions for a career change more in line with your dreams.

Love is still close to home for singles. Family connections play a role in love. There is probably nostalgia for an old flame. Often people reconnect with old loves (or people who remind them of old loves) in order to resolve old issues. A very happy love meeting happens from the 24th to the 27th, which reawakens love memories. (Be careful of overspending during that period.) Love is more emotional from the 6th onwards. It is about sharing feelings, giving and receiving emotional support. Last month, intellectual compatibility was important. This month, it is still important but you also want emotional compatibility.

Your financial planets are starting to move retrograde this month. Jupiter, your actual financial planet, goes retrograde on the 4th. Pluto, in your money house, will start to move retrograde on the 29th. While this will not stop earnings or prosperity, it will slow things down. More planning and review is necessary. Financial delays, though irritating, can actually work in your favour, giving you time to improve your product or service.

April

Best Days Overall: 4, 5, 14, 15, 23, 24

Most Stressful Days Overall: 1, 7, 8, 21, 22, 27, 28

Best Days for Love: 1, 2, 3, 14, 15, 23, 24, 27, 28

Best Days for Money: 4, 5, 14, 15, 17, 18, 23, 24

Monthly Career Peaks: 7, 8, 27

Monthly Personal Pleasure Peaks: 14, 15, 16, 17, 18

Most of the planets are in the Western, social sector of your chart. Your personal planet, Pluto, is retrograde. The message is clear: down-play personal will and self-interest and focus on other people. Success comes from the good graces of others and not so much from your personal abilities.

Most of the planets are still below the horizon (though this is soon to change). Continue to focus on the family and feeling right, rather than outer success.

Family still seems important on the love front as well. Emotional health, harmony and wellbeing will definitely draw love to you. Love opportunities are found close to home or through family connections. A sudden, surprise connection with an old flame happens from the 17th to the 20th. (This could also be someone who reminds you of an old flame.) Love is very tender and sentimental these days. Little things can hurt you or your lover – a gesture, a voice tone, body language, even a passing thought. Little things get magnified so be more aware here. Love is more about fun now, the giving and receiving of pleasure. Current relationships will be in a honeymoon period. Singles will be more interested in love affairs than in serious, committed love. After the 20th, you are mingling with people of high status and prestige who can help you career-wise. In general, this is a happy social and romantic month, especially after the 14th.

Health is good these days, though you have to be more careful after the 20th when another Grand Square pattern starts to form. Again, you are building something very big, either for yourself or for others. Try to rest and relax more. Enhance health by paying more attention to the arms, shoulders and lungs (until the 14th) and to the stomach and breasts afterwards. Diet plays more of a role in health after the 14th. Happily, there is a greater interest in health this month, and this is 90 per cent of the battle.

Though finances are slowing down, this is a prosperous month. Many wonderful and positive things are happening behind the scenes. Important financial deals and projects are being hatched. You might experience these things in a 'delayed reaction' kind of way, but they are nevertheless happening. This is a wonderful month for jobseekers. Lucrative positions will start manifesting after the 14th, perhaps even in foreign lands or with overseas companies. Family, social connections and your spouse or lover are all supporting your financial goals.

May

Best Days Overall: 2, 3, 12, 13, 20, 21, 29, 30

Most Stressful Days Overall: 4, 5, 18, 19, 25, 26, 31

Best Days for Love: 3, 14, 15, 22, 23, 25, 26

Best Days for Money: 2, 3, 12, 13, 14, 15, 20, 21, 29, 30

Monthly Career Peaks: 4, 5, 27, 31

Monthly Personal Pleasure Peaks: 12, 13, 14, 15

The Grand Square pattern of last month continues until the 21st. There is great achievement but also great expenditure of energy. Try to rest and relax more when you can. Enhance health through better nutrition and paying more attention to the stomach and breasts. It won't hurt to pay more attention to the thighs and liver either. Metaphysical therapies such as prayer are also more powerful this month. Harmony with your friends, spouse or lover is also important health-wise.

Most of the planets are still in the Western, social sector. Your 7th House is very strong and you are well into your yearly social peak, enjoying wonderful romantic and social experiences. Your personal planet is still retrograde so continue to down-play personal desires and self-interest, and put other people first. You will benefit from the grace of others.

Love is going well, and after the 4th you get more serious about it. You express your love by doing things for your beloved. Service is seen as the highest form of love. Love opportunities happen at the workplace, with colleagues or even bosses, as you have the aspects for the classic office romance these days. But your interest in health can also lead to romantic opportunity.

Finances are wonderful. Your financial planet is involved in a beautiful Grand Trine in the Water signs. Prosperity is happening slowly and steadily, unfolding like a flower in the spring. Parents (or parent figures), family and work are all contributing to your prosperity. With both of your financial planets still retrograde, you must continue to study important deals, investments and purchases carefully.

Your love planet re-stimulates eclipse points on the 11th and 12th. Be more patient with your lover or spouse those days as they are apt to be more temperamental. This might not even be related to you – some dramatic event could have caused it.

Mars re-stimulates an eclipse point on the 1st so there could be some disruption at the workplace.

June

Best Days Overall: 8, 9, 17, 18, 25, 26

Most Stressful Days Overall: 1, 2, 14, 15, 21, 22, 28, 29

Best Days for Love: 3, 4, 12, 13, 21, 22

Best Days for Money: 8, 9, 10, 11, 17, 18, 25, 26

Monthly Career Peaks: 1, 2, 3, 25, 27, 28, 29

Monthly Personal Pleasure Peaks: 8, 9, 10, 11

This month the planets move from the lower, night side of the horoscope to the upper, day side. The day side has been getting stronger over the past few months, but only on the 24th of this month do we see the day side becoming dominant. Both of the planets involved with the family and the home are retrograde this month. Your 10th House of Career gets very strong after the 3rd. So you can start shifting your attention from family and focus on your outer goals and desires. With dynamic Mars moving into your career house on the 3rd, your career is going to be hectic. You will have to take bold actions in that department, defending your own position – or that of your company – against fierce competitors. Career advancement can happen very suddenly.

Most of the planets are still in the West, and your love planet will be in your 7th House of Love until the 24th. You are still very much in your yearly social peak. Your personal planet, Pluto, is still retrograde. Like last month, down-play yourself, put other people first and cultivate your social skills.

Singles find love opportunities in the usual places this month. Love is in the air now. There could be financial disagreements with your beloved, but nothing too serious.

Health needs watching more carefully. Overwork is the main danger. Enhance health after the 3rd by paying more attention to the heart, spine, knees, teeth, skeleton and skeletal alignment.

This month, the North Node of the Moon makes a major change. It moves from your 6th House to your 5th House. For many this will bring an interest in children and fulfilment from being involved with them. Some of you might decide to have children now. For others, it brings an interest in the joy of life, a need to explore just being happy. For other Scorpios it will lead to greater personal creativity. Getting into a creative hobby brings much fulfilment. The North Node will be in your 5th House for some years to come and is a long-term trend.

The libido of Scorpio is legendary. This month, with the 8th House very strong, this libido is even stronger. Safe sex becomes more important than ever.

Also, being a natural 8th House personality, your natural interests are stronger. Career is important, but you are still very much interested in helping others to prosper, finding out secrets, personal transformation and learning more about the deeper things of life. Personal finance is mixed, although your line of credit should increase this month. Spousal support is also stronger.

July

Best Days Overall: 5, 6, 14, 15, 23, 24

Most Stressful Days Overall: 12, 13, 18, 19, 25, 26

Best Days for Love: 3, 4, 12, 13, 18, 19, 22, 23

Best Days for Money: 5, 6, 8, 9, 14, 15, 23, 24

Monthly Career Peaks: 20, 21, 25, 26

Monthly Personal Pleasure Peaks: 5, 6, 8, 9

The planets will start to shift to the East by the 21st. Until the 21st, the Western, social sector is still stronger. You are in a cusp-like month. Personal independence will get stronger, but you still need to adapt to conditions more often than not. This is another month for attaining ends through compromise and consensus. Bold, independent actions are not called for, except for in the career.

Most of the planets are still above the horizon, the day side of the horoscope. Your 10th House of Career is even stronger than last month – 40 to 50 per cent of the planets are either there or move through there, a huge percentage. The two planets involved with home and family are retrograde, so family issues need time for resolution and you might as well focus on your career. Your yearly career peak is in full swing and there is much advancement and opportunity. Jobseekers have sudden opportunity after the 21st, and those already in jobs could experience sudden changes. You or your company are fending off competitors and challengers. You thrive on competition these days. Plain, old-fashioned hard work and courage take you to career heights. You are learning that real life doesn't always follow your idealistic visions. The career planet re-stimulates eclipse points on the 1st and 2nd, bringing dramatic changes in your own career, the corporate hierarchy, or with a parent or parent figure. These events will work in your favour. There will also be dramatic events in the world on those days.

Finances are improving. Jupiter, the financial planet, starts moving forwards on the 7th. Financial judgement is getting stronger. Long-stalled deals or projects are starting to make progress. Earnings and earning opportunities come easily until the 21st, but afterwards there is more work and challenge involved. Prosperity is still strong but you are creating your own luck. Career progress is wonderful, but it may take time to see the results in the bottom line.

Your health needs watching all month, but especially after the 21st. Enhance health by paying more attention to the heart and small intestine. A healthy diet becomes more of a factor after the 21st. With your 6th House of Health basically empty this month (only the Moon visits on the 16th and 17th) the danger is that you might ignore your health, or let little problems fester. Try to rest and relax more and pace yourself better.

There is a crisis in love from the 14th to the 16th. Perhaps a current relationship has a 'near death experience', but true love will only improve and become purer because of this. Love will get tested again from the 25th to the 27th as the love planet re-stimulates eclipse points. Be more patient with your beloved during those periods. These can also bring dramatic experiences for your lover or spouse. Until the 19th, love is about passion and sexual expression. After the 19th, love is about philosophical and religious harmony. Until the 19th, singles are allured by sex appeal. After this date they are attracted to mentor types. Love opportunities come at universities or educational functions, in foreign lands or with foreigners, or in religious settings. After the

19th, you have the kind of aspects where the student falls in love with the professor. People of different ethnic or cultural backgrounds are alluring as well.

August

Best Days Overall: 2, 3, 10, 11, 19, 20, 29, 30

Most Stressful Days Overall: 8, 9, 14, 15, 21, 22, 23

Best Days for Love: 2, 3, 11, 14, 15, 21, 22, 31

Best Days for Money: 2, 3, 4, 5, 10, 11, 19, 20, 29, 30, 31

Monthly Career Peaks: 10, 11, 12, 13, 21, 22, 23

Monthly Personal Pleasure Peaks: 2, 3, 4, 5, 16, 17, 31

Many of last month's trends are still in effect. Most of the planets are above the horizon. Your 10th House of Career is still very powerful (40 to 50 per cent of the planets are either there or moving through there), and you are still in your yearly career peak. You can down-play home and domestic issues and take advantage of the strong career tide.

By the 13th, the Eastern sector – the personal side – of the horoscope becomes dominant. The shift that began last month is now established. Good comes to you because of who you are, what you do and your personal abilities. Social skills are less important now, except for in your career. It's time to start having life your way and on your terms.

Health still needs watching, especially until the 23rd. Rest and relax more. Enhance your health by paying more attention to the small intestine and the diet. Harmony with friends also seems important. If health problems arise, check your relationships with friends and repair them as best you can.

Your career is going great guns, and your spouse, lover or partner seems very supportive. Bosses are kinder and gentler (in general they have been stern and tough this year). Young women are also very helpful. Your career is enhanced by having the right social contacts. Attending, or hosting, the right parties also advances the career. This is a year when hard work and real achievement matter, but real achievement sometimes needs the right contacts.

Love trends are like last month until the 13th. You are attracted to educated and refined people who can teach you things. But after the 13th you are allured by power and prestige. People who can help you career-wise are interesting. Singles will have romantic opportunities with people of high social or professional status, perhaps bosses or elders. Romances of convenience wouldn't be a surprise. Love opportunities also come as you pursue your career goals. There is an interesting romantic opportunity with a neighbour from the 24th to the 26th.

Your 11th House of Friends becomes strong after the 23rd, showing more involvement with friends, groups and organizations. These things further the career too. Perhaps these are professional, career-related organizations. It looks like you will be doing voluntary work for them. Jobseekers can find opportunities at these organizations.

Prosperity is still strong but you are earning every penny. You are still building your financial muscles, but earnings will come much more easily after the 23rd.

Mars re-stimulates eclipse points from the 29th to the 31st. This can bring job changes, dramas with colleagues or dramatic changes in your health regime. It will be a turbulent period for the world at large as well.

September

Best Days Overall: 7, 8, 15, 16, 25, 26

Most Stressful Days Overall: 5, 6, 11, 12, 17, 18, 19

Best Days for Love: 1, 2, 11, 12, 20, 21, 30

Best Days for Money: 1, 7, 8, 15, 16, 25, 26, 27, 28, 29

Monthly Career Peaks: 17, 18, 19

Monthly Personal Pleasure Peaks: 1, 25, 26, 28, 29

There are two eclipses this month. Though they bring much change to people around you and to the world at large, you seem little affected. In fact, they will probably open doors for you.

The Lunar Eclipse on the 7th occurs in your 5th House. It will test a love affair (not a marriage). Dramatic events and changes will happen with your children, if you have them. Many of these changes are quite normal – the child goes off to school, changes their image, marries or moves out – but your relationship is now changed. (Children have been unusually rebellious for some time now, and during this eclipse they are likely to be more so.) Since the Moon is the Lord of your 9th House, these Lunar Eclipses always bring religious and philosophical changes. Your beliefs get tested by events. There are dramatic disturbances at your place of worship. Many change their church or spiritual leader under these eclipses. Since this eclipse occurs near Uranus – your home and family planet – moves, renovations or repairs to the home could happen. There could be changes to your family pattern or relationships. Dramatic events happen with a parent or parent figure. For students, this eclipse shows a change in the educational situation.

The Solar Eclipse of the 22nd occurs on the border of two signs and houses of your horoscope – the 11th and the 12th. It will probably impact on the affairs of both houses. Those on a spiritual path will change their practice and regime, probably due to a new revelation. Those not on a spiritual path might embark on one these days. There are disturbances and dramatic events in charities or causes you are involved in, which could change the nature of your relationship with them. Friendships get tested and there are usually dramas with friends. And, since the Sun is your career planet, there are career changes happening, and these are probably quite positive. In your chart, Solar Eclipses tend to bring dramatic events with parents or parent figures as well.

Finances are getting progressively better. You have pretty much paid your dues, and now it is time to reap the rewards. Pluto, in your 2nd House of Money, has been retrograde for many months. On the 4th it starts moving forwards again. Now both your financial planets are moving forwards, and by the 23rd will start receiving wonderful aspects. Everything you touch turns to gold.

If you can avoid being too critical, judgemental and analytical, love can be happy this month. If not, you can expect some sudden change.

October

Best Days Overall: 4, 5, 12, 13, 14, 22, 23, 24

Most Stressful Days Overall: 2, 3, 8, 9, 15, 16, 29, 30

Best Days for Love: 2, 3, 8, 9, 10, 11, 21, 22

Best Days for Money: 4, 5, 12, 13, 14, 22, 23, 24, 25, 26

Monthly Career Peaks: 15, 16, 22

Monthly Personal Pleasure Peaks: 1, 2, 22, 23, 24, 25, 26

Seventy to eighty per cent of the planets are in the independent Eastern sector of your chart. Your own sign of Scorpio is awesomely powerful – 50 to 60 per cent of the planets are either there or move through there in the month ahead. You are in a period of great independence when you can have things your way and life on your terms – so why not? (Of course, you can't be destructive about it.) The Higher Power is giving you a blank cheque – do, have, buy, create what you will. There is only one catch: you will have to live with the consequences of your creation. With great power comes great responsibility.

Happily, your 12th House of Spirituality is also very strong, perhaps as strong as your 1st House of Self. Thus, you seem more open to Higher Wisdom and guidance and are less likely to abuse your powers. Until the 23rd you are in an excellent period for inner spiritual growth. This is a good time for spiritual retreats, meditation seminars and involvement in spiritual and altruistic activities. Use this opportunity to review and digest the past year and set goals for your coming new year (which, in astrology, begins on your birthday). These spiritual interests are not only beneficial in their own right, but also set the scene for romantic opportunity.

This is also a month (especially after the 23rd) for living the good life, for the fulfilment of sensual fantasies, of physical, corporeal pleasures. Everything you desire is winging its way to you. There's not much you need to do – in fact, too much planning, manipulating and scheming could actually be a hindrance. Love, career opportunity and tremendous prosperity are pursuing you. You are having the peak sensual and financial experiences of a lifetime. It's all a 'done deal' so why interfere (and perhaps delay and complicate things) with your mental-emotional machinations?

By the 23rd there is another important shift when planetary power moves to the lower, night side of the horoscope. And though you still seem ambitious – and the world sees you that way – you are becoming more interested in emotional harmony. What good is all this money, love and career success if you don't feel right inside, if you are not at peace? So you will probably be more selective with the career and financial opportunity that comes. You don't want these things disturbing your family situation or emotional harmony. You are ambitious but not that ambitious.

The main impact of all these planets in your own sign will be on your health. If you've had any health problems this year, now they vanish – they are vaporized. Many of you will experience miraculous healings. Your own personal healing power is also enhanced. The only real health danger now is overindulgence in the good life. There is so much sensual delight open to you that you could easily overdo it if you're not careful. There will be a price tag on this later on.

November

Best Days Overall: 1, 9, 10, 19, 20, 28, 29

Most Stressful Days Overall: 5, 11, 12, 26, 27

Best Days for Love: 1, 5, 9, 10, 21, 30

Best Days for Money: 1, 2, 10, 20, 21, 22, 30

Monthly Career Peaks: 11, 12, 20

Monthly Personal Pleasure Peaks: 19, 20, 21, 22

Many of the trends of last month are still very much in effect. You are in the midst of your yearly (and probably lifetime) personal pleasure peak. Fifty to sixty per cent of the planets are still in (or moving through) your own sign and in your 1st House. This is another month for having things your way, creating the conditions of your personal happiness, of sensual delights and sensual fulfilment.

Like last month, self-esteem and self-confidence are unusually strong. You have the energy of 10 people. You get things done in a fraction of the time it normally takes. Your wish is the command of the universe.

You look great. You shine. Scorpios are always magnetic, charismatic people, but now even more so. Whatever your age or stage in life, sex appeal is enhanced and libido is increased. Love pursues you, probably even more than you can handle. Your lover or spouse goes out of their way to please you. You are catching the lucky breaks, both in love and money.

You are spending on yourself these days, and so you should. This is a great period to buy clothing, jewellery and personal accessories. With Venus in your own sign until the 22nd, your sense of style is outstanding and your choices will be good.

Progress is breathtaking this month – 100 per cent of the planets are moving forwards after the 20th. Until the 18th, 80 per cent are moving forwards.

Finance and personal pleasure are the main interests of the month, and both are very successful. Your financial planet makes a move from your 1st House into the 2nd House on the 24th, but this isn't going to change things much – prosperity is going to be just as strong (perhaps even more so) now and well into 2007. You have the golden touch and an instinct for profits.

Be more patient with your lover or spouse on the 29th and 30th when Venus re-stimulates eclipse points.

Health continues to be outstanding. Miraculous healings are still likely. The main danger health-wise, like last month, is overindulgence. The biscuit tin is open to you, but you don't need to eat the lot.

December

Best Days Overall: 6, 7, 16, 17, 25, 26

Most Stressful Days Overall: 2, 3, 8, 9, 10, 23, 24, 29, 30

Best Days for Love: 1, 2, 3, 9, 10, 11, 21, 22, 29, 30

Best Days for Money: 4, 8, 18, 19, 27

Monthly Career Peaks: 8, 9, 10, 18, 19, 20

Monthly Personal Pleasure Peaks: 16, 17, 18, 19

Most of the planets, like last month, are below the horizon. Though career is still important, you can shift more attention to the family and emotional issues. Your emotional wellbeing is more important than your career. The family situation seems a bit stressful this month, especially until the

22nd. Perhaps there are financial disagreements with family members, or your financial success stirs up old envies and jealousies. They may feel you are spending too much on yourself and not enough on them.

Most of the planets are still in the Eastern sector, the personal side of your chart. So you continue to be very independent, having things your way. Your way is the best way for you.

The main (and very unusual) headline this month is the immense power in your money house. Sixty to seventy per cent of the planets are either there or moving through there. The earning power here is stupendous and the aspects are favourable. Seventy per cent of the planetary genies are scheming and plotting to make you prosperous. Little things in your life – things you took for granted – have a hidden value that gets uncovered these days.

The main danger here is that you will start to define yourself in terms of your wealth. The lesson now is to put wealth in its proper perspective. There are certain things that money won't buy.

Though finance will be important all month, the 3rd House of Intellectual Interests becomes strong after the 22nd. This will be a good time to enjoy some of the fruits of wealth, to develop the mind and pursue mental interests. It's a good period for taking courses in subjects that interest you and for catching up on correspondence and phone calls.

Health is still excellent. You can enhance it further (after the 6th) by paying more attention to the liver and thighs.

Love is happy this month. Until the 11th, singles find love opportunities as they pursue their financial goals and with people involved in their finances. After the 11th, love happens in educational surroundings. Wealth and material gifts are alluring until until the 11th, but afterwards you want intellectual harmony and compatibility. You need someone you can talk to and share ideas with.

303

Sagittarius

♐

THE ARCHER

Birthdays from
23rd November to
20th December

Personality Profile

SAGITTARIUS AT A GLANCE

Element – Fire

Ruling Planet – Jupiter
    Career Planet – Mercury
    Love Planet – Mercury
    Money Planet – Saturn
    Planet of Health and Work – Venus
    Planet of Home and Family Life – Neptune
    Planet of Spirituality – Pluto

Colours – blue, dark blue

Colours that promote love, romance and social
    harmony – yellow, yellow-orange

Colours that promote earning power – black,
    indigo

SAGITTARIUS

Gems – carbuncle, turquoise

Metal – tin

Scents – carnation, jasmine, myrrh

Quality – mutable (= flexibility)

Qualities most needed for balance – attention to detail, administrative and organizational skills

Strongest virtues – generosity, honesty, broad-mindedness, tremendous vision

Deepest need – to expand mentally

Characteristics to avoid – over-optimism, exaggeration, being too generous with other people's money

Signs of greatest overall compatibility – Aries, Leo

Signs of greatest overall incompatibility – Gemini, Virgo, Pisces

Sign most helpful to career – Virgo

Sign most helpful for emotional support – Pisces

Sign most helpful financially – Capricorn

Sign best for marriage and/or partnerships – Gemini

Sign most helpful for creative projects – Aries

Best Sign to have fun with – Aries

Signs most helpful in spiritual matters – Leo, Scorpio

Best day of the week – Thursday

Understanding a Sagittarius

If you look at the symbol of the archer you will gain a good, intuitive understanding of a person born under this astrological Sign. The development of archery was humanity's first refinement of the power to hunt and wage war. The ability to shoot an arrow far beyond the ordinary range of a spear extended humanity's horizons, wealth, personal will and power.

Today, instead of using bows and arrows we project our power with fuels and mighty engines, but the essential reason for using these new powers remains the same. These powers represent our ability to extend our personal sphere of influence – and this is what Sagittarius is all about. Sagittarians are always seeking to expand their horizons, to cover more territory and increase their range and scope. This applies to all aspects of their lives: economic, social and intellectual.

Sagittarians are noted for the development of the mind – the higher intellect – which understands philosophical, metaphysical and spiritual concepts. This mind represents the higher part of the psychic nature and is motivated not by self-centred considerations but by the light and grace of a Higher Power. Thus, Sagittarians love higher education of all kinds. They might be bored with formal schooling but they love to study on their own and in their own way. A love of foreign travel and interest in places far away from home are also noteworthy characteristics of the Sagittarian type.

If you give some thought to all these Sagittarian attributes you will see that they spring from the inner Sagittarian desire to develop. To travel more is to know more, to know more is to be more, to cultivate the higher mind is to grow and to reach more. All these traits tend to broaden the intellectual – and indirectly, the economic and material – horizons of the Sagittarian.

SAGITTARIUS

The generosity of the Sagittarian is legendary. There are many reasons for this. One is that Sagittarians seem to have an inborn consciousness of wealth. They feel that they are rich, that they are lucky, that they can attain any financial goal – and so they feel that they can afford to be generous. Sagittarians do not carry the burdens of want and limitation – which stop most other people from giving generously. Another reason for their generosity is their religious and philosophical idealism, derived from the higher mind. This higher mind is by nature generous because it is unaffected by material circumstances. Still another reason is that the act of giving tends to enhance their emotional nature. Every act of giving seems to be enriching, and this is reward enough for the Sagittarian.

Finance

Sagittarians generally entice wealth. They either attract it or create it. They have the ideas, energy and talent to make their vision of paradise on Earth a reality. However, mere wealth is not enough. Sagittarians want luxury – earning a comfortable living seems small and insignificant to them.

In order for Sagittarians to attain their true earning potential they must develop better managerial and organizational skills. They must learn to set limits, to arrive at their goals through a series of attainable sub-goals or objectives. It is very rare that a person goes from rags to riches overnight. But a long, drawn-out process is difficult for Sagittarians. Like Leos, they want to achieve wealth and success quickly and impressively. They must be aware, however, that this over-optimism can lead to unrealistic financial ventures and disappointing losses. Of course, no Zodiac Sign can bounce back as quickly as Sagittarius, but only needless heartache will be caused by this attitude. Sagittarians need to maintain their vision – never letting it go – but must also work towards it in practical and efficient ways.

Career and Public Image

Sagittarians are big thinkers. They want it all: money, fame, glamour, prestige, public acclaim and a place in history. They often go after all these goals. Some attain them, some do not – much depends on each individual's personal horoscope. But if Sagittarians want to attain public and professional status they must understand that these things are not conferred to enhance one's ego but as rewards for the amount of service that one does for the whole of humanity. If and when they figure out ways to serve more, Sagittarians can rise to the top.

The ego of the Sagittarian is gigantic – and perhaps rightly so. They have much to be proud of. If they want public acclaim, however, they will have to learn to tone down the ego a bit, to become more humble and self-effacing, without falling into the trap of self-denial and self-abasement. They must also learn to master the details of life, which can sometimes elude them.

At their jobs Sagittarians are hard workers who like to please their bosses and co-workers. They are dependable, trustworthy and enjoy a challenge. Sagittarians are friendly to work with and helpful to their colleagues. They usually contribute intelligent ideas or new methods that improve the work environment for everyone. Sagittarians always look for challenging positions and careers that develop their intellect, even if they have to work very hard in order to succeed. They also work well under the supervision of others, although by nature they would rather be the supervisors and increase their sphere of influence. Sagittarians excel at professions that allow them to be in contact with many different people and to travel to new and exciting locations.

SAGITTARIUS

Love and Relationships

Sagittarians love freedom for themselves and will readily grant it to their partners. They like their relationships to be fluid and ever-changing. Sagittarians tend to be fickle in love and to change their minds about their partners quite frequently.

Sagittarians feel threatened by a clearly defined, well-structured relationship, as they feel this limits their freedom. The Sagittarian tends to marry more than once in life.

Sagittarians in love are passionate, generous, open, benevolent and very active. They demonstrate their affections very openly. However, just like an Aries they tend to be egocentric in the way they relate to their partners. Sagittarians should develop the ability to see others' points of view, not just their own. They need to develop some objectivity and cool intellectual clarity in their relationships so that they can develop better two-way communication with their partners. Sagittarians tend to be overly idealistic about their partners and about love in general. A cool and rational attitude will help them to perceive reality more clearly and enable them to avoid disappointment.

Home and Domestic Life

Sagittarians tend to grant a lot of freedom to their family. They like big homes and many children and are one of the most fertile Signs of the Zodiac. However, when it comes to their children Sagittarians generally err on the side of allowing them too much freedom. Sometimes their children get the idea that there are no limits. However, allowing freedom in the home is basically a positive thing – so long as some measure of balance is maintained – for it enables all family members to develop as they should.

Horoscope for 2006

General Trends

For some years now, many of you have been going through deep transformational processes. It has been a long and difficult journey. Many of you were forced to confront your personal underworld face to face – not a pleasant thing. You may have had near-death experiences. In recent years – 2001 to 2003 – this process was greatly accelerated. Some of you had health problems, surgeries, financial and marital crises and the like. (Some of this could have happened to your spouse or partner or people very close to you as well.)You were 'peering into the abyss of extinction'. But all of this was part of a great and wonderful plan. No Sagittarius got more than they could handle at any time. You were pushed to the edge but not over the edge. A whole new you was (and is) being born – the person you were meant to be. Your pains were labour pains, not punishments.

This year you are going to see some of the payoff for what you went through. You will enjoy the new you that has emerged, and you will understand why you needed each and every experience that you had.

Big, dramatic changes need to be made in your life, and now you have the confidence and the wherewithal to make them. Over the next few years, most of you will be in completely different conditions and circumstances – personally, socially, domestically and career-wise. It's going to be a very exciting ride.

Your major interests in the year ahead will be spirituality; the body, image and personal appearance; communication and intellectual interests; home, family and domestic life; religion, philosophy, higher education and foreign travel (always important interests, but especially in the year ahead).

SAGITTARIUS

Your paths to greatest fulfilment this year are spirituality; the body, image and personal appearance (after November 24th); children, fun and creativity (until June 23rd); home, family, domestic and psychological issues (after June 23rd).

Health

(Please note that this is an astrological perspective on health, not a medical one. At one time, both perspectives were identical, but in these times there could be quite a difference. For the medical perspective, please consult your physician or health professional.)

After what you've been through from 2001 to 2003, the year ahead is a snap. Health and vitality are vastly improved – only one long-term planet is in stressful aspect to you, two are in harmonious aspect and, later in the year, three will be in harmonious aspect. Your empty 6th House of Health shows that you don't need to pay any more attention than normal to this area. Nothing is wrong, so nothing has to be fixed.

You can enhance your already good health by paying more attention to the neck, throat, kidneys and hips. The neck, throat and hips (buttocks too) should be regularly massaged.

Sagittarius rules the liver and thighs, so it won't hurt to give these organs more attention as well. Thighs can be regularly massaged.

Venus is your health planet. Thus, for you, good health means good social health, healthy relationships and a healthy love life. Problems in relationships can very easily impact on your overall health. Any health problems that arise are probably coming from those kinds of things. If you bring your relationships back into harmony, chances are that the health problem will dissolve by itself.

Venus is a very fast-moving planet. During the year she will move through all the signs and houses of your horoscope. This means that health needs and powerful therapies can change from month to month. These short-term trends are discussed in the monthly reports.

Venus is retrograde from January 1st to February 8th, a pretty rare occurrence. This is not a time for making big and important changes to your diet, health regime or healing professionals. Rather, this is a time for studying these things more. If change is necessary, wait until after February 8th, when you'll have a very different perspective.

Personal transformation is still a big issue for many of you. Physical detox has been important for many years, and the trend continues this year. You may be tempted by cosmetic types of surgery, but much of the same effect can be obtained through spiritual disciplines such as yoga, meditation and nutrition. Their effects are slower and not as dramatic, but over the long haul they are more powerful.

The health of a parent or parent figure can be enhanced by paying more attention to the feet, ankles and spine. This person seems torn between new age and traditional types of medicine. The health of children and grandchildren seem status-quo. Children can enhance health through better nutrition and paying more attention to the small intestine. Grandchildren can enhance health by paying more attention to the spine, knees, teeth and overall skeletal alignment. Grandchildren seem more interested in and involved with health issues this year. If your spouse has a health problem there is good news about it. They benefit from detox regimes – mechanical or herbal. The liver, thighs, sexual organs, colon and bladder need more attention this year.

Health issues and regimes become more interesting for you from April 20th to May 20th and from May 29th to June 24th.

Home, Domestic and Family Issues

Ever since 2003, when Uranus began its flirtation with your 4th House, this area has been prominent and important. This will be so for many years to come.

Uranus is the planet of sudden, dramatic and drastic change. It likes to break barriers and assert its personal freedom. It can bring major rebellion or changes through new inventions and innovation. It is volatile and unpredictable.

So, this is the state of your home and family life these days. Over the course of the next few years you will see all of Uranus' scenarios happen. Many of you will break with your family or family members. Many of you will completely change your current domestic pattern. Many of you will move, perhaps a few times. Many of you will be constantly upgrading the home, renovating, rearranging and remodelling. Many of you are installing state-of-the-art communication equipment in the home.

At home, you are seeking maximum freedom. It's as if you resent *any* kind of limitation or obligation. Family members are mystified. (This could manifest the other way around too – it could be family members who are behaving this way, and you who are mystified.) It's as if the family tie, the family obligation, doesn't exist. Family members are very rebellious these days. In many cases, right or wrong has nothing to do with it. They rebel for the sake of rebellion.

While under the influence of a drug, normally sane and balanced people can do all kinds of strange things. The same is true under a planetary influence. The best way to handle these transits is to allow maximum freedom in the home – so long as it isn't destructive. Give freedom to your family, let go of your expectations of them, and give yourself freedom too.

Your emotional life also seems unusually volatile and extreme. Emotional highs are very high. The lows are ultra-low. Moods can shift in an instant. This can be with yourself or with family members. Your family can be extremely loving and co-operative one moment and in the next rebellious and nasty. This emotional volatility is behind all the changes we see in the home.

This is a time for cultivating emotional equilibrium. Try to steer a middle course between the highs and the lows, between love and hate and all emotional extremes. Try to separate yourself from your feelings.

This quest for more freedom in the home and with family is going to lead many of you into interesting and unusual experiments. It's as if you are throwing out all the old rule books, all the old traditions, and finding out how to do this on your own. True, you will have a few explosions here, but you will also have many successes. In the end, you will gain much new knowledge and wisdom – and this too is the purpose of the transit.

Children are making drastic and long-term changes to their image and personal appearance. They are also redefining their personalities these days. Adult children have a status-quo domestic situation. A parent or parent figure is spreading their wings, striking out in new ways and exploring their personal freedom. This, too, is probably contributing to the instability of the family situation. Grandchildren are having a more serious kind of year. Authority figures – perhaps uncles or aunts – are a little too harsh on them. They could use some bolstering of self-esteem. Adult grandchildren will probably move this year.

The urge to renovate and redecorate will be strong all year. April 14th to June 3rd and October 13th to December 16th are particularly good for renovation and heavy construction in the home. Redecorations or cosmetic home projects go better from April 6th to May 5th, July 19th to August 12th and October 24th to November 17th.

Love and Social Life

Neither your 7th House of Love and Marriage nor your 11th House of Friendships is particularly strong this year. This is not a major social year. I expect married Sagittarians will stay married and singles will stay single. It's important that you don't think there's anything wrong with you because you lack interest. In certain years it is very normal.

SAGITTARIUS

The lack of social interest could come from a sense of contentment. You seem satisfied with your present friendships, relationships and marital status, so there's no need to give undue attention to these things. Spiritual and psychological interests seem much more important in the year ahead. In fact, your social contentment frees up time and energy to develop yourself in other ways.

In any given year, even in an off-year, there will be times when social urges are stronger and expressed better than at other times. For you, these periods are January 1st to 4th, May 20th to June 21st and June 24th to July 19th.

For singles (those of you working on your first marriage) this is a year for preparing for true love, for making improvements in yourself, making yourself worthy of the beloved who will eventually come into your life. (The cosmos is already doing this to you, but you can co-operate with it.) It is also a year for learning to love your own company. (This will happen after November 24th.) If you don't love your own company, others won't either.

Those into their second marriage seem to have a crisis going on. Perhaps the relationship has become too practical and head-oriented, and some passion and feeling need to be injected there. The duties of marriage are weighing heavily on you. Those who are single, working on their second marriage, need patience. Perhaps marriage isn't even advisable. There will be romantic opportunities with money people – indeed you are allured by these kinds of people – but is the passion there? Those into their third marriage will have the relationship tested by the Solar Eclipse on September 22nd. This need not break it up but it will clear the air and bring necessary changes. Those who are single and working on their third marriage will have a status-quo year. This Solar Eclipse could make you re-evaluate your needs in love and attitudes to marriage. Singles who are working on the fourth marriage will have opportunity after November 24th. In general, 2007 will be a strong love year.

The marriage of parents or parent figures seems more unstable this year due to an almost compulsive need for freedom. Neither of them seems in the mood for compromise. Married siblings are facing crisis in their relationship. They need to bring back the feelings of romance. Single siblings probably shouldn't marry in the year ahead. Children of marriageable age have a status-quo year. Adult grandchildren are involved with glamorous people but affections seem too unstable for commitment.

Finance and Career

None of the houses involved with finance, career or work are prominent in the year ahead, so these areas seem status-quo. Again, as with love, don't feel there's anything wrong with you because of your lack of interest. Some years are like this.

This lack of interest in money, finance and career doesn't mean you won't have earnings or a career. These things are just on the backburner for a while. Your passions lie elsewhere – in the inner life, exploring your emotions and past history, in mental development and education.

Often, as mentioned earlier, this lack of interest can actually come from previous success and a feeling of contentment. And, after all, isn't this the purpose of wealth – to buy us the time and wherewithal to pursue our true passions?

When the 2nd House of Money and 10th House of Career are empty, the cosmos is giving you more freedom in these areas. So, if your personal horoscope (cast for your date, time and place of birth) shows great financial or career urges, this could be a spectacular year for you. But if it doesn't show these things, these areas will be status-quo. And that's wonderful too.

Last year (July 17th), your financial planet, Saturn, made a very important move from your 8th House to your 9th House. It will be in your 9th House for two more years. This shows earnings from the things you love to do – from travel, from connections to foreign countries, foreign investments or financial involvements with foreigners. Many of you can earn from teaching or from positions in academia. Religious ministry or the law will call many of you. More importantly, many of you will understand the true source of wealth and supply.

Even in an off-year there will be periods when finances and career will be more important (and happier) than at other times. For finance, your happiest and most active periods will be from January 1st to 20th, February 8th to March 5th, March 20th to April 19th, July 23rd to August 22nd and November 22nd to December 21st.

For career, these periods will be from August 20th to September 23rd, your yearly career peak.

The income of siblings is volatile. They can have some major reverses, but when they hit it big, it's really BIG. Their strong financial interests and drive are a big help for them. They are willing to overcome the challenges involved here. The income of parents or parent figures is status-quo, but a Solar Eclipse on March 29th might cause one of them to re-evaluate investments. Your spouse, lover and children have a stable year financially, as do grandchildren.

Self-improvement

With your financial planet in the metaphysical 9th House, the next two years are about reinforcing and deepening the knowledge you already have. More than any other sign in the zodiac, Sagittarius knows that wealth is spiritual, with its origins in the mind. The things we see all about us – the bank accounts, investments, homes, toys and so on – are only the symbols of wealth, the shadows projected from another level. The great illusion many fall under is to pursue the shadows – the things, the symbols – while ignoring the power that makes them happen. Perhaps some of you have fallen into this trap for a while, even though you know better. Now the cosmos is going to straighten it out.

Sagittarius is also the most religious and metaphysical of the signs, perhaps with the exception of Pisces. On the mundane level, the Sagittarius is like a jetsetter – they are the wealthy people of the planet. In their higher expression, they are the academic elite. And in the highest expression of all, Sagittarius represents the priesthood of the planet. They are our priests and philosophers. They interpret the spiritual laws for the rest of us and teach us how to approach and worship the Higher Power. They explain to us the meaning of life. Many of you are being prepared for these higher functions in the year ahead. Jupiter, your ruling planet, is now in the spiritual 12th House. Saturn is in your metaphysical 9th House. Many of you are having personal spiritual experiences and this is causing (as it should) a re-evaluation, a reordering of your religious and philosophical belief systems. There is a need to adjust the two. The dream life this year is hyperactive and very prophetic. In fact, with such a happy and active dream life, you may wonder why you bother getting up in the morning! ESP experiences are becoming everyday occurrences. There are many synchronistic kinds of experiences happening (strange coincidences and the like). The great inner world is letting you know of its existence and that it is on the case in your life. Go with the flow of this inner development as it will lead, eventually, to all the things you desire on the physical plane.

Month-by-month Forecasts

January

Best Days Overall: 6, 7, 15, 16, 25, 26

Most Stressful Days Overall: 3, 4, 10, 11, 17, 18, 19, 31

Best Days for Love: 8, 9, 10, 11, 17, 18, 19, 27, 28, 29, 30

SAGITTARIUS

Best Days for Money: 3, 4, 6, 12, 13, 15, 22, 23, 25, 27, 28, 31

Monthly Career Peaks: 17, 18, 19, 29, 30

Monthly Personal Pleasure Peaks: 22, 23, 25, 26

A rare Grand Square pattern shows that you are involved in some big project. You have to work harder than usual, which is affecting your finances and family life. There is some personal sacrifice involved as well – you can't indulge personal pleasures as much as you would like – but the payoff could be big.

The year begins with most of the planets in the East, the personal sector of your horoscope. Your 1st House of Self is strong, while your 7th House of Others is empty (only the Moon visits there on the 10th and 11th), so you are in a period of independence. You have more control over your life and happiness.

Most of the planets are below the horizon, in the lower, night side of the horoscope. Your 4th House of Home and Family is strong (and will get progressively stronger in coming months) while your 10th House of Career is empty – only the Moon visits there on the 17th, 18th and 19th. (That period, by the way, is your monthly career peak.) Another clear message: career and outer achievement can be down-played, and home, family and emotional interests can be emphasized.

You are getting your way in love, especially until the 4th. Love is there, pursuing you. Your spouse or lover is bending over backwards to please you; they are totally on your side, putting your interests ahead of their own. Your love planet, Mercury, moves very quickly this month. This shows much dating for singles and much social activity. Social confidence is strong, and needs in love change rapidly. Opportunity will come in different ways. After the 4th, romantic opportunity comes as you pursue your financial goals or with people involved in your finances. Singles are drawn to the wealthy, those who can help them financially. After the 22nd there is change. Now mental and intellectual harmony becomes important. Love opportunities come in educational settings, as well as with neighbours or locally.

The love planet will re-stimulate eclipse points on the 10th and 11th and from the 18th to the 20th. There is a need to be more patient with your beloved on those days as they are likely to be temperamental. Love can get tested and career can be turbulent. Parents, elders and bosses are more likely to be temperamental as well.

Though the financial planet is besieged and stressfully aspected – you are working very hard for earnings – this is still a prosperous month. Your money house is very strong, as is your interest in finance. With interest come the energy and the desire to overcome obstacles. You are getting a lot of help from your spouse or lover and social contacts. Jobseekers should be patient this month. Job offers need a lot of analysis and study before you accept them.

Health is excellent. With your health planet retrograde all month, avoid making drastic changes to your diet and health regime. In particular, avoid making permanent changes to the body. All of these things need more study. Next month, when your health planet starts moving forwards again, you will have a whole new perspective.

February

Best Days Overall: 2, 3, 11, 12, 21, 22

Most Stressful Days Overall: 1, 6, 7, 14, 15, 27, 28

Best Days for Love: 4, 5, 6, 7, 14, 15, 16, 17, 23, 24, 27, 28

Best Days for Money: 1, 2, 9, 10, 11, 19, 20, 21, 23, 24, 27, 28

SAGITTARIUS

Monthly Career Peaks: 14, 15, 27, 28

Monthly Personal Pleasure Peaks: 19, 20, 21, 22

The planets will start to shift from the East to the West after the 19th. Until then, most of the planets are still in the Eastern, personal sector of your horoscope. You continue to be independent and to create conditions as you like them. In coming months this will become more difficult, so act now while you can.

Like last month, most of the planets are below the horizon. Your 4th House of Home and Family becomes extremely powerful after the 19th, while your 10th House of Career is basically empty. Only the Moon will visit the 10th House on the 14th and 15th, and this will be your monthly career peak. You are in a night period of your year. Night is for dreaming, digesting and rejuvenating. And when the dawn breaks in your chart, you will be refreshed and energized to further your career.

Your ruler resides in the spiritual 12th House for most of this year. Your spiritual planet has been in your sign for many years now. And, this month, as the Sun moves into spiritual Pisces (on the 19th) your spirituality will increase even further. Aside from a greater interest in these kinds of subjects, you can expect increased spiritual experiences – enhanced ESP, prophetic dreams, an increase in the dream life in general, enhanced intuition, and more synchronistic experiences. You will probably be more sensitive to vibrations and need to be sure that you stay around only the most uplifting and positive kinds of people.

Health needs more watching this month, especially after the 19th. You can enhance health by paying more attention to the kidneys, hips, spine, knees, teeth and skeletal alignment. The health planet moves forwards on the 3rd, so this is a time to act on the health changes you've been contemplating.

Finances are stressful this month, but things will ease up after the 19th. Hang in there. Your financial muscles are getting stronger. With your financial planet retrograde, avoid making major financial changes, investments or purchases this month. This is a time for reviewing your financial life and seeing where you can improve your product or service. You are probably spending more on health and health products this month, but this field can also be a source of earnings. Colleagues or employees can have some very interesting financial ideas.

Love is still found close to home this month. Family or family connections play a role in love after the 9th. Singles might reconnect with an old flame, or with someone who reminds them of an old flame. This relationship might not be too serious; its purpose is to resolve old issues. Love is about nurturing and emotional support after the 9th. A current relationship is getting severely tested after the 18th. It looks like there's a power struggle going on. True love and commitment will survive, but anything less is in danger.

March

Best Days Overall: 1, 2, 10, 11, 12, 20, 21, 29, 30

Most Stressful Days Overall: 6, 7, 13, 14, 27, 28

Best Days for Love: 4, 5, 6, 7, 8, 9, 15, 16, 18, 19, 25, 26, 27, 28

Best Days for Money: 1, 8, 9, 10, 18, 19, 20, 23, 24, 27, 28, 29

Monthly Career Peaks: 13, 27, 28

Monthly Personal Pleasure Peaks: 18, 19, 20, 21

The Eastern and Western sectors of your horoscope are more or less evenly balanced this month. Neither one nor the other dominates. So this is a time for balancing personal interests with other people's interests, for sometimes being independent and sometimes cultivating social skills. In general, you will be more dependent on others from the 1st to the 12th and from the 29th to the 31st. You will be more independent from the 13th to the 28th.

Like last month, most of the planets are below the horizon. Your 4th House of Home and Family is very strong, especially until the 20th, while your 10th House of Career is basically empty. Only the Moon will visit there on the 13th and 14th, and this will be your monthly career peak. There is more excitement in the home these days. Perhaps renovations or upgrades are going on and your attention is needed there.

We have two eclipses this month. A Lunar Eclipse on the 14th – which is strong on you – and a Solar Eclipse on the 29th, which seems more benign.

The Lunar Eclipse is happening in your 10th House of Career. No doubt, your reviewing and digesting of this area is bringing on changes. They are probably good ones, but disruptive nevertheless. In coming months we see a 'detox' happening in the career. You are weeding out frivolous issues and focusing on essence. Those on a spiritual path will get new insight. An eclipse in the 10th House often shows shake-ups in your industry or corporate hierarchy. Since your career planet is retrograde from the 2nd to the 25th, don't make abrupt changes just yet. Study things more, let the dust settle, then make changes after the 25th. There can also be dramas with parents or parent figures this period. Reduce your schedule during this period. Your health needs watching more carefully until the 20th anyway, but especially during this eclipse period.

The Solar Eclipse of the 29th occurs in your 5th House. If you are involved in a love affair (not a marriage), it will be tested. Children make important changes in their lives. Since the Sun rules your 9th House of Religion and Metaphysics, religious beliefs get tested and there can be crises of faith. University students, or those preparing for university, make important changes in their education. People change their spiritual leaders or church affiliations under these kinds of influences as well.

Love still seems stressful. A power struggle with your beloved is in full swing. But with the retrograde of your love planet from the 2nd to the 25th, it is not wise to make any important love decision until after the 25th.

Finances improve dramatically after the 20th, but with your financial planet still retrograde, caution remains the financial watchword. Let progress happen steadily.

Health improves after the 20th. Until then, try to rest and relax and pay more attention to the ankles, massaging them regularly and giving them more support. Also, pay more attention to the heart. Miraculous – supernatural type – healings are likely from the 24th to the 27th. Metaphysical therapies seem unusually powerful during that period.

April

Best Days Overall: 7, 8, 17, 18, 25, 26

Most Stressful Days Overall: 2, 3, 9, 10, 23, 24, 29, 30

Best Days for Love: 2, 3, 4, 5, 14, 15, 16, 23, 24, 25, 26, 29, 30

Best Days for Money: 4, 5, 7, 14, 15, 17, 19, 20, 23, 24, 25

Monthly Career Peaks: 9, 10, 25, 26

Monthly Personal Pleasure Peaks: 14, 15, 17, 18

Career change is still very likely this period – perhaps this is due to the family situation or a move. With the career planet moving forwards, it is now a better time to go ahead than last month. Most of the planets remain below the horizon, and your 4th House of Home and Family is still strong. Even your career planet is in the 4th House until the 16th. Your 10th House of Career, by contrast, is mostly empty. The Moon will visit there on the 9th and 10th (your monthly career peak) but that's about it. Continue to pursue career goals through inner methods. Keep the focus on emotional harmony and right feeling. Work to stabilize the home base, which is not that easy.

On the 6th, the Western, social side of the horoscope becomes stronger than the Eastern, personal side. This is a time for cultivating social skills and for attaining ends through the grace of others.

The love crisis we've been seeing for some months now will start resolving after the 14th. Much depends on the depth of the love and commitment here. As in the past few months, love is about emotional nurturing and support. Emotional compatibility is very important, especially until the 16th. After the 16th, love is about fun. Singles don't appear interested in serious love. Playing the field and dating a lot seem the order of the day. With your love planet in fiery Aries, the tendency will be to rush into relationships too quickly. You are allured not by wealth, power or position but by the person who can show you a good time.

Your love planet will re-stimulate eclipse points on the 11th and 12th and the 22nd and 23rd. Be more patient with your beloved (and parents or parent figures) on those days.

Finances are good this month. The financial planet starts moving forwards on the 5th, restoring financial clarity and good judgement. Your financial planet also receives nice aspects, so you will wind up the month richer than when you began. Speculations are more favourable. You will earn in happier ways. Jobseekers have success this month, but issues of pay are the main sticking points. A sudden job opportunity can manifest itself from the 16th to the 19th. There might be some disruptions at work during that period as well. There seems to be some conflict regarding taxes, estates or insurance claims after the 14th. You will have to act boldly to resolve these things.

Health is good this period and you can enhance it by paying more attention to the ankles (until the 6th) and to the feet afterwards. Vigorous foot and ankle massage is powerful these days. Sudden and seemingly miraculous healings can happen from the 16th to the 19th. You might have to try a new and experimental therapy to resolve a long-standing health issue.

May

Best Days Overall: 4, 5, 14, 15, 22, 23, 29, 30

Most Stressful Days Overall: 7, 8, 20, 21, 27, 28

Best Days for Love: 3, 5, 6, 14, 15, 17, 22, 23, 27, 28

Best Days for Money: 2, 3, 4, 5, 12, 13, 14, 16, 17, 20, 21, 22, 29, 30, 31

Monthly Career Peaks: 7, 8, 15, 16

Monthly Personal Pleasure Peaks: 12, 13, 14, 15

Your personal planet, Jupiter, has been retrograde for a few months. This coincided with the shift of the planets to the West, which this month is even stronger than last month. Personal confidence and perhaps self-esteem is not as strong as usual, and this looks like a good thing. You are less likely to be overly assertive or belligerent. You are more likely to do what you should be doing: down-playing personal will, putting other people first and achieving aims through co-operation and consensus.

Your 7th House of Love and Romance becomes very strong after the 21st. You are entering your yearly social peak, enjoying wonderful romantic and social experiences. New friends – and prominent ones – are coming into the picture. A mentor or mentor type is involved in your love life, either personally or as an advisor. Love and love opportunities come in many ways this month: as you pursue leisure activities (until the 5th); at parties and social gatherings – the normal ways (from the 21st onwards); at the workplace or with people involved in your health, or as you pursue health goals (from the 5th to the 29th). Spiritual compatibility seems to be the main challenge in love. There is a need for tolerance here. You can be a Buddhist and your lover can be a born-again Christian. Romantic meetings could also happen in foreign countries.

Finances are still stressful, though earnings will come. It's just that there is a lot of work involved with them. This should improve after the 21st. But in spite of the challenges you are at least clear about your plans and goals, and your financial judgement is good.

Your health needs watching more carefully after the 21st. Enhance health through foot massage (until the 4th), through scalp and facial massage (after the 4th) and by paying more attention to the heart from the 21st onwards. Of course, keeping energy levels high is the most important thing, so rest and relax more and pace yourself. When your health planet moves into your 5th House (on the 4th), joy and fun will be important health tonics. A creative hobby will also improve overall health.

Venus, the health and work planet, will re-stimulate eclipse points on the 11th and 12th. This can bring some dramas at work or health changes, but they seem short-term and not serious.

Mars will re-stimulate eclipse points on the 1st, so avoid risky activities that day.

The love planet will re-stimulate eclipse points on the 30th and 31st. Be more patient with your lover, spouse and friends on those days, and also with parents or parent figures. Forewarned is forearmed.

June

Best Days Overall: 1, 2, 10, 11, 19, 20, 28, 29

Most Stressful Days Overall: 3, 4, 17, 18, 23, 24, 30

Best Days for Love: 3, 4, 8, 9, 12, 13, 17, 18, 22, 23, 24, 26, 27

Best Days for Money: 1, 8, 9, 10, 12, 13, 17, 18, 19, 25, 26, 28

Monthly Career Peaks: 3, 4, 25, 26, 30

Monthly Personal Pleasure Peaks: 8, 9, 10, 11

Most of the planets are still in the West, and your 7th House of Love and Social Activities is much stronger than your 1st House of Self. You are still very much in your yearly social peak. Continue to down-play self-interest and focus on other people. Cultivate your social skills now.

Love is still active and happy – not perfect, but more happy than stressful. There continue to be love opportunities in foreign lands or with people of different cultures. The workplace, gym or yoga studio are also scenes of romance. Love seems more harmonious from the 3rd to the 28th.

By the 24th the planetary power makes an important shift from the lower, night side of the horoscope to the upper, day side. Sixty to seventy per cent of the planets will then be in the upper half. So, it is time to de-emphasize the home, family and emotional life and start to express your outer urges, to pursue your career and life work. With your 4th House of Home and Family still strong – and with much change and ferment going on there – you won't be able to ignore it completely, but you can shift more attention to the career. The North Node of the Moon moves into your 4th House on the 23rd, where it will stay for a few years. This reinforces the importance of this area of life. Mainly, I read it as a need for more psychological development and understanding, and a fulfilment that will come from that.

Your health still needs watching until the 21st. Enhance health by keeping your energy levels high, through neck and throat massage (until the 24th) and arm and shoulder massage (after the 24th). Pay more attention to the lungs as well (after the 24th).

Finances are getting stronger day by day. Mars starts to travel with your financial planet on the 3rd, bringing great energy and enthusiasm to the financial life. Perhaps you have been overly conservative and cautious (basically a good thing, but sometimes we overdo it) and Mars will get you to take bold and necessary actions. Speculations are more favourable, but only under intuition. Money is earned in happier ways. Children have good financial ideas. Personal creativity can produce earnings, a wonderful aspect for artists and performers. Social contacts help earnings after the 28th. Parents and your spouse or lover also seem supportive. The prosperity of this month is only a taste of what is to come later in the year.

You are all travellers, but try to avoid unnecessary journeys from the 14th to the 16th and on the 30th when the Sun is re-stimulating eclipse points.

Your love planet re-stimulates eclipse points on the 1st and from the 8th to the 10th. Your spouse or lover, parents and sometimes friends can be more temperamental those days. Have patience.

July

Best Days Overall: 8, 9, 16, 17, 25, 26

Most Stressful Days Overall: 1, 14, 15, 20, 21, 27, 28, 29

Best Days for Love: 3, 4, 7, 8, 12, 13, 15, 20, 21, 22, 23, 24

Best Days for Money: 5, 6, 8, 9, 10, 11, 14, 15, 16, 17, 23, 24, 25, 26

Monthly Career Peaks: 1, 23, 24, 27, 28

Monthly Personal Pleasure Peaks: 5, 6, 8, 9

The fire element, your native element, is strong this month. You will want to get everything done in a hurry, but the many retrogrades going on will slow things down (up to 50 per cent of the planets are retrograde from the 3rd to the 7th, and 40 per cent thereafter). Make haste, but don't neglect the details or they will come back to haunt you.

Like last month, most of the planets are above the horizon. Your 10th House of Career will become powerful after the 21st, when Mars moves in. The planets involved with the home and family are retrograde, so many of these issues will have no quick fix and you may as well focus on your career. Doing right is more important than feeling right.

Career matters are complicated by the retrograde of your career planet, Mercury, from the 3rd to the 29th. Any career offers should be studied carefully as they may not be what they seem. Mars' move into your 10th House on the 21st will force important actions, but do your homework first. Your career seems happy, however, and you can enhance it through leisure pursuits, such as entertaining clients. Leisure activities can also lead to career advancement.

The Western, social sector of your chart is still stronger than the Eastern sector. Personal initiative and direct action are not as important as your social skills, except in your career. Who you know is more important than what you can do. Continue to adapt to situations and put other people first.

Though there is love in this chart, its status is cloudy. The retrograde of your love planet from the 3rd to the 29th puts things in doubt. It's good to review your relationships now and see where you can make improvements. Like last month, there are love opportunities at work or with colleagues (also with bosses after the 21st). From the 10th onwards love is about passion and sexual attraction. But there is also a 'detox' going on in your love and social life – you need to focus on essence issues.

The 9th House, your favourite house, is very strong this month. The cosmos pushes you to do what you most love to do, so there is more travel (try to schedule these things after the 7th) and higher education happening. You are able to pursue your interest in religion and philosophy. Philosophical revelation is not only good in its own right, but will also lead to financial improvement.

This month is a prosperous period. You spend more and you earn more. Again, foreign countries, foreigners, educators and academics play a big role here. The only problem is that you may have to sacrifice sensual pleasures and desires and focus on the bottom line.

Health is excellent this month. You can enhance it by paying more attention to the arms and shoulders (massage them regularly) and the stomach and breasts (after the 19th). Diet becomes more important after the 19th.

August

Best Days Overall: 4, 5, 12, 13, 21, 22, 23, 31

Most Stressful Days Overall: 10, 11, 17, 18, 24, 25

Best Days for Love: 2, 3, 11, 12, 17, 18, 21, 22, 23, 31

Best Days for Money: 2, 3, 4, 5, 6, 7, 10, 11, 12, 13, 19, 20, 21, 22, 23, 29, 30, 31

Monthly Career Peaks: 22, 23, 24, 25, 27, 28

Monthly Personal Pleasure Peaks: 2, 3, 4, 5, 29, 30, 31

Like last month, most of the planets are above the horizon in the day side of your chart. Your 10th House of Career becomes even stronger than last month, especially after the 23rd. Further, your career planet, Mercury, is now moving forwards (and quickly at that). You are in your yearly career peak, enjoying wonderful career experiences. And while there is much instability at home, focus most of your energy on the career. Deal with any family crisis that arises and get right back to business.

The planets make an important shift this month from the Western, social sector to the Eastern, personal sector. This will be established by the 28th, when Mercury crosses into the East. So your days of people-pleasing and adapting to situations are about over. You are becoming ever more independent, ever more able to have life on your terms.

Career is very hectic now. It's been that way for more than a month and becomes even more so now. You or your company face stiff competition. There are attacks on your position and you must defend yourself against them. And you will; you have the drive to do it. Career progress should be swift this month.

You advance your career not only by bold actions, but also by education, social connections, attending and hosting parties (especially after the 28th) and by strong ethics. Faith is an important ingredient in career success these days.

With the 9th House still powerful, there is more travel and educational opportunity, which is probably career-related. These opportunities look happy and you should take them if possible.

Your love planet moves quickly this month, passing through three signs and houses of your horoscope. Thus your needs in love will change quickly (Sagittarians are known for being fickle), and love opportunities will come in different ways. Until the 11th, love is about sexual attraction and chemistry. After the 11th, love is about philosophical and religious harmony. Mentor types attract you. Love is a way you can grow intellectually and is not just about sexual passion. Opportunities for love happen in educational or religious settings, perhaps also in foreign countries. After the 28th, the career is the scene of romantic opportunity. (There have been opportunities for love affairs in your career for a while, but now more serious love is possible.) Love affairs (not marriages) get tested from the 29th to the 31st, as Mars re-stimulates eclipse points.

Finances are still wonderful. Your financial planet has been moving forwards for some months and receiving very nice aspects. A lucrative job offer comes from the 25th to the 28th. Windfalls could also happen during that period.

Your health needs watching more carefully after the 23rd. Rest and relax more then. Enhance your health by paying more attention to the stomach, breasts and overall diet until the 13th, and to the heart afterwards.

September

Best Days Overall: 1, 9, 10, 17, 18, 19, 27, 28, 29

Most Stressful Days Overall: 7, 8, 13, 14, 20, 21

Best Days for Love: 1, 2, 3, 4, 11, 12, 13, 14, 20, 21, 22, 23, 30

Best Days for Money: 1, 3, 4, 7, 8, 9, 10, 15, 16, 17, 18, 19, 25, 26, 27, 28, 29, 30

Monthly Career Peaks: 5, 6, 20, 21, 22, 23

Monthly Personal Pleasure Peaks: 1, 25, 26, 27, 28, 29

In general, you are in a cycle of dramatic and sudden changes. These have been going on all year, but this month they are likely to accelerate. Two powerful eclipses impact strongly on you. With energy not up to its usual standards, you need to reduce your activities until the 23rd, especially around the eclipse periods.

The Lunar Eclipse of the 7th occurs in your 4th House and brings dramatic changes to the family pattern and relationships. Passions at home will run high. Sometimes families actually break up under these aspects. Sometimes there is only a clearing of the air. Often people move under these aspects. Sometimes they merely have to correct long-standing problems in the home. Your job is to maintain emotional equilibrium as much as possible. Cars and communication equipment will get tested. There could be drama or disruptions in your neighbourhood. Perhaps heavy construction is going on there, or old neighbours move out and new ones move in. Schoolchildren make important changes to their education.

The Solar Eclipse of the 22nd occurs on the border of your 10th and 11th Houses. Those of you born later in the sign of Sagittarius will feel it strongest, particularly those born between December 15th and 21st. This eclipse brings career change, upheavals with bosses or in your industry or corporate hierarchy, and dramas with parents or parent figures. Friendships will also get tested. Dramatic, out-of-the-ordinary experiences happen to friends. Your relationship to a professional or social organization changes.

Career is still very important this month, and you remain in your yearly career peak. But considering your energy levels, focus only on essence. Obstructions are getting blasted away by the Solar Eclipse of the 22nd. Let the dust settle.

Health is going to improve dramatically after the 23rd. In the meantime, enhance your health by paying more attention to the heart and small intestine (after the 6th). Diet is also important after the 6th.

This is a month when you are mingling with people above you in status. Your spouse or partner receives honour and recognition this month and seems supportive of your career. Singles are allured by power and prominence until the 13th. You seem to approach love from the head rather than the heart, but this is a short phase. After the 13th, you become more heart-oriented, romantic and interested in the feeling of love than in practical issues. Now you want someone who can be your friend and your equal.

October

Best Days Overall: 6, 7, 15, 16, 25, 26

Most Stressful Days Overall: 4, 5, 10, 11, 17, 18, 19

Best Days for Love: 2, 3, 4, 10, 11, 12, 13, 14, 21, 22, 23, 24

Best Days for Money: 1, 4, 5, 7, 12, 13, 14, 16, 22, 23, 24, 26, 27, 28

Monthly Career Peaks: 17, 18, 22, 23, 24

Monthly Personal Pleasure Peaks: 22, 23, 24, 25, 26

Things still seem hectic, volatile and unstable at home. You won't be able to ignore these things completely, but with most of the planets still above the horizon, keep your main focus on the career and your outer goals.

Like last month, most of the planets are still in the East, the personal sector of your horoscope. Your 1st House of Self is strong, while your 7th House of Others is basically empty (only the Moon will visit there on the 10th and 11th, your monthly social peak). Personal initiative and direct actions lead to achievement and happiness.

The 11th House of Friends and Group Activities is strong until the 23rd. Friends are better than the situations vacant for jobseekers. In fact, friendship seems more important than romance this month. This is also a month when you expand your knowledge of technology, astrology and science in general.

Your 12th House of Spirituality becomes unbelievably powerful after the 23rd. Fifty to sixty per cent of the planets are either there or moving through there. Some of you have trouble 'touching ground'. A little unworldliness is good at times, and this is one of them. You can expect all kinds of spiritual phenomena during this period. Psychic and ESP abilities, which have been strong all year, become even stronger. Dreams are in Technicolor, and perhaps more interesting than everyday life; they are also prophetic. You are going to receive much inner revelation on health and healing issues, your career (but more about your spiritual mission and not just the worldly career) and your love life. Psychics, gurus, astrologers and spiritual channels all play a greater role in your life now. This is a wonderful period for spiritual retreats, meditation seminars, introspection and review, and charitable activities.

All this spirituality could stress finances this month, but this is on the surface. It will force some needed adjustments to your financial life. Your interest in practical, bottom line issues is not as strong as usual. Your altruism can be so powerful that you give more to charity or those in need than you can really afford. You need to keep your giving in proportion.

Romance and career opportunity both happen in spiritual surroundings as well. Career needs inspiration, not some material action. Love is very idealistic now, and spiritual compatibility becomes very important.

Health is wonderful now. You can enhance it further by paying more attention to the kidneys and hips until the 24th. Hip massage is unusually effective. After the 24th, spiritual healing methods will be powerful, and many of you will experience miraculous healing. Perhaps you will be involved in the 'miraculous' healing of others as well. Practise safe sex and pay more attention to the colon and bladder after the 24th. Detox regimes will also be powerful during that period.

November

Best Days Overall: 3, 11, 12, 21, 22, 30

Most Stressful Days Overall: 1, 7, 8, 13, 14, 15, 28, 29

Best Days for Love: 1, 7, 8, 9, 10, 19, 20, 21, 28, 29, 30

SAGITTARIUS

Best Days for Money: 1, 2, 3, 10, 12, 20, 22, 23, 24, 30

Monthly Career Peaks: 13, 14, 19, 20

Monthly Personal Pleasure Peaks: 16, 17, 19, 20, 21, 22, 24

The spirituality and otherworldliness that we saw last month continues this month. Your 12th House of Spirituality is still packed with planets – 50 to 60 per cent of them.

After the 24th, the world will call to you. You will be grounded, in your body and enjoying all the sensual delights the world has to offer. Your otherworldly interests did not lead you to renunciation or monk-hood but to greater personal fulfilment. If anything, your otherworldliness led you to greater appreciation of being in a body, of being incarnate in this mortal world. Sagittarians are always high livers, but this month (and in coming months) even more so. Whether a Sagittarian is actually rich or not is never relevant. They live as if they are rich.

The main headline this month is when Jupiter (your ruling planet) moves from Scorpio into your own sign on the 24th. This is your month and your year.

Most of the planets are in the East. Your 1st House of Self is not only strong but packed with benevolent planets. If there was ever a time to have life on your terms, this is it. Every good gift is coming to you. Go boldly after your dreams.

Finances are temporarily stressed until the 22nd. This seems to come either from overgenerosity or from too much focus on otherworldly things. But this will change dramatically after the 22nd. Earnings will start to skyrocket. Financial judgement is good and speculations are favourable. If you keep your spending proportional, all will be well.

With Venus in your own sign after the 17th, this is a great period to buy personal items such as clothing, accessories or jewellery. Your taste is excellent and your choices will be outstanding.

Love is slower this month as your love planet is retrograde until the 18th. The love trends of last month apply now as well. Love happens in spiritual surroundings, or at charity or altruistic events. Astrologers, psychics and gurus have important love guidance for you. Spiritual compatibility in love is still very important.

Your career is also advanced in spiritual ways, through intuition and inspiration and more involvement in charitable and altruistic activities.

Health is excellent. You might make important changes to the diet and health regime on the 29th and 30th when your health planet re-stimulates eclipse points.

December

Best Days Overall: 1, 8, 9, 10, 18, 19, 27, 28

Most Stressful Days Overall: 4, 5, 11, 12, 25, 26, 31

Best Days for Love: 1, 4, 5, 9, 10, 11, 21, 22, 29, 30, 31

Best Days for Money: 1, 4, 8, 9, 10, 18, 19, 21, 22, 27, 28

Monthly Career Peaks: 9, 10, 11, 12, 18, 19

Monthly Personal Pleasure Peaks: 16, 17, 18, 19

The major headline this month is the convention of mostly beneficent planets in your own sign and in your 1st House. Sixty to seventy per cent of them are either there or moving through there. Energy levels are super-high: you have the energy to achieve any goal in life. You are not only in a yearly personal pleasure peak, but probably a lifetime one. Wonderful sensual experiences are happening. It is very easy to have things your way and to create happy conditions for yourself.

Your health is excellent. The main danger is overindulgence in the good life. Listen to your body. Seventy to eighty per cent of the planets are in your native Fire element. This, too, is an unusual percentage and shows a hyperactive month. The health danger here is burnout. You can enhance your already wonderful health by paying more attention to the liver and thighs until the 11th and to the spine, knees, teeth, bone structure and skeletal alignment afterwards.

Like last month, earnings are skyrocketing. Even the retrograde of your financial planet, Saturn, on the 6th can't stop wealth. It only counsels more homework and study. Career and job opportunities are running after you, and you are likely to be more selective now. You are not so career driven that you disturb your emotional harmony.

Love is pursuing you, and this is high-level love. Prominent people are eager for your favours. Love, like almost everything else in life, is on your terms. Your lover or spouse is bending over backwards to please you.

The good you experience this month is just the beginning as 2007 will also be an outstanding year.

Mars re-stimulates eclipse points from the 26th to the 28th. This could test a love affair. Avoid speculations or risky activities during this period.

Venus re-stimulates eclipse points from the 9th to the 12th. This can bring much needed changes to the diet and health regime. There can be some dramas at work.

Mercury re-stimulates eclipse points from the 17th to the 19th and from the 26th to the 28th. Be more patient with your lover, spouse, parent or parent figure those days as they are more likely to be temperamental.

Capricorn

♑

THE GOAT

Birthdays from
21st December to
19th January

Personality Profile

CAPRICORN AT A GLANCE

Element – Earth

Ruling Planet – Saturn
   Career Planet – Venus
   Love Planet – Moon
   Money Planet – Uranus
   Planet of Communications – Neptune
   Planet of Health and Work – Mercury
   Planet of Home and Family Life – Mars
   Planet of Spirituality – Jupiter

Colours – black, indigo

Colours that promote love, romance and social
   harmony – puce, silver

Colour that promotes earning power –
   ultramarine blue

CAPRICORN

Gem – black onyx

Metal – lead

Scents – magnolia, pine, sweet pea, wintergreen

Quality – cardinal (= activity)

Qualities most needed for balance – warmth, spontaneity, a sense of fun

Strongest virtues – sense of duty, organization, perseverance, patience, ability to take the long-term view

Deepest needs – to manage, take charge and administrate

Characteristics to avoid – pessimism, depression, undue materialism and undue conservatism

Signs of greatest overall compatibility – Taurus, Virgo

Signs of greatest overall incompatibility – Aries, Cancer, Libra

Sign most helpful to career – Libra

Sign most helpful for emotional support – Aries

Sign most helpful financially – Aquarius

Sign best for marriage and/or partnerships – Cancer

Sign most helpful for creative projects – Taurus

Best Sign to have fun with – Taurus

Signs most helpful in spiritual matters – Virgo, Sagittarius

Best day of the week – Saturday

341

Understanding a Capricorn

The virtues of Capricorns are such that there will always be people for and against them. Many admire them, many dislike them. Why? It seems to be because of Capricorn's power urges. A well-developed Capricorn has his or her eyes set on the heights of power, prestige and authority. In the Sign of Capricorn, ambition is not a fatal flaw, but rather the highest virtue.

Capricorns are not frightened by the resentment their authority may sometimes breed. In Capricorn's cool, calculated, organized mind all the dangers are already factored into the equation – the unpopularity, the animosity, the misunderstandings, even the outright slander – and a plan is always in place for dealing with these things in the most efficient way. To the Capricorn, situations that would terrify an ordinary mind are merely problems to be managed, bumps on the road to ever-growing power, effectiveness and prestige.

Some people attribute pessimism to the Capricorn Sign, but this is a bit deceptive. It is true that Capricorns like to take into account the negative side of things. It is also true that they love to imagine the worst possible scenario in every undertaking. Other people might find such analyses depressing, but Capricorns only do these things so that they can formulate a way out – an escape route.

Capricorns will argue with success. They will show you that you are not doing as well as you think you are. Capricorns do this to themselves as well as to others. They do not mean to discourage you but rather to root out any impediments to your greater success. A Capricorn boss or supervisor feels that no matter how good the performance there is always room for improvement. This explains why Capricorn supervisors are difficult to handle and even infuriating at times. Their actions are, however, quite often effective – they can get their subordinates to improve and become better at their jobs.

Capricorn is a born manager and administrator. Leo is better at being king or queen, but Capricorn is better at being prime minister – the person actually wielding power.

Capricorn is interested in the virtues that last, in the things that will stand the test of time and trials of circumstance. Temporary fads and fashions mean little to a Capricorn – except as things to be used for profit or power. Capricorns apply this attitude to business, love, to their thinking and even to their philosophy and religion.

Finance

Capricorns generally attain wealth and they usually earn it. They are willing to work long and hard for what they want. They are quite amenable to foregoing a short-term gain in favour of long-term benefits. Financially, they come into their own later in life.

However, if Capricorns are to attain their financial goals they must shed some of their strong conservatism. Perhaps this is the least desirable trait of the Capricorn. They can resist anything new merely because it is new and untried. They are afraid of experimentation. Capricorns need to be willing to take a few risks. They should be more eager to market new products or explore different managerial techniques. Otherwise, progress will leave them behind. If necessary, Capricorns must be ready to change with the times, to discard old methods that no longer work.

Very often this experimentation will mean that Capricorns have to break with existing authority. They might even consider changing their present position or starting their own ventures. If so, they should be willing to accept all the risks and just get on with it. Only then will a Capricorn be on the road to highest financial gain.

Career and Public Image

A Capricorn's ambition and quest for power are evident. It is perhaps the most ambitious Sign of the Zodiac – and usually the most successful in a worldly sense. However, there are lessons Capricorns need to learn in order to fulfil their highest aspirations.

Intelligence, hard work, cool efficiency and organization will take them a certain distance, but will not carry them to the very top. Capricorns need to cultivate their social graces, to develop a social style, along with charm and an ability to get along with people. They need to bring beauty into their lives and to cultivate the right social contacts. They must learn to wield power gracefully, so that people love them for it – a very delicate art. They also need to learn how to bring people together in order to fulfil certain objectives. In short, Capricorns require some of the gifts – the social grace – of the Libra to get to the top.

Once they have learned this, Capricorns will be successful in their careers. They are ambitious hard workers who are not afraid of putting in the required time and effort. Capricorns take their time in getting the job done – in order to do it well – and they like moving up the corporate ladder slowly but surely. Being so driven by success, Capricorns are generally liked by their bosses, who respect and trust them.

Love and Relationships

Like Scorpio and Pisces, Capricorn is a difficult Sign to get to know. They are deep, introverted and like to keep their own counsel. Capricorns do not like to reveal their innermost thoughts. If you are in love with a Capricorn, be patient and take your time. Little by little you will get to understand him or her.

Capricorns have a deep romantic nature, but they do not show it straightaway. They are cool, matter of fact and not especially emotional. They will often show their love in practical ways.

It takes time for a Capricorn – male or female – to fall in love. They are not the love-at-first-sight kind. If a Capricorn is involved with a Leo or Aries, these Fire types will be totally mystified – to them the Capricorn will seem cold, unfeeling, unaffectionate and not very spontaneous. Of course none of this is true; it is just that Capricorn likes to take things slowly. They like to be sure of their ground before making any demonstrations of love or commitment.

Even in love affairs Capricorns are deliberate. They need more time to make decisions than is true of the other Signs of the Zodiac, but given this time they become just as passionate. Capricorns like a relationship to be structured, committed, well regulated, well defined, predictable and even routine. They prefer partners who are nurturers, and they in turn like to nurture their partners. This is their basic psychology. Whether such a relationship is good for them is another issue altogether. Capricorns have enough routine in their lives as it is. They might be better off in relationships that are a bit more stimulating, changeable and fluctuating.

Home and Domestic Life

The home of a Capricorn – as with a Virgo – is going to be tidy and well organized. Capricorns tend to manage their families in the same way they manage their businesses. Capricorns are often so career-driven that they find little time for the home and family. They should try to get more actively involved in their family and domestic life. Capricorns do, however, take their children very seriously and are very proud parents, particularly should their children grow up to become respected members of society.

Horoscope for 2006

General Trends

Love, money and career have been the headlines for some years now. Social goals, such as marriage or a significant relationship, have been attained and you are cultivating friendships. Now you are focused on the prosperity of others – particularly your spouse or partner – rather than just on personal earning power.

The deeper things in life are also calling to you this year. Occult studies are interesting. You want to learn more about life after death and past lives. You want to delve deeply into the psyche. Personal transformation – the transformation of the physical body – is also an important interest. This will be a more serious kind of year.

Health should be vastly improved this year as there are no long-term planets in stressful aspect to you.

Your career was strong and happy last year, and now you want the payoff that comes with career success – the right kind of social life and friends, memberships in the right clubs and organizations.

Your major areas of interest this year are finance; communication and intellectual interests; the deeper things of life, personal transformation, life after death and past lives; tax, insurance and estate issues; friendships and group activities, astrology, astronomy, science and scientific pursuits; spirituality.

Your paths to greatest fulfilment in the year ahead are friendships and group activities (until November 24th); spirituality, charity and altruistic activities (after November 24th); home, family and domestic interests (until June 23rd); communication and intellectual interests (after June 23rd).

CAPRICORN

Health

(Please note that this is an astrological perspective on health, not a medical one. At one time, both perspectives were identical, but in these times there could be quite a difference. For the medical perspective, please consult your physician or health professional.)

As mentioned earlier, health looks excellent this year. If you have had a health condition in the past, this is a year for hearing good news about it. Overall energy and vitality are strong, which is the main factor at play. There are no long-term planets stressing you out.

Your 6th House of Health is basically empty. (Short-term planets will pass through there, temporarily enhancing interest, but there are no long-term planets there.) This lack of interest in health should be read as a good thing considering the overall ease of the aspects this year. You can sort of take good health for granted. You have no need to pay too much attention as everything is basically OK.

There are many things you can do to enhance your already good health. First off, as a Capricorn, it is always good to pay extra attention to the spine, knees, teeth, overall skeletal alignment (very important for you) and the gall bladder. This will enhance not only overall health but personal appearance as well.

With Mercury as your health planet, it is also good to pay more attention to the arms, shoulders, lungs and small intestine. Arms and shoulders can be regularly massaged.

Mercury is a very fast-moving planet. In a given year he will move through all the signs and houses of your horoscope. This means you are the kind of person whose health needs vary from month to month. Effective therapies will also vary monthly, and these short-term trends will be discussed in the monthly reports.

Saturn, your ruler, and one of the most important planets in your horoscope, will be in the 8th House all year. This is showing us many things. You are very interested in personal transformation, but especially of the body. Detox regimes are both interesting and powerful in the year ahead. This is also a wonderful year for weight-loss regimes.

When one's ruling planet is in the 8th House, there is usually a confrontation with death. This doesn't mean physical, literal death, but a psychological confrontation. It's as if the cosmos brings it close to you so that you are forced to come to terms with it. Often people have near-death experiences, or they experience death in their environment. They often have dreams or nightmares of death. When the 8th House is active in someone's chart they will often see dead animals as they walk the street or drive. Fear of death prevents people from living fully now, so it is good to confront and understand it.

The health of a parent or parent figure can be enhanced by new or alternative therapies. This person will benefit from regular foot and ankle massage, and from giving the ankles more support when exercising. Your spouse or lover, like you, benefits from detox regimes. Surgeries will probably be recommended as solutions to health issues, but a second (or even third) opinion is wise. If there is a health problem, your spouse or lover will hear good news after November 24th. The health of children seems status-quo. Grandchildren can enhance their health through foot and ankle massage. Friends' health is status-quo, though a good friend is making dramatic changes to their health regime. Siblings are taking on serious and disciplined health regimes; they seem orthodox and traditional in their approach to health. Like you, they need more care for the spine, knees, teeth, skeletal alignment, gall bladder and heart.

Home, Domestic and Family Issues

Even though your 4th House of Home and Family is not a House of Power this year, there could be some major changes in this area brought on by two eclipses. As the year begins you are still under the influence of the Lunar Eclipse of October 17th 2005, which occurred in your 4th House. On March 29th, there will be a Solar Eclipse in this same house, and the effects can last for up to six months or so.

I read this as follows: your lack of interest in home and family matters (your basically empty 4th House) could cause you to neglect this area, and the eclipses will force you back. If you've been neglecting family, dramas with family members will force you to pay attention. If you've been neglecting the physical house, the eclipses will show you what needs to be done by highlighting flaws or problems. If you've been on top of things with the home and family, these eclipses should be mild.

Overall, most of you will have more freedom and latitude with home and family matters, freedom to shape this area as you like. If you are going to do heavy construction in the home, June 3rd to July 21st and October 23rd to November 21st are good times. If you're going to entertain from home, redecorate cosmetically or buy art objects for the home, May 5th to 29th is a good time.

There could be dramas with a parent or parent figure this year, as the eclipses impact on them. I expect that this person will make important modifications to their image or personality. It will take time for family members to adjust to this. Adult children might feel cramped in their present living arrangements, but a move is not advisable. They just need to make better use of the space they have. Adult grandchildren will move either in late 2006 (after November 24th) or in 2007. Perhaps they are buying a run-down home and fixing it up. There is a lot of construction going on in their home. Siblings are leading a nomadic existence but their domestic situation seems status-quo.

Mars, your family planet, will move through at least eight different houses of your horoscope. When the aspects are kind to Mars, home and family issues will go smoothly.

When they are unkind, there are challenges. Thus the family situation will have its normal fluctuations this year, which will be discussed in the monthly reports.

Love and Social Life

As mentioned earlier, you have probably achieved your love and romantic goals in the past few years. Romance (especially for those working on or in your first marriage) is not a major priority. The real social action is happening in the area of friendships, and this looks very happy. New and prominent friendships are being formed. You have a happy involvement with groups and organizations that think like you.

There is a very interesting (and positive) 'mutual reception' aspect happening between Jupiter and Pluto, your spiritual and friendship planets. Each is a guest in the other's house, and co-operating very closely with the other. This gives us more fine-tuning as to what is going on with friendships. First, you are getting involved with spiritual people, altruistic types who can help you progress inwardly. It's not just that they are rich and prominent, which many of them are, but they have an advanced inner development as well. Many of your existing friends are likely to be turning to spiritual interests and pulling you along with them. The groups and organizations you join will probably be charitable or spiritually-oriented (not just professional or trade organizations). These are a great place for you to meet new friends as well. In general, this will be a more spiritual year, but aside from the inner benefits you receive, you will also make new and important friends. This trend is continuing for at least two years.

Even for singles (if there are any left), friendships are the major focus this year.

Even in an off-year, there will be periods when romance is happier and more active. For you this will be from June 21st to August 2nd.

Those working on their second marriage will have a status-quo year. Singles will tend to remain single and marrieds will tend to stay married. Those of you on their second marriage will have your relationship tested by two eclipses – a Lunar Eclipse on March 14th and a Solar Eclipse on September 22nd. This needn't break up the marriage – especially if love is true – but it will bring up issues that have long been swept under the rug so that corrections can be made. If love is true the relationship will be better than ever.

Those working on their third marriage will have a wonderful year romantically. Someone wealthy and very spiritual is coming into your life. Marriage or 'quasi marriage' is likely. Challenges and disagreements, especially over spiritual ideals and issues, can be worked out. Romantic opportunities are found at spiritual retreats, meditation seminars, charitable functions and the like.

The marriage of parents or parent figures is being tested this year, but it need not endanger the relationship. Siblings (especially the eldest) probably shouldn't marry this year. If they are already married, the marriage is in crisis. Issues of personal freedom are the cause. Single aunts or uncles are getting involved in serious romance, especially towards the end of the year. Marriage could happen in late 2006 or in 2007. Even if they are already married, there will be more romance in the marriage and a more active social life. Children of marriageable age will probably marry this year, or be involved in a significant relationship with marriage potential. Their love and social life in general is very positive this year. Adult grandchildren will have love – perhaps many loves – this year, but marriage is not advisable. If they are married, then the relationship is getting a severe testing.

Finance and Career

Finance is always important to you, Capricorn, and in the past few years it has been especially so. This trend continues in the year ahead. Not only do you have easy aspects, but your strong interest also gives you all the voltage you need to overcome any challenge. This will be a prosperous year.

As in the past few years, the planets involved with your finances – Uranus and Neptune – are in a beautiful 'mutual reception' relationship. Each is a guest in the house and sign of the other. Neptune rules your kingdom of intellectual interests and communication. So there is a very intimate and positive connection between these two kingdoms. Earnings goals depend on good communication, sales, marketing and public relations. Your intellect naturally gravitates towards money-making ideas. Industries and companies involved with communication, media and transportation are good as investments or could be important customers.

Your gifts of persuasion count a lot when it comes to negotiating loans or dealing with bankers and brokers.

You could be attending an educational event and meet an important client, customer or contact. Conversely, you could be pursuing financial goals and learn much new and important information, perhaps unrelated to finance.

With Uranus and Neptune in each other's signs (Uranus is in Pisces and Neptune in Aquarius), professional investors should look at the high-tech, oil, natural gas, energy and water sectors. Shipping and ship-building also look interesting.

On a deeper level, we see the role intuition is playing in finances these days. No-one is more hard-headed and practical than Capricorn. But when Capricorn learns to go with intuition – something unearthly, vague and nebulous to them – they become invincible.

Many of you will either be investing in or involved with the film, video and photography business this year. In many cases, these things are important to your present business, perhaps as marketing tools.

Your ruler is now in the 8th House for the next two years. Prosperity is forcing many of you to think more deeply about tax issues. Estate issues are also influential: many of you will inherit money or property or receive trust funds or insurance claims. You may be seeking outside capital to further your business, and this is likely to happen this year or next year.

On a more simplistic level, many of you have married recently, and you seem to be actively involved in your spouse's finances.

There are lessons we learn from failure and from lack, and there are lessons we can learn only in prosperity. This year you are learning the lessons of prosperity. Enjoy.

Self-improvement

This is going to be a very spiritual year. For some, it will mean getting on a spiritual path, one of the great steps a person can take. It will change – eventually – the whole course, tone and quality of your life. For those already on a spiritual path, this is a year for deepening it and finding success. Many are going to meet or be involved with spiritual gurus or mentors this year, another very important event in anyone's life. This will happen through friends or through involvement in altruistic activities. In some cases, an existing friend turns out to be the guru or mentor.

This is a year (especially after November 24th) when the inner world reveals itself to you. You Capricorns can be a hard-headed bunch. Though many of you do believe in the invisible world, your focus is more on what you can see, feel and touch. Practical, utilitarian forces are important. But this year the invisible will show you that it, too, is very practical, perhaps more practical (when understood correctly) than anything you experience with your five senses. You will have a very active dream life in the year ahead. Dreams will be both revelatory (giving you special messages and insights) and prophetic (advising you of things to come). You will have spiritual experiences – your ESP will be sharper and uncanny, and intuition will be strong. Synchronistic experiences will happen frequently, almost routinely. Everyday things – things you never bothered about because they were so simple – will now take on deeper meaning. That bird squawking, the way the sun glints off your car, the intricate pattern a cloud makes, the gestures of the little animals in your environment – all have a special message for you, and you will start to understand them if you pay attention. The invisible world is surrounding you with guidance and revelation through mundane things and events in your life.

Part of what is contributing to all this is your success. You are prosperous. You have love. And now a part of you asks, 'Is that all there is?'

This is a very good year for altruistic activities. These are not only good for the world, but also enjoyable for their own sake. They bring you a sense of inner joy and satisfaction, and help clear away old, negative karma. This is also a year for going on spiritual retreats. You will probably enjoy these more than worldly places of entertainment.

Month-by-month Forecasts

January

Best Days Overall: 8, 9, 17, 18, 19, 27, 28

Most Stressful Days Overall: 6, 7, 12, 13, 14, 20, 21

Best Days for Love: 8, 9, 12, 13, 14, 17, 18, 19, 20, 27, 28, 29, 30

Best Days for Money: 1, 2, 3, 4, 12, 13, 22, 23, 29, 30, 31

Monthly Career Peaks: 13, 14, 15, 20, 21, 27, 28

Monthly Personal Pleasure Peaks: 15, 16, 27, 28

CAPRICORN

You are in your yearly personal pleasure peak as the year begins. Most of the planets are in the independent East (70 to 80 per cent). Your 1st House of Self is strong while your 7th House of Others is empty (only the Moon visits there on the 12th, 13th and 14th). The message is clear: this is a time for having life on your terms, for pursuing personal happiness and sensual delight, for pampering the body.

Last month the planets shifted to the lower, night side of the horoscope. This shift gets even stronger on the 4th when Mercury moves below the horizon. Though you are always ambitious, this is a time to work on your ambitions in another way, in the night way rather than the day way, in an inner rather than outer way. This is seen in another way too: your career planet, Venus, is retrograde all month, so this is a time for review and digestion rather than overt action.

Your career planet is in your own sign all month. This shows that you don't need to chase after career opportunities; they are running after you. You can afford to be selective now. The world sees you as ambitious but really, home and family are more important these days. Important career decisions shouldn't be made this month. Research and consider these proposals but make decisions after February 3rd.

The year ahead is generally prosperous, but this month especially so. Beginning on the 20th, you are entering your yearly financial peak. Job opportunities (not just career moves) are pursuing you. Sales, marketing, communication, good use of the media and trading all enhance earnings. You have extra borrowing power this month, and outside investors are waiting for those of you with good ideas. Money can come from insurance claims, estates or tax refunds. Spousal support is stronger than usual. This is a good period to use extra earnings to pay off debts and to cut out useless expenses and get rid of old possessions.

Though you look great this month – your personal magnetism, charisma and sex appeal are at yearly highs – love seems status-quo. Your 7th House of Love is basically empty. There seems to be a lack of interest here. In general, your social life will be stronger from the 1st to the 14th and from the 29th onwards, the periods when the Moon – your love planet – waxes. But this only applies to serious love. Fun opportunities that will never lead to anything serious are plentiful and pursuing you all month. But again, you need to be selective here.

Health is excellent this month. You can enhance it by paying more attention to the liver and thighs (until the 4th); to the spine, knees, teeth, bone structure and skeletal alignment (from the 4th to the 22nd); and to the ankles (after the 22nd). You seem more interested in health this month as well, but this is more to do with vanity than health.

February

Best Days Overall: 4, 5, 14, 15, 23, 24

Most Stressful Days Overall: 2, 3, 9, 10, 16, 17

Best Days for Love: 4, 5, 6, 7, 9, 10, 14, 15, 17, 18, 19, 23, 24, 27, 28

Best Days for Money: 1, 9, 10, 19, 20, 25, 26, 27, 28

Monthly Career Peaks: 16, 17, 23, 24

Monthly Personal Pleasure Peaks: 11, 12, 23, 24

Like last month, most of the planets are still in the lower, night side of the horoscope. Continue to shift attention to the family and to attaining domestic stability. Though your career planet moves forwards on the 3rd and you are clearer as to where you want to go and what needs to be done, emotional harmony – right feeling – should come before the career. Career opportunities are still seeking you out. The opportunities that are most comfortable emotionally are the ones to look at. Continue to build the psychological foundations for future career success.

CAPRICORN

Most of the planets are still in the independent East. Your 1st House of Self remains strong, while your 7th House of Others is empty. (Only the Moon visits the 7th House on the 9th and 10th, and this will be the monthly social peak.) This is a time for standing on your own two feet and developing independence.

Your yearly financial peak continues all month. Many of last month's trends are still in effect. Getting the word out about your product or service seems the most important thing. With many planets in Pisces this month (including your financial planet), intuition will play more of a role after the 19th. Jobseekers continue to have success this month. Job opportunities are found locally – or perhaps neighbours or siblings have leads. There is a nice windfall on the 28th (but it could also happen early next month).

Health is excellent. You can enhance it by paying more attention to the ankles (until the 9th). After the 9th, pay more attention to the feet. Water therapies are very powerful after the 9th.

You look great. Venus in your own sign enhances personal beauty and your sense of style. Now that she is moving forwards, it is a good idea to buy clothing, jewellery or personal accessories – your judgement will be sound and the choices good.

Love is still status-quo, and this is probably a good thing. Your love life will be stronger, and you will have more enthusiasm for it, from the 1st to the 13th and on the 27th and 28th, when the Moon waxes. The Moon re-stimulates eclipse points on the 2nd, 3rd, 9th, 10th, 16th, 17th, 23rd and 24th. Be more patient with your lover, spouse or friends as they can be more temperamental.

Love affairs are still plentiful and seeking you out. These things will be tested from the 24th to the 26th when the Lord of your 5th House re-stimulates eclipse points.

357

March

Best Days Overall: 3, 4, 13, 14, 23, 24, 31

Most Stressful Days Overall: 1, 2, 8, 9, 15, 16, 17, 29, 30

Best Days for Love: 4, 5, 6, 8, 9, 15, 16, 18, 19, 20, 25, 26, 29, 30

Best Days for Money: 8, 9, 18, 19, 25, 26, 27, 28

Monthly Career Peaks: 15, 16, 17, 25, 26

Monthly Personal Pleasure Peaks: 10, 11, 23, 24, 25, 26

Like last month, most of the planets are still below the horizon in the night side of the horoscope. Your 4th House of Home and Family becomes very strong after the 20th, and there's a Solar Eclipse there to boot. Your 10th House of Career, by contrast, is mostly empty. Only the Moon will visit there on the 15th, 16th and 17th, and this will be the monthly career peak. So the focus is still on the home and family and on finding your emotional comfort zone.

Most of the planets are still in the independent East, though the percentage is not as strong as in previous months. This continues to be a time for changing conditions to suit yourself.

The Solar Eclipse of the 29th has a strong effect on you. You need to reduce your schedule from the 20th anyway, but especially around this eclipse. This is not a period for taking unnecessary risks. This eclipse will bring changes to the family and family pattern. Usually there is a clearing of the air with family members as long-seething issues surface. Flaws in the home, which perhaps you've been ignoring, now have to be dealt with. Dramatic events happen with parents or parent figures. Your spouse or partner is forced to make important financial changes. Perhaps there is a temporary disruption of spousal support. Insurance, estate and tax issues now take a dramatic turn. Emotions in the family will be volatile and temperamental. Understanding all of this will enable you to handle these things better.

The Lunar Eclipse on the 14th is much more benign. The eclipse occurs in your 9th House so students will make important changes. Your personal beliefs get tested. It is not unusual for people to change their place of worship or spiritual leader under these eclipses. And since the Moon, the eclipsed planet, is also your love planet, every Lunar Eclipse tests your marriage or current relationship. The air gets cleared. If love is true – if there is real commitment – there is nothing to fear. The relationship will be stronger because of it. This Lunar Eclipse also impacts on Pluto, your 11th House ruler. Thus friendships in general will get tested as well.

You need to rest and relax more after the 20th. Avoid making drastic changes to your diet or health regime from the 2nd to the 25th, when Mercury, your health planet, is retrograde. Wait until after the 25th when you will have a whole new perspective on these issues.

April

Best Days Overall: 1, 9, 10, 19, 20, 27, 28

Most Stressful Days Overall: 4, 5, 12, 13, 25, 26

Best Days for Love: 2, 3, 4, 5, 7, 8, 14, 15, 18, 23, 24, 27, 28

Best Days for Money: 4, 5, 14, 15, 21, 22, 23, 24

Monthly Career Peaks: 12, 13, 23, 24

Monthly Personal Pleasure Peaks: 7, 8, 19, 20

Continue to watch your health carefully until the 20th. Rest and relax more, and keep energy levels as high as possible. Enhance health and energy through foot massage and water-oriented and spiritual therapies until the 16th. After the 16th, scalp massage, vigorous physical exercise, good muscle tone and emotional harmony improve the health. Thermal therapies are good then too. Health will improve dramatically after the 20th.

Most of the planets are still below the horizon in the night side of your chart. Your 4th House of Home and Family remains strong, while your 10th House of Career is mostly empty (except for the Moon's visit on the 12th and 13th – your monthly career peak.) This means that family and emotional issues are more important than outer goals and achievements. The career is more in need of inspiration than just blind mechanical effort, and this will start happening after the 16th. Many of you will receive revelation after the 16th – not just about your worldly career but also about your mission for this life – a much deeper kind of insight.

The Eastern, independent half of your chart is still stronger than the Western half, but not by that much. You are balancing independence with dependence, and personal interests with the interests of others. But you can still change conditions to suit you. Later on, it will be more difficult.

Finances are still excellent this month. Money can come from pay rises and promotions; from your professional reputation; from parents or parent figures; from the government. If you have financial issues with the government, this is a good month to resolve them. As has been the case all year (and for many years), good marketing, sales and promotion are very important. Jobseekers find work locally or through neighbours until the 16th (the newspapers and situations vacant ads are also good then). Afterwards, family connections seem powerful.

Love becomes much more active this month as Mars moves into your 7th House on the 14th. This makes you more aggressive in love. Singles are more adventurous and risk-taking now. There is a tendency to leap into relationships and fall in love at first sight. This is not your normal nature, but a little of this is good for you. For married Capricorns or those already involved in a relationship, this transit can be stressful as it creates power struggles. A family member plays cupid. A parent or parent figure is interfering in the social life, probably from good motives. An old flame (or someone who reminds you of an old flame) can come into the romantic picture.

Be more patient with family members and parents from the 2nd to the 5th and on the 29th and 30th. Your family planet is re-stimulating eclipse points on those dates.

May

Best Days Overall: 7, 8, 16, 17, 25, 26

Most Stressful Days Overall: 2, 3, 9, 10, 22, 23, 29, 30

Best Days for Love: 2, 3, 7, 8, 14, 15, 16, 17, 22, 23, 27, 28, 29, 30

Best Days for Money: 2, 3, 12, 13, 18, 19, 20, 21, 29, 30

Monthly Career Peaks: 9, 10, 22, 23

Monthly Personal Pleasure Peaks: 4, 5, 7, 8, 9, 16, 17

This month, the Western, social sector of your chart begins to dominate. Personal independence is decreased and might not even be desirable. Your happiness seems dependent on the happiness of others.

Like last month, the planetary power is still mostly below the horizon. Your 4th House of Home and Family, though not as strong as in the past few months, is still stronger than the 10th House of Career. So it is wise to keep attention focused on domestic and family issues, and down-play the career. On the 4th, this is reinforced when your career planet moves into the 4th House. This is a good period to work more from home, if possible. Emotional comfort is still the dominating urge.

Prosperity remains very strong. Your financial planet is involved in a beautiful (and rare) Grand Trine aspect all month. Sure, there are a few challenges, especially after the 21st, but inherent prosperity and earnings are not really affected. Financial intuition is working well, though it won't hurt to get verifications. Family (and people who are like family) are supportive, and family connections play a huge role as well. Your charitable giving has increased all year, but this is even more the case this month. Jobseekers continue to have many opportunities in the month ahead. Until the 4th, family and family connections provide opportunities. After the 4th, opportunities come as you pursue leisure activities.

Health is excellent these days, and you can enhance it by paying more attention to the head and scalp until the 5th; to the neck and throat from the 5th to the 19th; and to the arms, shoulders and lungs from the 19th onwards. Health, in general, becomes more interesting to you after the 21st.

Love trends are pretty much as described last month. Mars remains in your 7th House of Love all month. Though power struggles are tempting, it is probably best to avoid them. There could be a business partnership forming with a family member. There is more entertaining from the home too. Be more patient with your lover or spouse on the 2nd, 8th, 9th, 15th, 16th, 21st, 22nd and 28th when the love planet re-stimulates eclipse points.

June

Best Days Overall: 3, 4, 12, 13, 21, 22, 30

Most Stressful Days Overall: 5, 6, 19, 20, 25, 26

Best Days for Love: 3, 4, 5, 6, 12, 13, 14, 15, 22, 25, 26

Best Days for Money: 8, 9, 14, 15, 17, 18, 25, 26

Monthly Career Peaks: 5, 6, 22

Monthly Personal Pleasure Peaks: 1, 2, 12, 13, 28, 29

CAPRICORN

Like last month, most of the planets are in the social West. Your 7th House of Others becomes very strong after the 21st, when you begin your yearly social peak. Your 1st House of Self, by contrast, is mostly empty – only the Moon visits briefly on the 12th and 13th. So this is a highly social month. It is a time to down-play the self and to put others first. Watch how your personal popularity grows as you do this.

This month the planets make an important shift to the day side, your favourite side of the horoscope. By now, most of you have found your emotional comfort zone. You have dreamed your career dreams. Now it is time to translate these things into action.

Career is enhanced this month the old-fashioned way: through work, service and genuine achievement. Social connections play a role, but performance is the essence.

Health is important this month. Your interest in health matters is strong. This is good news, as after the 21st you need to pay more attention here. Enhance health through rest and relaxation and through arm and shoulder massage (until the 3rd); more attention to the lungs (until the 3rd); more attention to the stomach, breasts and diet (from the 3rd to the 28th); and to the heart afterwards. Social disharmony can have an undue impact on health from the 3rd to the 28th. With your ruler, Saturn, receiving much stimulation, this month is excellent for detox and weight-loss regimes. Vigorous physical exercise seems interesting after the 3rd – you probably do this more from a sense of joy than for health reasons.

Love is active and happy. Singles have serious romantic opportunities. Marriage may or may not happen, but the people you are involved with are marriage material. Social contacts bring happy financial opportunity.

Intellectual interests and communication have been important for some years, but up till now your interest related to finance more than anything else. Now, with the

North Node of the Moon moving into your 3rd House for the next few years, these things become happy and fulfilling in their own right.

July

Best Days Overall: 1, 10, 11, 18, 19, 27, 28, 29

Most Stressful Days Overall: 3, 4, 16, 17, 23, 24, 30, 31

Best Days for Love: 3, 4, 5, 6, 12, 13, 14, 15, 22, 23, 24, 25, 26

Best Days for Money: 5, 6, 12, 13, 14, 15, 23, 24

Monthly Career Peaks: 3, 4, 23, 30, 31

Monthly Personal Pleasure Peaks: 10, 11, 25, 26

Both your financial planets are retrograde this month, but prosperity still seems strong. Again, intuition and social connections are the main engines of earnings growth. Many very positive things are germinating behind the scenes and will manifest later on. Important investments or purchases still need more homework. This is a good time to use excess cash to pay off debt. It is also a good time to borrow, as outside capital seems readily available.

Like last month, most of the planets are in the social, Western sector. Your 7th House of Love remains strong and you are well into your yearly social peak. Singles might not have marriage on their mind, but the opportunities are there. Love becomes romantic and has a honeymoon quality after the 19th. This is still a month to down-play personal will and self-assertion and to cultivate the good graces of others.

Adult children could marry these days or be involved in a very serious relationship.

The planetary shift to your favourite upper, day side of the horoscope gets even stronger after the 19th, as Venus crosses from the lower to the upper side. Seventy to eighty per cent of the planets will now be above the horizon, spurring the ambitions. Family and emotional issues can be down-played now as you act on your career dreams. Career is enhanced in the normal ways until the 19th – through hard work and productivity. After the 19th, career is advanced through social connections. In general, you are mingling with people of high status. Singles will have romantic opportunities with such people.

Health needs watching carefully until the 21st. Happily, you seem on the case. With your health planet retrograde from the 3rd to the 29th, many of you might feel that you can improve the 'doldrums' through some change to your diet or health regime. This is not advisable now. Enhance health by resting and relaxing more and by paying more attention to the heart, stomach and breasts. Harmony with friends and your spouse or lover is very important. Your diet is particularly important from the 10th onwards, but proceed gingerly.

With the 8th House of Transformation and Regeneration still very powerful, detox and weight-loss regimes go well. Many of you have been involved in personal transformation for a long time now, and these projects are succeeding.

Whatever your age and stage in life, this is a period for enhanced libido. Although this is a wonderful thing, don't abuse it.

August

Best Days Overall: 6, 7, 14, 15, 24, 25

Most Stressful Days Overall: 12, 13, 19, 20, 26, 27

Best Days for Love: 2, 3, 4, 5, 11, 12, 13, 19, 20, 21, 22, 23, 31

Best Days for Money: 2, 3, 8, 9, 10, 11, 19, 20, 29, 30

Monthly Career Peaks: 21, 22, 26, 27

Monthly Personal Pleasure Peaks: 6, 7, 21, 22

Many of the trends of last month are continuing now. Most of the planets are still in the Western, social sector of the horoscope. The 7th House of Love remains strong until the 13th. Though the social life is winding down, it continues to be a sociable month, and the focus still needs to be on others and their interests. Charm, and not direct action, will get you to your goals.

Most of the planets are still above the horizon, in the day side of your horoscope. It is time for outer achievement and career success. You can prepare for success by gaining more education in your chosen field – the 9th House is very strong this month. You need not ignore home and family, but the focus should be on your career as this is the best way to serve the family.

Love is still happy this month, but it seems to be more about libido and passion than romance. Sexual attraction seems the most important thing to you, especially after the 13th. Until then you are still mingling with people of high status and prestige – and allured by these kinds of people.

Finances are still good. Both your financial planets continue to be retrograde (like last month), and there is more work involved in earnings after the 23rd. Perhaps there is some financial dispute with a family member or your spouse. There may be added family expenses this month. These are just bumps on the road – the long-term trend is prosperous. Still, you need to do more homework on important investments and purchases.

Health is much improved now. You can enhance it by paying more attention to the stomach and breasts (until the 11th); the heart (from the 11th to the 28th); and the small intestine (after the 28th). With many planets in health-conscious Virgo after the 23rd, you are on the case.

Your 8th House of Transformation and Regeneration is still strong in the month ahead. Continue with detox and weight-loss regimes and with your projects of self-transformation. Those of you involved in occult studies or depth psychology also have an exceptional month. Libido, like last month, is stronger than usual. This is another good month to eliminate excesses from your life, whether these be physical possessions, impurities in the body, emotional patterns or negative character traits. It is also a good month to break addictions.

Your 9th House becomes strong after the 23rd. This brings religious and philosophical revelation for those who desire it. It also brings happy travel and educational opportunities.

Mars will re-stimulate eclipse points from the 29th to the 31st so avoid risky activities then. Encourage family members – especially parents or parent figures – to avoid risky activities too. Be more patient with them as they are likely to be more temperamental than usual.

Your love planet will re-stimulate eclipse points on the 5th, 6th, 11th, 12th, 18th, 19th, 25th and 26th. This is apt to make your lover or spouse (and perhaps friends) more temperamental, so be patient.

September

Best Days Overall: 3, 4, 11, 12, 20, 21, 30

Most Stressful Days Overall: 9, 10, 15, 16, 22, 23, 24

Best Days for Love: 1, 2, 3, 4, 11, 12, 15, 16, 20, 21, 22, 23, 30

Best Days for Money: 5, 6, 7, 8, 15, 16, 25, 26

Monthly Career Peaks: 20, 21, 22, 23

Monthly Personal Pleasure Peaks: 3, 4, 17, 18, 30

Most of the planets are still above the horizon, and your 10th House of Career gets very strong after the 23rd. You are entering your yearly career peak. A Solar Eclipse on the 22nd is probably also clearing the way for this so that you can proceed to your appointed destiny. Your family planet will also be in your 10th House of Career from the 8th onwards. This shows that your family understands your ambitions and is supportive. You are elevated personally, as is the family as a whole.

Along with two eclipses this month – which guarantee much change – there is also an important shift of the planets from the social West to the more personal East. By the 23rd, this shift will be established and you are becoming more independent. Social goals have probably been attained. You are getting ready to have life on your terms and to design things to your specifications.

The Solar Eclipse of the 22nd occurs right on the border of two houses – the 9th and 10th – and will impact on both of them. Those of you born early in the sign of Capricorn (from December 21st to 25th) will feel this stronger and should reduce your schedule. The eclipse brings important career changes. There can be dramas with parents or parent figures. This eclipse looks like it will catapult you to greater success and advancement, one way or another. Since the 9th House is involved in this eclipse, this has an impact on students. All of you will make changes to your personal religion and philosophy of life. These things will be tested, and you will almost have no choice but to make the changes. Many will change their religious affiliations, spiritual leaders and the like.

The Lunar Eclipse of the 7th occurs in your 3rd House, bringing long-term change to your locality or with neighbours. Cars and communication equipment get tested. Siblings can experience dramatic events. This eclipse occurs very near your financial planet, Uranus, showing that important financial changes are happening, probably related to the career. If there have been flaws in your financial thinking, planning or investments, you will find out about them now and be forced to make the necessary corrections. Every Lunar Eclipse tests marriages or current loves – the Moon is your love planet – but this is nothing to fear. Sometimes these eclipses bring break-ups but only in situations where the love and commitment weren't strong to begin with.

Try to rest and relax more after the 23rd. Enhance health by paying more attention to the small intestine (until the 13th) and to the kidneys, hips and heart afterwards. Metaphysical therapies such as prayer are powerful until the 13th. After the 13th, beauty becomes an important healing force. If you feel under the weather, go to a park, museum or art gallery and immerse yourself in beauty.

October

Best Days Overall: 1, 8, 9, 17, 18, 19, 27, 28

Most Stressful Days Overall: 6, 7, 12, 13, 14, 20, 21

Best Days for Love: 2, 3, 10, 11, 12, 13, 14, 21, 22

Best Days for Money: 2, 3, 4, 5, 12, 13, 14, 22, 23, 24, 29, 30

Monthly Career Peaks: 20, 21

Monthly Personal Pleasure Peaks: 1, 15, 16, 27, 28

Your 10th House of Career is awesomely powerful this month. Forty to fifty per cent of the planets are either there or moving through there. Major forces are conspiring to elevate you and grant you success. True, you are working very hard in this area (Mars is in your 10th House until the 23rd) but you are seeing the results of your work. So there are pay rises and promotions now, and more recognition for your professional achievements. Many of you will be more involved politically or in community affairs, perhaps being elected or appointed to government or community posts. The dreams you dreamed months ago are starting to bloom.

Family remains supportive career-wise. And outer success still seems the best way to serve your family.

Like last month, the planetary power is mostly in the East, so independent actions are powerful. This is a time for self-assertion, though you need not be rude or overbearing about it. If you are, you can expect some interesting kick-backs after the 23rd.

Love seems status-quo this month. Your 7th House of Love is mostly empty. Only the Moon will visit there on the 12th, 13th and 14th, and this will be the monthly social peak. I read this as a good thing. Love goals are basically achieved and you seem content with your romantic life. The power in the 11th House this month (which is even stronger than the 10th House after the 23rd) shows that the focus is on friendship and group activities. This is a very happy area of life. New and important friends are coming into the picture. You mingle with people of like mind and interests. If you are a member of a social or professional organization, your status there is elevated.

Children of marriageable age are having the peak romantic experiences of a lifetime. Marriages or significant relationships are still very likely (even more so than last month).

Health needs watching carefully until the 23rd. Enhance health by paying more attention to the heart, kidneys and hips (until the 2nd), and to the colon, bladder and sexual organs afterwards. Safe sex is more important these days. Detox regimes have been interesting all year, but now even more so. Keeping harmony with friends is also important.

Finances continue to be excellent, though you still need to do more homework with important purchases. Parents or parent figures are having a superb financial month. Your lover or spouse is more speculative after the 23rd.

CAPRICORN

November

Best Days Overall: 5, 13, 14, 15, 23, 24

Most Stressful Days Overall: 3, 9, 10, 16, 17, 30

Best Days for Love: 1, 9, 10, 19, 20, 21, 28, 29, 30

Best Days for Money: 1, 2, 9, 10, 19, 20, 26, 27, 28, 29, 30

Monthly Career Peaks: 16, 17, 21, 22

Monthly Personal Pleasure Peaks: 11, 12, 23, 24

Most of the planets remain above the horizon, and though your 10th House is not strong this month, outer ambitions are still more important than family and emotional issues. Your career is enhanced by having friends in the right places. You can also further the career by getting more involved in professional and social organizations.

With most of the planets in the East (a trend growing stronger day by day), it is good to be independent. During this period you might suffer from too much of a good thing – too much self-esteem, self-confidence and ego – and this can invite some nasty responses.

Like last month, romantic love doesn't seem to be a big issue for you. Your 7th House of Love is mostly empty. Only the Moon will visit there on the 9th and 10th, and this will be your monthly social peak. Again, friendship, rather than romance, is the main interest – and seems very happy. Old friends might be leaving the picture only to be replaced by new and better ones. Long-standing connections with organizations fall away from your life and you are involved with new and better ones. Children of marriageable age are still enjoying peak romantic experiences. Those of you working on your third marriage are likely to meet a special someone. In general, your social magnetism will be stronger from the 1st to the 5th and from the 20th onwards, when the Moon waxes.

This has been a spiritual year for you, a year of great inner growth and progress, and this trend is greatly strengthened this month. This is a period for going on spiritual retreats, attending meditation seminars, reading scripture and sacred writings, and for involvement in charities and altruistic activities. This trend is only going to get stronger next month. Your financial intuition, which has been strong all year, gets even stronger. This brings benefits to the bottom line, an attractive side-effect of your spiritual activities. Your inner focus reveals new sources of wealth and new wealth ideas. (These might come to you through friends as well, but they are only the mouthpiece for something higher.) You are more in touch with the true source of wealth.

December

Best Days Overall: 2, 3, 11, 12, 21, 22, 29, 30

Most Stressful Days Overall: 1, 6, 7, 13, 14, 15, 27, 28

Best Days for Love: 1, 6, 7, 8, 9, 10, 11, 18, 19, 20, 21, 22, 29, 30

Best Days for Money: 4, 6, 7, 8, 16, 17, 18, 23, 24, 25, 26, 27

Monthly Career Peaks: 13, 14, 15, 21, 22

Monthly Personal Pleasure Peaks: 9, 10, 11, 16, 17, 18, 21, 22

A very strange and amazing month for you down-to-earth Capricorns. There is no-one in the zodiac more level-headed, practical and sane as you. And now we have a period when the planets are holding a convention in your 12th House of Spirituality. Most of you have never experienced this kind of spiritual power. Sixty to seventy per cent of the planets are either in or moving through your 12th

House. Certainly, you are going to have to revise your notions of reality and how life should be conducted.

You have the kind of chart where you are so in love with the spiritual world that you want to leave everything and sit at the feet of the guru. Many of you will undertake religious and spiritual pilgrimages during this period. Others will go on spiritual retreats. You may be attending lectures by visiting holy men and women, reading more spiritual literature, and more involved with spiritual groups. All of you will become uncharacteristically altruistic. In fact, one of the problems of the month is that mundane financial issues don't seem interesting. Your otherworldliness is distracting you from the things of this world. Some of you might be more charitable than you should be – you can go overboard in this direction. But this is all temporary. Many of you will learn that there is a good reason for your practicality and focus on the material world. Glamorous as the spiritual world is, you have been sent here for a purpose, and your unique abilities are needed. You will now approach the material world from a whole new perspective.

Your otherworldliness will lead, eventually, to more personal fulfilment. After the 22nd, you are in your yearly personal pleasure peak. You've enjoyed the pleasures of the spirit, and now it's time to enjoy the pleasures of the flesh. This will keep things in balance.

Health is excellent and you can enhance it by paying more attention to the sexual organs, colon and bladder (until the 8th); to the liver and thighs (from the 8th to the 27th) and to the spine, knees, teeth, bone structure and skeletal alignment after the 27th. Spiritual therapies are extremely powerful from the 8th to the 27th. If you have had health problems, many of you will experience miraculous-type healings.

Love is status-quo this month and you seem content. Spiritual love seems more important and interesting than romantic love.

Aquarius

~~~

THE WATER-BEARER

Birthdays from
20th January to
18th February

Personality Profile

AQUARIUS AT A GLANCE

Element – Air

Ruling Planet – Uranus
    Career Planet – Pluto
    Love Planet – Venus
    Money Planet – Neptune
    Planet of Health and Work – Moon
    Planet of Home and Family Life – Venus

Colours – electric blue, grey, ultramarine blue

Colours that promote love, romance and social
    harmony – gold, orange

Colour that promotes earning power – aqua

AQUARIUS

Gems – black pearl, obsidian, opal, sapphire

Metal – lead

Scents – azalea, gardenia

Quality – fixed (= stability)

Qualities most needed for balance – warmth, feeling and emotion

Strongest virtues – great intellectual power, the ability to communicate and to form and understand abstract concepts, love for the new and avant-garde

Deepest needs – to know and to bring in the new

Characteristics to avoid – coldness, rebelliousness for its own sake, fixed ideas

Signs of greatest overall compatibility – Gemini, Libra

Signs of greatest overall incompatibility – Taurus, Leo, Scorpio

Sign most helpful to career – Scorpio

Sign most helpful for emotional support – Taurus

Sign most helpful financially – Pisces

Sign best for marriage and/or partnerships – Leo

Sign most helpful for creative projects – Gemini

Best Sign to have fun with – Gemini

Signs most helpful in spiritual matters – Libra, Capricorn

Best day of the week – Saturday

Understanding an Aquarius

In the Aquarius-born, intellectual faculties are perhaps the most highly developed of any Sign in the Zodiac. Aquarians are clear, scientific thinkers. They have the ability to think abstractly and to formulate laws, theories and clear concepts from masses of observed facts. Geminis might be very good at gathering information, but Aquarians take this a step further, excelling at interpreting the information gathered.

Practical people – men and women of the world – mistakenly consider abstract thinking as impractical. It is true that the realm of abstract thought takes us out of the physical world, but the discoveries made in this realm generally end up having tremendous practical consequences. All real scientific inventions and breakthroughs come from this abstract realm.

Aquarians, more so than most, are ideally suited to explore these abstract dimensions. Those who have explored these regions know that there is little feeling or emotion there. In fact, emotions are a hindrance to functioning in these dimensions; thus Aquarians seem – at times – cold and emotionless to others. It is not that Aquarians haven't got feelings and deep emotions, it is just that too much feeling clouds their ability to think and invent. The concept of 'too much feeling' cannot be tolerated or even understood by some of the other Signs. Nevertheless, this Aquarian objectivity is ideal for science, communication and friendship.

Aquarians are very friendly people, but they do not make a big show about it. They do the right thing by their friends, even if sometimes they do it without passion or excitement.

Aquarians have a deep passion for clear thinking. Second in importance, but related, is their passion for breaking with the establishment and traditional authority. Aquarians delight in this, because for them rebellion is like a great game or challenge. Very often they will rebel strictly for the fun of rebelling, regardless of whether the authority they defy is right or wrong. Right or wrong has little to do with the rebellious actions of an Aquarian, because to a true Aquarian authority and power must be challenged as a matter of principle.

Where Capricorn or Taurus will err on the side of tradition and the status quo, an Aquarian will err on the side of the new. Without this virtue it is doubtful whether any progress would be made in the world. The conservative-minded would obstruct progress. Originality and invention imply an ability to break barriers; every new discovery represents the toppling of an impediment to thought. Aquarians are very interested in breaking barriers and making walls tumble – scientifically, socially and politically. Other Zodiac Signs, such as Capricorn, also have scientific talents. But Aquarians are particularly excellent in the social sciences and humanities.

Finance

In financial matters Aquarians tend to be idealistic and humanitarian – to the point of self-sacrifice. They are usually generous contributors to social and political causes. When they contribute it differs from when a Capricorn or Taurus contributes. A Capricorn or Taurus may expect some favour or return for a gift; an Aquarian contributes selflessly.

Aquarians tend to be as cool and rational about money as they are about most things in life. Money is something they need and they set about acquiring it scientifically. No need for fuss; they get on with it in the most rational and scientific ways available.

Money to the Aquarian is especially nice for what it can do, not for the status it may bring (as is the case for other Signs). Aquarians are neither big spenders nor penny-pinchers and use their finances in practical ways, for example to facilitate progress for themselves, their families or even strangers.

However, if Aquarians want to reach their fullest financial potential they will have to explore their intuitive nature. If they follow only their financial theories – or what they believe to be theoretically correct – they may suffer some losses and disappointments. Instead, Aquarians should call on their intuition, which knows without thinking. For Aquarians, intuition is the short-cut to financial success.

Career and Public Image

Aquarians like to be perceived not only as the breakers of barriers but also as the transformers of society and the world. They long to be seen in this light and to play this role. They also look up to and respect other people in this position and even expect their superiors to act this way.

Aquarians prefer jobs that have a bit of idealism attached to them – careers with a philosophical basis. Aquarians need to be creative at work, to have access to new techniques and methods. They like to keep busy and enjoy getting down to business straightaway, without wasting any time. They are often the quickest workers and usually have suggestions for improvements that will benefit their employers. Aquarians are also very helpful with their co-workers and welcome responsibility, preferring this to having to take orders from others.

If Aquarians want to reach their highest career goals they have to develop more emotional sensitivity, depth of feeling and passion. They need to learn to narrow their focus on the essentials and concentrate more on the job in hand. Aquarians need 'a fire in the belly' – a consuming passion and desire – in order to rise to the very top. Once this passion exists they will succeed easily in whatever they attempt.

AQUARIUS

Love and Relationships

Aquarians are good at friendships, but a bit weak when it comes to love. Of course they fall in love, but their lovers always get the impression that they are more best friends than paramours.

Like Capricorns, they are cool customers. They are not prone to displays of passion or to outward demonstrations of their affections. In fact, they feel uncomfortable when their mate hugs and touches them too much. This does not mean that they do not love their partners. They do, only they show it in other ways. Curiously enough, in relationships they tend to attract the very things that they feel uncomfortable with. They seem to attract hot, passionate, romantic, demonstrative people. Perhaps they know instinctively that these people have qualities they lack and so seek them out. In any event, these relationships do seem to work, Aquarius' coolness calming the more passionate partner while the fires of passion warm the cold-blooded Aquarius.

The qualities Aquarians need to develop in their love life are warmth, generosity, passion and fun. Aquarians love relationships of the mind. Here they excel. If the intellectual factor is missing in a relationship an Aquarian will soon become bored or feel unfulfilled.

Home and Domestic Life

In family and domestic matters Aquarians can have a tendency to be too non-conformist, changeable and unstable. They are as willing to break the barriers of family constraints as they are those of other areas of life.

Even so, Aquarians are very sociable people. They like to have a nice home where they can entertain family and friends. Their house is usually decorated in a modern style and full of state-of-the-art appliances and gadgets – an environment Aquarians find absolutely necessary.

If their home life is to be healthy and fulfilling Aquarians need to inject it with a quality of stability – yes, even some conservatism. They need at least one area of life to be enduring and steady; this area is usually their home and family life.

Venus, the Planet of Love, rules the Aquarian's 4th Solar House of Home and Family as well, which means that when it comes to the family and child-rearing, theories, cool thinking and intellect are not always enough. Aquarians need to bring love into the equation in order to have a great domestic life.

Horoscope for 2006

General Trends

Money-making has been an important interest for many years now. You have been experimenting, trying this and that, upgrading, changing, going high and low. You've thrown out all the rule books in this department and have learnt much in the process. This is a real adventure – a journey – in your life. And this journey continues in the year ahead.

Last year, health and health regimes were very important but this has passed. Love and social issues are your focus now – but very challenging. Important love lessons are being learned.

Health needs watching carefully this year, and your tendency to neglect it can be a danger.

Where last year you were focused on educational issues and on expanding your mental horizons, this year it's about translating these expansions into the career. This is a wonderful year for money and career, perhaps one of the best in your life.

Neptune, the most spiritual of all the planets, is still in your own sign. Your ruling planet, Uranus, is in the most spiritual of all the signs, Pisces. So the interest in spirituality is still dominant, as it has been for many years. This, too, is a long-term journey. You are all under intense spiritual energies that are refining the physical body, helping you become aware of vibrations, and casting an otherworldly glamour on your image and personal appearance.

The major areas of interest in the year ahead will be the body, the image and personal appearance; finance; love, romance and social activities; career (until November 24th); friends, group activities, organizations, science, astrology and astronomy (all year but even more after November 24th).

Your paths to greatest fulfilment in the year ahead are career (until November 24th); friends, group activities, organizations, science, astrology and astronomy (after November 24th); communication and intellectual interests (until June 23rd); finance (after June 23rd).

Health

(Please note that this is an astrological perspective on health, not a medical one. At one time, both perspectives were identical, but in these times there could be quite a difference. For the medical perspective, please consult your physician or health professional.)

As mentioned, health needs watching carefully this year, especially until November 24th. For most of the year, two long-term planets are in stressful aspect to you. After November 24th, as Jupiter moves away from its stressful aspect, health and vitality should improve.

Health has been a big focus for a few years now. Many of you embarked on disciplined (and perhaps stern) health regimes and diets. But this interest seems to have waned this year, and this is a bit dangerous. More focus on health is called for; you will have to force yourself even though you lack the interest. The main thing now is to watch energy levels.

Aquarius rules the ankles, which are always important to you health-wise. Regular massage and good support are always beneficial. This year, your ruling planet is in the sign of Pisces (which rules the feet). This makes the feet important this year too and for many years to come, so add regular foot massage to your regime.

Saturn and Jupiter are putting stresses on your Sun this year. The Sun rules the heart (and the spleen as well, according to many astrologers). More attention therefore needs to be given here too.

Your health planet is the Moon. In the physical body, the Moon rules the stomach and breasts, so these also need more attention. Diet is more of an issue with you than for most people.

Since the Moon is the fastest-moving of all the planets – she will move through all the signs and houses of your horoscope in a month – your health needs can change from day to day. Beneficial therapies can also change on a daily basis. This is why Aquarians can be faddy about food and diets – they are always looking for that new treatment, that new supplement, that new miracle food, that new diet. We will deal with these short-term health issues in the monthly reports.

The times to be most watchful about health in the coming year will be January 1st to February 17th; April 20th to May 20th; June 3rd to August 23rd; October 23rd to November 21st. These are periods to rest and relax more and to pace yourself better. In any month there are days to rest and relax more as well, depending on the position of the Moon.

With Neptune in your own sign now for many years, there is a tendency to overindulge in alcohol and drugs. This is because the body is becoming more refined and sensitive. It feels pain, and other people's vibrations, more vividly, and one of the ways of coping is through alcohol or drugs. But there are other and better ways, such as knowledge and a spiritual discipline.

A parent or parent figure is making dramatic and long-term changes to their health regime but their overall health seems status-quo. This parent needs to be careful of overindulging in the good life this year. Children with health problems should have good news in the coming year. Grandchildren, like you, can enhance their health through regular foot and ankle massage and through taking better care of the feet and ankles. There are also new, cutting-edge therapies that might benefit them. The health of your spouse or lover seems status-quo. Their health can be enhanced by paying more attention to the spine, knees, teeth and overall skeletal alignment.

Home, Domestic and Family Issues

Your 4th House of Home and Family is not a House of Power this year. Things will probably be status-quo. Most of you seem more or less content with the home and the family situation and have no need to focus overly on it. The cosmos is taking a neutral stance towards you, pushing you neither one way nor another. Your personal free will plays a huge role this year.

There's no question that finance and career are more important than home and family in the year ahead. With career so happy and successful, it would be understandable if you 'neglected' the home for a time.

If you are married, your spouse might want to move, but you don't seem to care one way or another. If you are in a serious relationship, your lover will probably move to a bigger home. Your spouse seems interested in having children this year (for those of you who are of appropriate age), or even adopting them.

If you are doing heavy construction in the home, such as tearing down walls or ripping out pipes or wires, February

13th to 17th looks like a good time. If you're redecorating and beautifying the home in a cosmetic way, or buying things of beauty for the home, April 20th to May 20th and May 29th to June 24th are good times, and these are also good dates for entertaining from home and for family gatherings.

With fast-moving Venus as your family planet, family relationships and the domestic scene tend to be dynamic and rapidly changing. But these are short-term trends, best dealt with in the monthly reports.

One of the parents (or parent figures in your life) is travelling around a lot. They are prospering, living the good life and will probably have multiple moves or home renovations. The home is never finished – an eternal work in progress. Adult children have an uneventful domestic year, but their career is so exciting and changeable that it could cause domestic moves or upheavals. They may be transferred to another city or even country. Grandchildren of appropriate age have a status-quo domestic year – they may have moved last year.

Love and Social Life

An important and challenging area of life. Saturn, the great orderer, moved into your 7th House of Love and Marriage on July 17th 2005. It will be here all this year and all of 2007 as well, so this is a long-term trend.

This transit will test your marriage or serious, long-term relationship. This is a time for getting real about the partner. There is a need now to see the partner as they really are. Once this is done, we can decide whether we love this person and want to continue or not. This is not always a pleasant process, but it is healthy. Many will undoubtedly divorce under this transit. Saturn doesn't like relationships that aren't on a sound and realistic basis.

Many, however, will discover a new love for their spouse or partner. This process will deepen the love in the relationship. There is nothing like dealing with adverse conditions to test our love and commitment.

In general, the 7th House also rules our 'friendships of the heart'. The 11th House (which has also been undergoing much transformation for many years) rules 'friendships of the mind' – platonic friendship with people of like mind and interests. So, we are seeing a social process going on in you, accelerated over the next two years. This is a weeding-out process. Order and realism are being brought to bear on your love life. Friendships will also be tested. The good and true friends will remain, while the lukewarm ones will go by the wayside.

For singles working on their first marriage, this is not an especially good year. It is a time for rethinking your concepts of love, especially for understanding that love is not a free ride but carries with it burdens, duties and responsibilities. It is a time for taking a 'head approach' to love – and many of you will do so. There's nothing wrong with a head approach so long as you don't ignore the heart. But the heart approach without the head probably won't work this year. You'll need both.

The main challenge here is to use head knowledge appropriately – not in a romantic moment. Wait a day or so before analysing a current love or relationships. The lover who can satisfy your head *and* your heart is probably the best person to be with.

Love cannot be rushed this year. Marriage is a serious step, and you need to let love develop as it will.

Some of you singles might overly test love this year. The temptations here are great. But really there is no need to do so – you'll only complicate things even more. Let life, time and experience test your relationships. Enjoy each romantic encounter for what it is, without trying to project too far into the future.

When Saturn moves through the 7th House there is often disbelief in romantic love, even with normally romantic types such as you. Under this influence you may feel that marriage is not about romance – it's a job, a career move, like any other.

People involved with Aquarians this year will have to do much work to convince them of their love. The Aquarian will tend to be sceptical.

Those in, or working on, their second marriage will have a status-quo year. However, those working on their third marriage will probably hear wedding bells after November 24th or perhaps in 2007.

If one of the parents (or parent figures) is single, this could be a very powerful social year for them. Love is definitely in the picture. Children of marriageable age have been through a lot on the social level for many years but things are changing this year. A significant relationship will happen either after November 24th or in 2007. Siblings have a stable year socially. Adult grandchildren are preparing for marriage but it is not likely to happen this year. If they are already in a marriage, it will get tested and refined.

Finance and Career

Finances have been important for many years, and the trend continues in the year ahead. Career, which hasn't been that active for a while, becomes very powerful this year. In general, you are in one of the best career years of your life. Pay rises, promotions, honour and recognition are likely now. Career horizons are expanding. If there is anything to your talents and skills, the world is going to know about it.

Your friends are also having exceptional career years. In fact, many of them are helping in your own career. You seem to have friends in all the right places now, who bring you opportunities and promote you. Your naturally awesome networking skills are also playing a big role now. Career is furthered through your involvement in groups and organizations. Some of you will be elected to prestigious posts in these organizations. Others might be more involved in community affairs or local or national politics.

All of this, of course, helps the bottom line and boosts self-esteem and confidence. The year ahead looks very prosperous.

On the financial front, we are seeing the continuation of trends that have been going on for many years. You are investing in yourself – in your body, your image and personal appearance. Whatever your actual financial condition, you are dressing as if you are wealthy.

Your financial intuition is awesome these days. It really is the key to your success. One instant of true intuition is worth years of hard labour.

For many years you have been learning and applying the spiritual laws of affluence. It is through using these laws in our everyday lives that we learn more and deepen the knowledge we already have. If, in the coming year, you have periods of financial stress, the thing to do is get closer to spirit – the true source of all supply.

A major challenge is dealing with people who have a more materialistic approach to wealth than you have. The corporate community has a certain perspective on wealth, which is certainly valid on one level. They look at the visible and the measurable, but you are operating on a different level – the intuitive and creative level – and the perspective is radically different. Your faith in the invisible must be as strong as theirs is in the visible. Also, you will need to develop much tact and diplomacy in handling these people.

As in previous years, financial guidance is coming through dreams, spiritual leaders, psychics and astrologers.

Charitable giving has been important in previous years, and the trend continues this year. Many of you have got into a form of systematic and proportional giving.

Professional investors should look at oil, natural gas, shipping, water utilities and private-sector hospitals. High-technology and media companies also look very interesting.

You have a special feeling for these sectors and you should focus your energies here.

Speculations are very favourable all year. But of course this shouldn't be done blindly – only under intuition.

There is a strong connection between your image and appearance and your overall earning power. The better your look and the better your overall demeanour, the more you earn and the more financial opportunity comes. You have the kind of aspects often seen in models, actors and athletes.

Earnings will be strong all year but especially from January 20th to March 20th; May 21st to June 21st; and September 22nd to October 23rd.

Career success will happen all year but especially from February 19th to March 20th; June 21st to July 22nd; and October 23rd to November 21st.

One of the parents (or parent figures) is prospering greatly. This trend will continue for at least two years. Your spouse and children have a status-quo financial year but grandchildren are prospering and their overall net worth is increasing.

Self-improvement

Neptune, the most spiritual of all the planets, has been in your sign for many years now. It will stay there for many more years. This is having many effects on you – financially, image-wise and spiritually – but here we will discuss it from the health perspective.

The cosmos is working to refine and spiritualize the body. It wants you to have more conscious control over the body, to be able to shape and sculpt it according to your will. You are getting good at adopting any look you choose very quickly. This is a wonderful thing, but along with this comes hypersensitivity. You are feeling subtle vibrations (good or bad) in an actual physical way. Thus, if you are around someone with a heart or liver condition, you might feel it as if it were happening to you. And it really isn't. This sensitivity has caused more needless health problems than can be imagined. People have had unnecessary and dangerous operations because of this. There is a need now to become objective to the body, to observe sensations but stand separate from them, to differentiate sharply between actual symptoms and those emanating from others. This is a big and long-term project.

We are much more than our biochemistry. We are energy beings, receivers and radiators of energy. You can alter your body and its feelings by changing your energy. If you can pick up another person's condition, you can raise your own energy, and eventually this condition will just fall away. By learning how to change your energy you will also be able to heal others (or at least make them feel better) when they are around you. Rather than you picking up their condition, they will pick up your health, your optimism and positive qualities. This is a big subject beyond the scope of this report, but it's something for you to look into and explore.

Month-by-month Forecasts

January

Best Days Overall: 1, 2, 10, 11, 20, 21, 29, 30

Most Stressful Days Overall: 8, 9, 15, 16, 22, 23

Best Days for Love: 8, 9, 15, 16, 17, 18, 19, 20, 27, 28, 29, 30

Best Days for Money: 1, 2, 3, 4, 10, 11, 12, 13, 20, 21, 22, 23, 29, 30, 31

Monthly Career Peaks: 22, 23, 25, 26

Monthly Personal Pleasure Peaks: 1, 2, 3, 4, 19, 20, 29, 30, 31

There is a rare Grand Square pattern in the fixed signs this month, and you seem deeply involved in it. You are building something big, such as a business or institution. (Big projects are going on in the world as well.) This is a real challenge. It will be taxing on your energy levels so your health needs watching carefully until the 20th. Enhance health by resting and relaxing when you can and by working more rhythmically. Pay more attention to the heart, stomach and breasts. An empty 6th House this month shows that you might ignore legitimate health concerns.

Most of the planets are in the independent Eastern sector of the horoscope. Your 1st House of Self becomes powerful after the 20th. Although your 7th House of Others is also strong, the 1st House is stronger. This is a time to have things your way and to take responsibility for your own happiness.

This is also a very spiritual month. Your 12th House is strong until the 20th, and Neptune – the most spiritual of the planets – is in your own sign. Your spiritual practice will deepen and there is much revelation. This is a wonderful period for going on spiritual retreats, attending meditation seminars and lectures by visiting holy men. Since you have more independence, it is good to gain clarity on just what you want to create. Introspection and soul searching are useful for that. Charitable and altruistic activities are also good now. The dream life is more active and prophetic. ESP powers are enhanced. Intuition is solid. You march to a different drum than the rest of the world – and you seem to enjoy it.

This month the planets shift from the upper, day side of your horoscope to the lower, night side. Career is important this year – and will be very successful – but now is a time to pursue the career in the 'night way' rather than the 'day way' – through inner work rather than outer work; through dreaming, visualizing and digesting rather than overt action. Family and career vie with each other in importance and you are juggling both, but you can shift more emphasis to home and family.

It looks like there's construction going on in the home. If you have small children, keep them away from flammable or dangerous objects. Passions are running high at home – personally and with family members.

Finances are excellent this month. Happy windfalls and opportunities will happen towards the end of the month and early next month. Financial opportunities are seeking you out. Love, too, is seeking you and will find you after the 20th. Though love is in the air, singles should be cautious about marriage – processes are going on in your mind about love, and in a year or two you will have a whole new perspective on it. Let love develop slowly and methodically.

February

Best Days Overall: 6, 7, 16, 17, 25, 26

Most Stressful Days Overall: 4, 5, 11, 12, 19, 20

Best Days for Love: 4, 5, 6, 7, 11, 12, 14, 15, 17, 18, 19, 23, 24, 27, 28

Best Days for Money: 1, 6, 7, 9, 10, 16, 17, 19, 20, 25, 26, 27, 28

Monthly Career Peaks: 19, 20, 21, 22

Monthly Personal Pleasure Peaks: 1, 25, 26, 27, 28

Most of the planets are still in the independent East, and your 1st House remains powerful until the 19th. You are in the middle of your yearly personal pleasure peak, enjoying sensual pleasures and delights. You are having life more or less your way. (The Grand Square pattern is placing some limits on you until the 18th.)

Things at home and relations with family members are clarifying this month as your family planet, Venus, starts to move forwards on the 3rd. (She has been retrograde since the beginning of the year.) Family and home projects, which might have been plagued by delays, start to move forwards again. On a spiritual level, many of you are receiving revelation about your family and your relations with them. The roots of your issues lie in previous lifetimes.

With most of the planets below the horizon – in the night side of the horoscope – pay more attention to the home and family and to your emotional life. Many happy career opportunities are happening after the 19th, but you need to be more selective. Accept those that don't violate emotional harmony and comfort. In fact, the message this month is that you have no need to be over-ambitious – there will be many career opportunities that are more in harmony with you as you go along.

Love is still happy and continues to pursue you. Your lover or spouse goes out of their way to please you. Your spouse or lover seems financially supportive as well. Social connections play a big role in finance. After the 18th, siblings and neighbours are more supportive. The year as a whole is prosperous, but you are now in your yearly peak. Professional investors should look at gold, utilities, energy and gaming companies. Jobseekers will have better luck from the 1st to the 13th and on the 27th and 28th.

Until the 19th, singles are allured by physical attraction. However, after the 19th, wealth and material support are alluring.

Venus will re-stimulate eclipse points from the 24th to the 26th so be more patient with parents, parent figures and family members.

The Moon will re-stimulate eclipse points on the 2nd, 3rd, 9th, 10th, 16th, 17th, 23rd and 24th. Be more patient with colleagues or employees as they are apt to be more temperamental then.

Your health is much improved this month, especially after the 18th. You can enhance it by eating the right diet and paying more attention to the stomach and breasts.

March

Best Days Overall: 6, 7, 15, 16, 17, 25, 26

Most Stressful Days Overall: 3, 4, 10, 11, 12, 18, 19, 31

Best Days for Love: 4, 5, 6, 8, 9, 10, 11, 12, 15, 16, 18, 19, 20, 25, 26, 29, 30

Best Days for Money: 6, 7, 8, 9, 15, 16, 18, 19, 25, 26, 27, 28

Monthly Career Peaks: 18, 19, 20, 21

Monthly Personal Pleasure Peaks: 1, 5, 6, 7, 25, 26, 27, 28

Most of the planets are still in the East, and your 1st House of Self is stronger than your 7th House of Others. Continue to create your life as you desire it to be. If conditions displease you, take the actions needed to change them. Personal initiative is important these days.

Venus moves into your sign on the 6th. You have been looking good, been more magnetic and charismatic for some months now – and this trend continues. Your personal taste, sense of style and glamour are very strong. Women will be more beautiful now. Men will attract young women into their lives. This is a good month for buying clothing and personal accessories as your aesthetic sense is strong. Family members seem very much on your side and supportive. But perhaps you are feeling controlled, not by chains of iron or lead but by strings of gold. Love continues to pursue you. A sudden and happy romantic meeting happens on the 1st.

There are two eclipses this month, but both seem benign to you. Though the world in general gets disrupted, you are not affected too much. (Your personal horoscope cast for your exact date, time and place of birth could modify this.) The Lunar Eclipse of the 14th occurs in your 8th House and affects the income of your spouse or partner. Important and long-term changes are happening there. Financial thinking and planning need some adjustment, and the eclipse will be the spur to bring this about. Issues involving insurance, taxes and estates will take a dramatic turn, one way or another, and will move forwards. Since the Moon is your health and work planet, job changes are in store for many of you. This could be within your present company or at a different one. The conditions at work will change as well. Many of you will also make important changes to your diet and health regime.

The Solar Eclipse of the 29th occurs in your 3rd House and will test your car and communication equipment. It is often under these kinds of aspects that we decide, firmly, to get that new car or upgrade our computer or communication equipment. Dramatic events could happen with siblings and neighbours. Your locality could be undergoing radical change, such as major construction. Those of you who rely on dividend or interest income will have to make some financial adjustments – perhaps some companies cut their dividends or there is some dramatic move in interest rates. Every Solar Eclipse will test marriages or current love relationships, and this one is no different. True love and commitment will easily survive these things and probably get even better. But the weak relationships can be in danger.

Health is good and prosperity is still strong. Avoid speculations from the 2nd to the 25th, as Mercury is retrograde.

April

Best Days Overall: 2, 3, 11, 12, 13, 21, 29, 30

Most Stressful Days Overall: 1, 7, 8, 14, 15, 27, 28

Best Days for Love: 2, 3, 7, 8, 14, 15, 18, 23, 24, 27, 28

AQUARIUS

Best Days for Money: 2, 3, 4, 5, 12, 13, 14, 15, 21, 22, 23, 24, 29, 30

Monthly Career Peaks: 14, 15, 16, 17, 18

Monthly Personal Pleasure Peaks: 17, 18, 19, 21, 22, 23, 24

Most of the planets are still below the horizon. Your 4th House of Home and Family gets very strong after the 20th. Both your career planets are retrograde, showing a need for more planning and review there. So continue to build your stable home base and give more attention to the family.

Most of the planets are still in the independent East (though this is about to change) so continue to create your life on your terms. Make yourself happy and the world will be happy with you. Things get done through your personal initiative and not through people pleasing. Your social connections are wonderful things and should be cherished, but happiness is up to you.

Love is smooth and happy until the 20th. Intellectual compatibility is more important in love than wealth or material gifts. After the 20th (you have had your fill of talk) you want emotional nurturing and sharing. Emotional support is love. You give love that way and that is how you feel loved. Singles find love opportunities locally or with neighbours. Love is also found in educational surroundings. After the 20th, family connections or gatherings can lead to love. You feel sentimentally attached to old boyfriends or girlfriends, and might even reconnect with them, or with someone who reminds you of them. It's as if the cosmos gives you a 'do over' this period, and you can correct the mistakes you made in the past. Try a new tack with this person. Resolve old issues. Love gets challenged after the 20th by spiritual matters. You and your beloved are not on the same path or wavelength. Your cherished spiritual ideals get challenged – sometimes this is a good thing but if prolonged can be a problem. There is a need for more tolerance.

Prosperity is still strong this month and family continues to be very supportive. Speculations are favourable until the 16th. Professional investors should look at property. Jobseekers have success.

Health is good until the 20th but needs more watching afterwards. Enhance health by paying more attention to the heart, overall diet, stomach and breasts. Mars moves into your 6th House of Health on the 14th. This shows that vigorous physical exercise is important and you need good muscle tone now. If the muscles get weak, it can knock your whole body out of alignment. Detox regimes are beneficial, and more attention should be given to the colon, bladder and sexual organs.

Venus will re-stimulate eclipse points from the 27th to the 29th. Be more patient with family members then.

May

Best Days Overall: 9, 10, 18, 19, 27, 28

Most Stressful Days Overall: 4, 5, 12, 13, 25, 26, 31

Best Days for Love: 3, 4, 5, 7, 8, 14, 15, 16, 17, 22, 23, 27, 28, 31

Best Days for Money: 2, 3, 9, 10, 12, 13, 18, 19, 20, 21, 27, 28, 29, 30

Monthly Career Peaks: 12, 13, 14, 15, 25, 26

Monthly Personal Pleasure Peaks: 18, 19, 20, 21

The Eastern, independent side of your horoscope remains the strongest, but not as strong as it has been in recent months. Independence and personal initiative are still called for, but your need for social skills is getting stronger.

Like last month, most of the planets are below the horizon and your two career planets are retrograde. Career is more or less on hold now, and you might as well shift attention to the home and family. Being in emotional harmony will do more for you career-wise than hosts of overt, forced actions. Success is happening behind the scenes now.

Love remains problematic until the 21st. There are spiritual conflicts or incompatibilities, as discussed last month. There is still a need for tolerance. Though your spiritual life must come before everything – even your spouse and family – it is good every now and then to face some resistance to it, to have your ideals challenged. It gives you a chance to adjust and fine-tune them. But sometimes the challenge might be symptomatic of a basic, fundamental disharmony, and this revelation will lead you to some important decisions. Your beloved and your friends might not be in harmony this period as well, which further complicates your love life. For an Aquarius, this is a serious thing. But these issues get resolved, one way or another, by the 22nd when your attitude to love shifts again. Love is more about fun and having good times.

Health will improve after the 21st. In the meantime, like last month, rest and relax more and pay more attention to the heart, stomach, breasts, colon, bladder and sexual organs. Diet is still important, as is physical exercise and good muscle tone. Safe sex is more important as well.

Though you are in a prosperous year, finances are slowing down a bit. This should not alarm you as this is just part of the rhythm of Nature. Your financial planet will start to move retrograde on the 22nd. This will be a good period to review your products and services and see where you can make improvements. Financial intuition, which is like money in the bank for you, will need more verification after the 22nd. The intuition you receive might not be immediately feasible – it is something given to you for the future, perhaps months from now.

June

Best Days Overall: 5, 6, 14, 15, 23, 24

Most Stressful Days Overall: 1, 2, 8, 9, 21, 22, 28, 29

Best Days for Love: 1, 2, 3, 4, 5, 6, 12, 13, 14, 15, 22, 25, 26, 28, 29

Best Days for Money: 5, 6, 8, 9, 14, 15, 17, 18, 23, 24, 25, 26

Monthly Career Peaks: 8, 9, 10, 11

Monthly Personal Pleasure Peaks: 14, 15, 17, 18

This month, both your financial planets will be retrograde. Neptune, your actual financial planet, went retrograde on the 22nd of last month. Uranus in your 2nd House will go retrograde on the 19th. Much of what was said last month applies now. Don't lose heart. This slowdown is for your benefit – a blessing from on high. It is meant to be used creatively and constructively.

This month the Western, social sector of your horoscope becomes dominant. Now is the time to down-play personal interest and initiative and to cultivate your social skills. Avoid power struggles. Achieve ends by consensus and negotiation rather than by direct action. Watch how your popularity increases.

Your 7th House of Love starts to get very strong after the 3rd. You are entering your yearly social peak. Saturn has been in your 7th House all year, which has made you cautious in love, and slower to fall in love and enter into relationships – basically a good thing. But now Mars moves into the 7th House on the 3rd and urges you to jump into things, to abandon caution. Many of you will start becoming more aggressive in love and social matters, much more so than you have been all year. It seems to me that after a year of caution, a little risk-taking in love might be a positive thing. Love opportunities are found in educational surroundings, parties and places of entertainment, the workplace, or as you pursue health goals.

Until the 21st, love is about fun and good times. When the rough spots hit, you feel there is something 'wrong' and want out. After the 21st, you seem more serious about love. Love is about service to the beloved. It is about doing things for one another.

Your health needs watching, but happily you are very much on the case. Your 6th House is one of the strongest in the horoscope. Diet, health regimes and preventative medicine are all interesting now. You seem very concerned about the health of your lover or spouse too. Harmonious love relationships also play a role in health. Good health means more than just the absence of symptoms – it means a healthy love life as well. Continue to enhance health as discussed last month.

July

Best Days Overall: 3, 4, 12, 13, 20, 21, 30, 31

Most Stressful Days Overall: 5, 6, 18, 19, 25, 26

Best Days for Love: 3, 4, 5, 6, 12, 13, 14, 15, 22, 23, 25, 26

Best Days for Money: 3, 4, 5, 6, 12, 13, 14, 15, 20, 21, 23, 24, 30, 31

Monthly Career Peaks: 5, 6, 8, 9

Monthly Personal Pleasure Peaks: 5, 6, 7, 12, 13, 14, 15, 30, 31

With most of the planets in the social West and much power in the 7th House of Others, perhaps it is a good thing that Uranus, your ruler, is retrograde. Sure, self-confidence is weakened somewhat, but it will make you less likely to indulge in too much self-assertion and personal will. Meekness is a virtue now. You not only inherit the earth, but also win the heart of your beloved and friends. You are still in your yearly social peak, which is even stronger than last month. Much of what was said last month still applies. The workplace and the pursuit of health goals are roads to romance. After the 21st, social opportunity comes in the normal ways, at parties and gatherings. Love seems more serious now, and commitment more important. Perhaps you won't marry, but you will be interested in people who are marriage material.

This month the planets make an important shift from the lower, night side of the horoscope to the upper, day side. The day side is not yet completely dominant, but getting there. Career and outer achievement are becoming ever more important. And with Jupiter in your house of career starting to move forwards on the 7th, your career situation is starting to clarify as well. Stalled projects or developments start moving forwards again. So this is a month for shifting the gears.

Like last month, health needs careful watching. Enhance health through rest and relaxation, eating the right diet and paying more attention to the stomach, breasts and heart. Harmony with the family and in love also plays a more important role this month.

Last month, the North Node of the Moon moved into your 2nd House of Finance, where it will stay for another few years. This is a wonderful financial signal in its own right, for it shows happiness and fulfilment in your material pursuits. But, like last month, both your financial planets are retrograde. While overall prosperity is still intact, a breather now and then is a good thing. Continue to evaluate financial propositions more carefully. This is not your best month for earnings and you have to work harder than usual. Social bliss distracts you from bottom-line issues. Your spouse or partner seems less supportive than usual, and there may be some financial disagreements. Go the extra mile for earnings this period. You are building financial muscles.

The Sun re-stimulates eclipse points on the 1st and 2nd. This will bring dramatic events on a world level, but for you it shows a need to be more patient with your spouse, partner or current love. They are likely to be more temperamental than usual.

Venus will re-stimulate eclipse points from the 25th to the 27th. Be more patient with family members then.

August

Best Days Overall: 8, 9, 17, 18, 26, 27

Most Stressful Days Overall: 2, 3, 15, 21, 22, 23, 29, 30

Best Days for Love: 2, 3, 4, 5, 11, 12, 13, 21, 22, 23, 31

Best Days for Money: 2, 3, 8, 9, 10, 11, 17, 18, 19, 20, 26, 27, 29, 30

Monthly Career Peaks: 2, 3, 4, 5, 16, 17, 29, 30, 31

Monthly Personal Pleasure Peaks: 8, 9, 10, 11

By the 13th, the shift to the upper, day side of your horoscope will be complete. Seventy to eighty per cent of the planets will be in that side. So, it is time to make your career dreams happen. You can de-emphasize home and family issues and focus on your career.

Most of the planets remain in the West and your 7th House of Others is still strong. You are still in your yearly social peak. Social skills are more important than personal skills, knowledge or self-confidence. Negotiation, compromise and consensus will get you further than direct and arbitrary action.

Singles have many romantic opportunities with various types of people. You have a nice menu to choose from. Love is still romantic until the 23rd. After that, sexual chemistry seems the most important thing.

The 8th House becomes very strong after the 23rd. Your libido should be stronger than usual. This is a good period to pursue personal transformation and reinvention, for detox regimes on all levels. Your spouse or partner seems more prosperous and is likely to be generous. Perhaps they are travelling more on business. This is also a good time to pay off debts or refinance at more favourable rates. But with both your financial planets retrograde, all of this needs more homework. Tax and estate planning could be done well this month. This is also a time for delving into the deeper things of life, the mysteries of life, death, life after death and occult studies.

Health continues to need watching carefully, especially until the 23rd. With your 6th House still strong (until the 13th), you are on the case. Enhance health by paying more attention to the heart, stomach, breasts and diet; to the colon, sexual organs and bladder (until the 11th); and the kidneys and hips until the 13th. Emotional harmony with family and children plays an important role in overall health. You seem more active in the health of family members as well.

Finances are still stressful. You are overcoming many challenges, working harder and building financial muscles. Have no fear: all you need will be there.

Mars re-stimulates eclipse points from the 29th to the 31st. This will bring dramatic events on a world level. Reschedule risky activities for another time. Also, be more patient with siblings and neighbours as they are apt to be more temperamental.

September

Best Days Overall: 5, 6, 13, 14, 22, 23, 24

Most Stressful Days Overall: 11, 12, 17, 18, 19, 25, 26

Best Days for Love: 1, 2, 3, 4, 11, 12, 17, 18, 19, 20, 21, 22, 23, 30

AQUARIUS

Best Days for Money: 5, 6, 7, 8, 13, 14, 15, 16, 22, 23, 25, 26

Monthly Career Peaks: 1, 2, 25, 26, 28, 29

Monthly Personal Pleasure Peaks: 5, 6, 7, 8

Two eclipses this month shake things up in the world but you are relatively untouched on a personal level. People in your environment are affected, but for you these eclipses open up new opportunities.

The Lunar Eclipse of the 7th occurs in your 2nd House of Finance. It will show you where financial thinking and planning have been unrealistic. The things that happen now should be considered revelation and not punishment. Changes need to be made, but since both your financial planets are retrograde, proceed slowly and methodically. And since the Moon is also your work planet, this eclipse is showing job changes for many of you. Those who employ others have some shake-ups in their staff. Since this eclipse occurs near Uranus, your ruler, it will impact on your image, self-concept and personality. In coming months you will redefine your personality, and change your overall look. Sometimes impurities in the body come up for cleansing, but this should not be confused with sickness. If you've been watching your diet and your health, this probably won't happen.

The Solar Eclipse of the 22nd occurs right on the border of your 8th and 9th Houses, and will probably impact on both of them. Where the Lunar Eclipse brought changes to personal finance, this one brings similar changes to the finances of your spouse or partner. Financial thinking and planning need changing, and the eclipse provides the prod. Your partner can make changes faster than you can as their financial planet is moving forwards. You have to be more cautious. This eclipse will bring a turning point for legal matters in general, and especially if they involve estates,

403

taxes or insurance claims. Students in further or higher education make important changes to their plans. Foreign trips could be disrupted, delayed or postponed. Your religious beliefs get tested. Very often there is a crisis of faith. Since the Sun is also your love planet, every Solar Eclipse tests love, either the marriage or current love relationship. Long-seething issues can no longer be swept under the rug. There have been some tensions in love since last month, and this will be a good time to resolve them. Good relationships will get even stronger, but weak ones can easily dissolve. This eclipse delivers a glancing blow to Pluto, your career planet, so there could be career changes on the horizon as well. All of this will create opportunity for you.

Cultivating your social skills will be more challenging this month. Your self-esteem seems under attack. It is easy to be diplomatic when everyone is polite and nice, but not so easy when things get nasty. Yet, you should try.

October

Best Days Overall: 2, 3, 10, 11, 20, 21, 29, 30

Most Stressful Days Overall: 8, 9, 15, 16, 22, 23, 24

Best Days for Love: 2, 3, 10, 11, 15, 16, 21, 22

Best Days for Money: 2, 3, 4, 5, 10, 11, 12, 13, 14, 20, 21, 22, 23, 24, 29, 30

Monthly Career Peaks: 22, 23, 24, 25, 26

Monthly Personal Pleasure Peaks: 2, 3, 4, 5, 29, 30

The timing of the cosmos is exquisite. The planets are mostly above the horizon. Your 10th House of Career becomes amazingly strong after the 23rd with 50 to 60 per cent of the planets either there or moving through there. Both planets involved with your career are now moving forwards. (Pluto, your career planet, began moving forwards on the 4th of last month.) You are entering your yearly career peak, and probably, for many of you, your lifetime career peak. Even family members are supporting the career, and are perhaps even involved here. So, you can safely down-play home and family issues and focus on this rare, lifetime opportunity. You couldn't ask for better career aspects than what we have now.

However, it's very important to keep things in context. All of you are going to be elevated, honoured and recognized in some way, but your stage in life is a big factor. The filing clerk probably won't become managing director this month, but they will get promoted or be put on a management track. Students will do well and land dream jobs. People above you are favourably disposed to you. More importantly, you have friends in the right places who are also advancing, and they pull you along with them. You are jumping to a new and higher career track.

There will be pay rises and promotions. Your good professional reputation and your favour with people of power and prestige bring referrals to your business. Money can come from government grants, contracts or employees. Parents and parent figures seem supportive as well. In spite of the fact that both your financial planets are still retrograde, this is a prosperous month.

Your social life is also very happy this month, especially after the 23rd. Until the 23rd, you are attracted by mentor types, people who can teach you things. Under these aspects, students get involved with their teachers or professors. Ministerial types are interesting. Foreigners – the more exotic the better – are alluring. Love can happen at religious and educational settings. After the 23rd you start mingling with people above you in status. Often with these kinds of aspects there is the classic office romance. Singles are attracted by power and by people who can help them career-wise. Your spouse or partner is also advancing in their career and is supportive of your career. Love opportunities for singles come as they pursue career objectives.

Watch your health after the 23rd. Try to rest and relax more, and continue to pay more attention to the heart, stomach, breasts and diet.

November

Best Days Overall: 7, 8, 16, 17, 26, 27

Most Stressful Days Overall: 5, 11, 12, 19, 20

Best Days for Love: 1, 9, 10, 11, 12, 19, 20, 21, 30

Best Days for Money: 1, 2, 7, 8, 10, 16, 17, 20, 26, 27, 28, 29, 30

Monthly Career Peaks: 19, 20, 21, 22

Monthly Personal Pleasure Peaks: 1, 2, 3, 4, 5, 26, 27, 28, 29

Your yearly – and probably lifetime – career peak continues this month. Most of the planets are still above the horizon, and your 10th House of Career is packed with planets – 50 to 60 per cent of them are either there or moving through there. Success is unavoidable. Much of what was said last month applies now as well. By succeeding in the outer world, you are serving your family.

Aside from the career, many of you will be involved in political and community affairs. You are interested in governance now. Some of you will be elected or appointed to political office. In some cases, it will be to a prestigious post in an organization you belong to.

With this strong, worldly focus, it is only natural that your idealistic and spiritual side feels a bit thwarted. Integrating worldly success with your spiritual ideals and practice is the main challenge this month. You are so busy in the outer world that it is more difficult to practise your spiritual regime. You cannot allow even the rapturous events of the world to disturb your inner connection.

AQUARIUS

Last month was prosperous, and this month will be even more so. Your financial planet started to move forwards on the 29th of last month. Your other financial planet (Uranus in the money house) will start moving forwards on the 20th. Many a stalled deal or project is starting to progress again. Financial judgement is getting sounder day by day. Perhaps now, with all this success and opportunity happening for you, you can see the wisdom of the caution you exercised for many months.

Like last month, money comes from the career – from pay rises and promotions – from elders, bosses and authority figures, from the government and from your good professional reputation.

Love is still happy, especially until the 22nd. Very important love connections happen for singles. These people are marriage material but will it lead to marriage? Time will tell. Saturn in your 7th House suggests letting love develop in an unhurried way. Like last month, love happens at the workplace, as you pursue your career goals or with people involved in your career. People of power and status allure you. After the 22nd, love opportunities happen as you get involved with groups and organizations – your favourite activity. Friends can play cupid. Friendship is important in love: you want to be friends with the beloved as well as their lover.

Try to rest and relax when you can until the 22nd. Enhance health by paying more attention to the heart, stomach, breasts and diet. Keep your focus on things of essence and let the frivolous go.

December

Best Days Overall: 4, 5, 13, 14, 15, 23, 24

Most Stressful Days Overall: 2, 3, 8, 9, 10, 16, 17, 29, 30

Best Days for Love: 1, 8, 9, 10, 11, 18, 19, 20, 21, 22, 29, 30

Best Days for Money: 4, 5, 8, 13, 14, 18, 23, 24, 25, 26, 27, 31

Monthly Career Peaks: 7, 8, 16, 17, 18, 19, 25

Monthly Personal Pleasure Peaks: 23, 24, 25, 26

If ever there was an Aquarius heaven, this is it! Sixty to seventy per cent of the planets are either in or moving through your 11th House of Friends. Rarely do we see so many planets in any one sign or house.

It's as if the cosmos is forcing you to be who you are, to do the things you most love to do, to exercise your highest genius. These are peak experiences for sure. This is like giving a young child unlimited money and commanding them to go the amusement arcade and play all the video games. They can hardly believe their good luck!

Being who we really are – with integrity – is probably the most difficult achievement in life. Yet, there is nothing more worthwhile. And here, this month, the door is open and you can be who you are. It is not difficult – it is demanded of you.

So you are more involved with groups and organizations. Perhaps you are joining new ones. Your status in these organizations is elevated. New and important friends are coming into your life, and these are the real thing. These are people who support the manifestation of your 'fondest hopes and wishes'. With so much power in the sign of Sagittarius, group travel or tours seem happy, and there will be many opportunities for this.

In general, with so much power in your 11th House (and beneficent Jupiter moving in late last month) you will realize your dreams. And as you experience fulfilment, nothing is more certain than that you will formulate a whole new set of 'fondest hopes and wishes', perhaps grander than the previous ones. This is the nature of life. We always want more, more, more. Infinity has no limits.

Though your 10th House of Career is getting weaker, your career is still going strong. Your career planet, Pluto, is receiving powerful and positive stimulation. All these new friends and groups are enhancing the career – and perhaps your career is the cause of these things too.

Career success is not just about money – it's also about the people we meet at the top, and the social life we are exposed to. And this is what is happening now.

In general, your understanding of science, astronomy, technology and astrology becomes even stronger than usual. Much new knowledge and revelation comes to you.

This month you find it easier to integrate career success with your spiritual ideals and practice. You seem to have solved the problem.

Health is much improved over last month, and you can enhance it through paying more attention to the stomach, breasts and diet.

Pisces

☓

THE FISH
Birthdays from
19th February to
20th March

Personality Profile

PISCES AT A GLANCE

Element – Water

Ruling Planet – Neptune
  Career Planet – Pluto
  Love Planet – Mercury
  Money Planet – Mars
  Planet of Health and Work – Sun
  Planet of Home and Family Life – Mercury
  Planet of Love Affairs, Creativity and Children
    – Moon

Colours – aqua, blue-green

Colours that promote love, romance and social
  harmony – earth tones, yellow, yellow-
  orange

Colours that promote earning power – red, scarlet

Gem – white diamond

Metal – tin

Scent – lotus

Quality – mutable (= flexibility)

Qualities most needed for balance – structure and the ability to handle form

Strongest virtues – psychic power, sensitivity, self-sacrifice, altruism

Deepest needs – spiritual illumination, liberation

Characteristics to avoid – escapism, keeping bad company, negative moods

Signs of greatest overall compatibility – Cancer, Scorpio

Signs of greatest overall incompatibility – Gemini, Virgo, Sagittarius

Sign most helpful to career – Sagittarius

Sign most helpful for emotional support – Gemini

Sign most helpful financially – Aries

Sign best for marriage and/or partnerships – Virgo

Sign most helpful for creative projects – Cancer

Best Sign to have fun with – Cancer

Signs most helpful in spiritual matters – Scorpio, Aquarius

Best day of the week – Thursday

Understanding a Pisces

If Pisceans have one outstanding quality it is their belief in the invisible, spiritual and psychic side of things. This side of things is as real to them as the hard earth beneath their feet – so real, in fact, that they will often ignore the visible, tangible aspects of reality in order to focus on the invisible and so-called intangible ones.

Of all the Signs of the Zodiac, the intuitive and emotional faculties of the Pisces are the most highly developed. They are committed to living by their intuition and this can at times be infuriating to other people – especially those who are materially-, scientifically- or technically-orientated. If you think that money or status or worldly success are the only goals in life, then you will never understand a Pisces.

Pisceans have intellect, but to them intellect is only a means by which they can rationalize what they know intuitively. To an Aquarius or a Gemini the intellect is a tool with which to gain knowledge. To a well-developed Pisces it is a tool by which to express knowledge.

Pisceans feel like fish in an infinite ocean of thought and feeling. This ocean has many depths, currents and undercurrents. They long for purer waters where the denizens are good, true and beautiful, but they are sometimes pulled to the lower, murkier depths. Pisceans know that they do not generate thoughts but only tune in to thoughts that already exist; this is why they seek the purer waters. This ability to tune in to higher thoughts inspires them artistically and musically.

Since Pisces is so spiritually-orientated – though many Pisceans in the corporate world may hide this fact – we will deal with this aspect in greater detail, for otherwise it is difficult to understand the true Pisces personality.

There are four basic attitudes of the spirit. One is outright scepticism – the attitude of secular humanists. The second is an intellectual or emotional belief, where one worships a far-distant God figure – the attitude of most modern church-going people. The third is not only belief but direct personal spiritual experience – this is the attitude of some 'born-again' religious people. The fourth is actual unity with the divinity, an intermingling with the spiritual world – this is the attitude of yoga. This fourth attitude is the deepest urge of a Pisces, and a Pisces is uniquely qualified to pursue and perform this work.

Consciously or unconsciously, Pisceans seek this union with the spiritual world. The belief in a greater reality makes Pisceans very tolerant and understanding of others – perhaps even too tolerant. There are instances in their lives when they should say 'enough is enough' and be ready to defend their position and put up a fight. However, because of their qualities it takes a good deal of doing to get them into that frame of mind.

Pisceans basically want and aspire to be 'saints'. They do so in their own way and according to their own rules. Others should not try to impose their concept of saintliness on a Pisces, because he or she always tries to find it for him- or herself.

Finance

Money is generally not that important to Pisces. Of course they need it as much as anyone else, and many of them attain great wealth. But money is not generally a primary objective. Doing good, feeling good about oneself, peace of mind, the relief of pain and suffering – these are the things that matter most to a Pisces.

Pisceans earn money intuitively and instinctively. They follow their hunches rather than their logic. They tend to be generous and perhaps overly charitable. Almost any kind of misfortune is enough to move a Pisces to give. Although this is one of their greatest virtues, Pisceans should be more careful with their finances. They should try to be more choosy about the people to whom they lend money, so that they are not being taken advantage of. If they give money to charities they should follow it up to see that their contributions are put to good use. Even when Pisceans are not rich, they still like to spend money on helping others. In this case they should really be careful, however: they must learn to say no sometimes and help themselves first.

Perhaps the biggest financial stumbling block for the Pisces is general passivity – a *laissez faire* attitude. In general Pisceans like to go with the flow of events. When it comes to financial matters, especially, they need to be more aggressive. They need to make things happen, to create their own wealth. A passive attitude will only cause loss and missed opportunity. Worrying about financial security will not provide that security. Pisceans need to go after what they want tenaciously.

Career and Public Image

Pisceans like to be perceived by the public as people of spiritual or material wealth, of generosity and philanthropy. They look up to big-hearted, philanthropic types. They admire people engaged in large-scale undertakings and eventually would like to head up these big enterprises themselves. In short, they like to be connected with big organizations that are doing things in a big way.

If Pisceans are to realize their full career and professional potential they need to travel more, educate themselves more and learn more about the actual world. In other words, they need some of the unflagging optimism of the Sagittarius in order to reach the top.

Because of all their caring and generous characteristics, Pisceans often choose professions through which they can help and touch the lives of other people. That is why many Pisceans become doctors, nurses, social workers or teachers.

Sometimes it takes a while before Pisceans realize what they really want to do in their professional lives, but once they find a career that lets them manifest their interests and virtues they will excel at it.

Love and Relationships

It is not surprising that someone as 'otherworldly' as the Pisces would like a partner who is practical and down to earth. Pisceans prefer a partner who is on top of all the details of life, because they dislike details. Pisceans seek this quality in both their romantic and professional partners. More than anything else this gives Pisces a feeling of being grounded, of being in touch with reality.

As expected, these kinds of relationships – though necessary – are sure to have many ups and downs. Misunderstandings will take place because the two attitudes are poles apart. If you are in love with a Pisces you will experience these fluctuations and will need a lot of patience to see things stabilize. Pisceans are moody, intuitive, affectionate and difficult to get to know. Only time and the right attitude will yield Pisceans' deepest secrets. However, when in love with a Pisces you will find that riding the waves is worth it because they are good, sensitive people who need and like to give love and affection.

When in love, Pisceans like to fantasize. For them fantasy is 90 per cent of the fun of a relationship. They tend to idealize their partner, which can be good and bad at the same time. It is bad in that it is difficult for anyone to live up to the high ideals their Piscean lover sets.

Home and Domestic Life

In their family and domestic life Pisceans have to resist the tendency to relate only by feelings and moods. It is unrealistic to expect that your partner and other family members will be as intuitive as you are. There is a need for more verbal communication between a Pisces and his or her family. A cool, unemotional exchange of ideas and opinions will benefit everyone.

Some Pisceans tend to like mobility and moving around. For them too much stability feels like a restriction on their freedom. They hate to be locked in one location for ever.

The Sign of Gemini sits on Pisces' 4th Solar House (of Home and Family) cusp. This shows that the Pisces likes and needs a home environment that promotes intellectual and mental interests. They tend to treat their neighbours as family – or extended family. Some Pisceans can have a dual attitude towards the home and family – on the one hand they like the emotional support of the family, but on the other they dislike the obligations, restrictions and duties involved with it. For Pisces, finding a balance is the key to a happy family life.

Horoscope for 2006

General Trends

As is the case with the other mutable signs – Gemini, Virgo and Sagittarius – you are in a period of dramatic change in your life on almost every level. Learning to deal with the change, to deal with insecurity, to deal with facing the unknown is probably the most important lesson right now.

Along with the dramatic changes come metaphorical space flights. It's as if you blast out of the ordinary atmosphere of the earth and into space, reaching new heights and experiences. You are in a new realm.

Spirituality is always important to you but has become even more so in recent years. In fact, this spirituality has a great deal to do with the upcoming changes that are happening.

Health and health issues became important to you as of July 17th 2005, and this trend will continue in the year ahead.

Jupiter, the planet of abundance and good fortune, is making sensational aspects to you almost all year, until November 24th. So, though money in itself is not a big issue, you will prosper anyway. There is much career success, foreign travel and overall expansion of the horizons.

Career has been important for many years. You have had many 'death and rebirth' experiences career-wise, but the changes that come now will be very pleasant. You are entering one of the best career periods of your life.

Overall, your strongest interests this year are spirituality and charitable, altruistic activities; the body, image and personal appearance; health and work; foreign travel, religion, philosophy and higher education (until November 24th); career (all year but especially after November 24th).

Your paths to greatest fulfilment this year are foreign travel, religion, philosophy and higher education (until November 24th); career (after November 24th); finance (until June 23rd); the body, image and personal appearance (after June 23rd).

Health

(Please note that this is an astrological perspective on health, not a medical one. At one time, both perspectives were identical, but in these times there could be quite a difference. For the medical perspective, please consult your physician or health professional.)

Health and vitality are basically good this year. Only one of the long-term planets is in stressful aspect to you. Given this situation, the power in the 6th House of Health this year is no doubt indicating things other than disease. You are probably interested in preventative regimes. Or, more likely, given your strong spirituality, you are interested in healing others. This is definitely a year for disciplined and rigorous health regimes, diets and exercise programmes. With Saturn in your 6th House, you are not interested in quick fixes for health problems but in long-term cures.

As a Pisces, your feet are always important health-wise. Perhaps more than any other sign, you respond beautifully to foot massage and reflexology. The shoes you wear play an inordinate role in your overall wellbeing.

With Uranus in your own sign for the next five years or so, the ankles have also become important. It's good to massage them and give them extra support, especially when exercising, skiing, skating or biking.

Your health planet is the Sun. In the physical body, the Sun rules the heart (and some astrologers say the spleen as well). Paying more attention to these organs will enhance your already good health. Since the Sun is a pretty fast-moving planet – it will move through your entire horoscope in a given year – health needs and powerful therapies will tend to change from month to month. These things will be discussed in the monthly reports.

Saturn, which rules the spine, knees, teeth, gall bladder and overall skeletal alignment, is in your 6th House of Health for at least two more years. This shows that extra attention needs to be given to these organs, and to the bones in general.

Saturn rules your 11th House of Friends, so his position in your 6th House of Health has many other messages for us. You are actively involved with the health of friends. Social issue, such as disharmony with friends, could impact on physical health.

Generally, Saturn involved with health shows a traditional, non-experimental approach to health and health issues. But here Saturn is Lord of the 11th House, and tends to be more experimental than usual. I read this as someone who is cautiously experimental in health this year.

With Uranus in your own sign, there is a tendency now to test your physical limits. Yogis will try for that impossible posture, athletes for their personal best. There's nothing wrong with this of course, and many of you will learn that your physical limits were never what you thought they were. But these physical experiments need to be done mindfully. Stop if you feel undue pain or discomfort.

The health of your spouse or lover is also enhanced through foot and ankle massage. They are much more experimental in health than you are. There is good news about the health of a parent or parent figure this year. They can enhance health through detox regimes and paying more attention to the liver and thighs. Children will also benefit from these things. Overall, the health of children looks good. If there have been health problems there is good news ahead, especially after November 24th. Grandchildren are status-quo health-wise but may benefit from changes in their regime.

Home, Domestic and Family Issues

Though your 4th House of Home and Family is not a House of Power this year – you either don't need or don't want to pay too much attention here – there are many changes going on nevertheless.

With Uranus in your 1st House, you are more nomadic, travelling more, staying in different places for long periods of time. It's almost as if the road is your home. You seem satisfied with the status-quo this year – family relations are reasonable, your home seems OK – but other things in your life are causing changes.

Adding to this is Jupiter in your 9th House, the classic 'wanderlust' aspect of the zodiac. Rather than obstructing your freedom-loving urges, your family seems understanding and supportive.

Career will also be very happy and successful towards the end of the year, after November 24th. And these things often cause moves and domestic changes as a side-effect.

If you are planning heavy construction in the home, February 17th to April 4th is a good time. If you are redecorating or buying objects of beauty for the home, June 24th to July 19th is a good period – and this is also good for entertaining from home. Family issues in general will be more important from May 20th to June 21st.

Most of you have had difficulties with parents or parent figures over the years. Some have literally died. Others have had near-death experiences, surgeries and the like. Others have had spiritual death and rebirth experiences. Thus your relations with these people have undoubtedly changed – the old patterns have been broken in one way or another. The object here was never to break completely with the parent or parent figure, but to bring the relationship to a higher and more conscious level. The old way of relating needed to 'die'. Toxic connections were getting purified, a trend that continues in the year ahead.

Children of appropriate age seem more fertile in the year ahead. Pregnancies and new births are more likely. Some are considering adoption too. Their overall domestic situation, though, seems status-quo, although they might move in 2007. Your spouse might start agitating for a move (or for expensive items in the home) after November 24th. Business partners could move around that time too (or in 2007). Adult grandchildren could have many moves or renovations this year and in years to come. They are emotionally unsettled and are seekers of the dream home, as are parents and parent figures.

Love and Social Life

Your 7th House of Love and Marriage is not a House of Power this year. Personal freedom, spirituality, religion, travel and health all seem higher priorities in the year ahead. Generally, this shows a status-quo kind of year for love. Married Pisceans usually stay married and singles stay single.

This lack of interest can be read as a very good thing. Many of you have married in recent years; many are involved in significant relationships; and many are enjoying the single lifestyle. This lack of interest is an indication of contentment.

For singles, marriage might not even be advisable, as personal freedom seems your main interest. Pisceans are breaking loose now and exploring their freedom. Most are not interested in committed relationships.

Those of you who are married to Pisceans or involved with them romantically need to understand this. The only way these relationships will work is by granting them maximum freedom. If it isn't destructive, give them free rein, otherwise you'll have one rebellious and resentful person on your hands.

You also need to understand the many changes of image and self-concept that Pisces is going through these days. They are constantly exploring, changing and upgrading these areas. This can be bewildering for a partner. It's as if you are having multiple relationships with one person.

Since Pisceans have no idea where their experiments will go, they are as much of a mystery to themselves as they are to other people.

With fast-moving Mercury as your love planet, romantic opportunities will come in different ways and places throughout the year. These short-term trends will be discussed in the monthly reports.

Singles who are working on their second marriage will have serious love this year, and possibly marriage. This love is with someone prominent – someone above you in status who may be involved with your career. You can meet this person in various ways: as you pursue career goals, in foreign lands, at religious or university functions.

Singles working on their third marriage have a status-quo year. Romantic opportunities will come at work or as you pursue your health goals.

Singles working on their fourth marriage will have romantic opportunity, but it's best to stay uncommitted.

Siblings of appropriate age will be involved in a serious love relationship this year, which could lead to marriage. Business partnerships are also likely. A single parent (or parent figure) is likely to get involved in a serious romance, but after November 24th and perhaps in 2007. Adult children have a status-quo love year. For them, love opportunities happen with money people and those involved in their finances. Grandchildren of marriageable age are having a great overall year but marriage is status-quo.

Friendships and group activities are not that important this year either. But friendship opportunities will happen at work or as you pursue your health goals. Doctors and health professionals seem alluring.

Romance will tend to be most active from August 23rd to September 30th. A very important romantic opportunity will happen from October 2nd to December 8th.

Friendships and group activities seem happiest and most active from December 21st to January 19th and from July 23rd to August 22nd.

Finance and Career

This is more of a career year than a financial year. Your 2nd House of Finance is more or less empty, while your 10th House of Career is strong all year, and even stronger after November 24th.

You are dealing with eclipses in your money house for most of the year. The Lunar Eclipse of October 17th 2005 is still in effect until March, and a new Solar Eclipse on March 29th will happen in your money house. These will probably force you to reconsider your financial plans, thinking and strategy. Perhaps they have been unrealistic. Sometimes these changes happen through shock and disruption, but the end result tends to be good. In your case, you might be making financial plans based on too much pessimism. Many happy things happening in your career will nullify your gloomy thinking or strategy.

For the most part, though, the empty money house is showing contentment with things as they are. You seem satisfied with your income and this whole department of life and have no need (so you think) to make any major changes here. (This is why some of you need an eclipse or two this year to force you to make necessary changes.)

Though money in itself is not so interesting, it might be wise to force some interest here. The Moon's North Node shows that a focus here will bring happiness and fulfilment.

Career, however, remains the main headline of the year ahead. Your career planet, Jupiter, will be in the benevolent 9th House until November 24th. This shows career expansion, career opportunities in foreign lands or with foreigners, educational opportunities related to the career, and a general increase in your professional and social status. On November 24th (and you will feel this about a week before), Jupiter will cross your Midheaven, ushering in one of the best career periods of your life up until now. This not only brings career opportunity, pay rises and promotions but also honour and glory – recognition. Politicians often get elected or nominated to high office under these aspects, and this could happen to some of you too. Much depends on your stage and circumstance. People are often elected president of a community organization, a club, a residents' association and the like.

If you have been fretting about not being recognized or appreciated, relax. This is happening now.

You can also expect to be travelling more on business.

Those of you who have issues with the government – pending rulings or legal cases – can expect best case scenarios this year.

In general, elders, authorities, governments and people above you in status are favourably disposed to you.

A parent or parent figure starts to prosper after November 24th – this will be at least a two-year trend. Siblings have a status-quo financial year but their career is going well. Children are having a more difficult financial year. The problem isn't earnings, but managing what they have in a better way. They need to bring order and discipline into their financial lives. Grandchildren, if appropriate, are prospering, but it's not a free ride; they are working very hard.

Self-improvement

The spirituality of Pisces is legendary. In fact, most of the flaws attributed to the sign come precisely from this other-worldly spirituality which is so difficult for many people to comprehend (even some astrologers have trouble here). So, by temperament, you are very spiritual, but this innate gift and urge has been greatly magnified in recent years. Your ruling planet has been in the spiritual 12th House for many years. And, in 2004, your spiritual planet moved into your sign and will be there for many more years. Most of you are hardly touching the ground these days. Your whole life seems to be one long spiritual experience, a living dream. You know that the hard and fast reality you see around you is a dream made manifest. The invisible is just as real to you as the visible. Your dream life is so active, so interesting and so brilliant that it's amazing that you manage to get up in the morning! It's not easy to leave such spaces of great beauty. Inner playmates and invisible beings are as real as physical ones. Prophecy is so normal that it's 'ho hum'. Yet, you do manage to get up and be about your business. Why? Because you know that you are here for a purpose. You have a mission in life. As beautiful as your inner world is, the powers that be won't let you stay there. You must stay on the earth until your purpose is fulfilled.

This is a year when you will receive much revelation about this purpose. You will have revelation all year, but it will begin in earnest around November 24th. Once this is clear to you, life becomes a breeze, for in reality there is nothing else in life but your purpose. Not another's purpose but your own. And the carrying out of this purpose will lead you to all your other heart's desires. Anything not aligned with your purpose will have to go – and good riddance. It is wonderful to live in spiritual spaces, but this is not the be-all and end-all in life. It is nice to rest and refresh yourself there, but you've got a job to do so let's get on with it!

Month-by-month Forecasts

January

Best Days Overall: 3, 4, 12, 13, 14, 22, 23, 31

Most Stressful Days Overall: 10, 11, 17, 18, 19, 25, 26

Best Days for Love: 8, 9, 17, 18, 19, 27, 28, 29, 30

Best Days for Money: 3, 4, 12, 13, 22, 23, 31

Monthly Career Peaks: 22, 23, 24, 25, 26

Monthly Personal Pleasure Peaks: 1, 2, 3, 4, 29, 30, 31

Your year begins with most of the planets above the horizon. Your 10th House of Career is strong while your 4th House of Home and Family is basically empty – only the Moon visits there on the 10th and 11th. The message is clear: you are still in the day phase of your year, and can down-play family and emotional issues as you focus on your outer life and career. Happily, even family seems supportive of your career and seems to agree with your focus. Education is the best way to advance your career now, and for most of the year ahead. Mammoth career success will happen at the end of the year, so you need to make sure you are prepared. You can also advance the career through social and family connections until the 4th.

Most of the planets are in the independent East so this is a period for having things your way, so long as you're not destructive. Your personal happiness is important to the world, though some find this hard to believe.

Health is good this month. You can enhance it by paying more attention to the heart, spine, knees, teeth and overall skeletal alignment. This is a trend for the year, but especially in the month ahead. After the 20th, the ankles become important, and ankle massage will be very powerful.

Finances are complicated this month. Your financial planet is part of a Grand Square in the fixed signs. You are probably involved in a big financial project and many factors have to be balanced. If you get too bottom-line oriented, you could damage your status. But if you are too status conscious, you could suffer financially. Earnings are enhanced through good sales, marketing and promotion. This is a month when you build financial musculature. Overall, you are still in a prosperous year.

Your love planet, Mercury, moves very speedily this month, passing through three signs and houses of your horoscope. This shows a lot of social confidence, much dating, and finding love and social opportunities in different places and with different sorts of people. Until the 4th, love is linked to the career. After the 4th, friends become important in love. You want your partner to be your friend as well as your lover. Romantic opportunities happen at group functions in organizations. A friend might become more than that. After the 22nd, love happens at spiritual venues. Love is very idealistic during that period. Spiritual compatibility with the lover is very important.

Spirituality has been important for many years and this month it is more so, especially after the 20th. Always psychic, your powers are stronger these days. More introspection is called for now.

PISCES

February

Best Days Overall: 1, 9, 10, 19, 20, 27, 28

Most Stressful Days Overall: 6, 7, 14, 15, 21, 22

Best Days for Love: 4, 5, 6, 7, 14, 15, 16, 17, 23, 24, 27, 28

Best Days for Money: 1, 2, 3, 4, 5, 9, 10, 15, 19, 20, 25, 27, 28

Monthly Career Peaks: 19, 20, 21, 22

Monthly Personal Pleasure Peaks: 1, 8, 9, 18, 19, 25, 26, 27, 28

Like last month, the spiritual life is prominent in the month ahead, especially until the 19th.

Most of the planets are still in the East, and your 1st House of Self becomes ultra-strong after the 19th. Your 7th House of Others is mostly empty – only the Moon will visit there on the 14th and 15th, and this will be the monthly social peak. So this is still a time for creating conditions, not for adapting to them.

On the 19th, the planetary power shifts to the lower, night side of the horoscope. This is an important shift. Presumably, most career goals have been achieved by now. This is a time for reviewing and digesting the career and for visualizing future career goals. Inner work on the career will be more powerful than outer work. It is also a time for getting into the right emotional state and establishing a solid domestic base. With Mars moving into your 4th House on the 18th, you are probably making important repairs or renovations in the home. Looks like you are spending more on the home and on the family so the timing here is perfect.

With your 1st House strong, you are entering your yearly personal pleasure peak. This is a time for pampering yourself and giving the body its pleasures.

Health is good this month. Happily, you seem more interested in health as well. Health regimes and healthy lifestyles
appeal to you. There is a vanity component here as well. You
can enhance health through ankle massage (until the 19th)
and foot massage (after the 19th).

You are looking good these days. You are magnetic and
charismatic. The opposite sex takes notice. Love is pursuing
you and will find you after the 9th. Your lover or spouse
goes out of their way to please you.

Finances are getting easier as well, especially after the
18th. Until then, continue to go the extra mile for earnings.
Sales, marketing and promotion remain important until the
18th. After that, earnings come through the family, including parents or parent figures. Professional investors should
look at property, telecommunications, transportation and
media companies. Jobseekers have a fortunate month.
Dream job offers come after the 19th.

March

Best Days Overall: 8, 9, 18, 19, 20, 27, 28

Most Stressful Days Overall: 6, 7, 13, 14, 20, 21

Best Days for Love: 4, 5, 6, 8, 9, 13, 14, 15, 16, 18, 19, 25,
26, 27, 28

Best Days for Money: 1, 2, 6, 7, 8, 9, 15, 16, 17, 18, 19,
25, 26, 27, 28, 29, 30

Monthly Career Peaks: 8, 9, 10, 18, 19, 20, 21

Monthly Personal Pleasure Peaks: 24, 25, 26, 27, 28

Like last month, most of the planets are still in the lower,
night side of the horoscope. The two planets involved with
your career will be retrograde (the career planet goes retrograde on the 4th; Pluto in your 10th House goes retrograde
on the 29th). So the career is slowing down. You might as

well be happy, emotionally comfortable and pay more attention to the family.

The Eastern, independent sector of your horoscope is still stronger than the Western sector. Your 1st House of Self is powerful while your 7th House of Others is practically empty. Continue to create your own happiness.

Two eclipses this month guarantee a tumultuous period. Of the two, the Lunar Eclipse of the 14th seems to have the strongest effect on you. Be sure to reduce your schedule for a few days before and perhaps a day after. This eclipse occurs in your 7th House of Love and Marriage, and will test a current marriage or love relationship. Marriages have been tested for two years now, so only the strongest of them will survive. The same applies to other love relationships. (The retrograde of your love planet from the 2nd to the 25th is not helping matters either.) Singles, on the other hand, may decide to change their status. Love has been unstable for quite a while, and it is even more so now. Children are making important changes in their lives. Many of you are in the creative fields and there will be dramatic changes in your personal creativity, ultimately for the better.

The Solar Eclipse of the 29th is easier on you, but it will be strong for the world at large. This one occurs in your money house and shows long-term changes to your financial planning. These changes are long overdue, but now the eclipse forces the issue. There will probably be job changes as well. And since the Sun is also your health planet, there will be alterations to your diet and health regime, and to the people involved in your health.

Health is basically good this month. Not perfect, but more easy than difficult. You can enhance it through foot massage and water therapies until the 20th; through scalp massage, facial massage and thermal therapies after the 20th.

April

Best Days Overall: 4, 5, 14, 15, 23, 24

Most Stressful Days Overall: 2, 3, 9, 10, 17, 18, 29, 30

Best Days for Love: 2, 3, 4, 5, 9, 10, 14, 15, 16, 23, 24, 25, 26

Best Days for Money: 2, 3, 4, 5, 13, 14, 15, 23, 24, 25, 26

Monthly Career Peaks: 14, 15, 16, 17, 18

Monthly Personal Pleasure Peaks: 5, 6, 21, 22, 23, 24

Both your career planets are still retrograde, and the planetary power is mostly below the horizon. You can safely shift emphasis to the home, family and emotional issues now. Work on your career in the inner-oriented ways, through visualizing and dreaming.

Most of the planets are still in the independent East, and your 1st House of Self remains strong. You continue to be very much in your yearly personal pleasure peak. Creative powers are at their height now too. Personal initiative and direct action will lead you to happiness. Others are adapting to you, rather than vice versa. The important thing now is to build wisely and lawfully, for you are going to have to live with the result of your creation later on down the road.

Venus moves into your sign on the 6th. This enhances personal appearance and glamorizes the image. Your sense of style is excellent these days so it is a good time to buy clothing and personal accessories or otherwise beautify the image. Green, electric blue and yellow are suitable colours. Love continues to pursue you and there's nothing much you need to do. Love is tender, romantic and idealistic. Sensitivities in love are unusually strong so you need to watch your voice tones and body language with your beloved, and vice versa, but the highs of love will be very high. Love poetry will make interesting reading, and many of you will be writing your own.

Finances are strong this month. Your 2nd House of Finance is powerful until the 20th. Earnings come from work. Those in the health professions will have an especially strong month. After the 16th, social connections play a huge role in earnings. Business partnerships could form. Your spouse or current love plays an active role in your finances and seems supportive. On the 14th, the financial planet will move into your 5th House, making speculations more favourable.

Health is excellent and you can enhance it through scalp and facial massage, as well as heat therapies until the 20th; neck massage and earth-based therapies after the 20th. Mental health in general is important after the 20th. Since intellectual pursuits are important during this period, you will have a good opportunity to clear the mind of error.

Be more patient with family members and your beloved on the 11th, 12th, 22nd and 23rd as Mercury re-stimulates eclipse points. They are apt to be more temperamental.

May

Best Days Overall: 2, 3, 12, 13, 20, 21, 29, 30

Most Stressful Days Overall: 7, 8, 14, 15, 27, 28

Best Days for Love: 3, 5, 6, 7, 8, 14, 15, 17, 22, 23, 27, 28

Best Days for Money: 2, 3, 12, 13, 20, 21, 22, 23, 29, 30

Monthly Career Peaks: 12, 13, 14, 15, 19, 20, 21

Monthly Personal Pleasure Peaks: 18, 19, 20, 21

Major career developments are happening but mostly behind the scenes. They will take time to manifest. Continue to focus on the family and achieving a correct inner state.

Like last month, most of the planets are in the independent East, so it is time to build the conditions for personal happiness and have life on your own terms. Pretty soon the planets will shift and it will be harder to change conditions, so get it done as soon as possible.

Finances are wonderful this month, almost dream-like. Your financial planet is involved in a beautiful and rare Grand Trine pattern all month. Money is earned easily and effortlessly. Financial intuition is working overtime and is very bankable. Your good professional reputation is bringing referrals. Elders, bosses, authorities – even the government – seem kindly disposed to you. Speculations are favourable. Money is earned, or opportunities come, as you pursue leisure activities. You are probably spending more than usual on these things as well. 'Happy money' is in the picture this month. Professional investors should look at energy companies, utilities, precious metals – especially gold and silver – entertainment and gaming companies. Children have or inspire good financial ideas. Even Mars' (your financial planet) re-stimulation of an eclipse point on the 1st should be a good thing, a catalyst to wealth.

Love seems practical this period. You are allured by wealth until the 5th (and perhaps afterwards too). Love seems complicated – even stressful – from the 5th to the 19th. Friends, career, family and parents all vie for your attention, and perhaps your lover feels ignored. These other interests may distract you from your normal social life. A current relationship becomes unstable from the 25th to the 27th. If you can weather this, things will straighten out. Singles find love opportunities as they pursue their financial goals until the 5th. From the 5th to the 19th, love is found in the neighbourhood and in educational settings. After the 19th, love is close to home or comes at family gatherings or through family introductions. There is nostalgia for an old flame after the 19th, and a possible reconnection. (This can also be someone who reminds you of an old flame.)

Health needs watching carefully from the 21st onwards. Rest and relax more. Enhance health through neck massage or cranial-sacral therapies until the 21st, and through arm and shoulder massage afterwards. Diet becomes more of a health issue after the 21st. Earth-based therapies are powerful until the 21st, and air-based therapies are powerful afterwards.

June

Best Days Overall: 8, 9, 17, 18, 25, 26

Most Stressful Days Overall: 3, 4, 10, 11, 23, 24, 30

Best Days for Love: 3, 4, 8, 9, 12, 13, 17, 18, 22, 26, 27, 30

Best Days for Money: 8, 9, 10, 17, 18, 19, 20, 25, 26, 28, 29

Monthly Career Peaks: 8, 9, 10, 11, 30

Monthly Personal Pleasure Peaks: 10, 11, 14, 15, 17, 18

The planets now shift to the West after many months in the independent East. By the 24th, 60 to 70 per cent of them will be in the West, and personal independence is reduced. Now it is difficult to attain ends on your own. You need the co-operation of others.

Like last month, most of the planets are still below the horizon, and both your career planets are retrograde. You should place less emphasis on your career, although you can't ignore it completely, and the focus should be on the family and your emotional harmony. Once you are in a state of emotional harmony, you might be able to take advantage of some of the career opportunities happening this month. Career is furthered through leisure activities. Perhaps you make an important contact at a party or on the tennis court. Your passion will lead you to success.

Your financial planet moves out of the 5th House and into the 6th House. Money is earned through work, the old-fashioned way. Jobseekers will have opportunities, but they should ask themselves if they are the right ones to pursue. The main challenge now is not to let financial needs push you in ways that could damage your career or professional standing. Earnings opportunities will come through friends and organizations you belong to. Networking and technology play a role: perhaps on-line activities are involved here. Professional investors should continue to look at gold, utilities, gaming and entertainment, but also the health sector. Avoid rash speculation this period.

The North Node of the Moon will change signs this month, moving from the 2nd House of Finance to the 1st House of the Body, Image and Appearance. You will be happy to work on your body and image, getting it in shape and moulding it as you want it to be.

Health is good this period and you have a strong interest in it. With Mars now in your 6th House, you benefit from vigorous physical exercise. Health is also enhanced by paying more attention to the heart, spine, knees, teeth, skeletal alignment, large intestine, bladder and colon. Muscle tone and overall posture seem important. Until the 21st, health is enhanced through air-type therapies and arm and shoulder massage. After the 21st, water-based therapies are powerful.

Love is happy from the 3rd to the 28th, happy and carefree. Existing relationships should have more of a honeymoon quality. New ones are more about fun and entertainment than anything serious. Romantic opportunities come in the usual places – parties and entertainments.

July

Best Days Overall: 5, 6, 14, 15, 23, 24

Most Stressful Days Overall: 1, 8, 9, 20, 21, 27, 28, 29

Best Days for Love: 1, 3, 4, 7, 8, 12, 13, 15, 22, 23, 24, 27, 28, 29

PISCES

Best Days for Money: 5, 6, 8, 9, 14, 15, 16, 17, 23, 24, 27

Monthly Career Peaks: 1, 5, 6, 8, 9, 26, 27

Monthly Personal Pleasure Peaks: 9, 10, 12, 13, 14, 15

Overall retrograde activity increases this month, Pisces. For most of the month, 40 per cent of the planets will be retrograde. From the 3rd to the 7th, 50 per cent will be retrograde. Things in the world are slowing down and more patience is called for.

Like last month, most of the planets are in the social West. Your 7th House of Love starts getting strong after the 21st as well. Thus, regardless of your skills, gifts and personal attainments, this is a time when social skills matter.

Most of the planets are still below the horizon, in the night side of your chart. This will soon change, but for now continue to focus on achieving a correct inner state. Concentrate on the family and building up a stable home base. With your career getting ready to zoom to the stratosphere, you will be glad that you built a solid foundation. Family matters are a bit complicated this month as your family planet, Mercury, is retrograde from the 3rd to the 29th. And with Venus in your 4th House of Home and Family, you will probably want to buy art objects for the home or otherwise beautify and redecorate it. These things require more research now. Your sense of taste is very good, but your overall perspective will change after the 29th.

This is a month for working hard and playing hard. Your 5th and 6th Houses are the strongest this period. Having fun is an actual health tonic this month, especially until the 21st. Jobseekers could have interesting opportunities as they socialize or pursue leisure activities. Personal creativity matters for jobseekers now – don't be just a run-of-the-mill applicant. Spruce up your CV, research the company and present creative proposals to them.

Your career planet starts moving forwards on the 7th. Thus career issues, goals and projects are beginning to clarify and progress. You are not even close to your yearly peak yet, but things are in development.

Earnings are strong this month. Until the 21st, money comes from work or the health field. Colleagues or employees have interesting ideas. Earnings opportunities can also come as you pursue your health goals. After the 21st, earnings come through social connections, spousal support or business partnerships. Your financial life seems in the hands of others after the 21st. For the next few months, put other people's financial interests ahead of your own. Help others to prosper and your own prosperity will happen naturally. The main financial challenge now is earning in ways that don't violate your spiritual ideals. Financial intuition will also get tested.

Health is good this month and you are paying much attention here.

A power struggle in love will put a current relationship in danger. You should try to avoid it but it will be difficult. But with your love planet retrograde from the 3rd to the 29th, avoid making abrupt or drastic love decisions.

August

Best Days Overall: 2, 3, 10, 11, 19, 20, 29, 30

Most Stressful Days Overall: 4, 5, 17, 18, 24, 25, 31

Best Days for Love: 2, 3, 11, 12, 21, 22, 23, 24, 25, 31

Best Days for Money: 2, 3, 6, 7, 10, 11, 12, 13, 14, 15, 19, 20, 24, 25, 29, 30

Monthly Career Peaks: 2, 3, 4, 5, 29, 30, 31

Monthly Personal Pleasure Peaks: 8, 9, 10, 11

Like last month, most of the planets are still in the social West, and your 7th House of Others gets very powerful after the 23rd. You are entering your yearly social peak, having wonderful social and romantic experiences. Continue to down-play personal will and self-assertion and put other people first.

After the 23rd, the planetary power shifts to the upper, day side of your horoscope (and it will be even stronger after the 28th). Your career planet, Jupiter, is now firmly forwards. Outer ambitions are starting to call you. The right inner state you have been cultivating for many months will now translate into powerful and positive outer actions.

The crisis in a current relationship should resolve itself one way or another now. With your love planet moving forwards, your social confidence and judgement are good. Whatever your choice (and this is a free will issue), love is going to be happy this month. You probably won't marry now – Uranus in your sign is challenging any marriage – but you will be involved with people who are marriage material. Romance is blooming. Love opportunities happen at work – with colleagues or employees – this month. They can also happen as you pursue health goals. After the 28th, love can happen in the normal ways, at parties and social gatherings. Singles have a nice menu to choose from in the social sphere.

Health needs more watching after the 23rd, but you are on the case. Health is enhanced in many ways and through various kinds of therapies (there are many planets in your 6th House). Social harmony is unusually important this month. If there are problems, work to restore harmony with your lover, spouse or friends. Even if you split with a lover, the split can be done in the most harmonious and amicable way possible. Emotional health in general also seems important, especially from the 11th to the 28th. Family discord could be the cause of problems as well. The kidneys and hips need special attention after the 13th. And, as has been the case all year, continue to pay more attention to the heart, spine, knees, teeth and skeletal alignment. Health problems will begin in the posture, and faulty posture will knock other organs and limbs out of alignment.

The financial trends are the same as last month. Please review last month's discussion.

September

Best Days Overall: 7, 8, 15, 16, 25, 26

Most Stressful Days Overall: 1, 13, 14, 20, 21, 27, 28, 29

Best Days for Love: 1, 2, 3, 4, 11, 12, 13, 20, 21, 22, 23, 30

Best Days for Money: 3, 4, 7, 8, 9, 10, 13, 15, 16, 22, 23, 25, 26

Monthly Career Peaks: 1, 25, 26, 28, 29

Monthly Personal Pleasure Peaks: 5, 6, 7, 8, 23

This month there are two eclipses, both of which have a strong effect on you. Since health needs watching carefully until the 23rd anyway, it is sensible to reduce your schedule during this period, but especially around the eclipses.

The Lunar Eclipse of the 7th occurs in your own sign. This means it is strong and all Pisceans will probably be affected. The eclipse brings a redefinition of the personality and self-concept, leading to changes in your image and personal appearance. Few of us undertake this work unless we are pushed into it. And this is the function of the eclipse: it forces us to take actions we have long needed to take. So, perhaps you are under strong personal, verbal attack. Perhaps there are slanders and false rumours being floated around about you. Worse, others might be trying to define you in their way. So you need to define yourself – this is the best defence. In the end, these people will have done you a favour, even though that wasn't their intention. If you've been lax about health issues, impurities in the body can come up for cleansing. Your spiritual planet, Uranus, is involved in this eclipse, so there will be important changes in your spiritual regime. Sometimes these kinds of eclipses bring scandals, but if you have lived uprightly this shouldn't be a problem. Every Lunar Eclipse tests love affairs (not marriages), and this one is no different. Children will often make dramatic changes to their image and self-concept too. And sometimes normal, but dramatic, events in the lives of children cause changes in your relationship with them.

The Solar Eclipse of the 22nd occurs right on the border of your 7th and 8th Houses and will probably impact on both of them. Pisceans born late in the sign (March 15th to 20th) will feel this the most, and these people should definitely reduce their schedule this period. Marriages and serious relationships get tested. True love and commitment will certainly survive, but weaker relationships are in danger. (Mars in your 7th House is not helping matters here either.) Your spouse, partner or lover makes important financial changes. Spousal support can be temporarily shaken up. Issues involving estates, taxes and insurance claims take a dramatic turn (royalties are also affected here). Job changes are in store for many of you. But have no fear: it is probably a good thing. Your career is very bankable these days. Many of you need to be set free from a cage so that you can fly to the heights. In many cases, there will be long-term changes to the diet, health regime and with the people involved in your health. Dramatic events happen at work, with health professionals (in your sphere) and with aunts and uncles. Though the earth seems to be shaking, know that this is the prelude to much good.

For singles, this Solar Eclipse is probably a good thing. They will make long-term and important decisions about their status. Some might decide to marry under this eclipse, as they are dissatisfied with their present single status. Love is still good, whatever you decide.

Finances are improving after the 8th but the focus is still on helping others to prosper. Many of you will have a special insight into 'dead and near-dead' things – companies, properties or even people. You can see value in these things where others can't and can profit from them.

October

Best Days Overall: 4, 5, 12, 13, 14, 22, 23, 24

Most Stressful Days Overall: 10, 11, 17, 18, 19, 25, 26

Best Days for Love: 2, 3, 4, 10, 11, 12, 13, 14, 17, 18, 19, 21, 22, 23, 24

Best Days for Money: 2, 3, 4, 5, 6, 7, 10, 11, 12, 13, 14, 21, 22, 23, 24

Monthly Career Peaks: 16, 17, 22, 23, 24, 25, 26

Monthly Personal Pleasure Peaks: 2, 3, 4, 5, 10, 13, 14, 29, 30

The upper, day side of the horoscope still dominates. Seventy to eighty per cent of the planets are above the horizon. Your career planet, Jupiter, starts to receive unusual (and positive) stimulation, especially after the 23rd, while your 4th House of Home and Family is basically empty (only the Moon visits there on the 10th and the 11th). You are getting ready to enter your yearly (and for many of you, lifetime) career peak. And this is only the beginning.

It is understandable that you will now take advantage of the many career opportunities happening, and that you will down-play home and family issues. In fact, as time goes on, family will be very supportive here (after the 28th, they are thinking about it). The best thing you can do for your family now is succeed in the outer world.

The Western, social sector of the horoscope still dominates this month. This is soon to change, but in the meantime continue to cultivate your social skills, charm and grace.

The main headlines this month are the power in your 8th and 9th Houses. Forty to fifty per cent of the planets will either be in or move through the 8th House of Transformation this month. (The 9th House of Religion, Philosophy, Education and Travel will be even stronger after the 24th – 50 to 60 per cent of the planets will either be there or move through there!)

So this is a month for personal transformation, a strong interest for many years. Much progress will be made here. From a spiritual perspective, this is a month for 'alchemy' – for taking the lead of old habits, thoughts, emotional patterns and addictions and making gold out of them. Detox regimes of all sorts go well. Weight-loss programmes are successful. It is good to detox on the financial level as well by getting rid of old and useless possessions, waste and debt. This period is also beneficial for occult studies (one of your favourite subjects) and delving into past lives.

On the financial level, this is a good month for tax and estate planning. If you need access to outside capital this is a good month for attainment. Again, the prosperity of others is important to your own prosperity.

Whatever your age or stage, libido is stronger than usual.

The power in the 9th House (after the 24th) brings much religious and philosophical revelation, as well as great over-all optimism. Many of you will be travelling to exotic foreign countries. Students should do well in school. Those applying for higher education hear good news. In general, there are happy educational opportunities coming and you should take them. These seem to relate to the career.

Health is good this month, especially after the 23rd. Self-esteem and self-confidence might not be as high as you would like, and perhaps you are seen as a little weird, but your professional achievements are recognized and your status in society is elevated nonetheless. You can enhance health in the ways described in the yearly report and through paying more attention to the kidneys and hips (until the 23rd) and to the colon, bladder and sexual organs afterwards. Safe sex is more important this month.

November

Best Days Overall: 1, 9, 10, 19, 20, 28, 29

Most Stressful Days Overall: 7, 8, 13, 14, 15, 21, 22

Best Days for Love: 1, 9, 10, 13, 14, 15, 19, 20, 21, 28, 29, 30

Best Days for Money: 1, 2, 3, 9, 10, 19, 20, 28, 29, 30

Monthly Career Peaks: 1, 14, 15, 16, 19, 20, 21, 22, 23

Monthly Personal Pleasure Peaks: 1, 26, 27, 28, 29

The main headlines this month involve the power in the 9th and 10th Houses. The 9th House has 50 to 60 per cent of the planets, an unusually high percentage. Much of what was written last month applies now. Foreign lands call to you. Educational opportunities – and good ones – are coming. Your intellectual horizons are expanding. You are leading the abundant life now in many ways. Sometimes with these aspects people lead the high life, regardless of actual where-withal. Overspending is probably the main financial danger.

This is a month for sudden financial windfalls and opportunities. Your ideas of wealth are larger than life. Speculations are favourable now. Metaphysical techniques such as prayer are not only powerful from a health perspective, but also financially.

Success and boundless optimism often bring negative attacks from certain quarters. These are usually in proportion to your success, so when these things happen see them as signals of success. These things don't seem to impact at all on your professional and career status. Your achievements are recognized and there are pay rises and promotions.

Health is wonderful until the 22nd, but afterwards you need to rest and relax more when possible. Enhance health by paying more attention to the colon, bladder and sexual organs (until the 22nd) and to the liver and thighs afterwards.

Your love planet is retrograde until the 18th, so your love life is under review. Important decisions shouldn't be made. Love, though, is basically happy. There can be some short-term and minor differences of opinion with your lover or spouse. Fundamental compatibilities still seem strong. Try to compromise. You can enhance existing love by going on a 'honeymoon' trip to some exotic locale. For the unattached, foreign countries can be a source of love. Educational and religious settings are also likely scenes for romantic opportunity. Sexual magnetism, education and overall refinement are the turn-ons in love.

December

Best Days Overall: 6, 7, 16, 17, 25, 26

Most Stressful Days Overall: 4, 5, 11, 12, 18, 19, 31

Best Days for Love: 1, 7, 8, 9, 10, 11, 12, 18, 19, 21, 22, 29, 30

Best Days for Money: 1, 4, 8, 18, 19, 27, 28

Monthly Career Peaks: 6, 7, 8, 18, 19

Monthly Personal Pleasure Peaks: 23, 24, 25, 26

Fasten your seat belt and get ready to fly – physically and metaphorically! Sixty to seventy per cent of the planets are now in or moving through your 10th House of Career. This is an awesome percentage, rarely seen in any one sign or house. You are in a lifetime career peak, enjoying fantastic career experiences.

There is a cosmic conspiracy to elevate you, honour you and bring you undreamed-of success. These planetary powers are geniuses in their fields and they know how to bring these things about. If you are running for public office or angling for some promotion, you couldn't ask for better aspects than this. If you are too young to be thinking of your career, then elders are benevolently mapping out a happy future for you. Things are being prepared even now.

Now is the time for stardom in your chosen profession. If there is anything to your talent, rest assured that the world – those who count anyway – will know about it.

But this month is about much more than just worldly success. In many cases it is about learning what your true mission and purpose in life is all about. And, in reality, this is a person's true career. Large and grandiose assignments have probably been given to you, but no matter how large the undertaking, you are up to it.

Of course with elevation and success comes more responsibility. In the heavenly worlds everything is given without price. But here on earth, everything – even the most wonderful things – has a price tag attached, and not merely a financial one. So you will have to learn to use your power and authority in a right and proper way. Your challenges this month are not from powerlessness but from abuse or misuse of power. All this worldly activity – even in a good and noble cause – is going to cause changes in your spiritual regime. And some of you might feel that the call of the world is so strong that you are compromising your spiritual ideals. But it is good to examine this conflict and attain more clarity, which will bring adjustments to both the career and the spiritual ideals. They *can* coexist.

Health needs watching carefully this period. Yes, you are very busy in the world but try to make your actions more efficient and work with a rhythm. Enhance health through metaphysical therapies until the 22nd and by paying more attention to the liver and thighs. After the 22nd, enhance health in the ways discussed in the yearly report, paying attention to the spine, knees, teeth and overall skeletal alignment.